Frommer's®

Alberta

2nd Edition

by Christie Pashby

WILEY

John Wiley & Sons Canada, Ltd.

ABOUT THE AUTHORS

Christie Pashby has been writting for Frommer's for a decade, contributing to titles like *Frommer's Argentina, Frommer's Chile,* and *Best Hikes in British Columbia* and also authoring *Frommer's Banff and the Canadian Rockies Day by Day.* She divides her time between the Canadian Rockies and Bariloche, Argentina. A freelance journalist and translator, her website is www.patagonialiving.com.

Published by:
JOHN WILEY & SONS CANADA, LTD.
6045 Freemont Blvd.
Mississauga, ON L5R 4J3

ISBN 978-0-470-96422-4 (paper); 978-0-470-95209-2 (ebk); 978-1-118-01119-5 (ebk); 978-1-118-01120-1 (ebk)

Editor: Gene Shannon
Production Editor: Pauline Ricablanca
Editorial Assistant: Katie Wolsley
Cartographer: Lohnes&Wright
Production by Wiley Indianapolis Composition Services
Front cover photo: Jasper National Park, Alberta, Canada ©Carson Ganci / DesignPics / Aurora Images
Back cover photo: Bull rider at Calgary Stampede, Calgary, Alberta, Canada ©Henry Georgi / All Canada Photos / Alamy Images

For information on our other products and services or to obtain technical support, please contact our Customer Care Department within the U.S. at 877/762-2974, outside the U.S. at 317/572-3993 or fax 317/572-4002.

Wiley also publishes its books in a variety of electronic formats. Some content that appears in print may not be available in electronic formats.

Manufactured in the United States of America

1 2 3 4 5 RRD 15 14 13 12 11

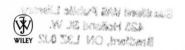

CONTENTS

10 EDMONTON 219

11 NORTHERN ALBERTA 246

APPENDIX: FAST FACTS, TOLL-FREE NUMBERS & WEBSITES 261

Index 269

LIST OF MAPS

ACKNOWLEDGMENTS

I'd like to thank my congenial editor Gene Shannon, as well as the staff at Travel Alberta and the Banff Lake Louise Tourism Bureau.

HOW TO CONTACT US

In researching this book, we discovered many wonderful places—hotels, restaurants, shops, and more. We're sure you'll find others. Please tell us about them, so we can share the information with your fellow travelers in upcoming editions. If you were disappointed with a recommendation, we'd love to know that, too. Please write to:

Frommer's Alberta, 2nd Edition
John Wiley & Sons Canada, Ltd. • 6045 Freemont Blvd. • Mississauga, ON L5R 4J3

AN ADDITIONAL NOTE

Please be advised that travel information is subject to change at any time—and this is especially true of prices. We therefore suggest that you write or call ahead for confirmation when making your travel plans. The authors, editors, and publisher cannot be held responsible for the experiences of readers while traveling. Your safety is important to us, however, so we encourage you to stay alert and be aware of your surroundings. Keep a close eye on cameras, purses, and wallets, all favorite targets of thieves and pickpockets.

FROMMER'S STAR RATINGS, ICONS & ABBREVIATIONS

Every hotel, restaurant, and attraction listing in this guide has been ranked for quality, value, service, amenities, and special features using a **star-rating system.** In country, state, and regional guides, we also rate towns and regions to help you narrow down your choices and budget your time accordingly. Hotels and restaurants are rated on a scale of zero (recommended) to three stars (exceptional). Attractions, shopping, nightlife, towns, and regions are rated according to the following scale: zero stars (recommended), one star (highly recommended), two stars (very highly recommended), and three stars (must-see).

In addition to the star-rating system, we also use six feature icons that point you to the great deals, in-the-know advice, and unique experiences that separate travelers from tourists. Throughout the book, look for:

special finds—those places only insiders know about

fun facts—details that make travelers more informed and their trips more fun

special moments—those experiences that memories are made of

overrated—places or experiences not worth your time or money

insider tips—great ways to save time and money

great values—where to get the best deals

The following **abbreviations** are used for credit cards:

AE	American Express	**DISC**	Discover	**V**	Visa
DC	Diners Club	**MC**	MasterCard		

TRAVEL RESOURCES AT FROMMERS.COM

Frommer's travel resources don't end with this guide. Frommer's website, **www.frommers. com**, has travel information on more than 4,000 destinations. We update features regularly, giving you access to the most current trip-planning information and the best airfare, lodging, and car-rental bargains. You can also listen to podcasts, connect with other Frommers. com members through our active-reader forums, share your travel photos, read blogs from guidebook editors and fellow travelers, and much more.

THE BEST OF ALBERTA

Alberta's fame—and international tourist reputation—is built on three pillars: mountains, cowboys, and more mountains. All right, that's two, but you get the point. This is an extravagantly gorgeous outdoor wonderland, and the Canadian Rockies are the main attraction. This is not to say all that is worthwhile is to be found at high altitudes. Calgary's growing, urbane charms are drawing more visitors every year, and in Edmonton, the second-largest Fringe Theatre Festival in the world has long been a magnet for international travelers. In the badlands, the strong pull of paleontology, anchored by the Royal Tyrrell Museum in Drumheller, draws more than half a million visitors every year.

But the mountains still receive top billing, and with good reason. A practiced mix of otherworldly natural beauty and creature comforts—the Alberta Rockies have within their midst some of the finest resorts, inns, and restaurants to be found anywhere in the world—there are few places on Earth where enjoying rugged wilderness can be so relaxing.

And if relaxing is not your idea of a good time, then take to the hills for world-class ski resorts, endless hiking trails, fly-fishing, and rock and ice climbing, to name but a few pastimes. Out here, the sky truly is the limit.

THE best TRAVEL EXPERIENCES

- **Cruising the length of Waterton Lake:** As the historic ferry boat chugs out of the harbor in Waterton Township, you can feel the chill rising off the glacial waters just a dozen feet below deck. In minutes, the tiny village vanishes, and you're chugging through nature as it must have been thousands of years ago. This is truly a preternatural experience: Ancient peaks rise up all around you; to the south, millennia-old glaciers loom in their rocky bowls. A round trip takes about an hour and a half, but it seems a moment unstuck in time. See p. 53.

o **Lunch at the Plain of the Six Glaciers:** This historic log-cabin teahouse has been drawing hikers for 90 years to its rustic setting beneath the imposing Victoria Glacier, at the back of Lake Louise. The 2-hour hike means you surely deserve a piece of chocolate cake. Take a bowl of homemade soup or a mug of hot chocolate outside and marvel at the six glaciers that cling to Aberdeen, Lefroy, Victoria, and Popes Peak. See p. 167.

o **Hiking Sunshine Meadows:** In the winter, there's all-natural snow for world-class skiing and boarding. In the summer months of July and August, Sunshine Meadows become the easiest alpine area to access in the Rockies. A school bus whisks you to the top of the hill. Anyone who can walk for 30 minutes can frolic in the wildflower-dotted meadows and soak up endless vistas of formations so massive and untouched that they seem more an artificial backdrop than real life. But real it is: Alpine lakes glisten in the sun, so cold your fingers ache on contact. Watch out for bears if you go; make lots of noise so they can hear you coming and get out of the way. See p. 57.

o **Sitting ringside at the Calgary Stampede:** These are the most coveted tickets at the annual rodeo, if you can get them, and they're not for the meek. Directly behind the holding pen, where 2 tons of bull is waiting to be released and buck off his rider, are a small collection of seats for the aficionado. You can smell the bull's rage as surely as you can smell the cowboy's fear. This is as close as—or closer than—you'd ever want to get, and it's a bona fide thrill. See p. 110.

o **Kayaking the North Saskatchewan in Edmonton:** The deep river valley of Alberta's capital provides it with a picturesque urban setting, but then there's the river itself. Deep, wide, and fast, it cleaves a path right through the city center. On a perfect summer evening as the sun is setting, the stillness on the water almost belies the fact you're in a city at all—except for the skyscrapers glowing sentinel-like just up the bank. See p. 238.

o **Afternoon tea at the Fairmont Chateau Lake Louise:** On a sunny day, the view from the Lakeview Lounge at the Fairmont Chateau Lake Louise (© **800/441-1414**) is well-nigh incomparable: the emerald waters of the lake just in front of you and the reflection of the Victoria Glacier at its southern end bouncing off it. Then there is the food: scones, finger sandwiches, clotted cream—all of it great, and none of it cheap. If the price tag troubles you, try to think of it as rent: You'd pay that and more just to sit here and stare, guaranteed. See p. 192.

o **Trail riding in Cowboy Country:** Saddle up at one of the private family ranches along the Cowboy Trail and give real cowboy-ing a shot. Places like **Sierra West Ranch Vacations** (© **403/628-2431**; www.sierrawestcabins.com) will let you ride for an hour, a day, or a few days, or even join in a real cattle drive. Remember to sit tall in the saddle! See p. 59.

o **Cruise to Spirit Island:** Board a boat on Jasper's quiet, vast, and mountain-cradled Maligne Lake. You'll journey to distant nooks and lakeside crannies before pulling into this picture-perfect island with a mysterious history. It's relaxing for parents and adventure-filled for kids. See p. 207.

THE best HISTORIC SITES

○ **Surveying the damage at the Frank Slide:** On April 29, 1903, the town of Frank, Alberta, disappeared. That morning, 82 million tons of mountainside came hurtling downward from its perch high above on Turtle Mountain, crushing everything in its path. The debris field, an historic site, remains a sight to behold: Boulders the size of suburban houses are strewn 150m (492 ft.) deep, 425m (1,394 ft.) high, and 1km (3,281 ft.) wide. These days, Highway 3 into British Columbia runs overtop the rubble field and trees poke out from between the rocks. And the excellent **Frank Slide Interpretive Centre** (© **403/562-7388**) offers you a chance to learn more about this massive cataclysm that happened in the blink of an eye. See p. 152.

○ **The origins of the cowboy trade at Bar U Ranch:** Bar U Ranch National Historic Site (© **888/773-8888**) tells the history of ranching in Alberta. It's on the site of what was once the most important corporate ranch along the Foothills southwest of Calgary, employing thousands of cowboys and running hundreds of thousands of cattle while in operation from 1882 to 1950. As ranches modernized and herds grew, Bar U owner Patrick Burns sold off parts of the vast ranch in 1950, bringing its dominance to a close. But the original Bar U site, with its horse barns, bunkhouses, mess hall, and office, remains intact. Authentic Cowboy hospitality welcomes visitors of all ages, with homemade treats, a darn good saddle maker and a ranch hand or two to lend character to a slice of Alberta history, perfectly preserved. See p. 153.

○ **Searching for David Thompson in Rocky Mountain House:** David Thompson is one of the most important figures in Canadian history. Using his base at Rocky Mountain House, the celebrated cartographer, explorer, and fur trader is credited with mapping as much as 20% of North America. His base was also a hotspot for fur traders of all kinds, drawn from both sides of the great rivalry between the Hudson's Bay Company and North West Company, both of whom operated out of Rocky Mountain House for 76 years. This little fort was like downtown in a vast wilderness of commerce and trade. See p. 156.

○ **Head-Smashed-In Buffalo Jump:** A high bluff facing east over the endless plains made this site the perfect bison killing field. Long before European contact, Native Canadians would stampede vast herds of bison over these bluffs, using the impact and the crushing weight of the herd to kill enough meat to last the winter. These days, a brilliant interpretive center (© **403/553-2731**) steps up the bluff in harmony with its surroundings; inside, an array of excellent exhibits explains the significance of this site to Native culture and history. See p. 152.

○ **Surveying the past at Lougheed House:** When Calgary was young, much of the city was built of sandstone from nearby quarries. But the material was high maintenance, and only a few buildings survive. One of the best is Lougheed House (© **403/244-6333**), a family mansion built for the prominent Lougheed family (Peter Lougheed was premier of the province from 1971 to 1985). Built in 1907, Lougheed House represents a perfectly preserved piece of the city's architectural history. See p. 112.

○ **Blackfoot Crossing Historical Park:** Long before there were cowboys, oilmen, and mountaineers in these parts, the Siksika people of the Great Plains roamed their vast domain. This re-created village—located an hour east of Calgary, where the landmark Treaty 7 between the Natives and Queen Victoria was signed in 1877—today shares the culture, history, and traditions of a people whose lands once spanned 181,299 sq. m (70,000 sq. miles), from British Columbia to Saskatchewan. It's a family-friendly spot that also has tipis available for overnight lodging. See p. 123.

○ **Lake Agnes Teahouse:** Canada's roots in mountaineering run deeper here than anywhere else. The Swiss guides, who were brought in by the Canadian Pacific Railway to usher their hotel guests up into the high alpine, were adventuring trailblazers working in one of the world's finest mountain landscapes. The historic teahouse (built in the 1920s as a day-hike destination) is a wonderful hike from the shores of Lake Louise up in to a majestic basin that gives you a front-row seat to alpine history, not to mention a good workout and mouth-watering home-baked treats. See p. 167.

THE best MUSEUMS

○ **The Royal Tyrrell Museum:** No offense to any of the province's other excellent institutions, but this one holds the trump card. A world leader in paleontology, the Royal Tyrrell (*☎* **888/440-2240**), found in the rich dinosaur fossil beds of Alberta's badlands near Drumheller, is truly a world-class facility, capitalizing on its location to draw some of the world's most accomplished scientists and exhibit designers in the field. No trip to Alberta would be complete without it. See p. 123.

○ **The Royal Alberta Museum:** Long on both the province's Aboriginal and natural history, Edmonton's Royal Alberta (*☎* **780/453-9100**) includes the Syncrude Gallery of Aboriginal Culture, which showcases 11,000 years of Native Canadian history. There also are extensive displays on the geological forces that shaped the province's spectacular, varied terrain and (every little kid's dream come true) a bug room! See p. 237.

○ **The Glenbow Museum:** Calgary's Glenbow Museum (*☎* **403/268-4100**) is a multipurpose institution, and it handles its multitasking role as the largest museum in the city with aplomb. It's a must for anyone with an interest in the history and culture of Western Canada. Especially notable is the third floor, with its vivid evocation of Native cultures—particularly of the local Blackfoot—and compelling descriptions of Western Canada's exploration and settlement. Other floors contain displays of West African carvings, gems and minerals, and a cross-cultural look at arms and warfare. See p. 101.

○ **The Art Gallery of Alberta:** In a gorgeous and avant-garde new building in what Edmonton hopes will be a reinvigorated downtown core, the Art Gallery of Alberta (*☎* **780/422-6223**) is one of the most daring contemporary art institutions in the country. It is a champion of First Nations contemporary art (think artists like Jane Ash Poitras and Carl Beam) and hosts a revolving door of some of the world's finest artists, from modern to classic—Degas, Goya, Whistler, or Yousuf Karsh, anyone? See p. 235.

○ **The Whyte Museum:** A little gem of a regional museum, the Whyte (*☎* **403/762-2291**), in Banff, chronicles the adventuresome town's founders and the indefatigable pioneer spirit that built it. The Whyte isn't limited to history; interesting touring exhibitions, like a recent show of contemporary landscape painting interpreting the varied Alberta landscape, keep a foot planted firmly in the present. See p. 176.

o **Remington Carriage Museum:** Special interest, to be sure, but this private museum (© 403/653-5139), in tiny Cardston, has been voted the "best indoor attraction in Canada" by Attractions Canada, and it's a thorough survey of transportation before the combustion engine ruled the roads. Every manner of carriage is present in the collection, along with a healthy dose of history. The museum also has one of the only carriage-restoration shops in North America. See p. 151.

THE best SMALL TOWNS

o **Rosebud:** A tiny prairie gem cradled in a river valley on a provincial byway, Rosebud is a thriving arts center just off the map. An art school, theater, and opera house are among the tiny hamlet's hidden pleasures, as are the meals to be had at the historic **Mercantile Dining Room** (© 403/267-7553). Art galleries and crafts by local artisans are for sale here, as well, most of them so good you'd swear you were in a town 100 times its size (Rosebud has a little over 100 permanent residents). See p. 125.

o **Vulcan:** The folks in Vulcan, Alberta, have a motto you've probably heard before: "Live long and prosper." Granted, the town was named well before Leonard Nimoy's pointed-eared alter-ego, Mr. Spock, became a cult legend. But never let it be said that an Albertan would let an opportunity to make a few bucks go to waste. The **tourist bureau** (© 403/485-2994) features a miniature *Starship Enterprise* as a welcoming sign, and the building itself looks lifted from the set of the late-'60s TV series *Star Trek*. Vulcan, a small farming community, celebrates Spock Days/GalaxyFest each June and brings in whatever tangentially Trek-related celebrity it can get (in 2010, the actor who played Tuvok on Star Trek: Voyager, Tim Russ, was the celebrity guest). See p. 130.

o **Canmore:** This has got to be one of the nicest small towns in North America! It has friendly residents, a gorgeous setting beneath the Three Sisters Mountain and next to Banff National Park, and an influx of moneyed weekenders—who've brought with them superb dining at places like the **Trough** (© 403/678-2820), shopping, and cafe-lingering. Canmore offers outdoor adventure and fine living, the best of both worlds. See p. 142.

o **Bragg Creek:** Not much more than a shopping plaza and a gas station, tiny little Bragg Creek, a short 45-minute hop west of Calgary, remains a draw as much for its excellent ice-cream shop as for its perch on the edge of Kananaskis Country. Since it is just a quick trip from Calgary, Bragg is starting to show its urbane side: There is a contemporary fusion restaurant, for one, and a day spa. But really, the attraction is the location: Bragg sits in the curl where the Rockies begin—picturesque, to say the least. Unlike Canmore, which is a bigger town nestled deep inside the mountains, Bragg Creek is sleepy and rural. See p. 154.

o **Lake Louise:** Just a half-hour west of Banff seems to make all the difference. Where Banff is crowded, noisy, and over-touristed at times, Lake Louise is peaceful and serene. An excellent, hippie-ish bakery and laid-back atmosphere make it all the more appealing. In Banff, you feel urged to do everything; in Louise, as the locals call it, you can be content to do nothing at all. See p. 190.

THE best LUXURY ACCOMMODATIONS

o **Fairmont Jasper Park Lodge** (📞 780/540-4454): Amid the grand old railway hotels of the bygone era, it is the most modest of them that remains the most alluring. The Jasper Park Lodge, set on 283 hectares (700 acres) of mountain meadow just outside the town of Jasper, with its bend-over-backward service, is the ultimate in civilized wilderness refuges. Guests stay in an array of cabins and separate buildings tucked around a pristine lakeshore, in units ranging from a hotel room to a full suite. Canoeing and golfing, horseback riding and swimming, and fine dining and cocktails give the lodge a feeling of nostalgic charm; like a camp for the entire family. The room service delivered on bicycle along the gentle path that runs alongside the lake doesn't hurt, either. See p. 210.

o **Hôtel Le Germain** (📞 403/264-8990): Calgary's newest downtown inn brings the bold style of Montréal to town, combining a boutique hotel with an office tower and 40 chic private residences—plus the hottest new restaurant in town in Charcut (see p. 90). Modern, sleek, spacious, and popular with celebrities and VIPs, there's finally some design-savvy flair amidst the sometimes dull sheen of Calgary. See p. 85.

o **The Kensington Riverside Inn** (📞 403/313-3733): It's a little slice of Malibu along the riverbank in Calgary. The Riverside, with its less than two dozen rooms, is private, intimate, modern, and sleek. Cocktails are served in the inn's comfortable, expansive lobby lounge—when weather permits, fireside. Warm grays, marble, dark leather, and wood define the aesthetic. There is nowhere else in the province where you're likely to feel as much like a Hollywood star on hideaway. See p. 85.

o **Mount Engadine Lodge** (📞 403/678-4080): This is roughing it in the best possible way. Tiny Mount Engadine Lodge is about a half-hour north of Canmore on a rough gravel road. Off the proverbial beaten track, there are few travelers here, if you don't count grizzly bears, wolves, and moose. At the lodge, perched on a bluff above a meadow frequented by moose, you can enjoy some of the finest home cooking in the Rockies while sipping wine on the patio. On any given day, you can hear a pin drop—or a moose bleat. See p. 143.

o **The Post Hotel** (📞 800/661-1586): Tucked away in a grove of trees in the secluded Lake Louise village, the Post is a wonderful antidote to Banff fatigue. Voted the best hotel in Canada by *Travel & Leisure* magazine in 2007, it's got proven European-styled hospitality wrapped up neat and tidy. Private, peaceful, and elegant while remaining homey, the Post has garnered an international reputation for impeccable service (it's part of the prestigious Relais & Chateau network) and easygoing comfort. Its award-winning restaurant, simply called the Post Hotel Dining Room, doesn't hurt, either: *Gourmet* magazine recognized it as one of its top-three rustic retreats in the world. See p. 193.

o **Fairmont Banff Springs Hotel** (📞 800/540-4406): The grande dame of the Rocky Mountain hotels, the Springs has been plenty touristed and tarted up over the years, most notably when its grand entrance was built over to provide a more efficient guest-processing experience. But the views of the Bow Valley from the Rundle Room are still nearly unmatchable, and the service, among the best you'll find anywhere, keeps the Springs an experience worth having. See p. 178.

○ **The Matrix Hotel** (© 800/465-8150): A very of-the-moment boutique hotel in a somewhat white-collar town, the Matrix is the urbanite's choice in downtown Edmonton. Sleek design and a soothing palette of browns and grays provide a perfect minimalist backdrop for whatever urban adventure you care to infuse it with. See p. 227.

○ **Alpine Village** (© 780/852-3285): Come to this pretty collection of red-roofed lodges next to the Athasbasca River south of Jasper for luxury and solitude. Grab a book, and sit by the river or next to a fire. Hike the wooded trails. Pop into town for groceries, then come back and stay close. It's like having the perfect mountain cabin, with the bonus of room service and housekeeping. See p. 210.

○ **Fairmont Hotel MacDonald** (© 866/540-4468): Perched high on the banks of the Saskatchewan River in Edmonton, the MacDonald surveys the valley with commanding grace. You can, too, from the expansive patio overlooking the river—or choose to view it from the stately rooms that recall an old-world elegance. See p. 226.

THE best FESTIVALS

○ **The Calgary Stampede:** Whether you want to call it a festival or not is your choice, but there's no denying that this is the biggest party Alberta has every year, bar none. Forget the thousands of tourists for a moment—it's Calgarians pulling on their boots, donning their Stetsons, and leaving work at noon every day (if they show up to work at all) that sets things alight. Oh, and there's that biggest-rodeo-on-Earth aspect, as well, but it's only part of the fun. It's a non-stop party, with event running from early in the morning (free breakfasts), through mid-day (parades), and on into the evening (live concerts by big names). This is the one event where an entire city goes to the same party. See p. 110.

○ **The Edmonton Fringe Festival:** After Edinburgh, the world's first and largest, Edmonton's Fringe Theatre Festival has no equal. This is a theater town, and it's never more apparent than during the 10 days in August when theater companies from all over the world descend on the Alberta capital with their finest, freshest work. This is truly a cross-section of the best contemporary theater the world has to offer—a can't-miss event for those in love with live performance. See p. 245.

○ **Wordfest:** Calgary's answer to Toronto's International Festival of Authors (one of the world's biggest), Wordfest is popular with readers and writers alike, including a tight selection of A-list novelists and journalists. Readings are open to the public and have included such luminaries as Richard Ford and David Adams Richards. It takes place each October. See p. 31.

○ **Big Valley Jamboree:** One of the biggest country music festivals in North America draws some seriously big names each summer (Martina McBride and Keith Urban headlined in 2010) to a wide field southeast of Edmonton near the town of Camrose. It's a mid-summer weekend with bull riding, a lumberjack show, and pancake breakfasts. Bring a tent and settle in. There's a family stage for the young 'ens, too.

○ **The Calgary Folk Music Festival:** There are bigger music festivals, and there may even be better ones (because music depends on your point of view, doesn't it?), but on a sunny July afternoon, the setting—on Prince's Island Park—can hardly be matched. And with a list of past headliners that includes Blue Rodeo, Ani

DiFranco, Kris Kristofferson, Calexico, Bedouin Soundclash, and Michael Franti, the music ain't bad, either. See p. 30.

o **Canmore Folk Music Festival:** Smaller than the folk fest in Calgary, more intimate than Edmonton's, and set just beneath the triple peak of the Three Sisters Mountain, Canmore's annual Folk Music Festival happens the first long weekend of each August. It's a casual 3-day festival showcasing folk, roots, blues, and world music. You'll be surprised at how great all the artists are. Bring a blanket and be prepared for any kind of weather—it's been known to snow! The outdoor food court and artisans fair are other draws.

o **Improvaganza:** Small but mighty, Edmonton's annual festival of improv comedy is a sight to behold. Held in June every year at the Rapid Fire Theater, it's about as many laughs as you could possibly handle in one place. Some of the best troupes from across the country come here, drawn by Edmonton's strong theater reputation.

THE best DINING

o **The Blue Pear** (© 780/482-7178): Set in an unassuming strip mall in Edmonton's 124th Street district, the Blue Pear might just be one of the best restaurants in the country. Run by a husband-and-wife team with a stout devotion to local, organic ingredients, the culinary results are no less than symphonic: lamb ravioli in a yoghurt brown-butter sauce; roast pork belly, crab cake, soya-pea puree with pancetta-wrapped enoki mushrooms—the list goes on. Each plate—there are three courses for C$59, no exceptions—arrives like a carefully constructed piece of art. But the real art is the flavor. See p. 232.

o **The Bison Mountain Bistro** (© 403/762-5550): On the second floor of a "green" building on Banff's Bear Street, the Bison exemplifies the best of Rocky Mountain cuisine, with an array of local ingredients simply prepared with flavor in mind. The name tells the tale: bison—burgers, steaks, or smoked—or venison pepperoni, all worked in to meals as thoughtful and flavorful as they are simple. A downstairs wine bar has smaller meals. This is the busiest place in town—and deserves to be. See p. 186.

o **Crazyweed Kitchen** (© 403/609-2530): Canmore's fine dining scene is constantly changing, but at the top of the list for a decade has been this one-of-a-kind restaurant. Original, alternative, trendy, and smart, Crazyweed's best asset is its chef, who brings Spanish, Indian, and Asian flavors together with local ingredients. Service and attitude can both be a bit questionable. But it's really about the food, isn't it? See p. 145.

o **Stampede Breakfast:** While there's nothing gourmet about pancakes, sausages, and thermos coffee, there's something truly heart-warming and authentic about the dozens of Stampede Breakfasts held in neighborhoods throughout Calgary during the Stampede. It's a great way to mingle with locals, and it's free! See p. 100.

o **River Café** (© 403/261-7670): With a full dose of Canadiana decor (canoes, an open-hearth fieldstone fireplace, etc.) and a menu that showcases only the best there is to offer in these parts (including beef tenderloin from Pincher Creek and elk carpaccio from northwest of Edmonton), this is my choice for the top restaurant in Calgary. Just getting here—you cross a bridge to Prince's Island Park—is lovely, especially on a warm summer's evening. Start with a fish-and-game platter and follow with local beef, pheasant, duck, lamb, or trout. You'll leave with a true appreciation for what makes Calgary (and Alberta) so special. See p. 90.

o **Mercato** (© 403/263-5535): One of Calgary's true see-and-be-seens, Mercato has both a high-end gourmet shop and an entertaining bistro centered around a wide-open kitchen, each oozing with fresh, traditional Italian flair. Book a spot at the counter to watch the chefs whip up sublime pastas, fresher-than-fresh salads, and of course, the Porterhouse-style classic *bistecca alla fiorentina* steak. There's a deep respect for the simplest ingredients like olive oil and balsamic vinegar.See p. 94.

o **Baker Creek Bistro** (© 403/522-2182): An unassuming spot on a secondary road that hooks through the mountains about 15 minutes east of Lake Louise, you'd be forgiven for driving by the red-roofed Baker Creek Chalets if looking for fine dining. The chalets are lovely, set alongside a burbling creek, but the dining room, in an unassuming log cabin, should be the main attraction. Fresh local food served with grace and contemporary panache by chef Shelley Robinson is a delight and surprise, and well worth a step off the beaten track. See p. 195.

o **Calgary's Farmers Market** (© 403/244-4548): If you love food, you can't miss the chance to mingle with local farmers, food producers, bakers, and proprietors of small gourmet stands. Held Fridays through Sundays, you can grab a bison burger, lamb sausage, ethnic food ranging from Cuban to Ukrainian, and just about anything Alberta-grown. Edmonton's Old Strathcona Farmer's Market (p. 222) is also worth a stop.

o **Evil Dave's Grill** (© 780/852-3323): The loyal following of locals should be your first clue that this Jasper resto, with its devotion to theme—"Malevolent" home-style Alberta beef meatloaf, or "Ex-Wife" spicy tomato penne with chicken and shrimp—is a keeper. Jasper can't match Banff or even Canmore in terms of dining, but the globally inspired menu here is refreshing and as close as Jasper gets to the Bow Valley's razor-sharp dining scene. See p. 216.

THE best SCENIC DRIVES

o **The Columbia Icefields Parkway:** Predictable, sure, but with good reason. You couldn't do this drive often enough to be anything but awed by it. As you drift past the silent majesty of millennia-old glaciers and millions of tons of age-old ice draped over the looming, ancient peaks, you may as well leave your jaw on the dashboard because, around the next bend, it'll just land there again. Easily and without a doubt the most dramatic stretch of highway in the province, if not the entire country. See p. 197.

o **The Bow Valley Parkway:** On the short stretch of the Trans-Canada Highway that links Banff to Lake Louise, there's a little-traveled side route called the Bow Valley Parkway (or Hwy. 1A). It's little-traveled with good reason, perhaps: Its two lanes wind through rock and forest, and probably double the travel time between the two points. But getting there, in this case, is half the fun. Little Highway 1A wends off along the base of Castle Mountain, one of the true massives of the local peaks, and getting underneath it offers the truest sense of its majesty. It's also along 1A where you're most likely to see wildlife—a giant elk grazing by the roadside or maybe even a black bear (don't even mention the bighorn sheep, which are as plentiful as squirrels). Sometimes, the road less traveled does, in fact, make all the difference.

○ **The Dinosaur Trail:** It's a short loop from the town of Drumheller around the Dinosaur Trail, but inside it is some of the most spectacularly barren scenery to be found anywhere. As you circle the route around Horse Thief and Horseshoe canyons, carved by the Red Deer River, picture yourself sailing through a massive, shallow inland sea, swarming with marine dinosaurs twice the size of your car. Then look down into the dark, desiccated canyons, and think how long it took the river to carve a space deep and wide enough to reveal this ancient history. It can make you feel tiny, indeed. See p. 121.

○ **Highway 40 through Kananaskis:** It's only open less than half the year, from June 15 to December 1, and with good reason: This is among the more rugged drives along the fringe of a major mountain range you'll ever take. The turn-off at Longview from Highway 22 warns you that the road is fraught with hazards, but on a beautiful summer day with the sunroof open, none of this seems to even be possible. As it transports you from bald prairie expanses to the towering peaks of the Rocky Mountains on the way to Highwood Pass, you'll have reached an elevation of 2,228m (7,310 ft.)—the highest elevation of any highway in the country. As you cruise close to the tree line, you'll find mounds of snow, even in high summer. But save your gawking for the wildlife, as elk, moose, mountain goats, and the occasional bear pause to watch you rumble by. See p. 144.

○ **The David Thompson Parkway:** Connecting Rocky Mountain House to the east with the Icefields Parkway, the David Thompson Highway is a direct route into the heart of the Rockies' high scenic drama. The foothills west of Rocky Mountain House give way quickly to the hard-rock mountains, which rise quickly in the west. The road is swallowed along the way, until you realize there are mountains ahead, behind, and all around you. The sense is of a massive natural fortress that you've slipped inside. See p. 156.

○ **The Cowboy Trail between Cardston and Bragg Creek:** Alberta's famed Cowboy Trail skirts the eastern edge of the Rockies, through rolling foothills and nothing much more at all, and that's its charm: hills upon hills, rolling gently toward mountains that seem close enough to touch. Passing through the occasional small towns like Black Diamond and Pincher Creek along the way offers a clue to the road's name: These are true West places, with pickup trucks and honky-tonk spirit to spare. The Trail continues through Cochrane and Rocky Mountain House, spilling out into high plains, which are less picturesque than the mountain vistas to be found further south. See p. 151.

THE best EXPERIENCES FOR KIDS

○ **Heritage Park:** With a petting zoo, steam engine train, paddle-wheel boat, and more cowboy and frontier fun than you can twirl a rope at, Calgary's Heritage Park offers a plethora of off-the-main experiences for the little ones. Easily a full day of distractions for the kiddies. And the grownups might learn a thing or two, as well. See p. 101.

- **The Royal Tyrrell Museum:** I know it's already been listed, but a special mention of the Tyrrell is deserved here for its amazing array of dinosaur diversions, such as interactive displays, films, animations, and hands-on experiences like a bucket full of T-Rex tooth fossils ripe for the handling. Slightly bigger kids (9 and over) can camp out overnight in the badlands and pick up real fossils from the dinos' final resting places. See p. 123.
- **Shaw Millennium Park:** With 6,968 sq. m (75,000 sq. ft.) of skate-able surface, basketball courts, and four sand volleyball courts on the western edge of downtown, Calgary's Shaw Millennium park is one of the largest skateboard parks in North America and draws skaters of all ages from all over the continent. A good bet for bigger kids; helmets and pads can be rented or purchased from the pro shop. See p. 101.
- **World Waterpark, West Edmonton Mall:** 2 hectares (5 acres) of waterslides and a wave pool in the massive West Edmonton Mall promise hours of wet and wild fun for kids. With the water kept at a bathtub-like 86°F (30°C), it's a little trip to the tropics in Northern Alberta. See p. 243.
- **Jasper Junior Naturalists:** The Friends of Jasper National Park runs a summer-long series of environmental awareness programs for kids 6 to 10. Look for bugs, get "lost" in the woods, learn about bears and birds . . . it's hand-on, full of adventure, and free Wednesdays through Sundays during summer at the Whistlers campground. You must pre-register. See p. 200.
- **Learn to ski or snowboard:** The scenery alone will motivate you, but with new equipment and fantastic snow, few places in the world can rival Banff for kids wanting to learn to shred or free ride. Sunshine Village is a great place to learn to snowboard, while Lake Louise is perfect for beginner skiers. Mt. Norquay has ski-by-the-hour rates, appealing for newbies. Best of all, each has a staff of truly world-class instructors that will make the whole process easy, not to mention fun.

THE best HIKING AND WALKING TOURS

- **Grassi Lakes:** The Canmore/Kananaskis area is overrun with great day hikes, but this one's a real winner. Short (5km/3.1 miles) but spectacular, the trail starts as a wide, rough road across from the Canmore Nordic Centre but quickly narrows and climbs past a towering waterfall and up, up, up an artfully-created trail to the lakes themselves, which are an intense hue of aquamarine, towering peaks all around them. People have been climbing to take in the view from Grassi Lakes for millennia; keep an eye out for Native Canadian pictographs just above the lakes themselves. See p. 148.
- **Crypt Lake:** A water taxi across icy-blue Waterton Lake in Waterton National Park takes you to the Crypt Lake trail head, a full-day hike that takes you up 700m (2,297 ft.) to the shores of the even-icier aquamarine Crypt Lake. There's much to take in along the way, too, including a 182m (597-ft.) waterfall and a natural tunnel. Acrophobes beware: There's also a dramatic cliff traverse. See p. 134.
- **Urban Safari:** For those who like their hiking not too far from a well-stocked bar, Calgary's **Urban Safari** tour (© **403/283-3158**) won't disappoint. Hike one of

Calgary's central neighborhoods, foraging for culinary delights at some of the city's best restaurants, all included in the package. See p. 112.

o **Lake Agnes and the Big Beehive:** Set out from the Chateau Lake Louise along the lake's south shore about 500m (1,640 ft.), and you'll be at the trail head for Lake Agnes, a short, popular, and utterly spectacular 11km (6.8-mile) loop that gradually climbs about 500m (1,640 ft.) over its span. First, you'll pass Mirror Lake and, above it, the Big Beehive, an aptly named rock formation that looms over the lake and offers gorgeous views of the Chateau and the lake below. This is civilized wilderness; a little higher up offers respite at the Lake Agnes Teahouse, a log cabin converted for tourism. Keep going; the farther you go, the thinner the crowd gets (many turn back at the teahouse), along with the air, and the better the spectacular scenery surrounding you. See p. 167.

o **Cavell Meadows:** For a chance to see wildflowers at their most colorful, come in early August to this loop trail on the northeast slope of Mt. Edith Cavell, south of the Town of Jasper. It's an 8km (5-mile) half-day hike that first passes by the toe of Angel Glacier. It's quite popular, so come early in the day for a quieter trail (and the best light for photography). See p. 230.

THE best OUTDOOR ADVENTURES

o **Wildlife-watching in Banff:** Dusk is the best time to head out on the picturesque Minnewanka Loop or Bow Valley Parkway near the town of Banff. There's a more-than-good chance you'll see elk and bighorn sheep. If you're lucky, you could also check mountain goats, black bear, moose, and grizzly bears off your list. **Discover Banff Tours** (© 877/565-9372) has regular tours with good local guides who'll do the driving, leaving you to worry about the photo opportunities. See p. 162.

o **Paddling the Athabasca River and climbing Morro Peak:** The **Jasper Adventure Centre** (© 800/565-7547) calls it their "ultimate adventure," and it's hard to argue, really. A 12km (7½-mile) paddle along the Athabasca River ends up at the foot of Morro Peak, where you'll climb 700m (2,297 ft.) to the rocky—and somewhat frighteningly narrow—ridge that is the mountaintop. Only one thing beats looking at the mountains here: Standing on top of one. Here's your chance. See p. 202.

o **Skiing Delirium Dive:** Only expert skiers and boarders need apply, and they must come prepared with avalanche equipment. If you qualify, there's no greater lift-accessed challenge in the Rockies than the Dive at **Sunshine Village** (© 877/542-2633). If you can't rope one of your buddies into joining you (and you must have a partner) one of Sunshine's ski school guides will lead you down. See p. 171.

o **Riding range on a cattle drive:** Sure, you can get all your cowboy experience at the annual Calgary Stampede (see p. 110), but if you want to go all the way, driving cattle is about as authentic as it gets. If you've seen *City Slickers,* where Billy Crystal and friends play, well, city slickers driving in the herd alongside real-life ranch hands, you've got the idea. **Home on the Range Adventure Tours** (© 866/760-8334) provides a link with real, live ranches in the Rocky Mountain foothills along the Cowboy Trail to ride range on the herd for a night or three. This is the real deal—right down to the smell.

o **White-water rafting the Horseshoe Canyon in Kananaskis Country:** The truth of it is, you could white-water raft on any number of mountain rivers all over Alberta and get a taste of the experience. But Horseshoe Canyon, in Kananaskis Country, offers the iconic mountain landscapes; a crisp, icy river; a plethora of water ledges to tumble over; and most importantly, plenty of white water. See p. 61.

o **Fly-casting on the Bow River near Calgary:** Ignore the skyscrapers and morning rush-hour traffic. Instead, set your mind to the trout. The Bow River, which runs right through downtown Calgary, is one of the world's great fly-fishing rivers. Put in just above Prince's Island Park and float down past the Glenmore Trail for a nice half-day outing. Local guides will bring all the gear and do the paddling. See p. 57.

ALBERTA IN DEPTH

2

Vast, broad plains; rolling foothills; jagged peaks; massive river delta; and the second-largest proven oil deposits on Earth—all this is contained within the provincial boundaries of Alberta, the second-most-westerly province in Canada. For many, Alberta is synonymous with the Rocky Mountains, and with good reason: More than three-quarters of the C$5 billion the province reaps from tourism every year is spent in and around the big-name National Parks of Banff and Jasper.

But in recent years, more has been done to promote the growing diversity of options to be found here, particularly the rapid ascent of urban centers like Calgary toward cosmopolitan, world-class status. While you're not likely to mistake Calgary for, say, Paris, it's a bustling, vibrant city with a unique and authentic identity. A vacation in Alberta now offers that rare combination of urbanity and natural wonder—a breadth of experience few places in North America share.

Alberta is the wealthiest province in Canada, with a GDP that is one of the highest in the world. This, of course, is due to skyrocketing oil prices and the province's glut of the valuable fuel, which has in turn brought wave upon wave of new residents from all over the country and around the world; the province is increasingly urban, multicultural, and cosmopolitan.

One of the great paradoxes here is that the Albertan identity remains strongly rooted to the land and the mountains, and yet—due to suburban sprawl and the gigantic industrial wasteland, the northern oil sands—it is also one of the least sustainable, least "eco-friendly" places on Earth. Don't make the mistake of associating Alberta's conservatism with conservation.

But the natural beauty is indeed spectacular. Just outside the city limits of Calgary and Edmonton, thousands of acres of ranchland sprawl through the foothills and on to the mountains, where cowboys ride range on their herds much as they might have more than a hundred years ago. All this comes to bear, of course, in the self-described "greatest outdoor show on Earth," the Calgary Stampede—the biggest rodeo in the world, which takes place every July. That's the splashiest display of Western pride, but it's evident every day in the countryside, through the rolling hills and high plains where the herds still roam and a good horse is worth its weight in gold.

ALBERTA TODAY

Alberta in the 21st century contains several of the fastest-growing urban centers in North America, which have experienced explosive economic growth thanks to the significant rise of oil prices in recent years. Of course, Albertans have seen this before, most notably in the late 1970s, when oil prices, inflated by resource rationing by OPEC, skyrocketed overnight—and created thousands of instant millionaires in the Alberta oil patch. The same pattern repeated itself in the 2000s, when rapidly escalating demand from places like India and China had oil prices soaring again.

When you consider that the second largest supply of oil in the world (after Saudi Arabia) sits in the province's northern oil sands, it's a safe bet that Alberta's a pretty happy place these days. Still, there is more austerity and caution in the air these days. Real estate values continue to grow, but at a slower pace than a few years ago. And the number of six-figure vehicles on the streets of Calgary has dropped considerably since 2008. A boomtown that has settled into its identity as a major city, Calgary continues to be the province's economic barometer. The most recent boom was different in less nuts-and-bolts ways, too; in the '70s, the province was oil-rich when oil was cheap. When the price of oil went up, there was the expected influx of outsiders from across the country, hungry for jobs, and when the bottom fell out, a great many of them went home.

Thirty years on, Alberta is older and wiser. After laying fallow, this time the province's growth spurt brought it an unprecedented spike in cosmopolitan diversity; international immigrants continue to flock to the province, looking not only to take part in the economic good times, but also to set up new lives. The result is the visibly changing face of a conservative province, settled by Scots Presbyterians but transforming into a cultural mosaic that seems to grow more diverse by the day.

And one of the principal assets of the first boom, the Heritage Fund—a multi-billion dollar trust established by the government of the day from its share of oil revenues—has, in the interim, fostered the new Alberta now enjoyed by the current generation. The Heritage Fund has financed public works projects all over the province, not the least of which have been investments in culture and education, dotting the province with state-of-the-art schools, arts venues, hospitals, and, of course, hockey rinks, among many, many other things. As a result, much of the province glitters with a sheen of surreal newness—a place where the future has already arrived. It also helps that the Prime Minister of Canada, Stephen Harper, is from Calgary and the roots of his popular political support are firm in Alberta. For the first time, Alberta is ruling the nation's political landscape.

A frequent criticism is that Alberta goes in only one direction: forward. The companion to that, of course, is that Albertans don't do enough looking back. There's good support for that criticism, too, when you consider that less than half the province's population was born here; as a society of newcomers, history is an abstract concept, at best.

But for those deep-seated Albertans, a worrying consequence of all the rapid growth has been a partial abdication of what made the province so attractive in the first place. And no, it's not just money; rather, it's the spectacular peaks of the Rockies and low, rolling green of the foothills in the run-up to the mountains, the broad plains of the Albertan prairie, and the deep river valleys and deltas that cradle much of the province's biodiversity.

As the boom has continued apace in recent years, much hand-wringing has taken place among long-time Albertans, as the northern Athabasca delta is increasingly fouled by the massive scale of extraction in the oil sands. Farther south, in Calgary and Edmonton, a similar alarm has risen as ever-sprawling suburbs claim thousands of acres of rolling foothills and plains—Alberta's signature landscape, the subtle geographic moments leading to the less-subtle mountains, and the places where farming and ranching, the province's early lifeblood, forged the identity some fear may be forever lost to development's continued march.

There is a sense, however, that public opinion in go-go Alberta—where they've learned to make hay while the sun shines because, as the early '80s bust showed, it doesn't shine every day—is starting to soften toward the preservation of its heritage.

While the right-leaning Progressive Conservative Party in Alberta has enjoyed uninterrupted rule and a lopsided majority of seats, since 1971, the most recent provincial election, in 2008, showed some chinks in the armor. This is not to say that the Conservatives walked away with less than a majority (they had one, and then some), but for the first time in memory, environmental issues and the hell-bent pace of oil-sands development were pushed to the center of the agenda. Perhaps for the first time ever, a majority of Albertans favored slowing the pace of the province's breakneck resource development—unheard of in a place where the industry-friendly Conservative government had, for decades, given Big Oil a relative carte blanche. In 2010, Calgary made history and showed its burgeoning new identity by electing Naheed Nenshi as mayor; he's the first visible minority (an Ismaili Muslim) to hold such an office in any major Canadian city.

This, in Alberta, is progress. In a place where the overriding ethic has always been money, the notion of heritage—the coveted cowboy culture (or "Western heritage," as they prefer) that gets trotted out for the Calgary Stampede each summer and then summarily shelved (for the city slickers, at least)—has typically been a footnote. But it's always been vital to a breed of Albertan for whom the land has been synonymous with their identity. And in the current generation, for the first time, that notion is growing—which may be why, among the most optimistic of Albertans, a favorite hope is edging closer to the truth: The first boom is when Alberta grew; the second one—cautiously continuing today—is when it grew up.

LOOKING BACK AT ALBERTA
Political History

The province of Alberta has been the province of Alberta for only a little more than 100 years; established in 1905 as a province of Canada, the year it joined Confederation under inaugural premier Alexander Rutherford was hardly the beginning of its story.

More to the point is that, not long before it became a Canadian province, the district of Alberta had been engaged in a long and committed campaign for autonomy from the nascent Dominion of Canada, which acquired the territory from the Hudson's Bay Company in 1870. As much as it longed for nationhood, Alberta finally gave in after the turn of the century, and so began the province's long-standing (and ongoing) resentment of the central Canadian government.

Alberta has always grumbled about being an afterthought in federal policy, at best—and blatantly exploited, at worst. The worst of times came during the first oil boom, when Pierre Trudeau was prime minister. In 1980, just before the boom went bust, Trudeau's government, the federal Liberals, instituted the National Energy Policy, which mandated Alberta sell its oil to the rest of Canada at less than world prices.

Needless to say, the policy didn't endear Albertans, fiercely independent-minded at the best of times, to their prime minister. Tension had been mounting for years; then-Calgary mayor Ralph Klein had intentionally stoked the flames of Western alienation with a number of aggressive attacks on not only the federal government, but also the constant influx of Easterners looking to cash in on Alberta's high times.

So when Trudeau took a tour through the West not long after the NEP was implemented, he was met with protest and ridicule in Alberta—culminating in a famous moment when Trudeau answered his Albertan critics from the window of a train with a middle-finger salute.

Not surprisingly, perhaps, 1980 was the year that saw the birth of a new political party in Alberta, the Western Canada Concept. It meant exactly what it said: A mandate to sever the four western provinces (Manitoba, Saskatchewan, Alberta, and British Columbia) from what it saw as the exploitive and resource-sucking power centers of Ontario and Quebec in the east.

The WCC was no joke; in the 1982 Alberta provincial election, Gordon Kesler won a seat in the provincial legislature, running as a WCC candidate. Kesler lost his seat not long after, but Western alienation had registered on the national radar as a very real, and very strong, political force.

Nobody could have guessed just how strong when, in 1987, Preston Manning, the son of Ernest Manning, a prominent Albertan politician and provincial premier for the right-wing Social Credit party from 1943 to 1968, founded the Reform Party, a resolutely arch-conservative party with western Canada at the top of its priority list.

Manning ran the party in federal elections but initially placed candidates only in western ridings; in its early days, it was a clear protest party—a statement by disgruntled Albertans that they believed none of the traditional parties had the West's interests at heart.

However, Reform took off. By 1993, with the Progressive Conservative government floundering, right-leaning voters fled en masse to Reform, handing them 52 of a possible 282 seats. The governing Liberals won 151, but Reform, a fringe project intended as protest only 5 years before, had arrived.

Then, in 2006, the impossible: Under the leadership of Calgary's Stephen Harper, the former Reform Party, now merged with the badly weakened Progressive Conservatives under the banner of the Conservative Party, formed the government of Canada.

Founding Alberta

Needless to say, Alberta has been a hotbed of political fervor over the years. Resolutely free-thinking, the roots of the maverick Alberta spirit can be seen in how it came to be. Initially explored as part of Rupert's Land, the vast area of the far northwest plied by trappers from the Hudson's Bay Company and its rival North West Company, Alberta's founding fathers are descended from hardy stock.

How else to describe early settlers who first arrived in the mid-18th century to a frozen wasteland—and decided to stay? Alberta's early draw was the fur trade, plied mostly in the far north, notably from Fort Chipewyan, a trading post so successful that it came to be known as "the emporium of the north" by trappers and explorers.

The far northern outposts were plied by disparate groups of French Canadians and Scotsmen from the Orkney Islands; while evidence of the French presence can still be found in bits and pieces throughout Alberta, the Scottish presence exists in full force. Scots Presbyterianism, in fact, is the foundation of the relatively devout Christianity that's still deeply embedded in rural Alberta today.

While the Hudson's Bay Company and North West Company battled for economic supremacy in the north, another battle—a spiritual one—was emerging alongside the business concern. Both the Roman Catholic Church, from its base in Montreal, and the Anglican Church of Canada sent missionaries into the desolate hinterland in the hopes of converting Native Canadians to their faith. Relics of the contest can be found throughout the province: At Fort Chipewyan in the far north, a surprisingly ornate Catholic Church, its ceilings painted a deep, celestial blue, sits on the shores of Lake Athabasca; in St. Albert, the body of Father Albert Lacombe, perhaps Alberta's most famous missionary, is entombed in the place where he first established a settlement in 1861.

The Catholic presence might seem particularly odd, given the fact that the province is named for Princess Louise Caroline Alberta, the fourth daughter of Queen Victoria and Prince Albert. But over the years, the western frontier has drawn immigrants from all corners of the globe, notably Ireland, Poland, and the Ukraine. But the Scots win the prize for place naming: Calgary, Airdrie, Canmore, and Banff, to name but a few, have the Scottish stamp (though the Princess scores points for Lake Louise and the tiny farming hamlet of Caroline, along the Cowboy Trail).

Alberta's eventual arrival at province-hood can be attributed to two men: Sir Frederick Haultain, the premier of the western territories, and Frank Oliver, the owner of Edmonton's *Bulletin* newspaper at the time. Their lobbying finally convinced Prime Minister Sir Wilfrid Laurier to include Alberta and Saskatchewan in Confederation on September 1, 1905. True to Alberta form, though, it wasn't without intrigue: Laurier, a federal Liberal, appointed Alexander Rutherford, also a Liberal, as the first provincial premier (Haultain, the more natural choice, was a Tory conservative).

Together, Rutherford and Oliver ensured that Edmonton, a largely Liberal town, would become the provincial capital over Tory Calgary (the grand Parliament buildings in Edmonton are the signature architectural landmark in the city). The political split—and the bitterness in Calgary—endures to this day.

Law, Lawlessness & the Native Presence

In its early days, Alberta was truly the Wild West. Settlers had to contend with all the ornery varmints of any Hollywood western: Cattle rustlers and horse thieves, gunslingers, and of course, a Native Canadian presence that didn't always take kindly to the newcomers' claims on a land they had always imagined as their own.

With a mind to encouraging agricultural development in the West, when the Dominion acquired the territories in 1870, it began negotiating treaties with various native bands, offering them reserve lands—tiny fractions of the province's geography—and perpetual government support in exchange for the vast majority of Alberta's best, most arable lands.

Around the same time, a new plague was being brought upon the natives, already decimated by Western disease like smallpox, brought by hunters and traders filtering in to Alberta from the American frontier. With them came whiskey—firewater, as the natives came to know it—which debilitated many tribes due to its abuse. All around them, the world they knew was falling apart; growing numbers of settlers and opportunistic hunters—some of them killing just for the thrill of it—were driving once-plentiful buffalo herds, the native population's primary food source, to near extinction. No small task, considering they had numbered in the tens of millions before the arrival of the white man. Callous "sportsmen" would open fire on herds from the windows of their trains, felling dozens of the giant creatures at a time for a laugh, their carcasses left to rot.

With the growing invasion and scarcity of food, the tensions between native bands themselves ratcheted up, culminating in 1870 with the Battle of Belly River (now the Old Man River), within the civic boundaries of modern-day Lethbridge. The resident Blackfoot tribe, devastated by smallpox, was set upon by a war party of Cree people looking to take advantage of the Blackfoot's weakness.

The war party stumbled across a Peigan tribe camp and, whipped into a frenzy, decided to attack without sending word back to their main camp. As the battle was waged the news spread to nearby main camps, including the Peigan, Blood, and Blackfoot, the initial targets. As these bands joined forces, the Cree war party was decimated; 300 Cree warriors were killed trying to escape.

 Throwing Sand on the Fire

Much of Calgary's central business district is built from sandstone from nearby quarries. Long-lasting, certainly, but significantly harder to move and build with than, say, wood frame. Why? In 1886, much of the nascent city of Calgary burned to the ground. Determined that would never happen again, civic fathers promoted the sandstone industry, thus giving the city its early architectural heritage.

It was the last battle between native bands on Canadian soil. But the tension it represented was starting to worry Ottawa, concerned about the uneasy mix of settlers, natives, and opportunistic Americans running wild in its newly acquired territories.

Then, in 1873, came the defining moment: In June, a party of American wolf hunters stormed into neighboring Saskatchewan, enraged that a large number of their horses had been stolen from their camp in Northern Montana. Unable to track their trail, the hunters arrived in the Battle Creek area, in the Cypress Hills, where two active trading posts were located next to a camp of about 300 Nakota people. An evening of too much whiskey and an argument about the missing horses resulted in the drunken hunters, along with local whiskey traders, opening fire on the Nakota camp. Twenty-three Nakota people were killed, along with one hunter.

It was called the Cypress Hills massacre, and it outraged Canadians across the Dominion, furious at the insult to their sovereignty that the reckless American hunters represented. The incident became the impetus for Sir John A. Macdonald, Canada's first prime minister, to found the North-West Mounted Police, initially headquartered right there in Cypress Hills. The North-West Mounted Police endure to this day as the Royal Canadian Mounted Police—or Mounties, as they're known, famous for their jodhpurs, red coats, and wide-brimmed hats.

Charged with policing the whiskey trade and enforcing the agreements the government had established with various native bands, the NWMP brought a great degree of calm to a rabidly lawless land.

THE LAY OF THE LAND

Much of the Albertan identity is derived from the land, from the prairies and badlands to the east, to the jagged Rocky Mountains to the west. All in all, it's a remarkable collection of geographic features for a region of its size.

The Badlands

East of Calgary and stretching to the south is a unique collection of high plains and deep canyons riven by ancient waterways like the Red Deer River, which Albertans have taken to calling the badlands. The Lakota people called the region *Makhóšiĉa*—literally, "bad land"—while early French trappers echoed the sentiment, deeming the region *les mauvaises terres à traverser*—"bad lands to cross."

There's good reason for this. The plains stretch out in every direction but drop off almost completely without warning into deep, eerie canyons too steep to descend into,

Looking Back at Alberta

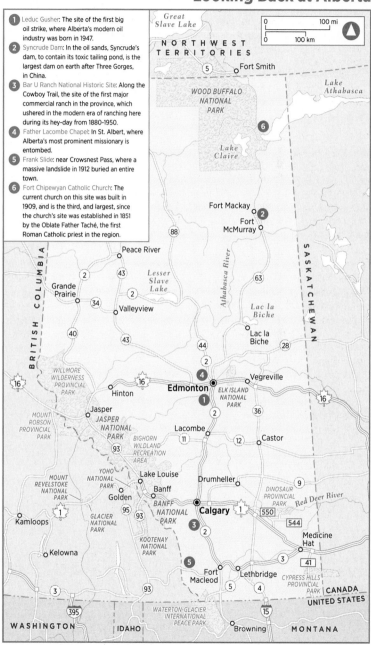

1 Leduc Gusher: The site of the first big oil strike, where Alberta's modern oil industry was born in 1947.

2 Syncrude Dam: In the oil sands, Syncrude's dam, to contain its toxic tailing pond, is the largest dam on earth after Three Gorges, in China.

3 Bar U Ranch National Historic Site: Along the Cowboy Trail, the site of the first major commercial ranch in the province, which ushered in the modern era of ranching here during its hey-day from 1880-1950.

4 Father Lacombe Chapel: In St. Albert, where Alberta's most prominent missionary is entombed.

5 Frank Slide: near Crowsnest Pass, where a massive landslide in 1912 buried an entire town.

6 Fort Chipewyan Catholic Church: The current church on this site was built in 1909, and is the third, and largest, since the church's site was established in 1851 by the Oblate Father Taché, the first Roman Catholic priest in the region.

thus forcing huge detours. The soil, clay and sand, is for the most part loose and dry, making it nearly useless for agriculture and subject to rapid and dramatic erosion.

For all these practical problems, the badlands are also starkly beautiful; hiking in Horse Thief Canyon, near Drumheller, for example, is an exceptional experience, one of preternatural beauty that makes you feel transported back thousands, if not millions, of years. Good thing you're not, though, or you'd encounter thousands of flesh-eating dinosaurs for whom the badlands are famous: The Drumheller region is one of the premiere paleontological regions in the world and contains one of the field's premiere museums in the Royal Tyrell.

The Mountains

This, of course, is the main attraction: Towering peaks cradling massive glaciers, icy blue-green lakes, the rare air of high altitude that tastes as fresh and pure as the time before man. The Rocky Mountains, which stretch north and west through Alberta from Montana's border, are undoubtedly one of the world's greatest geographical features, and the government of Canada, along with the province of Alberta, has been justifiably committed to preserving its alpine zones for the enjoyment and benefit of the entire planet.

The three Rocky Mountain national parks—Waterton Lakes, Banff, and Jasper—are all UNESCO World Heritage sites; and provincial alpine parks like those in Kananaskis Country do much to insulate the rolling foothills east of the mountains themselves from Alberta's rampant development. All of them are meticulously managed for maximum use with minimum impact: hiking trails, campsites, and guidance from the various parks authorities are first-rate.

Still, you shouldn't expect to have much time to yourself in most of these regions. As gorgeous as they are, they're extremely popular, especially in the summer months. If you don't want to brave the crowds, you might want to consider Waterton Lakes; no less spectacular than Banff or Jasper, but significantly less developed, Waterton is the wildest of all the alpine parks in the province. And it's hardly roughing it; quaint and rustic accommodation and a handful of good dining options make it a more authentic mountain experience than all the bells and whistles of Banff.

The Heartland

Just east of the rocky peaks are the low-rolling foothills, and beyond them, the broad prairies. Before oil was king here, Alberta's identity was built on agriculture—ranching and wheat farming, in particular—and for many a long-time Albertan, the province's culture still flows very much from the cowboy way.

At any given time, there are roughly 6 million beef and dairy cattle on Alberta ranchlands; annually, the province produces about 6.5 million metric tons of wheat annually, its biggest crop (barley is second, at around 4.5 million). Agriculture employs about 75,000 Albertans—only about 4% of the labor force, but as any farmer or rancher will tell you, it's a pretty significant 4%. "Farmers Feed Cities!" read the signs posted along Alberta's rural byways, and it's nothing but the truth: For all the glossy corporate sheen of Calgary and Edmonton, the vast expanses of farmland still dominate much of the provincial landscape.

But it's the land itself that has helped to forge the Albertan identity. Images of lonesome cowboys riding range in the ranchlands of the foothills are as much a part of Alberta's particular mythology as anything, perhaps even more so than the recent oil boom. Ranchers often are encouraging caution and fighting to stem further oil development in traditional natural areas. The land and its people are Alberta's history, and, as ranchers are reminding politicians and newcomers alike, an important part of its future.

In the headlong rush to development, long-time stewards of the land see Alberta's signature landscapes as threatened—by sprawling subdivisions, superhighways, golf courses, oil wells, you name it. Thankfully, there are still enough old-timers around to remind the newcomers of part of the reason why they came to Alberta in the first place—big skies, open places, and natural beauty. May it be ever thus.

The North

It's ironic to some that the source of Alberta's vast wealth is far out of sight of most of the people who reap its benefits. A little more than 400km (249 miles) north of Edmonton sit Alberta's oil sands, a massive store of crude oil—the world's second-largest proven supply, after Saudi Arabia—just north of the rapidly expanding town of Fort McMurray. Here, one of the largest-scale industrial excavations in history is taking place, as thousands of tons of bitumen—the oily muck in which the crude is trapped—is trucked to separating and refining plants on-site to extract the oil.

The relative invisibility of the oil sands projects, some believe, is part of the problem. There's a growing sense in the province that, if only most residents could see the devastating effect on the landscape, then the headlong rush to rapid development might slow down some. So far that hasn't happened, but growing public opinion here, for the first time, favors prudence over haste—not the Alberta way, historically, but perhaps a sign of better days ahead for conservation efforts.

The boreal forests of the north, after all, represent much of the province's most pristine wilderness. North of Fort McMurray lies the Athabasca River delta, the second-largest such wetland after the Amazon, and a cradle of tremendous biodiversity. Where it empties into Lake Athabasca sits Wood Buffalo National Park, the wildest of any of the wilderness parks in the province, with only one gravel road skirting its edge. It's also home to the last free-roaming herd of bison on Earth, all but eradicated during colonialism. The park is a throwback that way—a preserved portion of the Alberta that was. But it's also a powerful testament to what could be lost should the breakneck pace of development continue.

The Wildlife

Alberta veritably teems with wildlife—some places more than others, though often, it's just a matter of knowing where to look. On the prairies, it's in the ground, where millions of prairie dogs live much of their lives underground; or in the sky, where hawks, crows, owls, and ravens scan the flatlands for just such creatures—to them, a meal.

As you approach the mountains, larger mammals start to appear: deer, bighorn sheep, elk, and mountain goats, and the creatures that feed on them, like cougars, coyotes, and wolves—and Alberta's signature fearsome creature, the grizzly bear. Massive and imposing, grizzlies can get to be as tall as 3m (10 ft.) when on their hind legs; largely herbivorous, these massive creatures can (and will) eat almost anything if they get hungry enough, and their speed (they can run as quickly as 30kmph/19 mph), strength, and flesh-tearing teeth and claws make predation an easy option.

They tend not to disturb humans—as disinterested in bumping into you as you are them—but a grizzly caught by surprise, or one that believes a threat exists to her cubs, is as dangerous an animal as exists in the world. Historically, biologists have estimated that there are thousands of grizzlies in Alberta, but recent reports say there are approximately 700 in the province today (outside of national parks). So, the grizzly has been listed as a threatened species in Alberta. The dwindling numbers are due to habitat loss and low reproduction rates; hunting of grizzly bears is banned and strictly enforced in Alberta.

Farther north, in the boreal forests of the Athabasca delta, other large species, like moose, thrive on the rich wetlands. And, of course, the last free-roaming bison herd on Warth is safe and sound within the bounds of Wood Buffalo National Park.

Alberta's northern boundary extends into the frozen taiga and tundra, which means migratory herds of caribou pass through its borders, as well. And, of course, the northern lakes are home to many species of fish, such as lake trout and northern pike, which draw sport fishers from all over the world.

POPULAR CULTURE: FILM & TV, BOOKS & MUSIC

Alberta has a savvy film board, which encourages many productions from Hollywood to film in the province; but it also has a strong local culture of literature, theater, and music. A few examples follow.

Film & TV

Due to its spectacular landscapes and obvious cowboy culture, Alberta has been the site of many westerns over the years. One of the most recent—and most famous—is *Brokeback Mountain,* directed by Ang Lee and starring Jake Gyllenhaal and the late Heath Ledger as star-crossed lovers. Though the movie was set in Wyoming and Texas, Alberta was an able stand-in for both; the production was based in Calgary and was shot in various locations throughout the southern part of the province in 2004, including Kananaskis Country and the towns of Cowley and Fort Macleod. (Incidentally, while the movie was in production, the NHL's Calgary Flames were in the midst of their Cinderella run to the Stanley Cup finals. Lee, from Hong Kong, became so wrapped up in their playoff march that he became a rabid fan, going to every game; he remains a devoted Flames supporter to this day.)

But *Brokeback* is hardly the only movie to have been shot in and around the foot-hills: *The Assassination of Jesse James by the Coward Robert Ford,* starring Brad Pitt, in 2006; *Legends of the Fall,* a 1994 movie also starring Pitt and Anthony Hop-kins; and the Academy-Award winning *Unforgiven,* directed by and starring Clint Eastwood, along with Gene Hackman and Morgan Freeman, were all shot here; as was the decidedly more obscure—but chillingly realistic—2000 film *The Claim,* directed by Brit Michael Winterbottom, about a gold-rush town in the mountains of Northern California. And, just west of Lethbridge, Writing on Stone Provincial Park provided much of the backdrop for the zany Robin Williams comedy *RV.*

The iconic landscapes of the badlands, in the province's eastern reaches, have also provided a handy backdrop. Morgan Freeman's shack in *Unforgiven* was in Horseshoe Canyon, just outside Drumheller, which also provided the backdrop for *Shanghai Noon,* a western comedy starring Jackie Chan and Owen Wilson. Large chunks of *Superman 3* were also shot in the badlands, with Calgary's shiny office towers standing in for Metropolis. Kevin Costner's 2003 western Open Range was filmed mostly on the Stoney Nakota Reserve just east of Canmore.

The badlands' arid landscape has also managed to double for faraway locales, like Armenia in Canadian director Atom Egoyan's 2003 film *Ararat*, about the early 20th century Armenian genocide; nearby hamlet Nacmine provided the saloon that doubled for a Mexican cantina in *Dead Bang*, a 1989 movie starring *Miami Vice* star Don Johnson. The region also doubled for the decidedly less-exotic locale of nearby Montana in the 2001 film *Knockaround Guys*, starring Seth Green and Vin Diesel as the inept sons of Brooklyn mobsters sent to Montana to retrieve a bag of cash. (Naturally, things don't go as planned; fish-out-of-water mayhem ensues.)

Alberta has also been the site of some prominent TV shows, though far fewer; the best known, perhaps, is Stephen Spielberg's epic miniseries *Into the West,* from 2005.

The best example of Alberta proudly standing in for itself is the 2000 Canadian indie comedy *Waydowntown,* starring well-known Canadian actor Don McKellar and others, where a group of young Calgary office workers bet a month's salary on who can go the longest without stepping outside of the city's maze of glass towers, malls, interconnected walkways, and food courts into the fresh air.

Books

Alberta has produced many authors, but none so beloved as W.O. Mitchell. Mitchell, who died in 1998, was born in Saskatchewan but spent the majority of his adult life in Alberta, and was a significant influence on some of Alberta's major cultural institutions, including the Banff Centre, where he was director in the early '70s. Called Canada's Mark Twain by some for his ability to capture rural prairie life, his most celebrated work is likely *Who Has Seen the Wind* (McClelland & Stewart), about coming of age on the Canadian prairies. It's been described by some as Canada's *Catcher in the Rye*. Mitchell died in Calgary, aged 83.

Mitchell's stature as a writer helped spawn a new generation of authors in the province, among them Rudy Wiebe, an epic tragedy writer of the Canadian prairies (his 1973 novel *The Temptations of Big Bear* [McClelland & Stewart] won the Governor General's prize for fiction, his first of two), and William P. Kinsella, the author of *Shoeless Joe* (Houghton Mifflin Harcourt)—which became the Hollywood movie *Field of Dreams,* starring Kevin Costner—who was born in Edmonton and spent his formative years in the province before moving to British Columbia. Guy Vanderhaeghe, from neighboring Saskatchewan, penned one of the country's great novels, *The Englishman's Boy* (McClelland & Stewart), which hinges on the events of Alberta's Cypress Hills massacre.

Some of the most exciting new non-fiction writers are turning their gaze to the state of the province. Park warden Sid Marty's *The Black Grizzly of Whiskey Creek* (McClelland & Stewart) looks at Parks Canada's dealing with wildlife, while *Leaning on the Wind* (McClelland & Stewart) showcases life under the notorious Albertan Chinook winds. Calgarian travel writer Will Ferguson's hilarious *Beauty Tips from Moose Jaw* (Knopf Canada) and *How to Be a Canadian* (Douglas & McIntyre) give great insight into the local psyche. Journalist Andrew Nikiforuk's *Tar Sands: Dirty Oil and the Future of a Continent* (Greystone Books) takes a close and definitely uncomfortable look at the oil sands of the Fort McMurray area.

Music

While pop culture fans may grouse that he's far outstripped in notoriety, fame, and record sales by Alberta's best-known songstress, k.d. lang, or *Billboard* magazine's "Band of the Decade," Nickelback, there's little point disputing that Ian Tyson is the province's iconic troubadour. Tyson penned one of the best-known folk songs of all time, *Four Strong Winds,* with his wife Sylvia in the '60s and, since then, has cemented his reputation as one of the most prominent singer-songwriters of all time. Tyson still lives on his ranch along the Cowboy Trail and remains a devout Albertan. In 2006, when rampant oil development in southern Alberta seemed poised to threaten some of the wild foothills, Tyson led a protest group to government.

lang, meanwhile, also isn't one to shy away from political issues in her home province, but she's made more foes than friends. lang, a vegan, made a commercial for People for the Ethical Treatment of Animals where she denounced the beef industry: "If you knew how meat was made, you'd probably lose your lunch," she said. "I know. I'm from cattle country. That's why I became a vegetarian."

Needless to say, this didn't go over well in her tiny hometown of Consort, Alberta, in the heart of Alberta ranching territory; the sign that once proudly proclaimed it the "Home of k.d. lang" was defaced overnight.

But she's not the only superstar. After years of working the nightclub circuit in Calgary, native Calgarian Jann Arden broke through in 1994 with her hit single "Insensitive," which made it to #12 on the *Billboard* charts. Arden never looked back as she went on to register 17 Top-10 singles from eight albums. Still a devout Calgarian, until recently, Jann ran a restaurant with her family, the Arden Diner, on trendy 17th Avenue. It closed in 2007.

But the most prominent Albertans to reach rock stardom on a global scale are tiny Hanna, Alberta's Nickelback. Fronted by lead singer Chad Kroeger, their 2001 single "How You Remind Me" reached #1 on both Canadian and American charts; it finished 2002 as the *Billboard* Hot 100 #1 single of the year. The band has gone on to produce a string of hits, including "Hero" for the movie *Spider Man 2,* "Photograph," and "Rockstar."

FOOD & DRINK

For a long time, the typical Albertan menu would list beef, beef, and more beef, with a side of potato, and—what's that? Greens? Who needs that, we've got beef!

Thankfully, things have changed; particularly, as the cities have become more cosmopolitan and sophisticated (not to mention moneyed), the depth and breadth of cuisine has taken off.

Both Calgary and Edmonton now claim restaurants that are among the most innovative and creative in the country; and while beef still figures into a great many menus all over the province—and rightly so, as Alberta beef has legitimately gained a reputation as some of the best in the world—restaurants here were among the first to whole-heartedly embrace local-eating food trends, as well as exotic game meats.

Conservative Alberta has very much embraced the major contemporary food trends, and you're the beneficiary. It's hard to find a higher-end establishment that doesn't list entrees of bison or elk—both mild red meats with considerably lower fat content than beef—and makes a point of the provenance of each ingredient, many culled (seasonally, at least) from local farms and markets. In addition, you'll find a vast array of ethnic cuisines, from Middle Eastern to Asian to African, that reflect Alberta's burgeoning diversity; in the cities especially, there's something for every taste.

In smaller centers and in the heartland you'll likely find yourself relegated to meat and potatoes—or chain-style restaurants like Earl's and Moxie's, two Alberta staples that are actually quite good. But in urban centers like Calgary and Edmonton, or well-trod tourist destinations like Banff and Jasper, be sure to consult the dining guide for some remarkably cosmopolitan, sophisticated, and creative options.

There's far more to be found in these places than a superlative steak (though there's still plenty of that to be had, thankfully); even the most demanding foodies will find themselves satisfied, if not actually thrilled, at some of the offerings.

Frommer's Road-Tripping Favorites

Alberta is for drivers. With great open horizons and excellent highways, road-tripping is a regular activity in these parts. Most drives take you through picturesque little towns. Many have gems hidden on dusty main streets. So, pull over with for a hot mug and a special treat at these, my picks for best coffee shops and teahouses in the province:

○ **Buttercup Country Baker, Bragg Creek:** An old-fashioned bakery that specializes in artisanal breads, drop-ins can pair a coffee with a cupcake, cookie, or "bear's paw" donut. Bragg Creek Village Centre, 4–16 White Ave. © **403/949-2253.**

○ **Communitea Café, Canmore:** If you're en route to Banff and want to make a quick stop in Canmore, don't go anywhere but this downtown cafe for breakfast, lunch, or a snack. There are dozens of loose-leaf teas to choose from, the best espresso in the Bow Valley, and treats ranging from biscotti and macaroons to fresh croissants. 1001 6th Ave. © **403/678-6818.**

○ **Mother Mountain Teahouse, Delia:** A teeny, tiny little town en route from Calgary to Drumheller is home to this refurbished cabin. Relaxed, casual, and home to superb daily quiches. 102 1st Ave. © **403/364-2056.**

○ **Plain of the Six Glaciers Teahouse, Lake Louise:** This is the only one you have to hike into. It's a stunning 2½-hour hike (see p. 167) deep into an intense alpine landscape. You'll be rewarded with lemon squares and tea in this cozy log cabin that just may have the best patio in Canada.

○ **Sommerhouse Teahouse, Nanton:** In an historic home 45 minutes south of Calgary, slip into Victorian times with hand-stitched tablecloths, scones, and cream pies. 2202 21st St. © **403/646-1158.**

○ **Stone's Throw Café, Blairmore:** Everything is baked in-house at this warm cafe not far from the Frank Slide in the Crowsnest Pass. Spring and summer mean rhubarb crumble; winter calls for carrot cake. 13019 20th Ave. © **403/562-2230.**

PLANNING YOUR TRIP TO ALBERTA

3

"Western" is the applicable label for the province of Alberta, both geographically and in mindset. Sitting north of Montana, the province's western border is defined by the Rocky Mountain range that spills over into neighboring British Columbia, Canada's westernmost province.

With their strong economy and a true love for their province, Albertans are friendly and welcoming to visitors. The tourist industry here has a surfeit of tour operators, information bureaus, and a top-notch provincial travel authority in Travel Alberta.

Your trip can be equal parts wilderness adventure and city slicking; Calgary and Edmonton both offer superlative shopping, dining, and cultural activities. And Calgary, in particular, being only an hour from Banff National Park, is an ideal jumping-off point for outdoor adventures.

Once you've arrived in the province, you'll find getting around a breeze (especially if you have a car), unless winter conditions lead to treacherous driving conditions (which happens only about a dozen times a winter).

For additional help in planning your trip and for more on-the-ground resources in Alberta, turn to "Fast Facts," on p. 261.

WHEN TO GO

WEATHER Never forget: This is Canada, and that means in the winter, it's going to be cold. Mountain weather can be inconsistent, but you can generally rely on sub-freezing temperatures any time between early December and mid-March, though the southern portions of the province sometimes offer the respite of a mid-winter Chinook (see p. 86), which can temporarily elevate the temperature to spring-like warmth. Nonetheless, it would be imprudent to attempt driving in

Alberta in winter without at least snow tires, and if you're going into the mountains, some recommend chains, as well.

Naturally, the farther north you go, the colder it gets; excursions into the province's far north, like Wood Buffalo National Park, are only for the hardiest in the dead of winter, when temperatures can drop to –58°F (–50°C).

Still, Alberta, with its wealth of activities like downhill skiing, is one of the best places in the world for outdoor winter fun. Cold but completely sunny days are the norm. The winter season peaks over the Christmas/New Year's period, when prices can nearly double, and spring break, usually in March. If you can plan a late January or February winter vacation in Alberta, you'll save a fair amount of money. And you can see snow in parts of Banff well into spring.

Summer, though, is really tourist season, when parks like Banff and Jasper are brimming with tourist buses and campers. Summers are spectacular in Alberta, typically dry, warm, and sunny; the problem is that everyone knows it, and rates for everything, from hotels to tours, rise accordingly.

As a general rule, spring runs from early April to mid-May, summer mid-May to mid-September, fall mid-September to early November, and winter early November to late March.

As much of Alberta is at high altitude, prepare for cool evenings, even in the heat of summer. And if you venture north, have plenty of insect repellent on hand: the bugs are voracious in spring and early summer.

As a general guide: In Calgary, winter weather ranges from a low of about 9°F (–13°C) to around 30°F (–1°C); summer hovers typically around 68 to 77°F (20–25°C) but can get much hotter on exceptional days. In Edmonton, where it's typically colder, winter weather ranges from a low of 2°F (–17°C) up to 14 to 23°F (–10 to –5°C). In summer, temperature ranges from 50 to 77°F (10–25°C). In the mountains, where weather is changeable year round, Banff winter temperature ranges from about 5°F (–15°C) up to the high 20s (–2 to –4°C); and in summer, from 41 to 77°F (5–25°C).

HOLIDAYS　National holidays are celebrated throughout the country; all government facilities and banks are closed, but some department stores and a scattering of smaller shops stay open. If the holiday falls on a weekend, the following Monday is observed.

Canadian national holidays include New Year's Day, Good Friday, Easter Monday, Victoria Day (in mid- to late May, the weekend before U.S. Memorial Day), Canada Day (July 1), Labor Day (first Mon in Sept), Thanksgiving (in mid-Oct), Remembrance Day (Nov 11), Christmas Day (Dec 25), and Boxing Day (Dec 26). Alberta also celebrates Family Day on the third Monday in February and Heritage Day on the first Monday of August.

Alberta Calendar of Events

Alberta has some wonderfully unique festivals and special events, the granddaddy of them being the annual Calgary Stampede, the biggest rodeo in the world, which usually takes place the second week of July. The Edmonton Fringe Festival, an international theater event, takes place in October.

For an exhaustive list of events beyond those listed here, check http://events.frommers. com, where you'll find a searchable, up-to-the-minute roster of what's happening in cities all over the world.

JANUARY & FEBRUARY

Ice on Whyte Festival. On Edmonton's trendy Whyte Avenue; kids will surely enjoy the ice sculptures that line the active competition, not to mention the ice castle, ice slides, and ice maze. Edmontonians endure a long, cold winter; this is one of the ways they make the best of it; and then some. For more info, call ☎ **780/437-4182** or visit **www.iceonwhyte.com**.

Jasper in January Festival. Features wine and beer tastings, live music, and the annual Mountain Park Lodges Chili Cook-Off, all in a festive civic atmosphere in downtown Jasper. Canyon crawling, sleigh rides, and skating are added to the everyday winter activities of downhill and Nordic skiing. Jasper is always beautiful, but it's never so much fun as it is during this festival. For more information, contact Jasper Tourism at ☎ **780/852-3858** or **www.jasperinjanuary.com**.

Ice Magic Festival. An annual, nationally sanctioned ice-sculpting derby held at the Fairmont Chateau Lake Louise. The work here is world-class and a treat for kids and adults alike. For more information, call ☎ **403/762-0284** or visit **www.banfflakelouise.com**. There is no admission charge to view the sculptures.

MARCH

Taber Cowboy Poetry Festival. A favorite 1-day event in the heart of Alberta corn country. The name says it all: public readings at restaurants, bars, and the library, and all for free. For more info, see **www.albertacowboypoetry.com**.

APRIL

Rocky Mountain Food and Wine Festival. This festival tours the province from spring to fall, and its first stop is in Red Deer each April (it hits Banff in May, and Calgary and Edmonton in October). Expect tastings of wines from all over the world, served in concert with the best that each local venue's chefs have to offer. It's great fun for gourmands. For more info, call ☎ **866/228-3555** or visit **www.rockymountainwine.com**. Admission starts at C$23 adults, not including food or wine.

MAY

Calgary Beerfest. Beers from all over the planet are on offer here, as well as seminars and Q&As with brew masters who explain their craft to all in search of the perfect glass of suds. For more info, call ☎ **403/520-5433** or visit **www.get-a-life.ca/calgary beerfest**. Tickets are C$21 adults in advance or C$27 at the door.

Calgary International Children's Festival. An annual weekend-long festival that gives kids an array of experiences to help connect them to the performing arts. Dance, theater, music, and puppetry are all part of the many spectacles to be found here. For more info, call ☎ **403/294-7414** or visit **www.calgarychildfest.org**. Tickets for most performances start at C$13 adults.

MAY TO AUGUST

Banff Summer Arts Festival. From drama to opera, visual to musical, all of the arts are featured during the summer-long series of events held at the venerable Banff Centre (☎ **800/413-8368** or 403/762-6301; www.banffcentre.ca). Some of the best artists in the world showcase their talents in stunning settings.

JULY

Calgary Stampede. The greatest outdoor show on Earth, as it calls itself (and the biggest rodeo in the world) takes over the city for 10 days every July, transforming this urbane center into a hat-and-boots-wearing Wild West burgh. With carnival rides, to boot. See **www.calgarystampede.com** for more info. Admission to the Stampede grounds is C$14 adults; rodeo tickets start at C$25, through Ticketmaster (www.ticketmaster.ca).

Calgary Folk Music Festival. A big stop for big names on the folk circuit, this gathering in a green park on sunny Prince's Island ranges from funk to blues to world to folk. See **www.calgaryfolkfest.com** for more info; call ☎ **403/233-0904** for tickets.

Strathmore Heritage Days Stampede. It's the third-largest rodeo in Canada, but next to the flashy event in nearby Calgary, Strathmore feels intimate. There are six rodeo events and an annual running of the bulls. Thrill seekers only need apply. It's also a great value. General admission tickets are C$5 for adults, C$3 for seniors and children 11 to 15, and free for kids under 11. Call ✆ **403/934-5811** or visit **www.calgarychildfest.org** for more details.

AUGUST

Edmonton Folk Music Festival. In the height of summer in Edmonton's cool river valley, the folk fest, along with the Fringe Festival, is one of the city's biggest. Dozens of performers, spread over two days, make it a folk feast, with recent notables like Van Morrison, Ben Harper, John Pryne, and Los Lobos topping the bill. See **www.edmontonfolkfest. org** for more information, or call ✆ **780/429-1999** for tickets.

Edmonton International Fringe Theatre Festival. This world-class theater festival takes over the city for 10 days every late August. See performers from all over the world testing their freshest material with a local audience regarded by many to be among the most theater-savvy in the world. See **www.fringetheatreadventures. ca** for more info, or call ✆ **780/448-9000** for tickets.

Canmore Highland Games. The town's named for a legendary Scottish leader, so it's only natural that this Rocky Mountain town hosts a crowd of kilt-wearing, saber-tossing, piping, drumming, and dancing Celts each Labour Day weekend. For info see **www.canmorehighlandgames.com**, or call ✆ **403/678-9454**.

SEPTEMBER

Artcity Festival. Calgary's annual celebration of art, architecture, and design happens every September, with 10 days of exhibitions, performances, installations, lectures, and tours. Artcity leans toward the playful, interactive side of art, so expect some fun stuff. For more information, call ✆ **403/870-2787** or visit **www.artcityfestival.com**. All exhibitions and events are free and open to the public.

OCTOBER

Wordfest, Banff and Calgary. Alberta's biggest annual literary festival, with readings and interviews with famous authors spread throughout venues from Calgary to Banff. Visit **www.wordfest.com** for more info or call ✆ **403/237-9068** for ticket information.

NOVEMBER

Banff Mountain Film and Book Festivals. Hosted by the Banff Centre, the festival highlights the best mountain storytelling to be found anywhere, in either books or film. Documentary, non-fiction, and fiction are all on the docket here, a highlight for those fascinated with mountain lore. See **www. banffcentre.ca/mountainculture/festivals** for more information or call ✆ **800/298-1229** or 403/762-6369 for tickets.

DECEMBER

Cowboy Christmas. In tiny Hillspring, Alberta (in the south), you can treat yourself to a different kind of Christmas experience with the Great Canadian Barn Dance's Cowboy Christmas Ball; the venue hosts a variety of old-time country Christmas pleasures, like ice skating, hockey, caroling, and horse-drawn sleigh rides, finished off with turkey dinner and live entertainment (Christmas country crooners, of course!). For more info, call ✆ **866/626-3407** or visit **http://gcbd.ca/cowboy-christmas-ball**. Tickets are C$40 for adults, C$35 for seniors, C$30 for children 10 to 17, or C$13 for children under 10.

ENTRY REQUIREMENTS

Passports

If you are a U.S. citizen, you have to carry a U.S. passport to enter Canada and to re-enter the U.S. from Canada.

The Intelligence Reform and Terrorism Prevention Act of 2004 required that by January 1, 2008, travelers to and from Canada (and other neighboring countries) had to have a passport or other secure, accepted document to enter or re-enter the United States.

This is a change from prior travel requirements and affects all U.S. citizens entering the United States from countries within the Western Hemisphere who do not currently possess valid passports. For the latest information on entry requirements between the U.S. and Canada, see http://travel.state.gov/travel.

Permanent U.S. residents who aren't U.S. citizens must have their Alien Registration Cards (green cards). If you plan to drive into Canada, be sure to bring your car's registration papers and proof of insurance.

Citizens of most European countries, former British colonies, and certain other countries (Israel, Korea, and Japan, for instance) do not need visas but must carry passports. Entry visas are required for citizens of more than 130 countries. Entry visas must be applied for and received from the Canadian embassy in your home country. For more information on entry requirements to Canada, see the Citizenship and Immigration website's Visitors' Services page at www.cic.gc.ca/english/visit/index.asp.

Although it is rare, immigration officials may prevent the entry of visitors who appear to pose a health risk, those they doubt will be able to support themselves and their dependants in Canada, or those whose willingness and means to return to their home country is in question. Also, immigration officials can prevent the entry of foreign nationals who have a criminal record. This includes any convictions for driving while intoxicated.

For information on how to get a passport, go to the "Fast Facts, Toll-Free Numbers & Websites" appendix (p. 261)—the websites listed provide downloadable passport applications, as well as the current fees for processing passport applications. For a good list of updated entry requirements, visit the Government of Canada's Going to Canada website at www.goingtocanada.gc.ca.

Most visitors can stay up to 6 months in Canada. The date you must leave the country will be stamped in your passport.

It is advised to always have at least one or two consecutive blank pages in your passport to allow space for visas and stamps that need to appear together. It is also important to note when your passport expires. Many countries require your passport to have at least 6 months left before its expiration in order to allow you into the destination.

Visas

Citizens of a variety of countries require a visa from the Canadian Government to travel to the country. For information on obtaining a visa, please visit "Fast Facts," on p. 267. Many people do not require a visa to visit Canada. These include citizens of Andorra, Antigua and Barbuda, Australia, Austria, Bahamas, Barbados, Belgium, Botswana, Brunei, Croatia, Cyprus, Denmark, Estonia, Finland, France, Germany, Greece, Hungary, Iceland, Ireland, Israel (National Passport holders only), Italy, Japan, Korea (Republic of), Latvia (Republic of), Lithuania, Liechtenstein, Luxembourg, Malta, Monaco, Namibia, Netherlands, New Zealand, Norway, Papua New Guinea, Poland, Portugal, St. Kitts and Nevis, St. Lucia, St. Vincent, San Marino, Singapore, Slovakia, Solomon Islands, Spain, Swaziland, Sweden, Slovenia, Switzerland, the United States, and Western Samoa. No visa is required for persons lawfully admitted to the United States for permanent residence who are in possession of their Alien Registration Card (green card) or can provide other evidence of permanent residence, or for British citizens and British Overseas Citizens who are re-admissible to the United Kingdom.

(**Note:** This list was accurate at press time; for the most up-to-date list of countries exempt from visas, consult www.cic.gc.ca/english/visit/apply-who.asp.)

Customs

WHAT YOU CAN BRING INTO CANADA

Non-Canadian residents will pass through **Canada Border Services Agency** (📞 **800/461-9999** in Canada or 204/983-3500; www.cbsa-asfc.gc.ca) upon arrival. Customs regulations are very generous in most respects but get pretty complicated when it comes to firearms, plants, meats, and pets. You can bring in free of duty up to 50 cigars, 200 cigarettes, and 200g (7 oz.) of tobacco, provided you're over 18. Those of age (18 in Alberta) are also allowed about 1.15L (39 oz.) of liquor, 1.5L (51 oz.) of wine, or 24 355mL (12-oz.) containers of beer or ale. Dogs, cats, and most pets can enter Canada with their owners, though you must have proof of rabies vaccinations within the last 36 months for pets over 3 months old.

Canada has complex requirements, restrictions, and limits that apply to importing meat, eggs, dairy products, fresh fruits and vegetables, and other food from around the world. You can avoid problems by not bringing such goods into Canada.

As for firearms, visitors can bring rifles into Canada during hunting season and for the purposes of hunting. Handguns and automatic rifles are generally not allowed. Fishing tackle poses no problems, but the bearer must possess a nonresident license for the province or territory where he or she plans to use it.

WHAT YOU CAN TAKE HOME FROM CANADA

Returning U.S. citizens who have been away for at least 48 hours are allowed to bring back, once every 30 days, US$800 worth of merchandise duty-free. You'll be charged a flat rate of 3% duty on the next US$1,000 worth of purchases. Be sure to have your receipts handy. With some exceptions, you cannot bring fresh fruits and vegetables into the United States. Travelers 18 and older are allowed to bring back 1L (34 oz.) of alcohol, 100 cigars, or 200 cigarettes duty free. For specifics on what you can bring back, download the invaluable free pamphlet "Know Before You Go" online at www.customs.gov. Or contact **U.S. Customs & Border Protection** (1300 Pennsylvania Ave. NW, Washington, DC 20229; 📞 **877/287-8867**) and request the pamphlet.

U.K. citizens returning from Canada have a customs allowance of 200 cigarettes, 50 cigars, or 250g (8¾ oz.) of smoking tobacco; 2L (68 oz.) of still table wine; 1L (34 oz.) of spirits or strong liqueurs (over 22% volume); 2L (68 oz.) of fortified wine, sparkling wine, or other liqueurs; 60cc (mL) perfume; 250cc (mL) of toilet water; and £145 worth of all other goods, including gifts and souvenirs. People under 17 cannot have the tobacco or alcohol allowance. For more information, contact **HM Customs & Excise** at 📞 **0845/010-9000** (020/8929-0152 from outside the U.K.), or consult their website at www.hmce.gov.uk.

The duty-free allowance in Australia is A$900 or, for those under 18, A$450. Citizens can bring in 250 cigarettes or 250g (8¾ oz.) of loose tobacco, and 2.25L (76 oz.) of alcohol (for travelers 18 and older). If you're returning with valuables you already own, such as foreign-made cameras, you should file form B263. A helpful brochure available from Australian consulates or Customs offices is "Know Before You Go." For more information, call the **Australian Customs Service** at ☎ **1300/363-263** or visit www.customs.gov.au.

The duty-free allowance for New Zealand is NZ$700. Citizens over 17 can bring in 200 cigarettes, 50 cigars, or 250g (8¾ oz.) of tobacco (or a mixture of all three if their combined weight doesn't exceed 250g/8¾ oz.), plus 4.5L (152 oz.) of wine and beer, or 1.125L (38 oz.) of liquor. New Zealand currency does not carry import or export restrictions. Fill out a certificate of export, listing the valuables you are taking out of the country; that way, you can bring them back without paying duty. Most questions are answered in a free pamphlet available at New Zealand consulates and Customs offices: New Zealand Customs Guide for Travellers, Notice no. 4. For more information, contact **New Zealand Customs** (the Customhouse, 17–21 Whitmore St., P.O. Box 2218, Wellington; ☎ **04/473-6099** or 0800/428-786; www.customs.govt.nz).

WHAT YOU CAN BRING BACK INTO THE U.S.

It is forbidden to bring into the U.S. almost any meat products (including canned, fresh, and dried meat products such as bouillon, soup mixes, etc.). Generally, condiments (including vinegars, oils, and spices), coffee, tea, and some cheeses and baked goods are permitted. Avoid rice products, as rice can often harbor insects. Bringing fruits and vegetables is not advised, though not prohibited. Customs will allow produce depending on where you got it and where you're going after you arrive in the U.S.

Medical Requirements

Unless you're arriving from an area known to be suffering from an epidemic (particularly cholera or yellow fever), inoculations or vaccinations are not required for entry into Canada.

GETTING THERE & AROUND

Getting to Alberta

BY PLANE

The **Calgary International Airport** (airport code YYC; ☎ **877/254-7427** or 403/735-1200; www.calgaryairport.com) and the **Edmonton International Airport** (airport code YEG; ☎ **800/268-7134;** www.flyeia.com) are the main air hubs to access much of Alberta.

If you are heading anywhere in the south, including Banff National Park, fly to Calgary. To get to Banff, take either the **Banff Airporter** (☎ **888/449-2901** or 403/762-3330; www.banffairporter.com) for C$53 one-way, or **Brewster** Tours' airport shuttle (☎ **800/760-6934;** www.explorerockies.com) for C$49 one-way. Banff is 129km (80 miles) west of Calgary. It's about 90 minutes by car from the airport.

If you want to visit Jasper National Park or the north, fly to Edmonton (363km/226 miles east of Jasper; a 4-hr. trip by car).

To inquire about flights into Calgary and Edmonton, contact **Air Canada** (☎ **888/247-2262;** www.aircanada.ca), **Continental Airlines** (☎ **800/525-0280;** www.flycontinental.com), **Delta** (☎ **800/221-1212;** www.delta.com), or **WestJet** (☎ **888/937-8538;** www.westjet.com).

Many airlines from Europe and the United Kingdom fly to Calgary and Edmonton, as well.

To find out which airlines travel to Alberta, please see "Airline Websites," p. 268.

BY CAR

You can access Alberta from the province of Saskatchewan to the east, from the province of British Columbia to the west, or from the U.S. state of Montana to the south. There are many secondary roads, but the most popular highways are the Trans-Canada Highway 1, which enters Alberta near Medicine Hat and exits west of Banff, and Highway 16, also known as the Yellowhead Highway, which arrives east of Edmonton and exits Alberta west of Jasper. From the south, access Alberta via I-15, which comes north through Conrad, Montana.

There are scores of border crossings between Canada and the U.S.; however, not all of them keep the same hours, and some are closed at night. Be sure to double-check the hours of your border crossing before you set out.

In addition to having the proper ID to cross into Canada (See "Entry Requirements," earlier in this chapter), drivers may be asked to provide proof of insurance and ownership for their vehicle. If you're going hunting, remember that firearms are allowed into Canada only under special circumstances.

If you fly in and want to rent a car to explore the province, the options are plentiful. All the major car rental companies operate throughout the province, most of them with offices in all but the small towns.

Car rental agencies at the Calgary and Edmonton international airports include **Budget** (© 800/527-0700; www.budget.ca), **Hertz** (© 800/654-3131; www.hertz.ca), **National** (© 800/227-7368; www.nationalcar.ca), and **Thrifty** (© 800/367-2277; www.thrifty.com). They also have offices in the towns of Banff and Jasper, as well as Fort McMurray and Lethbridge.

As in the U.S., credit cards that offer insurance benefits are honored in Canada; check with your credit card company if you wish to choose this option.

For listings of the major car rental agencies in Alberta, see the "Fast Facts, Toll-Free Numbers & Websites" appendix (p. 261).

BY TRAIN

This is not an easy prospect for visitors arriving from the U.S.—while the closest passenger-rail entry point is on the British Columbia coast, you can nonetheless use **Amtrak** (© 800/USA-RAIL [800/872-7245]; www.amtrak.com) to link up with Canada's **VIA Rail** (© 888/VIA-RAIL [888/842-7245]; www.viarail.com) in Vancouver and make the day-long journey through the mountains to Edmonton, via Jasper (a 16-hr. journey, total). Canadian travelers can use VIA Rail to get to Edmonton from Vancouver to the west and Saskatoon to the east with three weekly VIA departures. VIA also has three weekly departures connecting Jasper, Alberta with Prince George and Prince Rupert, BC. VIA has no Calgary or Banff routes, but the privately owned **Rocky Mountaineer Vacations** (© 877/460-3200; www.rockymountaineer.com) has a stunning overnight trip that departs from Vancouver and stops in either Banff or Jasper (you select your destination at the changeover in Kamloops, BC).

Royal Canadian Pacific Luxury Rail Tours (© 877/665-3044; www.royalcanadianpacific.com) has a 6-day tour on a luxury heritage rail car that leaves Calgary, passes through the Canadian Rockies south of Banff, and loops back through Golden and Banff to Calgary.

BY BUS

Greyhound (© 800/661-8747; www.greyhound.ca) and **Brewster** (© 877/791-5500; www.brewster.ca) have daily trips from Vancouver to Edmonton and Jasper, including a 2-day drive with an overnight stay midway. Their routes from Vancouver to Calgary stop in Canmore and Banff. Greyhound's main routes through Alberta are along the Trans-Canada Highway 1 from Banff through Calgary and on to Regina and Winnipeg to the east; Highway 2, from Lethbridge through Calgary, Red Deer, and Edmonton; and the northern Yellowhead Highway from Saskatoon to the east through Edmonton to Jasper National Park and on to Prince George, BC. Greyhound serves dozens and dozens of towns across Alberta. There is no service connecting Alberta with the U.S. state of Montana to the south.

Getting Around

Alberta's a big place, and the car rules here. It's your best bet for traveling from center to center, as well as picking up on beautiful scenery along the way.

Once you're in the big cities, you can fairly rely on public transit (both Calgary and Edmonton have extensive bus and light-rail services) or your own two feet to explore the neighborhoods to be found there. Calgary, in particular, has an impressive network of bike paths—one of the largest in North America—so that's a nice way to explore that city, as well.

Still, as you navigate Alberta, it's a real benefit to have four wheels under you for the freedom to explore.

BY PLANE

Air Canada (www.aircanada.com) sells flight passes for unlimited travel. The least expensive, and most relevant here, is the Western Commuter pass, which offers 10 flights between the cities of Calgary, Edmonton, Vancouver, and Victoria. The pass is good for 1 year and costs C$2,990. Along with their regional carrier, Jazz, Air Canada flies into airports in Edmonton, Calgary, Fort McMurray, Lethbridge, Medicine Hat, and Grande Prairie.

WestJet (www.westjet.com) flies in and out of Calgary, Edmonton, Fort McMurray, and Grande Prairie.

BY CAR

Even in the cities, here, in the heart of the new West, you'll either miss out on a lot of the action or spend a fortune on cabs if you don't have a car. Plus, if you plan to explore the countryside, some of the most incredible scenery can be seen from behind the wheel.

If you're visiting from abroad and plan to rent a car in Canada, keep in mind that foreign driver's licenses are usually recognized, but you should get an international one if your home license is not in English or French.

Check out Expedia.ca, Travelocity.ca, and Priceline.ca, all of which offer competitive online car rental rates. For car rental agencies, see the "Getting There" section (above) or the appendix "Fast Facts, Toll-Free Numbers & Websites" (p. 261).

The roads in Alberta are generally top-rate; speed limits on the major highways—those with four lanes—are typically 110kmph (68 mph), with secondary routes usually at 90kmph (56 mph). In the cities, unless otherwise posted, the maximum is 50kmph (31 mph).

Running east-west through Calgary and on to Banff is Highway 1, the Trans-Canada Highway. Perhaps the most gorgeous drive on the continent, the Icefields Parkway (Hwy. 93), stretches through 230km (143 miles) of spectacular mountains and glaciers, between Lake Louise and Jasper. Turn north just past Lake Louise to get on Highway 93.

The Queen's Highway, or Highway 2, connects Calgary and Edmonton to the north, a distance of 286km (178 miles), and Calgary and Montana to the south, where it becomes U.S. Route 89. From Edmonton, the Yellowhead Highway (Hwy. 16) links the city to Jasper, and then continues on to Prince Rupert, BC.

BY BUS

Bus travel is often the most economical form of public transit for short hops between cities, but it's certainly not an option for everyone. **Greyhound** (*©* **800/661-8747;** www.greyhound.ca) is the sole nationwide bus line. International visitors can obtain information about the **Greyhound North American Discovery Pass.** A 7-day pass costs C$239 per person, while a 30-day pass is C$439 per person. The pass can be obtained from foreign travel agents or through www.discoverypass.com for unlimited travel and stopovers in the U.S. and Canada.

Greyhound links all the major and minor centers in the province. There are several departures daily from the major centers, and usually at least one per day in the smaller centers. Consult the website for prices and a timetable.

MONEY & COSTS

THE VALUE OF THE CANADIAN DOLLAR VS. OTHER POPULAR CURRENCIES

Can$	US$	UK£	Euro (€)	Aus$	NZ$
C$1	US$0.95	£0.61	€0.75	A$1	NZ$1.35

Frommer's lists exact prices in the local currency. The currency conversions quoted above were correct at press time. However, rates fluctuate, so before departing, consult a currency exchange website, such as www.oanda.com/convert/classic, to check up-to-the-minute rates.

In general, prices for goods and services are comparable between Canada and the U.S.—with the Canadian dollar now stronger than it has been in many years, Canadian prices are not as low as they once were for travelers using U.S. dollars. On a day-to-day basis, traveling in Canada will cost about the same as traveling in the U.S., as long as restraint is used when making hotel selections. European travelers using euros and the British pound will find that Canadian prices for comparable goods and services are generally lower than those in their home countries.

Alberta has no provincial sales tax. There's only the 5% national Goods and Services Tax (GST), plus a 5% Accommodations Tax.

WHAT THINGS COST IN ALBERTA	C$
Taxi from the airport to downtown Calgary	45
Double room, moderate	140
Double room, inexpensive	100
Three-course dinner for one without wine, moderate	30–35
Bottle of Molson Canadian beer	5.50–6
Bottle of Coca-Cola	2.50
Cup of coffee	1.75–2.25
1L (¼ gal.) of premium gas	0.95
Admission to most museums	5–9
Admission to national parks	9.80

CURRENCY

Canadian currency is counted in dollars and cents, just like the currency system in the U.S. However, in addition to pennies, nickels, dimes, and quarters, there are one- and two-dollar coins (there are no dollar or two-dollar bills). Dollar coins are bronze-plated coins and bear the picture of a loon—hence their nickname "loonies." There's also a two-toned C$2 coin sometimes referred to as a "toonie." Paper currency begins with C$5 bills.

Exchanging currency is pretty straightforward, particularly if you are changing U.S. dollars into Canadian. Most banks on both sides of the border will exchange U.S. and Canadian currency, even if they don't normally advertise as foreign exchange services. However, the easiest way to procure Canadian currency is simply to withdraw money from an ATM.

Often, Canadian businesses will accept U.S. dollars in payment, making the conversion at the till. If you do spend American money at Canadian establishments, you should understand how the conversion is done. Often, by the cash register, there's a sign offering a standard exchange rate. This percentage, say 10%, is the "premium"—it means that for every U.S. greenback you hand over, the cashier will see it as $1.10 in Canadian dollars. Thus, for an C$8 tab, you need pay only $7.27 in U.S. bills. However, currency conversions at the till rarely provide the best rates of exchange, so it's best to shop around for the best rate, which is usually found in banks.

It's a good idea to exchange at least some money into Canadian currency—just enough to cover airport incidentals and transportation to your hotel—before you leave home so you can avoid lines at airport banks or ATMs. You can exchange money at your local American Express or Thomas Cook office, or your bank. If you're far away from a bank with currency-exchange services, American Express (✆ 800/807-6233; www.americanexpress.com) offers traveler's checks and foreign currency, though with a C$15 order fee and additional shipping costs.

ATMS

The easiest and best way to get cash away from home is from an ATM (automated teller machine)—often called an ABM in Canada. The **Cirrus** (✆ **800/424-7787;**

www.mastercard.com) and **PLUS** (© **800/843-7587;** www.visa.com) networks span the globe; look at the back of your bank card to find out which network you're on, then call or check online for ATM locations at your destination. Be sure you know your personal identification number (PIN) before you leave home and find out your daily withdrawal limit before you depart. Also, keep in mind that many banks impose a fee every time a card is used at a different bank's ATM, and that fee can be higher for international transactions (up to C$5 or more) than for domestic ones (where they're rarely more than C$1.50). On top of this, the bank from which you withdraw cash may charge its own fee. Ask your bank about international withdrawal fees.

You can also get cash advances on your credit card at an ATM. Keep in mind that credit card companies try to protect themselves from theft by limiting the funds someone can withdraw outside their home country, so call your credit card company before you leave home.

If your ATM is associated with a small community bank or credit union, it may not work at all ATMs in Canada, particularly the nonbank ATMs found in convenience stores and public facilities. In such cases, simply find a bank ATM that will honor the card as long as it belongs to a major ATM network like Cirrus or Plus.

TRAVELER'S CHECKS

Traveler's checks are something of an anachronism from the days before the ATM made cash accessible at any time. Traveler's checks used to be the only sound alternative to traveling with dangerously large amounts of cash. They were as reliable as currency but, unlike cash, could be replaced if lost or stolen.

These days, traveler's checks are less necessary because most cities have 24-hour ATMs that allow you to withdraw small amounts of cash, as needed. However, keep in mind that you will likely be charged an ATM withdrawal fee if the bank is not your own, so if you're withdrawing money every day, you may be better off with traveler's checks—provided that you don't mind showing identification every time you want to cash one.

You can get traveler's checks at almost any bank. American Express offers denominations of C$20, C$50, C$100, C$500, and (for cardholders only) C$1,000. You'll pay a service charge ranging from 1% to 4%. You can also get American Express traveler's checks over the phone by calling © **800/221-7282;** Amex gold and platinum cardholders who use this number are exempt from the 1% fee. AAA members can obtain checks without a fee at most AAA offices.

Visa offers traveler's checks at Citibank locations nationwide, as well as at several other banks. The service charge ranges between 1.5% and 2%; checks come in denominations of C$20, C$50, C$100, C$500, and C$1,000. Call © **800/732-1322** for information. MasterCard also offers traveler's checks. Call © **800/223-9920** for a location near you.

If you carry traveler's checks, be sure to keep a record of their serial numbers separate from your checks in the event that they are stolen or lost. You'll get a refund faster if you know the numbers.

CREDIT CARDS

Credit cards are a safe way to carry money, they provide a convenient record of all your expenses, and they generally offer good exchange rates. You can also withdraw cash advances from your credit cards at banks or ATMs, provided you know your

PIN. If you've forgotten yours, or didn't even know you had one, call the number on the back of your credit card and ask the bank to send it to you. It usually takes 5 to 7 business days, though some banks will provide the number over the phone if you tell them your mother's maiden name or some other personal information. Your credit card company will likely charge a commission (1% or 2%) on every foreign purchase you make, but don't sweat this small stuff; for most purchases, you'll still get the best deal with credit cards when you factor in things like ATM fees and higher traveler's check exchange rates. However, if you are planning on putting a lot of purchases or cash advances on a credit card, you should inquire about the commission charged for exchanging currency. The rates vary from card to card.

Canadian businesses honor the same credit cards as in the U.S. Visa and Master-Card are the most common, though American Express is also normally accepted in hotels and restaurants catering to tourists. Discover and Diner's Club cards are somewhat less frequently accepted.

For tips and telephone numbers to call if your wallet is stolen or lost, go to "Lost & Found" in the "Fast Facts, Toll-Free Numbers & Websites" appendix (p. 264).

Beware of hidden credit-card fees while traveling. Check with your credit or debit card issuer to see what fees, if any, will be charged for overseas transactions. Recent reform legislation in the U.S., for example, has curbed some exploitative lending practices. But many banks have responded by increasing fees in other areas, including fees for customers who use credit and debit cards while out of the country—even if those charges were made in U.S. dollars. Fees can amount to 3% or more of the purchase price. Check with your bank before departing to avoid any surprise charges on your statement.

STAYING HEALTHY

Alberta has state-of-the-art medical facilities and top-flight physicians throughout the province.

In general, Canada poses no particular health threats to travelers. Nonetheless, you may want to check the CDC's (Centers for Disease Control) travel advisory site at www.cdc.gov/travel for any last-minute alerts.

Regional Health Concerns

One thing you should be aware of if you're in the national parks of Alberta is giardiasis (also identified as "beaver fever"). *Giardia* is a parasite sometimes found in mountain lakes and streams. As long as you can resist the temptation to drink directly from some of those pristine, icy-blue waters—and the parks authority warns you not to—you'll be fine. If not, a cycle of metronidazole will take care of it.

DIETARY CONCERNS   In the major centers, there's something for everybody, from the most devout vegan to the observers of kosher and halal diets. Smaller towns may not be so well-versed in these kinds of dietary requirements, so plan ahead.

BUGS, BITES & OTHER WILDLIFE CONCERNS   In Alberta, where much of the land is wild, common sense reigns (some of it is to be repeated in upcoming chapters). When hiking in grizzly bear country, for example, make plenty of noise so as not to surprise the bears. If you happen upon a grizzly, speak calmly so that it can identify you as human, don't make eye contact (which it can take as threatening), and back away slowly—if you run, the bear may give chase.

Most animals you might encounter in Alberta are more afraid of you than you are of them; even the big predators have no more interest in crossing paths than you do. If you make plenty of noise and, if camping, secure your food and any lotions with aroma well up in a tree, out of scent range of bears and other critters, you'll likely encounter no problems.

Bugs, however, are another thing. While they tend to be rare at higher altitudes in the mountains, in summer, you can be besieged by voracious swarms of mosquitoes, black flies, horseflies, and deerflies in many parts of Alberta. They're particularly ferocious in the northern wetlands of the province. All of them bite; some take blood, others a chunk of flesh. Some of them really, really hurt. A thick coating of repellent is a must, but it may not deter all of them. Long sleeves, pants, and a hat are your best bets; so, too, is not going north until September, when insects start to die off. Also be on the lookout for wood ticks—small, flat-bodied, spider-like insects that bite humans and can carry Rocky Mountain spotted fever and Lyme disease (although the latter is rare in the Rockies).

RESPIRATORY ILLNESSES   While Ontario, a couple of thousand kilometers to the east, suffered a SARS scare in 2003, it was well-contained and quickly defeated. No such ailment ever came close to being this far west.

HIGH-ALTITUDE HAZARDS   One thing to bear in mind is that much of Alberta is at high altitude, meaning the air has less oxygen than at sea level. Your lungs will work harder here—not noticeable at a sidewalk cafe, perhaps, but potentially an issue high on a mountainside. Remember to pace yourself accordingly, especially during your first couple of days at altitude. Drinking a lot of water and keeping up good sleep habits also help.

SUN/ELEMENTS/EXTREME WEATHER EXPOSURE   Being at high altitude also means less atmosphere between you and the harmful rays of the sun. Especially in the mountains, a strong sunblock and sun hat are essential, in summer or winter.

Speaking of winter, remember: This is Canada. That means cold. In the northern parts of the province—Edmonton and beyond—you can usually rely on sub-freezing temperatures from December all the way through March; in the prairie regions, the winds can get painfully stiff, so be aware of wind chill and signs of frostbite.

The south, where the province narrows because of the mountains, is unpredictable because of that proximity. Weather systems move through the Rockies with alarming speed at times, and a sunny day can become a blizzard with disturbing quickness. The only real advice is to be prepared for anything, because that's what could happen.

If You Get Sick

In most cases, your existing health plan will provide the coverage you need. But double-check; international visitors, in particular, may want to buy travel medical insurance. (For more detailed information on this, see "Insurance," on p. 263.) Bring your insurance ID card with you when you travel.

If you suffer from a chronic illness, consult your doctor before your departure. For conditions such as epilepsy, diabetes, or heart problems, wear a Medic Alert Identification Tag (© **800/825-3785;** www.medicalert.org), which will immediately alert doctors to your condition and give them access to your records through Medic Alert's 24-hour hotline.

Pack prescription medications in your carry-on luggage and carry prescription medications in their original containers, with pharmacy labels—otherwise, they won't make it through airport security. Also, bring along copies of your prescriptions in case you lose your pills or run out. Don't forget an extra pair of contact lenses or prescription glasses. Carry the generic name of prescription medicines in case a local pharmacist is unfamiliar with the brand name. Canada's health care system is similar to that in the U.S., except that its health insurance for Canadian citizens is managed nationally by the federal government. Hospitals have emergency rooms open 24 hours for emergency care.

In addition, most cities also have walk-in clinics where nonemergency treatment is available. Look in the local Yellow Pages under "Clinics, Medical" for walk-in clinics; these clinics usually take credit cards, though they may be able to bill your private insurance directly. You can also inquire at your hotel, as some hotels have relationships with private practitioners to treat the emergency needs of guests.

Pharmacies are common, and most large cities have at least one 24-hour operation. You'll have no trouble getting prescriptions filled; in fact, prescription drugs are substantially cheaper in Canada than in the U.S. We list **emergency numbers** in "Fast Facts," p. 262.

CRIME & SAFETY

Like the majority of Canada, Alberta is a highly lawful society with very little violent crime. Common sense is your best companion when it comes to staying safe, but even in the big cities, and even late at night, you'd probably have to go looking for trouble to find any.

By reputation, at least, Alberta is very socially conservative and may not be overly welcoming to some alternative lifestyles; but on the whole, Albertans are progressive, accepting, and almost overwhelmingly friendly people.

In the mountains, be aware that almost any slope is a potential avalanche chute—and even small avalanches can be deadly. Drivers should avoid stopping in places where there are signs reading NO STOPPING, AVALANCHE AREA. Anyone venturing out into the backcountry should know how to recognize and travel safely in avalanche terrain. Call Parks Canada at © **403/762-1460,** in Banff, for the latest avalanche reports. See "Getting Around By Car," for more information on road safety.

Don't leave valuables in your car or unattended in public spaces throughout Alberta.

Gay and lesbian rights are enshrined as part of the federal Bill of Rights. It's unlikely that travelers will encounter discrimination while visiting Canada. It's possible to get into heated conversations regarding U.S. foreign policy, but little discrimination will result from this kind of dispute over political issues.

SPECIALIZED TRAVEL RESOURCES

In addition to the destination-specific resources listed below, please visit Frommers.com for other specialized travel resources.

LGBT Travelers

Canada is one of the most gay-tolerant travel destinations in the world. Gay marriage is legal in Canada, and the entire nation has nondiscrimination protection for gays and lesbians. While not every rural village will express the same level of tolerance, most gay travelers will encounter little adversity.

In Alberta, gay culture is celebrated in both Calgary and Edmonton with annual Gay Pride parades (in June and Sept, respectively); large gay communities, that until relatively recently kept a low profile in conservative Alberta, are now highly visible parts of both cities. Bars, clubs, and restaurants specific to the scene abound; see the specific city chapters for details.

A good clearinghouse for information on gay Canada is the website www.gaycanada.com, which features news and links to gay-owned or -friendly accommodations and businesses across Canada. Another guide for gay-based travel information for destinations worldwide is www.gay.com.

For more gay and lesbian travel resources visit www.frommers.com/planning.

Travelers with Disabilities

Most disabilities shouldn't stop anyone from traveling. There are more options and resources out there than ever before. A clearinghouse of official Canadian federal government information on disability issues, including those related to travel and transportation, is available from Persons with Disabilities Online (www.pwd-online.ca). The **Canadian Paraplegic Association** (© **613/723-1060;** www.canparaplegic.org) can offer advice for mobility-challenged travelers, as well as address issues for those with spinal cord injuries or other physical disabilities. From the national website, you can click to find provincial organizations.

A World of Options, a 658-page book of resources for travelers with disabilities, covers everything from biking trips to scuba outfitters. It costs C$30 (C$18 for members) and is available from Mobility International USA (132 E. Broadway, Ste. 343, Eugene, OR 97401; © **541/343-1284** voice and TTY; www.miusa.org).

Most museums and visitors centers are wheelchair-accessible, and most hotels now have at least one wheelchair-accessible floor.

For more on organizations that offer resources to disabled travelers, go to www.frommers.com/planning.

Family Travel

If you have enough trouble getting your kids out of the house in the morning, dragging them thousands of kilometers away may seem like an insurmountable challenge. But family travel can be immensely rewarding, giving you new ways of seeing the world through smaller pairs of eyes.

Alberta makes an especially great family-vacation destination because of its fantastic national park system and abundance of recreational activities. Destinations such as the Canadian Rockies are especially attractive, as outfitters make it easy to arrange guided hiking, biking, white-water rafting, and horseback-riding excursions simply by talking to your hotel's concierge. The big cities offer a range of options, from historical parks to zoos, and the prairies feature guest ranches and Old West activities.

Throughout this guide, kid-friendly activities are marked with a "Kids" icon—these destinations feature activities or facilities that your children may enjoy. In addition, most hotels offer free lodging for children under 16 (or even under 18 at some hotels) traveling with parents, and also offer complimentary continental breakfast. For a quick list of our choices for best family-friendly experiences in Alberta, see Chapter 1, and for a list of reasons why Waterton Lakes National Park (in Alberta's southwest corner) makes a great family vacation destination, see p. 135.

Remember that even children traveling with parents will be required to have some sort of official ID. This can be either a passport or a birth certificate. Children under the age of 18 traveling alone to Canada will need to have a signed letter from parents. For other guidelines for traveling with children, see "Entry Requirements," earlier in this chapter.

For a list of more family-friendly travel resources, visit www.frommers.com/planning.

Women Travelers

Canada is one of the most polite and nonviolent places on Earth, and most women will have no problems traveling in Alberta, either alone or with other women. A little common sense should prevent dangerous or uncomfortable situations. It's never a good idea to hitchhike alone, and walking alone late at night in cities isn't recommended.

In the Rocky Mountains, women-specific outdoor adventures are run by the **Alpine Club of Canada** (© **403/678-3200**; www.alpineclubofcanada.ca), and by **Yamnuska Mountain Adventures** (© **866/678-4164**; www.yamnuska.com).

For general travel resources for women, go to www.frommers.com/planning.

Senior Travel

Mention the fact that you're a senior while traveling in Alberta, and frequently, you can receive discounted admission prices to cultural and tourist attractions. In most Canadian cities, people over the age of 65 qualify for reduced admission to theaters, museums, ski resorts, tours, and other attractions, as well as discounted fares on public transportation. It is less common to receive discounts on lodging, though it does happen, so it is worth asking when you make your lodging reservations. Most of the major U.S. airlines have canceled their senior discount and coupon book programs; Air Canada does not offer senior discounts.

Members of AARP (formerly known as the American Association of Retired Persons; 601 E St. NW, Washington, DC 20049; © **800/687-2777** or 202/434-2277; www.aarp.org) can get discounts on hotels, airfares, and car rentals. AARP offers members a wide range of benefits, including *AARP: The Magazine* and a monthly newsletter. Anyone over 50 can join. The Canadian affiliate can be reached at www.carp.ca.

Parks Canada offers a discounted annual pass to the Canadian national park system for those 65 years of age and older. The discount amounts to about one-quarter off the regular adult rate.

For more information and resources on travel for seniors, see www.frommers.com/planning.

Student Travel

Alberta has always been a great place for young people. The seasonal tourist industry means that the resorts load up on students in the summer, usually from all over the world; Banff, most summers, seems to have more Australians than Canadians. It's also known as party central for the thousands of early-20s types that flock here.

The bigger resorts have dorm-style accommodations for staff. For those merely passing through, the network of hostels offer cheap beds for everyone—assuming they choose to use them.

Check out **International Student Travel Confederation (ISTC;** www.istc. org) for comprehensive travel services information and details on how to get an **International Student Identity Card (ISIC),** which qualifies students for substantial savings on rail passes, plane tickets, entrance fees, and more.

It also provides students with basic health and life insurance, and a 24-hour helpline. The card is valid for a maximum of 18 months. You can apply for the card online or in person at **STA Travel** (✆ **800/781-4040** in North America, 132 782 in Australia, or 0871 2 300 040 in the U.K.; www.statravel.com), the biggest student travel agency in the world; check out the website to locate STA Travel offices worldwide. If you're no longer a student but are still under 26, you can get an **International Youth Travel Card (IYTC),** which entitles you to some discounts, from the same people. **Travel CUTS** (✆ **866/246-9762;** www.travelcuts.com) offers similar services for both Canadians and U.S. residents.

RESPONSIBLE TOURISM

Alberta's reputation as an oil and gas powerhouse contrasts with the superbly eco-friendly nature of visiting the national parks of the Canadian Rockies (Waterton Lakes, Banff, and Jasper) or the eerily pristine badlands of the province's southeast. In the national parks, the environment comes first, and all tourists are expected to be respectful of nature at all times.

Meanwhile, plush executives from Calgary's shiny skyline make their fortune off exploitive and non-renewable resources—the oil sands near Fort McMurray in Northern Alberta have been called "Canada's worst eco-disaster." These same execs then jet off to their mountain paradises on the weekends to take sanctuary in nature. And so Alberta is indeed a place of contrasts.

The province includes a vast and diverse geography, from grasslands and badlands to glaciers and tall alpine peaks. Each area is vulnerable and fragile, and the simple rules of "leave no trace" should apply. For more information, visit www.leavenotrace.ca.

Albertans themselves are quick to ensure that visitors keep up with their eco-habits, from recycling to non-idling (if you're stopped by a train, please turn off your engine!). Locals also know to stay away from wildlife as much as possible.

If you're very keen to reduce your carbon footprint during your travels in Alberta, stick with public transit (the main carrier is Greyhound; see p. 78). For example, you can take a shuttle van from the Calgary airport to Banff and then ride the mountain town's electrical public bus system. You could even camp at the Tunnel Mountain Campground just outside town, thereby limiting your use of wastewater and electricity.

The more time you spend in the wilderness of Alberta, whether you're riding a bike along the North Saskatchewan River in Edmonton or backpacking through Kananaskis Country, the more you'll appreciate the need to care for the environment.

You can also use your fork to go green in Alberta by eating in one of the many restaurants in this book that serve locally sourced, organic foods. Better yet, head to one of the province's many farmers' markets and buy fresh produce right from the source.

Many major car rental agencies, including Budget and Hertz, now offer hybrid vehicles.

Animal-Rights Issues

The Calgary Stampede continues to come under fire for what various animal rights groups call the cruel treatment of rodeo animals. It's hard to argue, sometimes, when the chuck-wagon races, in which a team of horses pull wagon and driver around a track in close proximity to other wagons, seem to result in at least one dead horse each year (in

GENERAL RESOURCES FOR green TRAVEL

In addition to the resources for Alberta listed above, the following websites provide valuable wide-ranging information on sustainable travel:

- **Responsible Travel** (www.responsibletravel.com) is a great source of sustainable travel ideas; the site is run by a spokesperson for ethical tourism in the travel industry. **Sustainable Travel International** (www.sustainabletravelinternational.org) promotes ethical tourism practices and manages an extensive directory of sustainable properties and tour operators around the world.
- In the U.K., **Tourism Concern** (www.tourismconcern.org.uk) works to reduce social and environmental problems connected to tourism. The **Association of Independent Tour Operators (AITO;** www.aito.co.uk) is a group of specialist operators leading the field in making holidays sustainable.
- In Canada, **www.greenliving online.com** offers extensive content on how to travel sustainably, including a travel-and-transport section and profiles of the best green shops and services in Toronto, Vancouver, and Calgary.
- In Australia, the national body that sets guidelines and standards for ecotourism is **Ecotourism**

Australia (www.ecotourism.org.au). **The Green Directory** (www.thegreendirectory.com.au), **Green Pages** (www.thegreenpages.com.au), and **Eco Directory** (www.ecodirectory.com.au) offer sustainable travel tips and directories of green businesses.
- **Carbonfund** (www.carbonfund.org), **TerraPass** (www.terrapass.org), and **Cool Climate** (http://coolclimate.berkeley.edu) provide info on "carbon offsetting," or offsetting the greenhouse gas emitted during flights.
- The **Hotel Association of Canada** (www.hacgreenhotels.com) has a Green Key Eco-Rating Program, which audits the environmental performance of Canadian hotels, motels, and resorts.
- Visit **www.eatwellguide.org** for tips on eating sustainably in the U.S. and Canada.
- For information on animal-friendly issues throughout the world, visit **Tread Lightly** (www.treadlightly.org).
- **Volunteer International** (www.volunteerinternational.org) has a list of questions to help you determine the intentions and the nature of a volunteer program. For general info on volunteer travel, visit **www.volunteerabroad.org** and **www.idealist.org**.

both 2009 and 2008, horses were killed—one had a heart attack following the chuck-wagon races and another was euthanized after a collision; in 2007, three horses were killed—one instantly when its neck snapped following a collision in the chuck-wagon races). Those with animal cruelty sensitivities might not care to attend this event.

For information on animal-friendly issues throughout the world, visit **Tread Lightly** (www.treadlightly.org).

SPECIAL INTEREST & ESCORTED TRIPS

There's something for everybody here, from low-key relaxing vacations to adventures and intense experiences that will teach you something new. For information about active vacations, see chapter 4.

Academic Trips

Don't be surprised if you're inspired while exploring Alberta! There are a superb range of art courses, from writing to opera, offered at the world-class **Banff Centre** (© **403/762-6100;** www.banffcentre.ca). They also have an excellent centre for leadership development, focusing on business, cultural and non-profit sectors.

Adventure & Wellness Trips

The Canadian Rockies are surely one of the great hiking and outdoors destinations in the world. See Chapter 4 for a complete listing of guided adventure tours. Or relax and take things a bit deeper in the yoga and meditation retreats lead by Canmore-based Tracey Delfs of **Balance Quest** (www.balancequest.net).

Volunteer & Working Trips

Banff National Park's new **Volunteer Program** has a tourist-friendly "pitch-in" event called Helping Hands. For more information, visit www.pc.gc.ca/eng/pn-np/ab/banff/edu/edu5v.aspx.

To volunteer on one of a dozen different Albertan farms, visit the website for **World Wide Opportunities for Organic Farms** (www.wwoof.ca) and search under Alberta.

Escorted General Interest Tours

Escorted tours are structured group tours, with a group leader. The price usually includes everything from airfare to hotels, meals, tours, admission costs, and local transportation.

Brewster Transportation and Tours (P.O. Box 1140, Banff, AB T1L 1J3; © **866/606-6700;** www.brewster.ca) offers a wide variety of tours throughout Canada, both escorted and independent. Their offerings include motor coach and train excursions, ski and other winter vacations, city and resort combination packages, chartered day tours by bus, and independent driving tours. Highlights include a visit to the Columbia Icefield in Jasper National Park and one to Yellowknife, Northwest Territories, to see the aurora borealis. Many packages in the Rockies include stays at guest ranches.

Travel by train lets you see the Rockies as you never would in a bus or behind the wheel of a car. **Rocky Mountaineer Vacations** (369 Terminal Ave., Ste. 101, Vancouver, BC V6A 4C4; ☏ **877-460-3200;** www.rockymountaineer.com) bills its Rocky Mountaineer as "The Most Spectacular Train Trip in the World." During daylight hours between mid-April and mid-October, this sleek blue-and-white train winds past foaming waterfalls, ancient glaciers, towering snowcapped peaks, and roaring mountain streams. The Rocky Mountaineer gives you the options of traveling east from Vancouver; traveling west from Jasper, Calgary, or Banff; or taking round trips. A new rail service offers travel to and from Vancouver and Jasper via Whistler and Prince George. There's also a tour offering a VIA Rail connection from Toronto, or packages that include links to the Inside Passage from Prince Rupert to Victoria. Tours range from 2 to 12 days, with stays in the mountains and cities. A number of large travel companies offer extended trips that include some train travel, usually starting in Calgary and finishing, via the train, in Vancouver. These include **Tauck World Discovery** (☏ **800/788-7885;** www.tauck.com), which stops at all three of the lovely Fairmont hotels in Banff and Jasper, a mid-winter bus tour with **Collette Vacations** (☏ **800/340-5158;** www.collettevacations.com) and Australia's **APT Touring** (☏ **800/290-8687;** www.aptouring.com.au), which has a tour linking the Canadian Rockies with Alaska, among others.

For more information about escorted general-interest tours, including questions to ask before booking your trip, see www.frommers.com/planning.

STAYING CONNECTED
Mobile Phones

Phones from virtually all major American wireless providers, such as Verizon and T-Mobile, will function on one of the major Canadian networks (Telus, Rogers, or Bell). However, wireless charges will be very high for roaming outside your home country.

If you prefer, once you arrive in Canada, there are several options for temporary, pay-as-you-go phoning. Places like Best Buy and Future Shop—big chain stores that are virtually everywhere—sell pre-paid phones starting at C$50 (plus airtime). Virgin Mobile is your best bet, with no activation charge and a C$10 card that gets you about 40 minutes.

CellularAbroad (www.cellularabroad.com) will rent you a cell phone in Canada starting at C$49 for 7 days, plus airtime at C38¢ a minute.

Internet & E-Mail
WITH YOUR OWN COMPUTER

Almost all hotels have free wireless Internet available to guests; Starbucks locations throughout Alberta now offer wireless access through the Bell network for a fee. Many other cafes and restaurants offer free wireless. Consult www.jiwire.com; its Hotspot Finder is the world's largest directory of public wireless hotspots. Its Alberta listings top out at nearly 400.

WITHOUT YOUR OWN COMPUTER

Most major airports have **Internet kiosks** that provide basic Web access for a per-minute fee that's usually higher than cybercafe prices. Check out copy shops like

FedEx Kinko's, which offers computer stations with fully loaded software (as well as Wi-Fi).

For help locating cybercafes and other places where you can go for Internet access, please see "Internet Access" in the "Fast Facts, Toll-Free Numbers & Websites" appendix (p. 264).

Newspapers & Magazines

The two most important daily newspapers in Alberta are the *Calgary Herald* and the *Edmonton Journal.* National dailies are the *Globe and Mail* and the *National Post,* both published in Toronto. Virtually every small town in Alberta has a weekly community newspaper.

Local magazines that may be of interest include the left-leaning *Alberta Views,* the stylish *Avenue,* and the business-friendly *Alberta Venture.*

Telephones

The Canadian telephone system closely resembles the U.S. model. All operators (dial 0 from Canada to get one) speak English, as well as French, and respond in the appropriate language as soon as callers speak to them.

There are two area codes in Alberta: 403 in the south and 780 in the north. All of the province requires 10-digit dialing.

Pay phones in Alberta require C50¢ for a 3-minute local call. Directory information calls (dial ✆ **411**) are free of charge. Both local and long-distance calls usually cost more from hotels—sometimes a lot more, so check. As in the U.S., paper directories come in White Pages (residential) and Yellow Pages (commercial).

TO CALL ALBERTA FROM THE U.S.   Calls between Canada and the U.S. do not require the use of country codes. Simply dial 1 plus the three-digit area code and seven-digit number.

TO CALL ALBERTA FROM THE U.K. OR AUSTRALIA   First dial the international access code 00 (from Australia, dial 0011). Follow that with the Canadian country code 1, then the three-digit area code, and the seven-digit number.

TO CALL THE U.S. FROM ALBERTA   Simply dial 1 plus the three-digit area code and seven-digit number.

TO CALL THE U.K./IRELAND/AUSTRALIA/NEW ZEALAND FROM ALBERTA   First dial 011, then the country code (U.K. 44, Ireland 353, Australia 61, New Zealand 64), then the number.

TOLL-FREE NUMBERS   Phone numbers that begin with 800, 888, 877, and 866 are toll-free. That means they're free to call within Canada and from the U.S. You need to dial 1 first. Remember that some hotels will charge you for all phone calls you make, including toll-free ones.

Many convenience groceries and packaging services sell **prepaid calling cards** in denominations up to C$50. Many public pay phones at airports now accept American Express, MasterCard, and Visa.

For **reversed-charge or collect calls,** and for person-to-person calls, dial the number 0, then the area code and number; an operator will come on the line, and you should specify whether you are calling collect, person-to-person, or both. If your operator-assisted call is international, ask for the overseas operator.

For **directory assistance** ("Information"), dial _𝒞_ **411** for local numbers and national numbers in the U.S. and Canada. For dedicated long-distance information, dial 1, then the appropriate area code and 555-1212.

TIPS ON ACCOMMODATIONS

Being the tourist destination that it is, you'll encounter fluctuating room rates at most Alberta hotels, particularly seasonally; in summer, Banff and Jasper hotels will typically take whatever they can get, and deciphering their "code"—rack rate, walk-in rate, weekend rate, etc.—can be somewhat akin to learning a new language.

Hotels in Calgary, Edmonton and Fort McMurray depend mainly on business travel; their rates are therefore more expensive Monday through Friday. Understand that your bargaining power is weakest in the midst of a sunny July; if you're able to travel in late September, you could very well find yourself a deal or two.

Some of the online services, such as Expedia.ca and Priceline.ca, offer pricing that you won't find directly at the hotels. Try them before booking your accommodation.

Most accommodations in this book offer complimentary in-room or in-lobby Internet or Wi-Fi access. For hotels that charge for Internet or Wi-Fi, the price is stated in the review, otherwise it is generally "free" or included in the room price.

For tips on surfing for hotel deals online, visit www.frommers.com/planning.

ACTIVE VACATION PLANNER

M ost people don't come to Alberta with the intention of sticking to the cities. Blessed with extraordinary mountain terrain; beautiful rolling foothills; vast prairie land; and endless, big blue sky (most of the time), the province of Alberta cries out to be seen from the outside in.

There are wildlife to glimpse and diverse ecosystems to observe, and in the far north, there's the Athabasca, the second largest river delta in the world (after the Amazon), with wetlands that cradle more than 55 species of mammals and more than 200 species of birds. The national parks of Waterton Lakes, Banff, Jasper, and Wood Buffalo are all UNESCO World Heritage sites and offer unique opportunities to explore nature—albeit with wildly varying degrees of solitude.

Even urban Albertans often embrace the outdoors, so you'll also find plenty of opportunities for cycling in Calgary and Edmonton on an expansive and well-connected system of bicycle paths. In the winter, these paths can be used to cross-country ski, as well—always an interesting sight amid the downtown skyscrapers.

Whether you're intent on adventure or just want to try something new, this is the place to get out of the car and stretch yourself. This chapter lays out your options, from tour operators who run multi-activity packages to the best spots to visit outdoors (with listings of tour operators, guides, and outfitters that specialize in each), and provides an overview of Alberta's parks.

NATIONAL PARKS

Alberta's extraordinary natural environment features a wealth of protected areas, wildlife reserves, and archaeological zones. National parks, provincial parks, and nature preserves make up a significant chunk of Alberta's most beautiful and environmentally sensitive areas. Some are much more developed than others; the mountain parks are important tourist destinations and therefore are quite strenuously patrolled and regulated.

The discussion below lists all of Alberta's national parks (four), but it couldn't possibly comprise all the provincial parks, wilderness preserves, and bio-zones in the province (for that, go to the province's parks website, www.albertaparks.ca). Rather, it details the ones that are the most famous, most accessible, and most rewarding for visitors, including several of the largest and most biodiverse on the planet.

The national parks all require a visitor's permit: entry costs C$9.80 per person per day, C$20 per group or family per day (a "family" is considered up to 7 people in a single vehicle). If you stay more than a few days, it makes sense to buy an annual membership, which is C$68 per person or C$136 for a group or family. The Annual Discovery Package pass includes unlimited entrance into 27 national parks and national historic sites for a calendar year. The price is C$84 per person per year, C$166 per group or family per year. This pass is a good idea if you will be visiting at least a handful of national parks. If you go with an organized tour, the tour operators almost always take care of the bureaucratic details and include the fees in their package price.

Banff & Jasper National Parks

One of the most famous parks in the world, Banff—with its jagged peaks, rushing mountain streams, glacier-fed lakes, and world-class skiing and hiking—is also, not surprisingly, one of the most traveled.

Jasper, connected to Banff as the Rockies stretch north, is for some a welcome alternative to Banff's bustle. (Both parks have a central town with the same name; the Town of Banff and the Town of Jasper, also known as the "townsites.") Where Banff's townsite is busy and can feel commercialized during the peak season, Jasper can still feel quaint and lively, though not overcrowded. Either way, once you're outside both townsites, these two parks together comprise 17,519 sq. km (6,764 sq. miles) of vigilantly protected nature area. That's plenty of space for everybody.

The parks are traversed by one of the most scenic highway systems in Canada, making seeing them both in a single trip a relatively simple and shockingly gorgeous experience; innumerable nature trails leading to more remote valleys and peaks are interwoven throughout. This is hiking and skiing heaven.

Whichever destination you choose (if you choose), you'll find no shortage of incredible outdoor options. Whether it's a boat cruise on Maligne Lake in Jasper (p. 207) or hiking on high to the alpine meadows near Lake Louise in Banff (p. 166), it's easy for both towns to vanish quickly as you set out into the wilderness on the hundreds of kilometers of park-maintained trails.

Mountain bikers will particularly enjoy the Canmore Nordic Centre Provincial Park (p. 147); situated just east of Banff's gates on Highway 1, the center, built for

Nordic events in the 1988 Winter Olympics, offers a huge network of alpine bike trails in summer that will satisfy even the most ambitious cyclist. In winter, it's a world-class Nordic ski center.

Waterton Lakes National Park

For those seeking the road less traveled among the mountain parks, Waterton Lakes, tucked in the province's southwest corner, is it. Deer lounge on the front lawns of the few sweet little homes in the Waterton Townsite, while bighorn sheep wander the main street. The occasional bear or cougar wanders through, too, the town folk say, but they're equally comfortable with—or oblivious to—the human presence.

The best tour to be taken in Waterton is undoubtedly on the HMV *International*, an old steamer that takes passengers from Waterton Townsite south the full length of lower Waterton Lake and into Glacier National Park in Montana (p. 131). The towering mountains and glaciers surrounding you on the journey are extraordinary.

What to Bring

Outdoor and adventure travel in Alberta requires some special gear, and it's a good idea to come prepared; though you'll have no problem buying all your gear in, say, Banff, you may not much like the tourist premium you'll pay. You can rent some equipment, such as crampons for ice climbing, but you'd be wise to bring most nontechnical items with you.

The most basic items for travelers who are doing any sort of light adventure, such as trekking, are (already broken-in) hiking boots (it's not a bad idea to take them in a carry-on or wear them on the plane, to avoid their loss), outdoor apparel such as fleece pullovers and a good rain jacket, and a daypack.

Essential gear for almost all travelers includes

- Sun hat and sunscreen
- Wool ski hat and gloves (even in the summer)
- Water-repellent, wind-resistant, and cold-weather clothing
- Light trekking shoes or boots
- Several pairs of thick socks

For light adventure, bring

- Good backpacking or climbing boots
- Base layer (thermal underwear or a wicking-quality shirt)
- Insect repellent
- Pocketknife
- Toilet paper
- Flashlight or headlamp
- Mosquito net
- Sleeping bag
- Energy bars or other trail snack foods
- Sports sandals or comfortable shoes (for post-climbing and trekking, or for river and wet-weather wear)
- Metrodinazole (the recommended treatment for giardiasis)
- Water bottle or other portable hydration system
- Good internal-frame backpack

For backcountry adventure travel, bring

- Food supplies and cooking equipment
- First-aid kit
- Compass and whistle
- Tent, camping stove, and cookware
- Adequate fuel
- Insulated inflatable mattress
- Topographical maps of trails

The boat takes you to the trail head for the Crypt Lake hike (p. 134), which you start by ferrying across the lake. As you ascend the trail, you pass four waterfalls before arriving at Crypt Lake, which is nothing short of otherworldly.

On nearby Cameron Lake (p. 134), you can also rent boats in summer to cruise the crystal blue waters. A massive glacier sits cradled in a mountain bowl at the far end of this small lake. You can paddle close enough to feel the chill of the melting ice.

Wood Buffalo National Park

When it comes to remote, no park in Alberta can touch Wood Buffalo, in the province's far north. It is the largest expanse of protected wilderness reserve in North America and among the largest in the world. Straddling Alberta and the Northwest Territories, Wood Buffalo is largely a reserve of high boreal plain, serviced by a single road that skirts its northeastern edge from the Territories; there is no road access from Alberta at all. Much of the park is accessible only by water or air.

From Alberta, you can fly in on a chartered plane from Fort McMurray or arrange passage by water via the remote town of Fort Chipewyan, where there's a park office.

Wood Buffalo is a wild place, to be sure. You'll find no places to rent bikes or boats, no restaurants, no shopping—and no plumbing. As such, it's not everyone's cup of tea. But flying or ferrying to Sweetgrass Station (p. 258), from which you can hike, camp, or canoe the high boreal plains in search of the last free-roaming wild bison herd on Earth, is an experience that can't be had anywhere else.

SKIING

One of the most enjoyable (and most vigorous) ways to see the majesty of Alberta's Rockies is via its world-class alpine ski resorts. People travel from all over the world to ski here, and with good reason: The Rockies boast some of the best skiing to be found anywhere. Lift tickets range from C$58 to C$78 per day (adults), with tickets for children a bargain at approximately one-third the cost of the adults'.

High-speed lifts spirit you to the top of snowy peaks, from which you descend through fluffy, powdery snow; if you get cold, each resort has state-of-the-art lodges to warm you up. And after a day of high altitudes and fresh air, the various amenities of the nearby towns—Banff, Lake Louise, Canmore, or Jasper—can offer you every imaginable comfort.

The largest of Alberta's ski areas—and one of the largest in North America—is **Lake Louise** (✆ **877/956-8473** in North America or 403/552-3555; www.ski louise.com), near Banff, which sprawls over several peaks. With its 1,680 skiable hectares (4,151 acres) and 113 named runs, Lake Louise has been named the most scenic ski area in North America by *Ski* magazine.

Sunshine Village (✆ **877/542-2633** in North America or 403/705-4000; www. skibanff.com), 15 minutes west of Banff off Highway 1, receives more snow than any ski area in the Canadian Rockies—more than 9m (30 ft.) per year!

Banff Mount Norquay (✆ **403/762-4421**; www.banffnorquay.com) is just next to the town of Banff. Norquay caters to family skiing and offers day care, instruction, and night skiing. They also have skiing by the hour, great for half-days.

In Kananaskis Country, just east of Banff, you'll find **Nakiska** (☏ **800/258-7669** or 403/591-7777; www.skinakiska.com), where skiers can follow in the tracks of past Winter Olympians; Nakiska was built for the 1988 Calgary Winter Olympic games, and is still an operating ski area.

In Jasper, you'll find **Ski Marmot Basin** (☏ **866/952-3816** or 780/852-3816; www.skimarmot.com), located 19km (12 miles) west of Jasper on Highway 93. Marmot is generally underrated as a ski resort; it doesn't get the crowds of Banff, but is a great ski area with a ton of varied terrain.

For some urban skiing, try Calgary's **Canada Olympic Park** (☏ **403/247-5452;** www.coda.ab.ca). Located on a slope on the west side of town, the facility was heavily spruced up for the Olympics, adding ski jump, luge, and bobsled facilities to the old ski-area terrain (all of which you can sample as a tourist, if you like).

Cross-country skiers will find endless pleasure in exploring the **Canmore Nordic Centre Provincial Park** (☏ **403/678-2400**), also built for the 1988 games. More than 70km (43 miles) of trails are available to skiers all winter; Trail Sports (on-site) offers ski rentals, skill-building courses, and guided excursions.

HIKING & MOUNTAIN CLIMBING

This is a big one in alpine Alberta. I suggest that you consult the specific chapters of Banff & Jasper (chapter 9), Kananaskis & Canmore (chapter 8), and the Waterton Lakes National Park section of chapter 7 for substantial hiking information; the options are far too numerous to list here; *Frommer's Banff & the Canadian Rockies Day by Day* also boasts a number of reviews.

In a nutshell, Alberta's varied alpine terrain and transition zones offer hiking enthusiasts endless choices for all kinds of excursions, from short trips through rolling foothills and spare forest, and along swift-running alpine creeks and rivers; to multi-day excursions up and over mountain passes, past towering waterfalls and massive glaciers, through the Continental Divide—on and on and on. There are a lifetime of options.

Some regions are particularly conducive to hiking excursions (read: the mountains); read on for some guidelines, including where to find trail maps and tour operators.

In the Canmore/Kananaskis area, **Tourism Canmore** (☏ **866/CAN-MORE** [866/226-6673] or 403/678-1296; www.tourismcanmore.com) has a comprehensive guide of hiking trails near town, as well as throughout the vast Kananaskis Country to the south; here, just east of Banff, the terrain is a little more varied—a mixture of alpine and foothills. For guided tours, contact **Inside Out** (☏ **888/999-7238;** www.insideoutexperience.com) in Canmore; they can set you up with a huge variety of guided hikes in the area. Costs per person for half-day hikes are C$69 (C$59 for children, or groups of eight or more), for full-day hikes C$139 (C$129 for children or groups). All guided tours include shuttle service to the trail head. **Mahikan Trails** (☏ **866/776-HIKE** [866/776-4453] or 403/609-2489; www.mahikan.ca) will lead you to archaeologically significant First Nations sites in the area (p. 123). Full-day rates are C$600 for a group of four people, with an additional C$124 for each extra person up to eight. Banff National Park offers an almost immeasurable number of hiking options (1,600km/994 miles' worth), from short day trips to multi-day treks. Not all of them are difficult (though many are), but be aware that the easier hikes tend to draw the most crowds in summer. It's wise to check with the park to find the right trail for you. Parks Canada's website for Banff (www.pc.gc.ca/banff) has many maps and good tips, as well as regularly

 ## Outdoor Safety

Most tours and activities are extremely safe, but there are risks involved in any adventure activity. The risks in activities such as mountain climbing and white-water rafting can be considerable. But even hiking puts you in new terrain, where there are many unknowns, so be prepared. Know and respect your own physical limits and skills (or lack thereof) before undertaking any high-risk activity, especially in the mountains.

Also, be prepared for extremes in temperature and rainfall, and wide fluctuations in weather. A sunny morning hike can quickly become a cold and wet ordeal, so always carry some form of rain gear when hiking in the mountains; bring sufficient protection against the cold at high altitudes and have a dry change of clothing waiting at the end of the trail. Be sure to bring plenty of sunscreen, no matter where you travel.

If you do any trekking or camping, exercise caution with wildlife. Be aware of large mammals like bears; make plenty of noise along the trails and let them know you're coming—they have as little interest in running into you as you do them. (See p. 149 to find out what to do if you encounter a bear.) If you're camping, make sure to store your food safely out of reach and scent, preferably hoisted at least 3m (9¾ ft.) in the air over a tree branch.

If you are bitten by a raccoon, a marmot, or another creature (such as a bat), there is a small risk of rabies (there have been 24 reported cases in all of Canada since 1924, but an elderly man in Alberta died in 2007 after being bitten by a rabid bat). Wash out the wound thoroughly with soap and water, and seek medical attention.

Avoid drinking from mountain rivers, streams, and lakes; the waters can contain microbes—like *Giardia,* a parasite that causes extreme nausea and vomiting—that will wreak havoc on your digestive system. If you want to use water from streams or lakes, either boil it for at least 5 minutes or bring some kind of water filtration system with you (available at most outdoors stores).

Having said all that, Alberta's bounteous nature needs to be protected from visitors more than visitors need to be protected from it. A fundamental component of enjoying nature is leaving the natural environment undisturbed. The responsible outdoor traveler's maxim is: Take nothing but memories (and photos); leave nothing but footprints. Do not cut or uproot plants or flowers. Pack out everything you pack in, and never litter. Leave places the way you found them. If you see garbage lying around in protected areas, pick it up and pack it out, along with your own trash. Don't scratch your name or any other graffiti on trees or monuments. Bury your excrement as far as possible from the trail you're on.

updated trail reports. Or call them at ✆ **403/762-1550.** Guided hikes and overnight backpacking trips are led by a number of companies, including **WildTrips** (✆ **403/678-0929;** www.wildtrips.ca) and **Yamnuska Mountain Adventures** (✆ **866/678-4164;** www.yamnuska.ca). The **Sunshine Meadows** guided hike (p. 168), run by **White Mountain Adventures** (✆ **403/762-7889**) takes you above the Sunshine Village ski area and into a gorgeous alpine meadow. Group hikes cost C$35 per person.

In Jasper, your best bet for hiking isn't the local tourist authority, **Jasper Tourism** (✆ **780/852-3858;** www.jaspercanadianrockies.com), though they are able to help with hiking guides and trail maps. The *real* hiking authority in Jasper is the *Hike Jasper* guide, a tremendous online resource run by local enthusiasts. On their website, www.hikejasper.com, you'll find their take on the best hikes summer and winter, night-time hiking, and a listing of the best guides plying the park and their offerings (a top one is a 5-day guided hike retracing the route of legendary explorer David Thompson as he pushed through the Rockies and on to the Pacific Ocean).

Waterton Lakes National Park is considerably less developed than the other national parks in Alberta—which, overall, is a good thing. At the **park office** (✆ **403/859-2252;** www.pc.gc.ca/pn-np/ab/waterton/index.aspx), you'll find all the information you need, from maps of hiking trails to weather conditions. They'll also let you know if there's been a bear or cougar sighting recently—handy info if you plan to venture forth on foot.

However, Waterton's relatively untrammeled wilderness will make finding a guide a little tougher. You can try the one outfitter in town, **Tamarack Outdoor Outfitters** (✆ **403/859-2378**), which may be able to hook you up with a game local; otherwise, follow the guidelines the parks service provides and be aware of wildlife: This is the wildest of Alberta's mountain parks.

FISHING

Alberta's fast-running mountain rivers and streams, as well as its northern lakes, offer a great many opportunities for anglers. The north in particular, in the Peace-Athabasca delta, is a favorite; hundreds of remote lakes throughout the wetlands offer sport fishers ample opportunity to trawl for lake trout, northern pike, and walleye. Fly-fishers will want to cast into the Bow River and wade the rivers of the Crowsnest Pass.

Keep in mind that you need a license (C$26 for Canadians and C$71 for non-Canadians) to catch fish in Alberta. Most fishing outfitters in the province sell them, as well as many sporting goods stores. You also need a permit from Parks Canada to fish in Banff. They cost C$10 per day or C$34 for an annual pass.

Fort McMurray Tourism (✆ **780/791-4336;** www.fortmcmurraytourism. com) offers a list of approved fishing tour operators and lodges, most which fly you in to the lakes on tiny floatplanes (there are very few roads in the north) for 2 days or longer of angling in the northern wilderness. **Mikisew Sport Fishing** (✆ **888/ 268-7112** or 780/743-8218; www.mikisewsportfishing.com) is one of the oldest of such tour operators; it offers trips to more than a dozen remote lakes all over the north with an assortment of 5-day packages.

In the national parks, you'll find tour operators (far too many to list here) that offer anything from hip-wading fly fishing in the rivers to trawling the mountain lakes. Be warned: Unless you're an experienced fly fisher or very familiar with the area, do not attempt to wade into the mountain rivers on your own. The water is ice-cold, and the current is unpredictable at different points in the river and at different times of the year. An imprudent wade in the wrong place or at the wrong time could easily kill you.

In Canmore, **Inside Out** (✆ **888/999-7238;** www.insideoutexperience.com), the one-stop-shopping tour center, can find you a reputable guide. In Banff, both **Banff Fishing Unlimited** (✆ **403/762-4936;** www.banff-fishing.com) and Big Jim Dykstra (a fair name, since Jim stands 6'5"), the owner/operator of **Hawgwild Flyfishing** (✆ **403/678-7980;** www.flyfishingbanff.com), will pick you up and take you to various favorite spots in Banff, and in and around the Canmore/Kananaskis area. Banff Fishing Unlimited offers fly fishing, as well as lake fishing; Dykstra specializes in fly fishing only—and guarantees a catch or your money back.

In Jasper, you can take a guided fishing trip on Maligne Lake with **Maligne Tours** (✆ **780/852-3370;** www.malignelake.com). They include equipment, lunch, and hotel transportation. **Currie's Guiding** (✆ **780/852-5650;** www.curriesguiding jasper.com) specializes in fishing in Jasper, so if you're looking for a longer or more varied excursion with hardcore anglers, they're a good bet.

The Crowsnest Pass area of southwestern Alberta is another fly-fishing hotspot. Contact **Crowsnest Angler** (✆ **403/564-4333;** www.crowsnestangler.com) for guided fishing, equipment, and insider's tips.

BIRD WATCHING

Being on the migratory route for hundreds of species of birds, Alberta is a great option for those looking for alpine birds, prairie species, and the many species that nest in the Northern Alberta Wetlands.

Banff National Park has more than 277 recorded species, and birding is good even in the winter. Look for magpies; Clark's nutcrackers; whiskey jacks; and black-capped, boreal, and mountain chickadees.

Inside and all around Wood Buffalo National Park, in the far north, is the Peace-Athabasca delta, one of the biggest inland freshwater deltas in the world, where migratory birds from all four North American flyways pass through each spring and autumn. The park also protects the last remaining wild nesting area of the endangered whooping crane, as well as some nesting sites of the threatened peregrine falcon.

McLennan, or the "Bird Capital of Canada," is located about an hour and a half northeast of Grande Prairie. It's one of the most significant waterfowl staging areas in Northern Alberta, where more than 206 species have been identified. Visit the Kimiwan Lake area, an internationally renowned wetland; here, the Interpretive Centre, staffed from May through September, has plenty of info on the many shorebirds and waterfowl that populate the area.

In Grande Prairie, the rare trumpeter swans are so numerous that in late April the town celebrates their arrival at nearby Crystal Lake with a weekend festival.

The Clifford E. Lee Nature Sanctuary, southwest of Edmonton, is one of Alberta's "Special Places," as designated by the provincial government. Trails wind their way through marshes, sand hills, meadows, and aspen and pine woods. May through August is the best time to visit.

Newell Lake, near Drumheller, is a good place to see white pelicans and American avocets in the summer. And Jasper National Park is chock full of species, with its range of habitats from alpine meadows and tundra to forested valleys. Visit Talbot Lake for waterfowl, and Cottonwood Slough for owls. Late March through September is best.

Tour operators that specialize in birding are few and far between: Wayne Millar, of Edmonton-based **Watchable Wildlife Tours** (✆ **780/405-4880;** www.bird sandbackcountry.com) can tailor a bird-watching excursion to your tastes; his rates start at C$225 per person for a 12-hour tour, minimum two people. Most of the major tour operators in places like Banff and Jasper, mentioned elsewhere in this chapter, can steer you to birding excursions in their locality.

HORSEBACK RIDING

When you're in Alberta, a horse is never too far away. Tours range from an afternoon—or as little as an hour—to a week through the back country, to riding range on a cattle herd on a real working ranch. This is cowboy country, after all; horses aren't just tourist curiosities—they're workers.

There are plenty of riding options in the mountain parks, and you can hardly go wrong riding into the midst of the majestic peaks that surround you. The **Alberta Outfitters Association** (✆ **800/742-5548;** www.albertaoutfitters.com) represents the trail-riding industry. Their website lists all affiliated operators throughout the province.

Just before you reach Waterton Lakes National Park, you pass through the aptly named hamlet of Mountain View, from which the Rockies loom in the near distance. Here, you'll find not much more than gas and a general store, but just off Route 5 is the Nelson Ranch, home of **Mountain Meadow Trail Rides** (✆ **866/653-2413;** www.mountainmeadowtrailrides.com). The Nelson family has owned this ranch, a 809-hectare (2,000-acre) spread tucked into the province's southwest corner, since 1898. It's also become a guest ranch in recent years, which means the family's 50 horses are put into regular service for trail rides for greenhorns passing through. Mountain Meadows charges C$38 per person for a 90-minute ride; a 3-day/2-night package, all meals included, is C$630 per person.

In the park itself, **Alpine Stables** (✆ **403/859-2462**), across from the golf course on the way to the townsite on Entrance Road, offers guided rides on more than 250km (155 miles) of trails; tours range from 1 hour to overnighters. One-hour rides are C$30 per person; full days are C$135. Overnighters start at C$375 per person.

In Banff, try **Warner Guiding and Outfitting** (✆ **800/661-8352** or 403/762-4551; www.horseback.com). Multiday trail rides, which start at C$825 per person for a 3-day lodge-to-lodge trip and peak at C$1,406 for a 6-day backcountry tenting trip, explore some of the most remote areas of the park.

Some rides climb up to backcountry lodges, which serve as base camps for further exploration; other trips involve a backcountry circuit, with lodging in tents. Shorter day rides are also offered from two stables near the townsite. An afternoon ride goes for C$151 per person.

Operating out of Lake Louise, **Timberline Tours** (**©** **888/858-3388** or 403/522-3743; www.timberlinetours.ca) offers day trips to some of the area's more prominent beauty sites, starting at C$65 per person for 90 minutes of riding. Three- to ten-day pack trips are also offered.

In Jasper, for a short ride, call **Pyramid Stables** (**©** **780/852-7433**), which offers 1- to 3-hour trips (C$55–C$95 per person) around Pyramid and Patricia lakes.

Long-distance trail rides take you into the backcountry. **Skyline Trail Rides** (**©** **888/582-7787** or 780/852-4215; www.skylinetrail.com) offers a number of short day trips costing roughly C$43 per person for 75 minutes, as well as 3- to 4-day trips to a remote, albeit modernized, lodge. Sleigh rides are offered in winter.

Of course, most will tell you the best place to ride is in the foothills, among the working ranches and herds, many of which offer guest packages that include all meals and accommodations. Alberta has been ranch country for well over a century, and the Old West lifestyle is deeply ingrained in Albertan culture. There's also the long Alberta tradition of guest ranches, where you can spend a few days indulging in a cowboy fantasy.

At Seebe, in Kananaskis Country near the entrance to Banff National Park, are a couple of the oldest and most famous ranches. **Rafter Six Ranch** (**©** **888/267-2624** or 403/673-3691; www.raftersix.com) has a beautiful old log lodge. The original Brewster homestead was transformed in 1923 into the **Brewster's Kananaskis Guest Ranch** (**©** **800/691-5085** or 403/673-3737; www.kananaskisguestranch. com).

The **Black Cat Guest Ranch** (**©** **800/859-6840** or 403/865-3084; www. blackcatguestranch.ca)—near Hinton, just east of Jasper—was once a winter horse camp.

At all of these, horseback riding and trail rides are the main focus, but other western activities, such as rodeos, barbecues, and country dancing, are usually on the docket.

Close to Calgary is the **Homeplace Ranch** (**©** **877/931-3245** or 403/931-3245; www.homeplaceranch.com), a guest ranch run by the McKinney family in the glorious environs of the high foothills. The McKinney family homesteaded here in 1912 and still run a cattle ranch on their vast property, but they welcome guests for riding tours and lessons. Packages start at C$866 per person for 4 days and 3 nights, and include all meals, accommodations, and riding.

A night at a guest ranch usually ranges from C$90 to C$200, depending on what style of room you choose, and includes breakfast. Full bed-and-board packages are available for longer stays. There's usually an additional fee for horseback riding. Home stays at smaller working ranches are also possible. Here, you can pitch in and help your ranch-family hosts with their work, or you can simply relax. For a stay on a real mom-and-pop farm, obtain a list of member ranches from **Alberta Country Vacations Association** (**©** **403/722-3053;** www.albertacountryvacation.com).

MOUNTAIN BIKING

Where to begin? Some of the earliest adopters in the annals of this sport were rabid cyclists in Alberta, and the province remains one of the hotbeds of mountain biking. In Canmore, the site of the Nordic events for the 1988 Calgary Winter Olympic Games, the lasting legacy is the **Canmore Nordic Centre Provincial Park** (1988 Olympic Way, Canmore; ℭ **403/678-2400**), which is probably ten times as busy in summer as in winter thanks to the adaptability of the ski trails to world-class mountain biking. More than 70km (43 miles) of trails are taken over by mountain bikers in summer, and Trail Sports (on-site) offers bike rentals, skill-building courses, and guided rides.

Mountain biking in the national parks is a little bit trickier, given the sensitive nature of the environment, not to mention the throngs of tourists that might be meandering the trails at any given time. Banff National Park has more than 190km (118 miles) of mountain-biking trails, but it's permitted on only a select number of the hiking trails. You are subject to fines if you are caught biking on a hiking-only trail. The park's website (www.pc.gc.ca/banff) has a good list of biking trails. The same is true of Jasper, where information, trail maps, and excluded areas can be found at www.explorejasper.com/recreation/biking.htm. And remember, be bear aware!

To avoid conflicts and ensure everyone's safety, read and abide by the Rules of the Trail, as set by the International Mountain Bicycling Association (www.imba.com). Keep in mind that many trails go through remote areas, so be prepared for potential mechanical difficulties far from a bike shop.

For an experienced mountain biking guide through Kananaskis Provincial Park, near Canmore, as well as Banff and Jasper, try **Inside Out** (ℭ **888/999-7238;** www.insideoutexperience.com), an experienced, multi-faceted tour operator that can hook you up with guides for almost anything (not just mountain biking).

To rent a bike in Jasper, contact **Freewheel Cycle** (ℭ **780/852-3898;** www. visit-jasper.com/freewheel.html). Mountain-bike rental costs C$12 to C$15 per hour or C$45 to C$50 per day. In Banff, contact **Bactrax** (ℭ **403/762-8177;** www.snowtips-bactrax.com), which rents mountain bikes for C$44 to C$63 per day.

WHITE-WATER RAFTING

Compared to some of the major white-water destinations, Alberta is fairly tame; the mountain rivers and streams here are relatively small, and the water not terribly white, most of the time.

That's not to say there's not fun to be had; and if you're a neophyte, it can be a good place to, ah, get your feet wet. In Kananaskis, near Canmore, the Kananaskis and Bow rivers are the main draw. Inside Out Experience, above, can provide more information on rafting packages. Also, the **Canadian Rockies Rafting Company** (ℭ **877/226-7625;** www.rafting.ca) is among the most established rafting-tour companies in the area, with a range of different trips—the more gentle ride along the Kananaskis River, to the white-water rush of the Bow River's Horseshoe

Canyon (with rapids as high as Class IV). Full-day trips start at C$79 for adults or C$70 for children 12 to 15 (children under 12 not permitted). These are mountain rivers, so bear in mind that the water is very cold. **Chinook Rafting** (© **866/330-7238;** www.chinookrafting.com) operates out of Banff and offers very similar adventures.

And, even though it's not like rafting the mighty Colorado River, rafting here is not without its dangers. If you're just experimenting with river rafting, stick to Class II and III rivers. If you already know your way around a raft and a paddle, there are Class IV and even a few Class V sections to run.

SUGGESTED ALBERTA ITINERARIES

Getting your head around the vast distances and wide-open spaces of Alberta can be daunting. There's a lot to see out here, but some parts of it are more interesting than other parts. Assuming that you're here to see spectacular scenery, not open expanses of plains, sticking to the western portion of the province is the best idea if you have limited time. But combining the mountains with another area—the badlands or the province's southeast, for example—makes for a more diverse journey. It all depends on time and inclination. If you have plenty of the latter and not so much of the former, this chapter should help.

5

THE BEST OF THE CANADIAN ROCKIES IN 1 WEEK

If you're nimble and have a car, you can get a taste of Alberta's must-sees—urban and mountain—in a week. You can do this itinerary in reverse if you prefer; Calgary is closest to the mountains and might be an easier final destination at the end of your trip if you're tired of driving. Edmonton is a fairly dull 3½-hour drive from the mountains, maybe best gotten out of the way at the outset.

1 Exploring Calgary

Take a day to explore this bustling boom town, currently flush with the promise of oil prices staying high. This day can all be done on foot. (See "The Best of Calgary in 1 Day," later in this chapter, for more details.) Get your bearings 191m (627 ft.) up off the ground at the **Calgary Tower** (p. 99). You can see the Rockies and the foothills to the west, downtown and the Bow River below, and the far horizon stretching past the suburbs in every other direction. Hop up the street to visit the **Glenbow Museum** (p. 101) to hear the story of the West, ripe with characters like cowboys, mavericks, chiefs, and groundbreakers.

Exiting on the north side of the museum lands you at the **Stephen Avenue Mall** (p. 79), the city's historic downtown strip, where you'll find plenty of restaurants, as well as the entry points to several of Calgary's swanky downtown malls. Head over another block east to **Olympic Plaza** (p. 101), a public square across the street from the sandstone Old City Hall. Built for the medal ceremonies of the 1988 Winter Olympics, this is still where Calgarians come to celebrate everything, from hockey victories to Reggaefest.

Cross south and head to the hip blocks of **Uptown 17th Avenue SW** for an afternoon coffee break at one of the area's great cafes. Give yourself time to pop into a few boutiques like **Junk Star Vintage** (p. 114) and **Gravity Pope** (p. 114).

For dinner, head to the **River Café** (p. 90) on **Prince's Island Park** (p. 105), a lush island in the middle of the Bow River.

2 & 3 Banff & Kananaskis

From Calgary, you'll take Highway 1 west through the foothills and into the mountains. In an hour, you'll have passed the entrance to Kananaskis Country. Start with a mid-morning coffee break and stroll through the picturesque mountain town of **Canmore** (p. 139). Continue west on Highway 1 through the **Banff National Park** (p. 164) gates. A short drive—watch your speed, the legal limit drops to 90kmph (56 mph) in the park—will land you on **Banff Avenue** (p. 173), the main drag of this ritzy tourist town brimming with opportunities to separate you from your money. Here, you'll find everything from motels to grand hotels, fast food to haute cuisine. You could pass the day shopping—Louis Vuitton, anyone?—but Banff, for all the glitz, is one of the most spectacular places on Earth. So, get out of town! Head to **Lake Minnewanka** (p. 176), look into float trips down the **Bow River** (p. 170), or hike **Johnston Canyon** (p. 166) up to the Ink Pots. If it's all too active—or too far—you can take in some majestic scenery right in the Banff townsite by riding the **Sulphur Mountain Gondola** (p. 173).

On Day Two, start with a morning hike up **Tunnel Mountain**. If it's summer, saddle up for an afternoon horseback ride with **Holidays on Horseback**. Then, treat yourself to traditional afternoon tea in the castle that is the **Fairmont Banff Springs Hotel** (p. 178). Rest your bones at dusk at the **Upper Hot Springs** (p. 176).

4 Lake Louise

A stone's throw—okay, 45 minutes—west of Banff, Lake Louise has its own particular charms. Calm and low-key where Banff is wild and frantic, Louise boasts the same or better beauty with less of the tourist-culture hassle. Start by picking up a lunch-to-go at one of the delis in Lake Louise Village's **Samson Mall**. Continue up the hill, parking next to the lovely **Fairmont Chateau Lake Louise** (p. 192) and hiking around the back of the lake. Continue hiking 90 minutes to the historic **Plain of the Six Glaciers Teahouse** (p. 167) for jaw-droppingly dramatic landscapes and yummy baked treats. Back in the car,

Bradford West Gwillimbury Public Library

Customer ID: 696524

Items that you checked out

Title: Not dark yet
ID: 33328900591195
Due: 15-Jun-2021

Title: Bryant & May off the rail
ID: 33328001563846
Due: 29-Jun-2021

Title: Cook, eat, repeat :
ID: 33328900585387
Due: 29-Jun-2021

Title: Frommer's Alberta.
ID: 33328001755871
Due: 29-Jun-2021

Title: Original highways :
ID: 33328900308384
Due: 29-Jun-2021

Title: Yearbook
ID: 33328900590270
Due: 29-Jun-2021

Total items: 6
Account balance: $0.00
June 8, 2021 9:26 AM
Checked out: 25
Overdue: 1
Hold requests: 17
Ready for pickup: 0

Phone: 905-775-3328

The Canadian Rockies in 1 Week

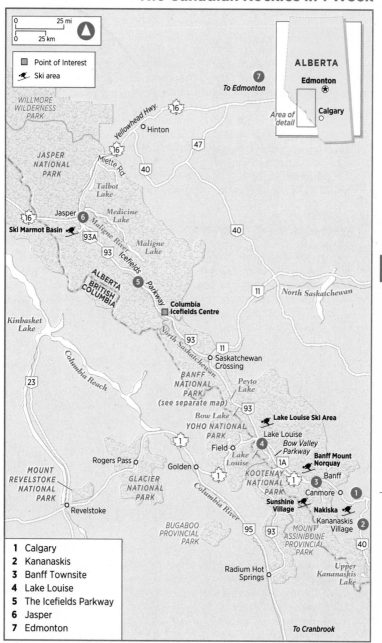

1 Calgary
2 Kananaskis
3 Banff Townsite
4 Lake Louise
5 The Icefields Parkway
6 Jasper
7 Edmonton

make a short stop at the serene **Moraine Lake** (p. 191)—trail head for more outstanding hikes. To cap things off, there's dinner at the **Post Hotel** (p. 193), if you can handle the sticker shock; a low-key culinary hotspot, it's routinely rated among the best in Canada.

5 The Icefields Parkway

You'll want a whole day to travel this spectacular route between Lake Louise and Jasper. As you travel through **Sunwapta Pass** (p. 198), past the mind-blowing views of the **Columbia Icefields** (p. 197), you'll want to savor every moment. Plan to spend at least 2 hours at the Icefields and don't miss the Columbia Glacier **Icefield Experience** (also known as the "Snocoach;" p. 197), a chance to walk on the Athabasca Glacier. This is an ancient place, one that gives pause. Take your time, but be warned: Gas up in Lake Louise. The only filling station along the way, at the Saskatchewan River crossing, gives new meaning to the term "tourist trap." Fuel prices are 50% higher here than anywhere else. It's another 90 minutes to Jasper from the Icefields.

6 Jasper

Jasper's not quite so crassly commercial as its southern cousin Banff, so a stroll through town can be as relaxing as a trail hike. Then again, you could do both at one go—trails start right in town. **Maligne Lake** (p. 207) is a half-hour drive away, where a spectacular cruise to **Spirit Island** (p. 207) awaits, over icy blue waters in the heart of the Rockies. You could also drink in the scenery from a more comfortable distance, on the patio of the **Fairmont Jasper Park Lodge** (p. 210), where a lovely lunch menu is served, staring the majesty of Edith Cavell Mountain in the face.

7 Edmonton

Take the Yellowhead Highway east from Jasper to Edmonton. You'll eat a good chunk of this day driving—3½ hours or so—but worry not: Edmonton's low-key enough that you can get a good feel for it in an afternoon. Allow yourself a little self-indulgent shopping stroll along **Whyte Avenue** (p. 243) before heading to the stunning new **Alberta Art Gallery** (p. 235). Keen naturalists may prefer the eco-displays at the **Royal Alberta Museum** (p. 237). From there, you're conveniently within blocks of the outstanding and stylish **Blue Pear** (p. 232), probably Edmonton's finest restaurant, showcasing local cuisine.

THE BEST OF SOUTHERN ALBERTA IN 1 WEEK

Alberta's a big place, and there's plenty of ground to cover—especially out here in the badlands and portions of the south, where the prairie seems to roll without end in every direction. Just accept you're going to spend some time behind the wheel—and that you'll be rewarded for your efforts—and you'll be fine.

1 Drumheller & the Royal Tyrrell Museum

Fly into Calgary and set out for Drumheller, on Highway 2 North, exiting at Highway 9 East. It'll take you about an hour and a half. Head straight for the **Royal Tyrrell Museum** (p. 123), an extraordinary world-class facility that's as fascinating for adults as it is for dino-crazed kids. After the museum, take a spin on the **Dinosaur Trail** loop (p. 121), stopping at viewpoints for **Horse Thief Canyon** and **Horseshoe Canyon** (p. 120), carved out of the rough sandstone terrain over millennia by the Red Deer River.

2 Dinosaur Provincial Park

From Drumheller, you're about 2 hours to **Dinosaur Provincial Park** (p. 125), where fascinating field guides and a fantastic interpretive center are there to offer tours of this area that was once a vast, ancient inland sea. Some of the most significant discoveries of the Cretaceous period have been found here—whole skeletons of massive aquatic dinos from millions of years ago. As you walk the valley floor, be aware of the fossilized bone fragments crunching underfoot.

3 & 4 Waterton Lakes National Park

From Dinosaur Park, you're about 4 hours across bald prairie to **Waterton Lakes National Park** (p. 131), a spectacular mountain park that's also the least traveled of the three in Alberta (the others being Banff and Jasper). Take a nice long cruise the length of Waterton Lake on the historic **HMV International** (p. 53) to Goat Haunt, Montana, at the lake's south end, while an expert guide fills your mind with fascinating history and geology along the way. Or rent a canoe on nearby **Cameron Lake** (p. 134) and marvel at the snow-laden bowls hanging above you from the peaks. You can hike at Cameron Lake, as well, or trudge deep into **Red Rock Canyon**. Or you could spend an afternoon at high tea at the **Prince of Wales Hotel** (p. 135), gazing out the spectacular south-facing windows at the lake and glacier-laden mountains beyond.

5 The Southern Cowboy Trail

From Waterton, drive to Pincher Creek on Highway 6, then turn west on Highway 3, toward Crowsnest Pass. Not far along, you'll come across **Frank Slide** (p. 152), the site of a dramatic landslide that saw millions of tons of rock tumble down and crush the town of Frank in 1903. Back east on Highway 3 to Highway 22 North, you reach the beautiful **Cowboy Trail** (p. 150), Alberta's storied western heritage highway along the fringe of the Rocky Mountains. Just south of Longview on Highway 22, **Bar U Ranch National Historic Site** (p. 153) was one of the first, and biggest, ranches in Western Canada; it remains a perfectly preserved relic of that era. Continue west to Canmore and enjoy dinner beneath the Three Sisters Mountain at the innovative and smart **Crazyweed Kitchen** (p. 145).

Southern Alberta in 1 week

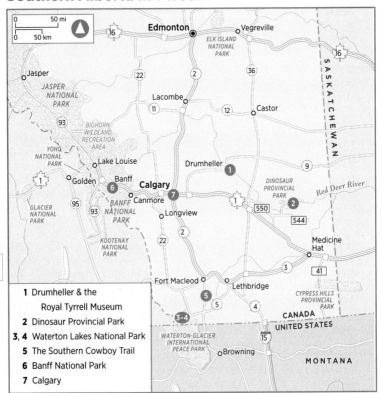

1 Drumheller & the
   Royal Tyrrell Museum
2 Dinosaur Provincial Park
3, 4 Waterton Lakes National Park
5 The Southern Cowboy Trail
6 Banff National Park
7 Calgary

6 Banff

Can you see Banff National Park in a day? Well, it's tight, but it's certainly worthwhile. The first stop is the town of Banff, including a ride up the Sulphur Mountain Gondola (p. 173), the easiest peak to reach in the Rockies. Cruise past Bow Falls, and then into the Fairmont Banff Springs Hotel (p. 178) for lunch. After lunch, it's more than worth the 45-minute drive to Lake Louise (p. 190), where you can stretch your legs by walking around from the parking lot, in front of the Fairmont Chateau Lake Louise and on to the back of the lake in 45 minutes.

7 Calgary

At the end of a long road, Calgary's urbane comforts will beckon. Pop into the **Glenbow Museum** (p. 101) to soak in culture and soothe those travel-weary bones, and a pleasant afternoon of shopping among the boutiques of the

Mission district (p. 114) is a restorative unto itself. Finish up on the patio of **Mercato** (p. 94), a Calgary hotspot with some of the best traditional Italian food you'll ever have.

A SKI WEEKEND IN THE ROCKIES

You're probably better off to make it a long weekend, given the number of resorts and the mixture of terrain. But if you have only a couple of days, you can still hit three ski areas.

1 Friday Night: Night Skiing at Mount Norquay

Just above the town of **Banff** (p. 172) and across the Trans-Canada Highway sits the relatively compact—and steep—**Mount Norquay** (p. 164) ski area. This is the only ski area in the Rockies that lights a portion of its runs for Friday night skiing, so take advantage; this is how you'll pack the most runs into your limited time and get your ski legs warmed up.

2 Saturday: Sunshine Village

Sunshine Village (p. 171) is reached by a high gondola that runs from a base just about 20 minutes west of Banff. The added elevation means that this is some of the best, most consistent snow you'll find in Banff. The scenery is sky-high, as well. Skiing above the tree line at Sunshine, one of the biggest ski areas in Canada, can also mean some of the highest winds in the Rockies, so bundle up and be prepared. Intermediates will want to hit up the runs beneath the new high-speed Strawberry lift. Experts can't miss Goat's Eye.

3 Sunday: Lake Louise

This is the granddaddy of the Banff-area ski resorts, with multiple lodges, 1,700 skiable hectares (4,200 acres), and 139 runs. **Lake Louise**'s (p. 164) vast terrain runs the gamut, from beginner to extreme, sprawling over several peaks and spilling down the "back side" of the mountain. This is the place in Banff for purists. Lunch at Temple Lodge is a classic.

A WEEK OF OUTDOOR ADVENTURE

The opportunities to explore the great outdoors are boundless in Alberta, especially in the south and west, where Banff and Kananaskis are well-stocked with tour operators and activities. Start in Calgary and head west.

1 White-Water Rafting in Kananaskis

Take your pick: The wild white water of the Bow River through the Horseshoe Canyon, or the more gentle drift offered by the Kananaskis River. Either way, you'll be surrounded by spectacular scenery—and drenched by the icy mountain river water. See p. 150.

2 Mountaineering at the Yamnuska Centre

Take a mountaineering course, learn to ice or rock climb, or take guided hikes along some of Kananaskis's most gorgeous trails with **Yamnuska Mountain Adventures** (p. 148). Bank on two things: You'll end the day tired and happy.

3 Trail Riding at Boundary Ranch

A couple hours on horseback into Kananaskis's high country will give your trail-weary legs a break—if not your butt. Relax at **Boundary Ranch's** (p. 150) outdoor patio with a beverage and burger afterward.

4 Mountain Biking at the Canmore Nordic Centre

Built for the 1988 Calgary Winter Olympics, the **Canmore Nordic Centre Provincial Park** (p. 147) is a world-class cross-country ski facility that doubles as a premiere mountain biking venue in the summer, with 65km (40 miles) of trails for all ability levels. Bike rentals are available on-site at **Trail Sports** (p. 147).

5 Go Underground at Grotto Mountain

Dive down into the underpinnings of the majestic mountains surrounding you on a caving expedition under Grotto Mountain. **Canmore Caverns** takes guided tours into the cool, damp caves, which can be a bit of a tight squeeze for claustrophobes at times.

6 Hike Sunshine Meadows

Outside ski season, **Sunshine Village's** (p. 168) ski area is relatively vacant, save for beautiful meadows of wildflowers, glistening alpine lakes, whistling marmots and tiny pikas roaming the rocks, and clear alpine air. A bus does all the hard work, taking you up the dirt road 2,150m (7,054 ft.), at the meadow's doorstep. A **guided hike** (p. 168) leads you to some of the most spectacular views to be found anywhere.

7 Explore Lake Louise

After all that activity, you might need a break. **Lake Louise** (p. 164) can help. Take the **Lake Louise Gondola** (p. 191) up to a spectacular alpine meadow for a bit of gentle high-altitude meandering. Finish off with a stroll around scenic **Lake Louise** itself, with a refreshment waiting on the patio at the posh **Fairmont Chateau Lake Louise** (p. 192).

THE BEST OF CALGARY IN 1 DAY

You can easily do the best Calgary has to offer in a day—and best of all, you can do most of it on foot (save a cab ride or two). See "The Best of the Canadian Rockies in 1 Week," earlier in this chapter, to work this day into a longer Alberta itinerary.

1 Stephen Avenue Mall

Start with breakfast at the **Avenue Diner** (p. 93), home to the best Eggs Bennie in town on the pedestrian-only downtown heart, **Stephen Avenue Mall**

A Ski Weekend in the Rockies & a Week of Outdoor Adventure

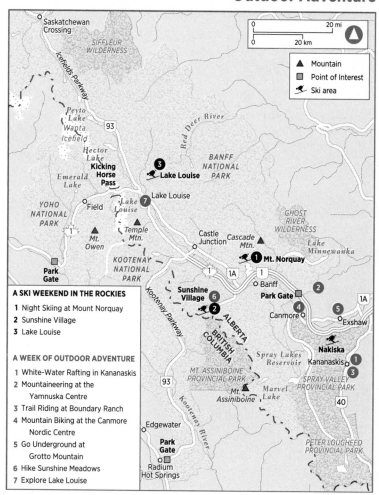

Legend

- ▲ Mountain
- ■ Point of Interest
- ⚡ Ski area

A SKI WEEKEND IN THE ROCKIES

1. Night Skiing at Mount Norquay
2. Sunshine Village
3. Lake Louise

A WEEK OF OUTDOOR ADVENTURE

1. White-Water Rafting in Kananaskis
2. Mountaineering at the Yamnuska Centre
3. Trail Riding at Boundary Ranch
4. Mountain Biking at the Canmore Nordic Centre
5. Go Underground at Grotto Mountain
6. Hike Sunshine Meadows
7. Explore Lake Louise

(p. 79). Businessmen rushing off to the office mingle with artists working at nearby galleries.

2 Downtown

At 9th Avenue SW, head indoors to the central area's interconnected urban malls for a bit of shopping. Pay special attention to **Holt Renfrew** (p. 113), power-suit central for Calgary's moneyed set.

The Best of Calgary in 1 Day

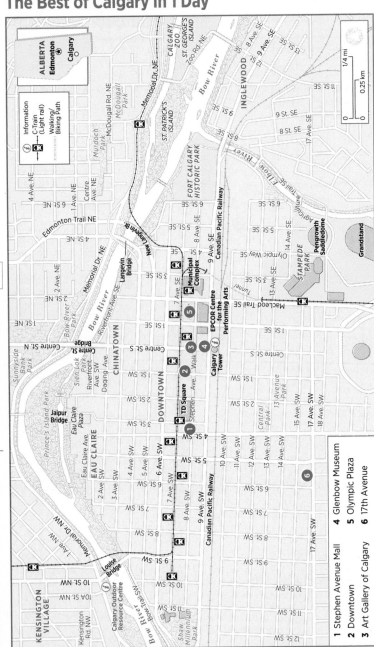

1 Stephen Avenue Mall
2 Downtown
3 Art Gallery of Calgary
4 Glenbow Museum
5 Olympic Plaza
6 17th Avenue

3 Art Gallery of Calgary

Along Stephen Avenue is the **Art Gallery of Calgary** (p. 97), a small but interesting institution in a gorgeous old sandstone heritage building. You'll find interesting local and international contemporary art here, with a small sidewalk cafe on the mall, to boot.

4 Glenbow Museum

Near the east end of the mall is the **Glenbow Museum** (p. 101), one of the country's premiere museums for natural history and Aboriginal culture.

5 Olympic Plaza

At the east end of the Mall is **Olympic Plaza** (p. 101), a large public square across from **Old City Hall** (p. 104) that served as the presentation point for medals during the 1988 Winter Olympics. Still a popular spot for concerts, the plaza is a skating rink in winter and a wading pool in summer. A favorite relaxation spot for office workers on break or at lunch.

6 17th Avenue

Hop in a cab for **17th Avenue** (p. 114), a stretch of trendy boutiques, bars, and restaurants that serves as the city's most vibrant social stretch. Shop at some of the trendy fashion-forward stores like Divine or Goodfoot (p. 114) before retiring to one of the many patios for refreshments, and a prelude to a fabulous dinner at any one of the many options to be found here. Try Mercato or The Coup (p. 95).

THE BEST OF EDMONTON IN 1 DAY

Due to the deep river valley running through the city, Edmonton's core is not as walkable as Calgary (though it is quite walkable in spots). But it's easy enough to conquer in a day with some occasional driving.

1 Downtown

Start your day with a walk through downtown (pick up a muffin and coffee at **Holt's Café** [p. 130] en route) and some pick-me-up inspiration at the sparklingly modern **Art Gallery of Alberta** (p. 235). It offers some of the most interesting Canadian contemporary art to be found anywhere, with an emphasis on contemporary Aboriginal expression.

2 High Street/124th Street Area

A short drive takes you from the bustling downtown to a leafy residential neighborhood. The **High Street** (p. 243) area boasts more mature art galleries, cafes, and the very good **Royal Alberta Museum** (p. 237), which features extensive natural and Aboriginal history displays, as well as large traveling expeditions and plenty for kids to explore.

The Best of Edmonton in 1 Day

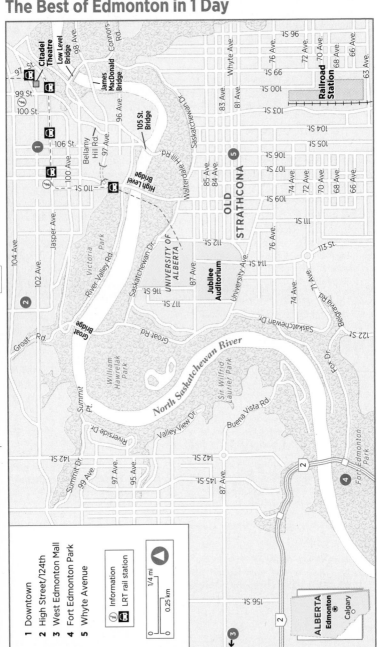

1 Downtown
2 High Street/124th
3 West Edmonton Mall
4 Fort Edmonton Park
5 Whyte Avenue

ℹ Information
🚇 LRT rail station

1/4 mi
0.25 km

ALBERTA
Edmonton ✱
Calgary

Citadel Theatre
Low Level Bridge
James MacDonald Bridge
105 St. Bridge
High Level Bridge
Railroad Station
UNIVERSITY OF ALBERTA
OLD STRATHCONA
Jubilee Auditorium
North Saskatchewan River
William Hawrelak Park
Sir Wilfrid Laurier Park
Victoria Park
Groat Bridge

3 West Edmonton Mall

While it wouldn't be hard to spend a weekend here, if you've got only a few hours, I suggest hitting up the roller coasters, waterslides, and wave pool. See p. 243.

4 Fort Edmonton Park

Across the North Saskatchewan River, off Fox Drive, is **Fort Edmonton Park** (p. 235), a pioneer village that preserves the way of life on which the city was founded. An ancient trolley car takes you around the dusty streets, where you can see re-enactments of pioneer "urban" life.

5 Whyte Avenue

Just a few blocks away from Fort Edmonton Park is Whyte Avenue, a lively stretch of **Old Strathcona** (p. 219) in Edmonton where the majority of the social activity takes place. Tons of restaurants, bars, clubs, boutiques, and theaters cluster along here. Many of the restaurants have sidewalk patios, the better for people-watching. Dinner here at one of the many dining options—try Packrat Louie (p. 234) or Da-De-O (p. 233)—serves as a good prelude for an evening of live theater at one of the many venues to be found within a few blocks' radius of this vibrant district.

6 | CALGARY

Straddling two mountain rivers, the Bow and the Elbow, the city of Calgary rests in a wide river valley where the great plains to the east start to buckle and toll on their way west to the Canadian Rocky Mountains. Calgary has come a long way in a relatively short period of time: From its beginnings as Fort Calgary, an outpost of the Northwest Mounted Police, in 1876, the city has evolved in just over 130 years to a bustling, dynamic urban center of more than a million souls and a center of international commerce.

The 1988 Winter Olympic Games helped put Calgary on the international map, and its legacy has been one of enduring tourism. Visitors now associate Calgary with the mountains, even if they are still another hour's drive west. The Olympics also brought enduring high-level athletics, as well. Much of Canada's Olympic team training takes place in Calgary (although this is now shared with the new facilities in Vancouver and Whistler), thanks both to its legacy facilities—the University of Calgary enjoys state-of-the-art athletic facilities that are the equal of any in North America, to say nothing of a full-sized, covered skating oval—and its high altitude (the city sits almost 1,067m/3,500 ft. above sea level, making its thin air ideal for building lung capacity).

But despite some Calgarians' protestations to the contrary, this is an oil town, first and foremost. More than 90% of the country's oil, gas, and energy business is right here, as are more than half of the coal companies. Calgary's fortunes have ever followed the price of oil, and the city is well acquainted with the boom-and-bust cycle. A favorite bumper sticker through the '80s and '90s—a down period following the boom cycle of the late '70s—told the tale: "Dear Lord, please let me have another oil boom. I promise not to piss it all away this time!"

Boom or bust, business rules here. People in this city are entrepreneurs and risk takers, and when the good times are rolling, they roll right along with them, flaunting their wealth and doing their best to live large. Posh restaurants and cafes are routinely jammed, and high-end retail shopping is practically a contact sport here as flush Calgarians seem hurried to spend their money as quickly as they can. Real estate here is outrageously expensive, given the city's size and stature.

This is a city that works hard and plays hard. With an average age hovering around 30, it certainly has the stamina. The workday starts not long after 6am, for many, and ends around 4pm (despite their protestations of staunch independence, their fortunes remain tied to the Toronto Stock Exchange, two time zones away). You'll find them pursuing their leisure time just as aggressively, as the city empties out on summer weekends and the nearby mountains and parks—some of the most breathtaking on Earth, such as Banff and Kananaskis—fill up with Calgarians in hot pursuit of down time.

Never let it be said that Calgarians are the reserved sort. Showiness is in the blood of the city—infused, perhaps, by the fickle cycle of the oil industry. After all, as any Calgarian oilman can tell you, we're here for a good time, not a long time.

This is clearly evident in the cityscape, where shiny new towers crowd the compact downtown skyline, and climbing cranes—a sign of more to come—rise up along with them. In every direction on the city's fringes, new suburbs are sprouting and sprawling as fast as they can clear the land and frame them up—to many a rural Albertan rancher and even long-term Calgarians' dismay.

Calgary has long been criticized for rushing forward at the expense of burying its past. But in this era of rapid growth, a strong citizen movement has grown on two fronts: to preserve the spectacular lands that surround the city and to promote urban density. A visitor today will see the fruits of that, as Calgary no longer grows only out, but up: For the first time in its history, the towers that cluster around downtown aren't just offices, but condominiums.

With the influx of money has come a flood of cultural facilities and awareness, too. The city is more cosmopolitan than at any time in its history, and the common phrase that seems to be gaining momentum here tells the tale: During the first oil boom, Calgary grew; in the second one, it grew up. This leaves Calgary, ever-ambitious, looking to join the top shelf of North American urban centers—if, as many Calgarians believe, it's not there already.

ESSENTIALS

Getting There

BY PLANE **Calgary International Airport** (© 877/254-7427; www.calgary airport.com) lies 16km (10 miles) northeast of the city. You can go through U.S. Customs right here if you're flying to or coming from the U. S. via Calgary. The airport is served by **Air Canada** (© 888/247-2262; www.aircanada.com), **Delta** (© 800/221-1212; www.delta.com), **American Airlines** (© 800/433-7300; www.aa.com), **United** (© 800/241-6522; www.united.com), **Continental** (© 800/525-0280; www.continental.com), and the homegrown **WestJet** (© 800/937-8538; www.westjet.com), a Calgary-based carrier with dozens of destinations across North America. Being a hub of international commerce, Calgary is also served by several commuter lines.

Cab fare to downtown hotels comes to around C$25. Several downtown hotels provide shuttle service from the airport; the only devoted airport shuttle is the new **Allied Downtown Shuttle Service** (© 403/299-9555; www.airportshuttle calgary.ca; one-way C$15 adults, C$10 children), which now runs only pre-arranged shuttle service.

BY CAR   From the U.S. border, Route 89 in Montana becomes Highway 2 at the Carway border crossing and runs to Calgary. It continues north to Edmonton (via Red Deer). From either Vancouver in the west or Regina in the east, take the Trans-Canada Highway.

BY TRAIN   The nearest VIA Rail station is in Edmonton (see chapter 10). You can, however, take a scenic train ride to/from Vancouver/Calgary on the Rocky Mountaineer, operated by **Rocky Mountaineer Vacations** (© **800/665-7245** or 604/606-7245; www.rockymountaineer.com). The lowest-priced tickets begin at C$609 for 2 days of daylight travel, which includes four meals and overnight accommodation in Kamloops; many other packages are available.

BY BUS   Greyhound buses (© **800/661-8747** or 403/260-0877; www.greyhound. ca) link Calgary with most other points in Canada, including Banff and Edmonton, as well as towns in the United States. The depot is at 877 Greyhound Way SW, west of downtown near the corner of 9th Avenue SW and 16th Street SW.

Visitor Information

The downtown **Visitor Service Centre** (© **800/661-1678** or 403/263-8510; www.tourismcalgary.com), at the base of the Calgary Tower (101 9th Ave. SW) and at the airport near the luggage carousels, provides free literature, maps, and information. The friendly white-hatted volunteer greeters at the Calgary Airport can also point you in the right direction.

City Layout

Central Calgary lies between the **Bow River** in the north and the **Elbow River** to the south. The two rivers meet at the eastern end of the city, forming **St. George's Island,** which houses a park and the zoo. South of the island stands **Fort Calgary,** birthplace of the city. Before meeting the Elbow, the Bow River makes a bend northwest of downtown, and in this bend nestles Prince's Island Park and the Eau Claire Market. The Canadian Pacific Railway tracks run between 9th and 10th avenues; Central Park and Stampede Park, scene of Calgary's greatest annual festival, stretch south of the tracks. Northwest, across the Bow River, is the University of Calgary's campus. The airport is northeast of the city.

Calgary is divided into four segments: northeast (NE), southeast (SE), northwest (NW), and southwest (SW), with avenues running east-west and streets north-south. The north and south numbers begin at Centre Avenue, the east and west numbers at Centre Street—a recipe for confusion if ever there was one.

Calgary's Neighborhoods in Brief

Despite its comprehensive cycling path system, Calgary is a driver's city, with hundreds of acres of sprawling suburbs and freeways. Still, there are a handful of areas in and around the downtown area that draw shoppers, diners, and revelers. If not downtown itself, a couple of satellite neighborhoods near the core contain much of the action.

DOWNTOWN

Downtown, which sprung up out of virtually nowhere in the 1970s oil boom, has often been criticized as an empty canyon of office towers, and for the most part, it's been a fair assessment. After 6pm on a weekday in years past, you could practically watch the tumbleweeds rolling down the street. That's changed a little in the past 5 to 10 years, as the **Eau Claire Market,** in downtown's south side near the Bow River, has brought in shoppers and, more importantly, some densely clustered residents in a series of riverside condominium towers.

The reclamation of **Stephen Avenue Mall** (8th Ave., btw. Centre St. and 7th St. SW) as a bona fide shopping and eating pedestrian stroll (it had been, in years past, a relatively derelict stretch) also gives downtown some much-needed vitality. Between the **Eaton Centre, Banker's Hall,** and the **TD Centre,** a good cluster of high-end retail can be found here. It's hopping the most during lunchtime.

The east end, anchored by the **Epcor Centre for the Performing Arts** and **Olympic Plaza,** gives downtown a much-needed shot in the arm after dark, too. But the more things change, the more they stay the same: In 2008, Penny Lane, a small cluster of historic buildings just west of Stephen Avenue that contained a nice complement of shops, eateries, and popular bars, was cratered to make way for a new skyscraping office tower. To the north is Calgary's Chinatown, an entirely authentic ethnic enclave, with the best dim sum, Vietnamese food, and tea shops in the city.

With the population booming and some of those new towers now including some condominiums, downtown Calgary is pushing toward colonization outside of business hours. Stay tuned and see.

17TH AVENUE SW

Undoubtedly Calgary's most vibrant, urban-feeling zone, the relatively compact axis of 17th Avenue and 4th Street SW is ground zero for Calgary's social scene. 17th Avenue tends toward the younger crowd more than 4th Street (also known as **the Mission**—see below) and overflows with lounges, bars, and restaurants.

A high-end plaza of street-side boutiques is at **Mount Royal Village,** on 16th Avenue and 8th Street SW (here, the block between 17th and 16th aves. is a stretch of park; the shops face onto it, visible from 17th Ave.).

This was also the site of the semi-notorious **Red Mile,** where thousands of

fans of the city's National Hockey League team, the Calgary Flames, gathered every night during the Flames' improbable run to the Stanley Cup finals in 2004. The Flames have tasted nothing like that success since, but fans still gather on game nights at the area's sports bars in fair numbers.

THE MISSION/CLIFF BUNGALOW

Going south of 4th Street SW from 17th Avenue SW is the Mission, a quaint cluster of low-rise buildings, and shops and restaurants housed in old homes or historic 3-story brick buildings (this being Calgary, there are a couple of strip malls for good measure, as well).

An urbane little stroll stretching south to the Elbow River at 26th Avenue, the Mission is a more grown-up version of 17th Avenue: great and interesting restaurants, boho cafes, and relatively serene places for a drink. Decor and fashion, while not over-emphasized here, are nonetheless features of this strip, which quickly falls away to quiet residential zones on either side of 4th Street. In warm weather, there's no better place in town to sit street-side on a patio, sip your latte or Pinot Grigio, and watch the world go by.

INGLEWOOD

Inglewood is sort of Calgary's version of Marlon Brando in *On the Waterfront:* could have been a contender, but never really seemed to get up off that mat. After decades of awaiting a wave of gentrification to wash through its historic streets and deliver it back to the center of city life, Inglewood—the oldest part of the city, where Calgary began—is still waiting, even as condo towers sprout all over downtown and real estate skyrockets to untold heights.

As it stands, Inglewood remains an endearingly shabby strip of historic buildings, some of them occupied with eclectic design stores, galleries, and artist studios, and some of them not occupied at all. Minutes away from downtown, across the river and over a bridge to the east, Inglewood remains a city unto itself—a village just outside the urban swirl.

KENSINGTON/SUNNYSIDE

Just north of downtown, across the Bow River, sits Kensington, probably the city's most earthy, bohemian quarter. There's little presence here of the city's wildly moneyed set; low-key restos and pubs are the order of the day here, along with vintage clothing, the city's venerable repertory cinema, **The Plaza** (1133 Kensington Rd. NW; ✆ **403-283-3636**), and a great second-hand record store, **Hot Wax** (114 10 St. NW; ✆ **403-283-0055**).

Kensington is perhaps the most eminently walkable area in the city. Clustered around the axis of 10th Street NW and Kensington Avenue, you can find all you need within a few blocks and a short stroll—whether it's a fair-trade organic Americano, a Guatemalan cotton pullover, or a copy of Coltrane's *Blue Train* on vinyl.

However, Kensington is not untouched by development—the imposing complex at the corner of 10th Street and Memorial Drive, by the river, has a Red Robin chain restaurant, and pricey fashion and design can be found along Kensington Avenue—but it remains a comfy pocket of earthiness amid the sparkle of a high-gloss metropolis.

GETTING AROUND

BY TRANSIT Calgary Transit System (✆ **403/276-1000;** www.calgarytransit.com) operates buses and a light-rail system called the C-Train. You can transfer from the light rail to buses on the same ticket. The ride costs C$2.75 for adults and C$1.75 for children; the C-Train (a light rail train that runs above ground) is free (buses are not) in the downtown stretch between 10th Street and City Hall. Tickets are good for travel in only one direction.

BY CAR Car-rental firms include **Avis** (211 6th Ave. SW; ✆ **403/269-6166**), **Budget** (140 6th Ave. SE; ✆ **403/226-1550**), and **Hertz** (227 6th Ave. SW; ✆ **403/221-1300**). Each of these has a bureau at the airport.

BY TAXI To summon a taxi, call Checker Cabs (✆ **403/974-1111**), Red Top Cabs (✆ **403/974-1110**), or Yellow Cabs (✆ **403/299-9999**).

ON FOOT As a whole, Calgary is not a terribly walkable city. Suburbs sprawl outward in every direction, connected to the center and each other by a network of freeways, known here as "Trails." In the city core, though, there are a handful of pedestrian-friendly areas—though you might have to drive or take transit just to get to them. Stephen Avenue, a pedestrian zone along the southern boundary of the financial district, is a pleasant place for a stroll, past sidewalk cafes and, at the far end, Olympic Plaza, a public space where medals were awarded during the 1988 Winter Olympics. Other walkable zones near the core can be reached on foot, if the connection isn't entirely pleasant. South of downtown lie the vibrant districts of 17th Avenue SW and the Mission, which can be reached from downtown by walking under a railroad bridge at either 4th or 8th streets SW. You'll traverse several semi-occupied blocks before you reach your destination. To the north, across the Bow River, lies Kensington, which you can walk to by going over the pedestrian bridge next to 9th Street after meeting the pathway west along the riverbanks from **Eau Claire Market** (200 Barclay Parade SW; www.eauclairemarket.com). Continue over the bridge and along Memorial Drive to the corner of 10th Street SW and Kensington Road NW—this is the heart of probably the city's most walkable district.

A Word about Walking

The "Plus 15" system is a series of enclosed walkways connecting high-rise downtown buildings, 4.5m (15 ft.) above street level. These walkways enable you to shop in living-room comfort, regardless of the weather. Watch for the little "+15" signs on the streets for access points. All the downtown malls are connected, as are several office towers. If you are in a downtown hotel, test yourself by getting from Banker's Hall building up to the Sheraton Suites across from Eau Claire Market.

BY BICYCLE Calgary has an extensive bicycle path system that connects the central core to some of the far-flung suburbs, and everything in between. All in, Calgary had more than 500km (311 miles) of devoted bike paths throughout the city—the most of any city in North America—with even more planned. Ride alongside the Bow River, through downtown, and off and around the Glenmore Reservoir without ever seeing a city street. This ride, and many more, can be found on the city's website, www.calgary.ca (search "cycling"). Also see the suggested "Cycling Tours," later in this chapter.

To ride, of course, you need wheels, and a number of places are happy to rent you a bike—in the summer months, at least. **Bike Calgary** (www.bikecalgary.org), a local riders' association, is a good place to start for current listings, as they tend to be seasonal and offer different services—or cut them off—year to year. But **Sports Rent** (4424 16th Ave. NW; © **403/292-0077;** www.sportsrent.ca) is a reliable option. They rent basic mountain bikes for C$25 per day, with kiddie bikes at C$10 per day.

[FastFACTS] CALGARY

Airport The **Calgary International Airport** is located 17km (11 miles) northeast of downtown. For general inquiries, call © **403/735-1200** or visit www.calgaryairport.com. For flight information, see "Getting There," above.

American Express The office at 421 7th Ave. SW (© **403/261-5982**) is open Monday to Friday 9am to 5pm.

Area Code Calgary and Southern Alberta are in the 403 area code.

From anywhere in Canada and the U.S., simply add "1" to the number you're dialing, a 10-digit number. When dialing locally in-city, you must use 10-digit dialing; add "403" before every seven-digit number.

Babysitting Hotel concierges can usually provide a list of approved sitters. You can try CanadianSitter at © **866/221-7918** or www.canadiansitter.ca.

Business Hours Most banks are open weekdays 10am to 4pm,

and Saturdays for a few hours in the morning or afternoon. Most shopping centers are open Monday to Friday 10am to 9pm, Saturday 10am to 6pm, and Sunday noon to 5pm.

Currency Exchange Being a tourist center, change bureaus abound, but your best bet is to use your bank card at any of the hundreds of ATMs in town. If you must trade cash or traveler's checks for Canadian currency, your best bets are any of the major chartered banks found downtown, at shopping malls, and in neighborhoods all over the city: CIBC, Bank of Montreal, Scotiabank, Royal Bank, or TD Canada Trust. **Travelex** (_C_ **403/221-1866;** www. travelex.com) is a currency exchange with branches at the airport and throughout the city.

Dentist Many dental clinics are open evenings and weekends. Ask your hotel to recommend one or visit the **Alberta Dental Association** website at www.abda.ab.ca to find one.

Directory Assistance Dial _C_ **411** to get local and long-distance directory help. You'll pay a fee from a private phone, but if you dial Directory at a payphone, it's free.

Doctors If you need non-emergency medical attention, check the phone book for the closest branch of **Medicentre,** a group of walk-in clinics open daily 7am to midnight. Also see their website, www.medicentres.com, for a list of locations.

Drugstores Check the phone book for **Shoppers Drug Mart,** which has more than a dozen stores in Calgary, most open till midnight. The branch at the **Chinook Centre** (6455 Macleod Trail S.; _C_ **403/ 253-2424**) is open 24 hours.

Emergency As with most urban centers in North America, _C_ **911** will put you in touch with emergency police, fire department, or ambulance services.

Fishing Licenses If you're planning to fish, either in the city or outside of it, you need to obtain a license. They're available at most sporting goods stores, convenience stores, and gas stations at a cost of C$26 per day for Canadians, C$27 per day for non-Canadians. Children under 16 and seniors over 65 can get licenses for free.

Hospitals If you need immediate attention, the following hospitals have emergency departments: **Foothills Hospital** (1403 29th St. NW; _C_ **403/670-1110**), **Alberta Children's**

Hospital (1820 Richmond Rd. SW; _C_ **403/229-7211**), and **Rockyview General Hospital** (3500 26th Ave. SW; _C_ **403/541-3000**).

Libraries The main branch of the **Calgary Public Library** is downtown, near the municipal buildings, at 616 Macleod Trail SE (_C_ **403/260-2600;** www.calgarypublic library.com). Branches are located throughout the city, most with Internet access.

Newspapers Calgary's two dailies, the _Calgary Herald_ (www.calgaryherald.com) and the _Calgary Sun_ (www.calgarysun.com), are both morning papers. _Fast Forward Weekly_ (www. ffwdweekly.com) is a youth-oriented newsweekly and a good place to look for information on the local music and arts scene.

Police The 24-hour number is _C_ **403/266-1234.** Dial _C_ **911** in emergencies.

Post Office The main post office is at 207 9th Ave. (_C_ **403/974-2078**). Call _C_ **403/292-5434** to find other branches.

WHERE TO STAY

A thriving hub of international commerce makes finding a cheap bed in Calgary difficult. Downtown offers a full complement of international business-class brands like Sheraton, Westin, and Delta, with few independents and little to distinguish between them, save location. Newer modern and sleek hotels like Le Germain and Hotel Arts have livened things up a bit.

Less expensive rooms, if they're available at all, tend to cluster around the motel strips: Macleod Trail S, or 16th Avenue NW, which is what the Trans-Canada Highway becomes as it passes through the city. A few deals can be found downtown at cheaper chains like **Best Western** (www.bestwestern.com), **Sandman**

Inn (www.sandmanhotels.com), or **Travelodge** (www.travelodge.com). There is a dearth of accommodation outside the central financial core and motel strips, unfortunately, notably in trendy neighborhoods like the Mission.

If you like B&Bs, try the **Bed and Breakfast Association of Calgary** (www.bbcalgary.com), which has several dozen listings for the city. The many hotels in Motel Village (see below), which link to the city center via the C-Train, are another option; you can often find these rooms at discount hotel websites.

Downtown

VERY EXPENSIVE & EXPENSIVE

Delta Bow Valley ☺ From the outside, Delta's Bow Valley property looks like a fairly generic business hotel. Inside, the Delta's lobby is a quiet oasis of soothing calm just outside the main bustle of the city's constantly churning core. Many of the rooms have been renovated and are generously sized, but some are definitely worn-out. The location, along the Bow River, is a peaceful choice for someone who wants to be within walking distance of downtown, but it's the furthest from the core of any of the big chain hotels. The breakfast is expensive for the quality. The Bow Valley is also welcoming to children: kids under 17 stay free with a parent. At meals, kids under 6 eat free, while kids under 12 eat at half price. The hotel also features a children's "creative center," where kids can be parked to indulge their artistic urges with art supplies and computers. The Delta Bow Valley is also the only hotel in Calgary that offers a complimentary sedan service within the downtown core, making the slightly inconvenient location easier to manage.

209 4th Ave. SE, Calgary T2G 0C6. © **800/665-8571** or 403/266-1980. www.deltahotels.com. C$149–C$189 double; C$249–C$349 suite. Family & senior rates available. AE, DC, DISC, MC, V. Parking Fri & Sat C$11, Sun–Thurs C$17. **Amenities:** Restaurant; lounge; concierge; health club; whirlpool; indoor pool; 24-hr. room service; sauna; spa. *In room:* A/C, TV, hair dryer, Internet, minibar.

The Fairmont Palliser ★ Opened in 1914 as one of the Canadian Pacific Railroad hotels, the Palliser remains Calgary's landmark historic hotel, its most visible expression of old-world luxury and upper-crust class. The vast marble-floored lobby, surrounded by columns and lit by gleaming chandeliers, is the very picture of Edwardian sumptuousness. You'll feel like an Alberta Cattle King in the Rimrock Dining Room, with vaulted ceilings, period murals, a massive stone fireplace, and hand-tooled leather panels on teak beams, although it's a bit grandfatherly to some. Guest rooms are large for a hotel of this vintage—the Pacific Premier rooms would be suites at most other properties—and they preserve the period charm while incorporating modern luxuries. Fairmont Gold rooms come with their own concierge and a private lounge with breakfast, drinks, and hors d'oeuvres included. In early 2010, a C$30-million renovation delivered new carpets, upholstery, and furniture throughout.

133 9th Ave. SW, Calgary T2P 2M3. © **800/441-1414** or 403/262-1234. www.fairmont.com/palliser. 405 units. C$179–C$499 double; C$259–C$579 suite; C$1,800–C$2,500 suite w/multiple bedrooms. AE, DC, DISC, MC, V. Valet parking C$30–C$37; self-parking C$25. **Amenities:** Restaurant; lounge; babysitting; concierge; concierge-level rooms; health club; indoor pool; 24-hr. room service; spa. *In room:* A/C, TV, hair dryer, minibar, Wi-Fi.

Hotel Arts ★ You can still feel the old skeletons of the Holiday Inn it once was, but ever since this hotel reopened in 2006, it's been the city's see-and-be-seen destination. Raw Bar, the hotel's lounge, is a cocktail hotspot and a popular sushi

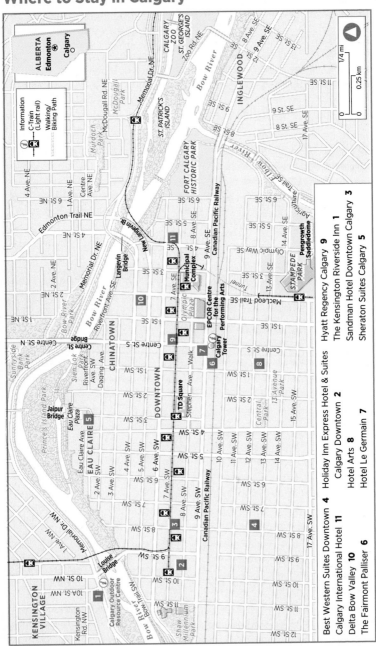

Best Western Suites Downtown **4**
Calgary International Hotel **11**
Delta Bow Valley **10**
The Fairmont Palliser **6**

Holiday Inn Express Hotel & Suites
Calgary Downtown **2**
Hotel Arts **8**
Hotel Le Germain **7**

Hyatt Regency Calgary **9**
The Kensington Riverside Inn **1**
Sandman Hotel Downtown Calgary **3**
Sheraton Suites Calgary **5**

bar, while Saint Germain, its dining room, is one of the top-rated fine-dining experiences in the city. Keep your eyes peeled for one or two players from the Calgary Flames, the city's NHL hockey team, leaving their Porsches with the valet. An interior courtyard sports a nice-sized open-air pool, which in turn sports a ring of poolside tables with cocktail and dinner service. The rooms, meanwhile, do their best to be chic, with long draping curtains, large plasma screens, and faux-fur throws on their Egyptian-cotton-clad beds. All come with small balconies, as well, ideal for surveying the city's late-night skyline. Rooms, generally, are small; and the bathrooms, in particular, feel dark and tiny when compared to other hotels in new buildings. But the common spaces are vast and inspired, dotted with contemporary art and dark velvet.

119 12th Ave. SW, Calgary T2R 0G8. © **800/661-9378** or 403/266-4611. www.hotelarts.ca. 185 units. C$269 double; C$359 suite. AE, DC, MC, V. Valet parking C$30; free self-parking. **Amenities:** Restaurant; bar; concierge. *In room:* A/C, TV, hair dryer, minibar, Wi-Fi.

Hotel Le Germain ★★   Calgary's newest hotel is a breath of fresh air in a brand new building right downtown. Le Germain, a chain from Montréal, brings a modern and stylish flair to their 143 rooms (too many to be called "boutique," even if they try). Guests are chic business folks and cosmopolitan travelers from places like New York and Europe. Staff, many of whom are bilingual, will go beyond the call of duty to ease your stay. Dark browns and purples mix with retro white chairs and mirrors in spacious and very comfortable rooms. There are large work spaces, a good music system, and all the bells and whistles for those with work to be done. Smart extras, like a hidden ironing board and individual climate control, hit the mark, as well. Bathrooms are all very large, with a bright separated shower and plenty of light. The gym connects with the next-door apartments, so it can be crowded. The ground level restaurant, Charcut (see p. 90), is the best in town.

899 Centre St. SW, Calgary T2G 1B3. © **877/362-8990** or 403/264-8990. www.germaincalgary.com. 143 units. C$279–C$529 superior double; C$309–C$559 deluxe double; from C$759 suite. AE, MC, V. Parking C$35. **Amenities:** Restaurant; lounge; concierge. *In room:* A/C, TV, hair dryer, minibar, Wi-Fi.

Hyatt Regency Calgary   Posh and relatively new (about 10 years old), the Hyatt is linked to the Telus Convention Centre and is convenient to shopping and arts venues that run along the Stephen Avenue Mall. Guest rooms are large, measuring roughly 37 sq. m (398 sq. ft.), with comfy furniture and great views. Suites are truly spacious, with most of the comforts of home. The hotel's Stillwater Spa (© **403/537-4474**) is a full-service day spa, with a combination of massage and hydrotherapies, body wraps, and beauty treatments. The fitness center and saline pool offer majestic views across the city skyline to the Rockies. The Hyatt flanks historic Stephen Avenue; rather than leveling the 1890s stone storefronts, the Hyatt cleverly incorporates them into the hotel's facade. Original art worth C$2 million is on display in the hotel lobby and corridors.

700 Centre St. SE, Calgary T2G 5P6. © **800/233-1234** or 403/717-1234. www.calgary.hyatt.com. 355 units. From C$189 double; from C$349 suite. AE, DC, DISC, MC, V. Valet parking C$35; self-parking C$25. **Amenities:** Restaurant; lounge; babysitting; concierge; health club; Jacuzzi; indoor pool; 24-hr. room service; sauna; spa. *In room:* A/C, TV, hair dryer, minibar, Wi-Fi.

The Kensington Riverside Inn ★★★   At all of two stories high and half a block from the city's vibrant—and eminently walkable—Kensington District, the Riverside

Inn is a delightful surprise. A chic redo in recent years has erased its country charm, replacing it with a sleek, sophisticated aesthetic. It's private, secluded, and quiet. The large salon features a fireplace and couch-side cocktail and appetizer service from its award-winning restaurant, the Chef's Table. The 19 rooms are ample and have all the comforts, including plush down pillows and duvets. A short walk across the footbridge lands you on Prince's Island Park, perhaps the city's most appealing urban oasis, which sits in the shadow of the downtown office towers. With its just-close-enough-to-downtown location, the Riverside is Calgary's top boutique hotel, without a doubt.

1126 Memorial Dr. NW, Calgary T2N 3E3. ✆ **877/313-3733** or 403/228-4442. Fax 403/228-9608. www.kensingtonriversideinn.com. 19 units. C$209 double; C$309 suite. Rates include breakfast. AE, DC, MC, V. Free parking. **Amenities:** Restaurant; bar; concierge. *In room:* A/C, TV, hair dryer, minibar, Wi-Fi.

Sheraton Suites Calgary   The Sheraton Suites overlooks the Eau Claire Market area, just steps away from both the Bow River Greenway and downtown business towers. As an all-suite hotel, the Sheraton offers large and thoughtfully designed rooms that put luxury and business ease foremost. The decor is strikingly modern, with quality and notably comfortable furniture, plus easy access to high-tech tools to help a business traveler multitask. The built-in cabinetry makes it feel very home-like, as do the Prairie-influenced art, plants, and two TVs in every room. Corner king suites are especially nice, with huge bathrooms, tiled showers, and Jacuzzi tubs. If being near green space is important to you and you'll be staying for a few nights, this should be your top choice.

 Chinooks

It's an old saying in the mountains: If you don't like the weather, wait 5 minutes. The implication, of course, is that wild, unpredictable weather patterns coursing over the lush valleys on the western slope of the Rockies invariably transform as they climb up and over the mountains themselves, throwing them into chaos.

East of the mountains, as they are in the Bow River Valley, Calgarians are nonetheless well-acquainted with the vagaries of mountain weather systems. You'd be hard-pressed to find a Calgarian with more than a decade in town under their belt who hadn't seen at least one snowstorm in July.

That's the downside. Happily, there's an upside, too. On occasion, warm, moist air traveling east from the Pacific Ocean travels up into the mountains. The moisture condenses and falls as precipitation on the mountains themselves. The air, now dry, tumbles down the Rockies' eastern slope, gaining speed and warming, according to weather officials, at a rate of about 6°F (3°C) per 305m (1,000 ft.).

By the time the wind—typically stiff and consistent, not gusty—reaches the city, it's warmed up enough to bestow upon Calgarians mid-winter days that spike up beyond 68°F (20°C). When a Chinook's in town, there's often a signature arch of cloud in the west, an inversion of cloud and sky. The Chinook arch is a welcome feature in the western winter sky, melting snow and ice, and bathing the city in temporary warmth. Calgarians know it can't last—a week is a long time for a Chinook to stick around—but their occasional arrival makes a long, often frigid, winter that much more bearable.

255 Barclay Parade SW, Calgary T2P 5C2. ☏ **888/784-8370** or 403/266-7200. www.sheratonsuites. com. 323 units. C$127–C$295 suite. Additional adult C$30. AE, DC, DISC, MC, V. Valet parking Sun–Thurs C$38, Fri & Sat C$27. **Amenities:** 2 restaurants; lounge; babysitting; concierge; exercise room; Jacuzzi; indoor pool; 24-hr. room service; sauna; Wi-Fi (in public spaces). *In room:* A/C, TV w/games & movie channels, fridge, hair dryer, Internet.

MODERATE & INEXPENSIVE

Always a challenge in money-mad Calgary, there are nonetheless a handful of perfectly comfortable choices in the city core. Don't expect white-glove service, but clean, convenient, efficient, and well-maintained are the main benefits of the hotels in this section. Luckily, the light-rail system makes it easy to stay outside the city center—particularly in Motel Village in Northwest Calgary and along the C-Train line south along Macleod Trail—yet have access to the restaurants and sights of downtown.

Best Western Suites Downtown This well-maintained older hotel is an excellent value. The rooms, all considered suites, are quite large, some almost apartment-size, and are fitted with quality furniture; some come with efficiency kitchens. It's located between downtown and trendy 17th Avenue.

1330 8th St. SW, Calgary T2R 1B6. ☏ **800/981-2555** or 403/228-6900. www.bestwesternsuitescalgary. com. 123 units. C$119–C$169 junior suite; C$169–C$199 1-bedroom suite; C$169–C$269 2-bedroom suite. Additional adult C$20. Children 17 & under stay free in parent's room. Senior, weekly & monthly rates available. AE, DISC, MC, V. Free parking. **Amenities:** Restaurant; Jacuzzi; sauna. *In room:* A/C, TV, fridge, hair dryer, Internet, kitchenette.

Calgary International Hostel ⚜ The 120 beds at the Calgary hostel are the city's most affordable lodgings—but there are reasons beyond economy to stay here. The hostel is on the edge of downtown, convenient to bars and restaurants along Stephen Avenue and theaters near the performing-arts center. There is a games room and Internet access, it has homey—if somewhat dated—common areas, and it's clean as a whistle. It's very highly rated by guests from all over the world. There are 110 dorm-style beds with two family rooms available. A small convenience store is on-site.

520 7th Ave. SE, Calgary T2G 0J6. ☏ **866/762-4122** or 403/269-8239. www.hihostels.ca. Members C$26–C$30 shared room, C$69–C$100 private room; nonmembers C$30–C$35 shared room, C$77–C$110 private room. MC, V. Free parking.

Holiday Inn Express Hotel & Suites Calgary Downtown This conveniently located older hotel has just undergone a major makeover, emerging as part of the Holiday Inn Express chain. The rooms are large and nicely furnished; all have balconies and large workstations with high-speed Internet access. It's just a block from the C-Train, which will put you in the heart of things in 5 minutes. With free parking, this is one of the best deals in the downtown area. Be wary of the noisy bar next door.

1020 8th Ave. SW, Calgary T2P 1J2. ☏ **888/465-4329** or 403/269-8262. www.hiexpress.com/calgar-ydt. 56 units. C$148–C$209 double; C$239–C$359 suite. Rates include hot breakfast. AE, MC, V. Free parking. **Amenities:** Restaurant; pub; fitness center. *In room:* A/C, fridge, hair dryer, Internet (free).

Hotel Alma Located on the campus of the University of Calgary, this new hotel is a bit far from the city center, but the value and the design make up for it with ease. Rooms are a bit reminiscent of a college dorm in size, but their European styling (ergonomic chairs, wide desks, orange and brown accents) and many bonuses (free local and North American long distance calls, free breakfast and Wi-Fi) will keep you very pleased and surprised. The best surprise, though, is the young, friendly, unpretentious, and very professional staff that seem truly thrilled that you are staying with them. With parking at only C$7 a night and public transit a few blocks away, you can leave car worries behind. This offers a great value for those ready to think a bit outside the box.

169 University Gate NW, Calgary T2N 1N4. ✆ **877/498-3203** or 403/220-3202. www.hotelalma.ca. 98 units. C$109–C$239 double. Rates include breakfast. AE, MC, V. Parking C$7. **Amenities:** Restaurant; access to nearby fitness center & pool. In room: A/C, fridge, Wi-Fi.

Sandman Hotel Downtown Calgary ★ 🔥 This hotel on the west end of downtown is one of Calgary's best deals. The Sandman is conveniently located on the free rapid-transit mall, just west of the main downtown core. The standard rooms are a good size, but the real winners are the very large corner units, which feature small kitchens and great views. Rooms may be dated, but they are clean and cared for. The Sandman is a popular place with corporate clients, due to its central location and good value. It also boasts a complete fitness facility. Its private health club, available free to guests, has a lap pool, three squash courts, and aerobics and weight-training facilities.

888 7th Ave. SW, Calgary, AB T2P 3J3. ✆ **800/726-3626** or 403/237-8626. www.sandmanhotels.com. 301 units. C$99–C$139 double. Children under 16 stay free in parent's room. AE, DC, DISC, MC, V. Parking C$6–C$16. **Amenities:** Restaurant; bar; concierge; health club; indoor pool; limited room service. In room: A/C, TV, fridge, hair dryer, Wi-Fi.

Motel Village

Northwest of downtown, this triangle of more than 20 large motels, plus restaurants, stores, and gas stations, forms a self-contained hamlet near the University of Calgary. Enclosed by Crowchild Trail, the Trans-Canada Highway, and Highway 1A, the village's costlier establishments flank the highway, and the cheaper ones lie off Crowchild Trail. If you're driving and don't want to deal with downtown traffic, just head here to find a room; for C-Train service, use the Lions Park or Banff Park stops. Except during the Stampede, you'll be able to find a vacancy without reservations. Use a discount hotel website such as Travelocity to find deals here. Popular chain hotels and some independents are located here, including **Comfort Inn** (2369 Banff Trail NW; ✆ **403/289-2589**), **Calgary Motel Village** (2369 Banff Trail NW; ✆ **800/228-5150** or 403/289-2581), **Best Western Village Park Inn** (1804 Crowchild Trail NW; ✆ **888/774-7716** or 403/289-4645), **Travelodge North** (2304 16th Ave. NW; ✆ **800/578-7878** or 403/289-0211), and the **Quality Inn University** (2359 Banff Trail NW; ✆ **800/661-4667** or 403/289-1973). You can expect rates of about C$120 to C$140 for a double.

Macleod Trail South

All the usual suspects are here, lining Macleod Trail, a wide, noisy, cluttered commercial strip that leads south out of town and eventually turns into Highway 2. This is big-box-retailer heaven (or hell, depending on your perspective), capped off with Southcentre, one of Calgary's largest suburban malls, at the intersection of Macleod Trail and Anderson Road. Paralleling Macleod Trail is the C-Train line, which will whisk you downtown from its southernmost point near Midnapore (an even-farther-out 'burb) to the core in about 45 minutes. In the south, motels tend to cluster between Heritage Drive (the farthest north) to Anderson Road (the farthest south), so your trip would be closer to half an hour. Closer to downtown, motels can be found along Macleod as soon as you crest Cemetery Hill out of downtown, starting around 42nd Avenue SW and stretching to about 58th Avenue SW—too far to walk, but a reasonable cab ride away. As with Motel Village, use sites like Expedia or Travelocity to hunt out the deals; posted rates are sometimes as low as C$69. A few of your best bets are **Travelodge Hotel Calgary Macleod Trail** (9206 Macleod Trail S; ✆ **800/578-7878** or 403/253-7070), **Comfort Inn and Suites South** (4611 Macleod Trail S; ✆ **403/287-7070**), and **Inn on Macleod Trail** (4206 Macleod Trail S; ✆ **866/554-0162** or 403/287-2700).

Airport

There are a slew of hotels close to the Calgary International Airport. The only one that deserves a special mention here is the new **Acclaim Hotel ★★** (✆ **866/955-0008** or 403/291-8000; www.acclaimhotel.ca), the best airport hotel in town, by far. Located just 5 minutes from the airport, the hotel's style is sophisticated, Euro-modern, and thoughtful. They have free parking for those of you on the out-bound portion of your trips. This is a relaxing way to start or finish your trip. Doubles are C$139 to C$159.

Camping

The **Calgary West Campground** (✆ **403/288-0411;** www.calgarycampground. com), on the Trans-Canada Highway west of the city, allows tents and pets. Facilities include washrooms, toilets, laundry, a dumping station, hot showers, groceries, and a pool. The price for full hook-up with two people is C$45 per night; tent sites are C$29 to C$32 per night.

WHERE TO DINE

Gone are the days when the Calgarian restaurant scene offered a vast array of dishes featuring Alberta beef—generally acknowledged as some of the best in the world—and little else. Recent economic boom times and an influx of outsiders from around the country and all over the world have bestowed upon the city a vibrantly eclectic, cosmopolitan dining scene. As is the case with most things here, a fresh, contemporary take dominates most menus, and the emphasis on organic and local ingredients seems to grow by the day. Don't be shocked to find local bison and elk on a great many menus around town, if accompanied by such cutting-edge culinary trends like molecular gastronomy (ginger-celeriac foam, anyone?)

The city's most vibrant dining districts can be found either in or on the edge of the city core. Downtown, both workers on their lunch breaks and travelers lodging in the many nearby hotels have a huge variety of options, most along Stephen Avenue Mall or 9th Street. The handful of blocks around 17th Avenue SW, between about 8th Street and 2nd Street, and 4th Street SW, between 17th Avenue and 25th Avenue (also known as the Mission) are also dense with choices.

Both earthy and urbane, eating your way through all of Calgary's worthy restaurants could take months—not to mention a fair chunk of most people's savings.

Flush with oil wealth as it is, Calgary's restaurants, which tend to cater to the new-money set, are rarely a bargain, with high-end restaurants pushing into the C$40-to-C$50 range for signature dishes like Bison tenderloin or filet mignon. What follows are some worth the pain.

Downtown
EXPENSIVE

The Belvedere ★ CONTEMPORARY A favorite power-lunch spot for flush oilmen, the very stylish Belvedere, on Stephen Avenue Mall, is one of the most impressive of Calgary's restaurants. The dining room exudes a darkly elegant, 1930s atmosphere. The menu blends traditional favorites with stand-up-and-take-notice preparations. Foie gras frequently appears as an appetizer, perhaps seared with a brioche, chili-battered onions, and black pepper foam. Main courses feature local meats and seasonal produce; favorite main courses include an elk rack with melon salsa, Digby scallops with mango and chilies, and duck breast with black truffle chutney. The bar is a quiet and sophisticated spot for a drink. They also have what is probably Calgary's best wine list.

107 8th Ave. SW. ℂ **403/265-9595.** www.thebelvedere.ca. Reservations recommended. Main courses C$24–C$44. AE, DC, MC, V. Tues–Fri 11:30am–2pm & 5pm–midnight; Sat 5:30–10pm.

Charcut ★★ GRILL This is the evolution of the steakhouse, a gorgeous and hot new restaurant that moves beyond the typical Alberta chunk of beef (tenderloin, New York strip, T-bone) and looks at being a locavore and carnivore in a whole new light. The locally sourced menu is relaxed and simple, encouraging sharing. For example, split a butter-like bone marrow au gratin to start; then, pass around a pig's head mortadella with pistachios and truffles on house-made brioche or a lamb neck terrine with garden rhubarb. The simply prepared meat comes next, charbroiled, wood smoked, or hot off a rotisserie. There's a marbled and flavorful butcher steak, lamb leg, prime rib, or heritage chicken. Non-carnivores can enjoy the whole fish on the bone. Good value, an extensive beer list, and smart service only add to the highly satisfying experience.

101-899 Centre St. SW. ℂ **403/836-7482.** www.charcut.com. Reservations recommended. Main courses C$19–C$29. AE, DC, MC, V. Mon & Tues 11am–11pm; Wed–Fri 11am–1am; Sat 5pm–1am; Sun 5–10pm.

Murietta's West Coast Grill REGIONAL CANADIAN Just around the corner from the vibrant Stephen Avenue restaurant scene, Murietta's is a popular and stylish bar and dining room that combines the best of historic and contemporary Calgary. Located on the second story of the 1890s Alberta Hotel, Murietta's huge bar is a favorite watering hole for urban professionals, and the art-filled, two-story stone-walled dining room is the place for Alberta steaks and local lamb, pork, and game. For appetizers, choose PEI mussels or shucked oysters. And if red meat's not your thing, Murietta's offers a daily changing selection of fresh fish with a choice of sauces—perhaps saffron vanilla butter on wild Pacific salmon. A nice selection of sandwiches, pastas, and flatbread pizzas will please lighter eaters.

200-808 1st St. SW. ℂ **403/269-7707.** Reservations suggested. Main courses C$12–C$45. AE, DC, MC, V. Mon–Wed 11am–10pm; Thurs–Sat 11am–11pm; Sun 4:30–10pm.

River Café ★★ CONTEMPORARY If you have one meal in Calgary, it should be here. You might have a slightly better meal at, say, Téatro, but nothing touches

Where to Dine in Calgary

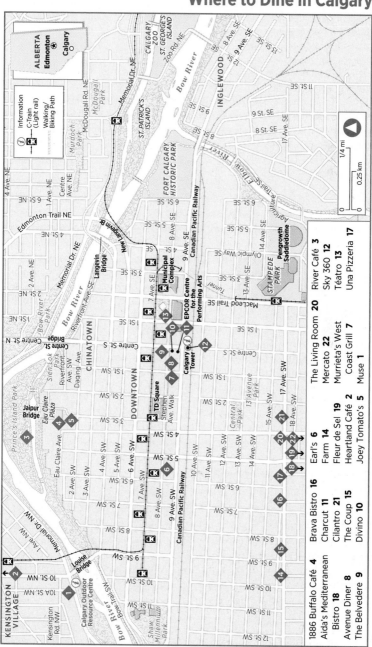

1886 Buffalo Café **4**
Aida's Mediterranean Bistro **18**
Avenue Diner **8**
The Belvedere **9**
Brava Bistro **16**
Charcut **11**
Cilantro **21**
The Coup **15**
Divino **10**
Earl's **6**
Farm **14**
Fleur de Sel **19**
Heartland Café **2**
Joey Tomato's **5**
The Living Room **20**
Mercato **22**
Murrieta's West Coast Grill **7**
Muse **1**
River Café **3**
Sky 360 **12**
Téatro **13**
Una Pizzeria **17**

the River Café's combo of cuisine and location. To reach the aptly named River Café, it takes a short walk through the Eau Claire Market area, then over the footbridge to pretty Prince's Island Park. On a lovely summer evening, the walk is a plus, as are the restaurant's park-side decks (no vehicles hurtling by). Wood-fired, free-range, and wild-gathered foods teamed with organic whole breads and fresh-baked desserts form the backbone of the excellent menu. There's a wide range of appetizers and light dishes—many vegetarian—as well as pizza-like flat breads topped with zippy cheese, vegetables, and fruit. Specialties from the grill include braised pheasant breast with mustard spaetzle, black-cherry oil, and roasted apple. Menus change seasonally and read like a very tasty adventure novel.

25 Prince's Island Park. ✆ **403/261-7670.** www.river-cafe.com. Reservations recommended. Main courses C$24–C$49. AE, MC, V. Mon–Fri 11am–3pm, Sat & Sun 10am–3pm; daily 5–11pm (5–10pm in winter). Closed Jan.

Sky 360 REGIONAL   There's more than just spectacular views 762 steps (or a quick elevator ride) up the Calgary Tower. The menu here is now much more gourmet-focused and upscale than in years past, but it's also full of crowd-pleasers like goat cheese penne, grilled salmon, tenderloins, and strip loins. The elevator fee is included in your meal; the wine list is surprisingly good, and with the place rotating on a 45-minute schedule, you'll get a couple of full city views in with a meal.

101 9th St. (in the Calgary Tower). ✆ **403/532-7966.** www.sky360.ca. Reservations recommended. Main courses C$22–C$42. AE, MC, V. Mon–Sat 11am–2pm, Sun 10am–2pm; daily 5–10pm.

Téatro ★★ ITALIAN   Located in the historic, spectacularly renovated Dominion Bank building, Téatro is about entertainment. It's just across from the Centre for the Performing Arts, and the restaurant's open kitchen and chic atmosphere offer distraction and drama. Oh, and the chef delivers the best New Italian cooking in Calgary. The high-ceilinged dining room is dominated by columns and huge panel windows, bespeaking class and elegance. The extensive menu is based on "Italian market cuisine," featuring what's seasonally best and freshest; some of the best dishes come from the wood-fired oven that dominates one wall. For lighter appetites, there's a large selection of antipasti, boutique pizzas, and salads; the entrees, featuring Alberta beef, veal, pasta, and seafood, are prepared with flair and innovation. Lobster-and-scallop ravioli is a favorite. Service is excellent.

200 8th Ave. SE. ✆ **403/290-1012.** www.teatro.ca. Reservations recommended. Main courses C$22–C$50. AE, DC, MC, V. Mon–Fri 11:30am–2pm; daily 5pm–midnight.

MODERATE & INEXPENSIVE

1886 Buffalo Café ★★★ TRADITIONAL/BREAKFAST   The name means what it says: Founded in 1886 (the "Buffalo" was added in recent years) and made moderately famous by a sweet Visa ad made for the 1988 Calgary Winter Olympics, it's probably the longest-running breakfast in town, if not the whole country. With good reason—the hash browns are piled high, the bacon and sausages fresh and perfectly cooked, the flapjacks come in towers, and the array of egg dishes is dizzying. All served in the noisy din of the cafe's resoundingly authentic, pioneer-era environment (clapboard shack exterior, rough old-wood interior), it's an experience not to be missed. The cafe got here first, but the city has built up around it; 1886 is now surrounded by gleaming office towers and the condos of Eau Claire Market (which is right across the street), but its authenticity remains undiminished. Try Kenny's Special, a mountain of egg, cheese, green pepper, and mushroom; plan to

| Clean |

Maybe it's the overall newness, maybe it's the relatively sparse population in the city center itself, or maybe it simply speaks to a general fussy, fastidious self-consciousness of a city rapidly climbing the international urban ladder, but for a city of a million people, Calgary is remarkably clean and tidy—so much so, in fact, that in 2007 it was ranked the #1 Cleanest City in the World by Mercer Quality of Living, an annual survey of the world's most livable cities (in that broader ranking, Calgary placed 24th overall).

skip eating the rest of the day. You can also try the Barley Mill (✆ 403/290-1500), a large pub that is its sister property, right next door, for good, unpretentious, reasonably priced pub fare.

187 Barclay Parade SW. ✆ **403/269-9255.** Reservations not accepted. Main courses C$9–C$15. MC, V. Mon–Fri 6am–3pm; Sat & Sun 7am–3pm.

Avenue Diner Along the Stephen Avenue Mall pedestrian strip, the Avenue is a reasonably priced alternative. Their specialties are breakfasts and lunches. In fact, they're not even open in the evenings. There's a cool retro feel to the scene, and the menu has some blast-from-the-pasts, as well—namely, their signature macaroni and cheese made with aged white cheddar and truffle oil. The Eggs Bennys are vegetarian-friendly; try the one with vine-ripened tomatoes, basil, and reduced balsamic. Come mid-morning on a weekday; it can be tough to get a table for weekend brunch.

105-8th St. ✆ **403/263-2673.** www.avenuediner.com. Reservations not accepted. Main courses C$6–C$18. Mon–Fri 7am–3pm; Sat & Sun 8am–3pm.

Divino ★ BISTRO This estimable bar and restaurant calls itself a "wine and cheese bistro," and while a casual spot for a drink and cheese platter is welcome on busy Stephen Avenue, Divino offers a lot more. This bustling, stylish gathering spot offers intriguing light entrees, from sandwiches (lamb confit melt with fig jam) to pasta (cannelloni filled with lobster and chanterelles), in addition to full-flavored and satisfying main courses such as roast chicken with herb mustard gnocchi. A class act.

113 8th Ave. SW. ✆ **403/234-0403.** www.crmr.com/divino. Reservations recommended. Main courses C$17–C$37. AE, DC, MC, V. Mon–Thurs 11am–10pm; Fri 11am–11pm; Sat 5–11pm; Sun 5–10pm. Closed Sun Oct–June.

Earl's CONTEMPORARY For a good meal at a reasonable price, this popular chain is always a can't-miss option. The downtown location is no exception. Well-located in the base of the Banker's Hall tower, Earl's is jammed at lunch time, and with good reason: There are few places downtown where one can find fresh, moderately inventive fare for less than C$20 a plate. As a result, it tends to be jammed with tourists and aspiring junior executives whose paychecks don't quite match their ambitions. The menu is a catch-all, with samplings of multicultural fare (Thai green curry, south Indian curry, stir-fried Shanghai noodles), and an array of burgers, sandwiches, and salads. You can push yourself into the high-dollar range by ordering a steak for C$35, but if that's your plan, you'll want to go elsewhere. If you're looking for a quick lunch in a vibrant setting that won't break the bank, then Earl's is your place. It also features a lounge popular with the after-work set.

Level 1, 315 8th Ave. SW. © **403/265-3275.** www.earls.ca/LocationList/Earls_Bankers_Hall.htm. Main courses C$11–C$35. AE, DC, MC, V. Mon–Fri 11am–11pm; Sat & Sun 11am–midnight.

Joey Tomato's ITALIAN   In the popular Eau Claire Market complex, the lively Joey Tomato's serves Italian/Asian fusion cooking to throngs of appreciative Calgarians. And no wonder it's often packed with the city's young and tanned: The food is really good, the prices are moderate (by the city's standards), and there's a lively bar scene. The broad menu includes steaks, fresh fish, and stir-fried veggies. It's always a fun, high-energy place to eat.

200 Barclay Parade SW. © **403/263-6336.** www.joeyrestaurants.com. Reservations not accepted. Main courses C$12–C$35. AE, MC, V. Sun–Thurs 11am–midnight; Fri & Sat 11am–1am.

17th Avenue & the Mission (4th St.)
EXPENSIVE

The Living Room ★ CONTEMPORARY   Along the burgeoning 17th Avenue cluster of boutiques, bars, and restaurants, the Living Room offers an inventive contemporary menu in an almost cottage-like setting. Set in an old bungalow—a holdover from much earlier days in this development-mad city—the dining room is cozy and homey, with modern design flair, and the expansive street-side patio, under the cover of lush trees, is an urban oasis perfect for summer evening dining. The solid wooden fence that separates the patio from the sidewalk is a perfectly calculated height: short enough to observe the dynamic street scene, but just tall enough to feel apart from it. The restaurant features an "interactive" component (which is just a fancy way of saying it makes dishes for two, to share) and offers an array of local fare (bison, lamb, and beef) prepared in inventive ways, such as the Hamilton Farms Black Angus tenderloin, with seared Quebec foie gras, sun choke and salsify ragout with ginger cider and beet reduction. Also, an updated version of fondue can be found here—perfect for the waning, chilling days of patio season in the fall.

514 17th Ave. SW. © **403/228-9830.** Reservations recommended, particularly for patio. Main courses C$26–C$39. AE, MC, V. Mon–Fri 11:30am–2pm & 5–11pm.

Mercato ★★★ ITALIAN   One of Calgary's true see-and-be-seen hotspots, Mercato serves up gorgeous traditional Italian fare with outstanding flair and panache. It's a casual environment with an open kitchen and, when it fills up at lunch and dinner—as it almost always does—it's a loud, boisterous, fun affair. Attached to the restaurant is a culinary boutique, where specialty cheeses, breads, and pastas can be found; particularly appealing are the barrel-sized kegs of Uncle Luigi's olive oil and balsamic vinegar, which the staff bottle before your eyes. The menu features a sublime selection of pastas, including a killer traditional fettuccine carbonara and a linguini with fresh ricotta, arugula, and *prosciuttino* (crisped prosciutto). Adventurous diners can tuck into such dishes as braised rabbit legs in a wild mushroom, tomato, and olive *ragu,* a recent feature (the menu changes regularly), or requisite beef and poultry dishes, served with elegance.

2224 4th St. © **403/263-5535.** Reservations strongly recommended. Main courses C$16–C$40. AE, MC, V. Daily 11:30am–2pm & 5:30–11pm.

MODERATE

Aida's Mediterranean Bistro 🍴 MIDDLE EASTERN   An unassuming hidden gem along this busy main drag in the Mission, Aida's consistently serves up basic, tasty Middle Eastern fare in a no-nonsense, although comfortable, environment. Homemade old standards include a falafel platter with hummus and a chicken *shawarma* plate. Or share a few mezzos to sample a variety. Don't miss the desserts, either baklava or *knafi*. It lacks outdoor seating, but for a quick, easy, and inexpensive meal, Aida's is a port in trendy Mission's typically high-priced restaurant storm.

2208 4th St. SW. *©* **403/541-1189.** www.aidasbistro.ca. Main courses C$15-C$20. MC, V. Mon 11am-9pm; Tues-Thurs 11am-10pm; Fri & Sat 11am-11pm; Sun 4-9pm.

Brava Bistro NEW CANADIAN   Brava began as an offshoot of a successful catering company and has now evolved into an approachable Mediterranean-style bistro. In the relaxed, beautifully lit dining room, you can try anything, from elegant appetizers and boutique pizzas to contemporary main courses. For an appetizer, try seared scallops with buttered spinach and truffled vichyssoise. Among the entrees, the sautéed salmon with beets and horseradish is deliciously complex and colorful, while the homey rotisserie chicken or beef ribs with creamy polenta are tempting when comfort food feels more appropriate. Mussels and frites are a staple. The wine list is large and well-priced. They have a lovely street-level patio.

723 17th Ave. SW. *©* **403/228-1854.** www.bravabistro.com. Reservations recommended. Main courses C$16-C$31. AE, DC, MC, V. Mon-Sat 11:30am-3pm; Sun-Wed 5-10pm, Thurs-Sat 5pm-midnight.

Cilantro INTERNATIONAL   Cilantro's upscale and casual atmosphere has been a hit in Calgary for 20 years. Look past the forlorn stucco storefront on an urban strip of 17th Avenue. The walls hide a tucked-away garden courtyard with a veranda bar. The food here is always excellent; it's eclectic, with feints toward California and Santa Fe. You can snack on sandwiches, pasta, or burgers (in this case, an elk burger), or have a full meal of grilled buffalo rib-eye or grilled sea bass. The wood-fired pizzas—with mostly Mediterranean ingredients—are great for lunch.

338 17th Ave. SW. *©* **403/229-1177.** www.crmr.com/cilantro. Reservations recommended on weekends. Main courses C$24-C$42. AE, DC, MC, V. Mon-Thurs 11am-10pm; Fri 11am-11pm; Sat noon-11pm; Sun 5-10pm.

The Coup ★ VEGETARIAN   Calgary's best vegetarian food comes with a healthy, fresh, and creative fusion vibe at this hip spot on 17th Avenue. Most ingredients are organic and local. There are jam-packed salads, falafel quesadillas, and a dragon bowl that has steamed veggies, tofu, and brown rice. Flavors stem from all over the map, Latin to Asian. There's also a fun cocktail list. This place is always busy, but you can have a drink at the sister lounge next door called Meet while you wait.

924 17th Ave. SW. *©* **403/541-1041.** www.thecoup.ca. Reservations not accepted. Main courses C$7-C$16. AE, MC, V. Tues-Fri 11:30am-3pm, Sat & Sun 9am-3pm; Tues-Thurs 5pm-10pm, Fri & Sat 5pm-11pm, Sun 5pm-9pm.

Farm ★ REGIONAL   Owner Janice Beaton is a locavore leader in these parts. As the name suggests, this is a place to sample wholesome, simple food. Modeled after the Slow Food movement (Beaton is one of the founders of the local chapter), the food is more precious than pastoral. Small plates and platters make sampling from the outstanding cheese and cold cuts a good idea. The bubbly and mildly spicy signature mac 'n' cheese is by far the best in town. Trout and steak are larger options. The ambience is as relaxing as the countryside.

1006 17th Ave SW. *C* **403/246-2276.** www.farm-restaurant.com. Reservations recommended for dinner. Main courses C$9–C$19. Mon–Fri 11:30am–2pm; Mon–Thurs 5–10pm, Fri 5–11pm; Sat 10:30am–11pm; Sun 10:30am–10pm.

Fleur de Sel ★★ BISTRO   Locals don't get more local than this. With its rich, red walls and black-and-white tile, everything about Fleur de Sel screams "French!"—including its boisterous owner and chef, Patrice. Like most of his staff, he knows most of the customers by name—many of them from the dense neighborhood nearby or from up the hill in tony Mount Royal—and greets them with the enthusiasm of a favorite uncle. This is not a place to observe your cholesterol intake—Fleur de Sel, with its lovely, liberal application of butter and cream, takes the credo "fat is flavor" quite literally; what it is, though, is a place to throw caution to the wind for a moment, sit back, and enjoy the ride. This is the kind of homey place where strangers at adjacent tables can quickly become friends, brought together by a love for cuisine. If you enjoy your confit with a side dish of possibility, then Fleur de Sel is the place for you.

#2-2015 4th St. SW. *C* **403/228-9764.** www.fleurdeselbrasserie.com. Reservations recommended. Main courses C$29–C$39. MC, V. Tues–Fri 11:30am–2pm; daily 5:30pm "'til the last guest!"

Una Pizzeria ★ PIZZERIA   The best pizza in Calgary is at this chic wine bar on 17th Street. There's nothing avant-garde about a staple like the *margherita,* but the toppings—*flor di latte* mozzarella—are certainly gourmet. You can also opt for a flatiron steak with salsa *verde* and caper berries or a stunningly simple (there's that word again) appetizer of marinated zucchini with lemon, olive oil, and Romano cheese. The wine list includes 25 to 30 wines by the glass.

618 17th Ave. SW. *C* **403/453-1183.** www.unapizzeria.com. Reservations not accepted. Main courses C$13–C$21. MC, V. Daily 11:30am–1am.

Kensington
EXPENSIVE

Muse ★ CANADIAN/FRENCH   Tucked away on à quiet side street in perhaps Calgary's most walkable district, Muse resides in an adobe-type building that evokes a modern Mediterranean experience. The building's patchwork floor plan includes several levels, some open to small patios, and tucks diners into small, intimate

Sun City

Despite its sometimes-extreme swings in unseasonal weather, Calgary is the sunniest city in Canada. On average, the sun shines in Calgary 333 days each year, closely followed by another Albertan spot, Medicine Hat, with 330. By contrast, Toronto, Canada's largest city, counts 303 sunny days per year.

And while Calgarians suffer some long, cold winters, they don't lack for sunshine to lessen the blow: In December, January, and February, Calgary averages 366 hours of sun each winter—good enough for number 1, and edging out Winnipeg, the runner-up with 358.

spaces within the larger building. The menu, which breaks down into four courses, is focused on fresh, local ingredients and modern takes on traditional French fare. The smoked Pembina pork rack, with *"primeurs"* vegetables, Yukon potato hash, and grainy mustard jus is outstanding fare, both light and hearty, while the BC halibut with quinoa and cherry tomato salad, prosciutto-wrapped asparagus, and *vierge* sauce is a field-fresh, summery delight. All in, Muse is an intimate, urbane, yet ultimately casual experience with can't-miss cuisine—a winning combination.

107 10A St. NW. ✆ **403/670-6873.** Reservations recommended. Main courses C$15-C$38. AE, MC, V. Tues-Thurs & Sun 5-10pm; Fri & Sat 5-11pm. Closed Mon.

INEXPENSIVE

Heartland Café ★ CAFE   A little east of the main drag of 10th Street NW, this traditional Kensington spot, tucked amongst the houses, is an original and one of the best cafes in town. Counter-service sandwiches, coffee, and decadent baked goods all served in a homey general store environment, Heartland feeds the soul at the same time as the belly.

940 2nd Ave. NW. ✆ **403/270-4541.** Sandwiches from C$6. AE, MC, V. Mon-Fri 8am-8pm; Sat & Sun 8am-5pm.

Elsewhere

Calgary sprawls into distant suburbs in every direction, making culinary adventures in the far-flung corners a time-consuming, confusing affair. However, at least a couple of spots, new this year, are worth the geographical challenge. Near the Calgary Zoo is the acclaimed and decidedly high-brow **Rouge** (✆ **403/531-2767;** www.rougecalgary.com), which was recently listed amongst the top 60 restaurants in the world by the esteemed S. Pellegrino awards. Their French-inspired cuisine is dainty and precise, and a summer meal on their patio is a perfect special-occasion splurge. On the far south side of Calgary is **The Ranche** (✆ **403/225-3939;** www.crmr.com/theranche), set inside a heritage ranch home in Fish Creek Park. The menu is heavy on meat and game. Great for weekend brunch.

EXPLORING CALGARY

Calgary's relatively compact center belies its actual size, which stretches out for miles in every direction. Despite its population of 1 million, its footprint is among the largest in North America—bigger than Toronto, Canada's most populous city with more than double its population. As such, it can be a difficult place to negotiate without a car. The C-Train is an excellent link north to south, running right down the middle of the city in the south, along Macleod Trail, before cutting west through downtown and continuing north. Still, Calgary is a driver's city, and if you hope to see much outside the city's core, prepare to spend some time behind the wheel.

Downtown

Art Gallery of Calgary ★★   A small but mighty faction of contemporary-arts advocates here have been lobbying for years for funding to build a large-scale contemporary art gallery along the lines of the Vancouver Art Gallery or Toronto's Art Gallery of Ontario, but thus far have had no success. With Edmonton's stunning new Art Gallery of Alberta, the fight has gotten even tougher for them to see their

Calgary Attractions

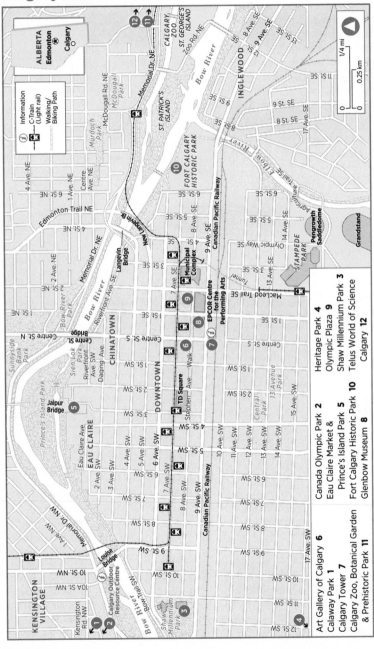

Art Gallery of Calgary **6**
Calaway Park **1**
Calgary Tower **7**
Calgary Zoo, Botanical Garden
& Prehistoric Park **11**

Canada Olympic Park **2**
Eau Claire Market &
Prince's Island Park **5**
Fort Calgary Historic Park **10**
Glenbow Museum **8**

Heritage Park **4**
Olympic Plaza **9**
Shaw Millennium Park **3**
Telus World of Science
Calgary **12**

dreams become a reality. But, knowing Calgary's limitless ambitions, they will. And in the meantime, there's the very good Art Gallery of Calgary on downtown's Stephen Avenue Mall, a mostly pedestrian stretch in the heart of the city's financial district. Housed in an historic building, the gallery's constantly changing program features prominent contemporary artists from all over the city and around the world in virtually every discipline—you will see well-curated photography (both documentary and conceptual), painting, and avant-garde sculpture, all with a smart, contemporary edge. It also offers a cafe (© 403/410-9358) with a lovely sidewalk patio for people-watching.

117 8th Ave. SW. © **403/770-1350.** www.artgallerycalgary.org. C$5 adults, C$2.50 students, free for children 5 & under. Tues-Sat 10am-5pm; first Thurs of every month 10am-9pm. Closed Sun & Mon.

Calgary Tower ☺   Make this your first stop, for there's no better place to get your bearings. Reaching 762 steps—or 191m (627 ft.)—into the sky, this enduringly touristy landmark offers brilliant views from its observation terrace, from which you can take in the city, the mountains, the Bow River, and the prairies beyond. The elevator whisks you to the top in just 63 seconds. A stairway from the terrace leads to the rotating restaurant Sky 360 (see "Where to Eat," earlier in this chapter). Photography from up here is fantastic.

101 9th Ave. SW (at Centre St. SW). © **403/266-7171.** www.calgarytower.com. Elevator ride C$14 adults, C$12 seniors, C$10 children 6-17, C$6 children 5 & under. Sept-May daily 9am-9pm; June-Aug daily 9am-10pm. C-Train: 1st St. E.

Eau Claire Market & Prince's Island Park   Eau Claire Market is part of a car-free pedestrian zone north of downtown on the banks of the Bow River; it links to lovely Prince's Island Park, a bucolic island lined with paths, shaded by cottonwood trees, and populated by hordes of Canada geese. This is where much of downtown Calgary comes to eat, drink, shop, sunbathe, jog, and hang out in good weather. The market itself no longer offers much for the traveler except a few eateries (better options are the pubs in the plaza outside the market), though it remains busy with a four-screen cinema and an IMAX theater (© **403/974-4629**) that has a five-story domed screen. The riverside park area and the island are your absolute best bets for a bit of outdoor urban Calgary; on a gorgeous summer day, a meander through Prince's Island, followed by a little window-shopping at the eclectic booths at the market, can't be beat.

200 Barclay Parade SW (near 2nd Ave. SW & 3rd St. SW). © **403/264-6450.** Free admission. Market building Mon-Sat 9am-9pm, Sun noon-4pm; shops & restaurants hours vary. C-TRAIN: 3rd St. W.

Fort Calgary Historic Park   On the occasion of the city's centennial in 1975, Fort Calgary became a public park of 16 hectares (40 acres), spread around the ruins of the original Mounted Police stronghold. In 2001, volunteers completed a replica of the 1888 barracks using traditional methods and building materials. The Interpretive Centre captures the history of Calgary, from its genesis as a military fort to its 20th-century beginnings as an agricultural and oil boomtown. Kids can do time in the 1875-era jail or dress up as a Mountie. There are a number of interesting videos and guided displays; always in focus are the adventures and hardships of the Mounties a century ago. The rigors of their westward march and the almost unbelievable isolation these pioneer troopers endured now seems incredible. If all this history whets your appetite, cross the Elbow River on 9th Avenue and head to the Deane

House. This historic home was built by a Fort Calgary superintendent nearly 100 years ago and is now the Deane House Restaurant (© **403/269-7747**), operated by Fort Calgary.

THE CALGARY stampede

The tagline is "the greatest outdoor show on Earth"; most Calgarians would agree, though most would apply the label to more than just the rodeo it ostensibly refers to. Since 1912, the Stampede has become more than a rodeo; it's a civic party. The first week in July, banks, restaurants, bars, offices, the airport, and shops pile hay bales around their front doors and erect clapboard door frames over the modern glass and steel, and button-down office workers don their boots, hats, and jeans for a hootin' hollerin' good time. For Calgarians, Stampede is not a spectator sport: By lunchtime, most offices sit vacant as the majority of the working crowd have gone in for some serious "Stampeding"—local code for going to (and staying too long in)—the city's numerous (and packed) bars.

A curious counterpoint to all the nocturnal social activity is the Stampede tradition of a "Stampede breakfast." Served daily—and early, and free!— every day of the Stampede at parking lots, shopping malls, and corporate offices all over town, it usually consists of flapjacks, sausages, orange drink (not to be confused with juice), and coffee. There may be some kind of hangover remedy embedded in this combination— heaven knows most of the indulgers could use it—but one thing's certain: If you pay for a single breakfast during Stampede, you're just not paying attention. See www.flapjackfinder.com for complete listings and reviews of the nearly 100 breakfasts offered.

The main event, of course, is the rodeo, the largest and most prestigious of its kind in North America, in which cowboys from all over the world compete in such events as bull-riding, steer-roping, and chuck-wagon races for prize money totaling more than C$1 million.

Parts of Stampede Park, just off Macleod Trail (near 25th Ave. SW), become amusement areas, whirling, spinning, and rotating with rides. Other areas are just for the kids, who romp through Kids' World and the Petting Zoo. Still other sections host livestock shows, a food fair, handicraft exhibitions, an art show, lectures, a bazaar, a casino, lotteries, and entertainment on several stages.

Reserving accommodations well ahead is essential—as many months ahead of your arrival as you can possibly foresee. Some downtown watering holes even take reservations for space at the bar; that should give you an idea of how busy Calgary gets.

The same advice applies to reserving tickets for Stampede events. Park admission is C$14 adults, and tickets to the top rodeo events begin at C$25 but go up from there, depending on the event, the seats, and whether the event takes place in the afternoon or evening. A number of centennial projects are also in the works for the 100th anniversary year in 2012 (visit their website closer to the date for details), which are sure to bring Calgary major global attention and make tickets extra hard to come by. For mail-order bookings, contact the Calgary Exhibition and Stampede (P.O. Box 1060, Station M, Calgary, AB T2P 2K8; © **800/661-1767;** fax 403/223-9736; www.calgarystampede.com).

750 9th Ave. SE. (C) **403/290-1875.** www.fortcalgary.com. C$11 adults, C$10 students & seniors, C$7 children 7-17, C$5 children 3-6, free for children under 2. Daily 9am-5pm. C-TRAIN: Bridgeland.

Glenbow Museum ★ One of the country's finest museums, the Glenbow is a must for anyone with an interest in the history and culture of western Canada. What sets it apart from other museums chronicling the continent's Native cultures and pioneer settlement is the excellence of its interpretation. The walls and halls come alive with engaging storytelling. Especially notable is the third floor, with its vivid evocation of Native cultures—particularly of the local Blackfoot—and compelling descriptions of western Canada's exploration and settlement.

130 9th Ave. SE (at 1st St.). (C) **403/268-4100.** www.glenbow.org. C$14 adults, C$10 seniors, C$9 students & children 7-17, free for children under 6; C$32 families. Mon-Sat 9am-5pm; Sun noon-5pm. C-TRAIN: 1st St. E.

Olympic Plaza ★★ Not to be confused with Canada Olympic Park, Olympic Plaza is a public square just across the street from Calgary's stately, sandstone Old City Hall. Plunked at the eastern end of the Stephen Avenue stroll, the plaza was built for the Winter Olympics in 1988. It served as a very public place for medal winners to receive their awards and has continued in the celebratory vein. This is now where Calgarians come to celebrate everything from hockey victories to Reggaefest. Bands play here in the summer—the regular being every Wednesday at lunch time—and a host of events play out here, as well. When it's not occupied, the summertime plaza features a wading pool for kids—and sweaty office workers—to cool off in. In the winter, the plaza is a popular public skating rink. It includes a Legacy Wall, with plaques commemorating medal winners from the Calgary Olympic Winter Games.

228 8th Ave. SE. (C) **403/268-2489.** Free admission. Open 24 hours a day. C-TRAIN: Olympic Plaza.

Shaw Millennium Park ☺ This massive park, maintained by the City of Calgary, is the largest free, outdoor 24-hour skateboarding park in North America. There's a gnarly street course with ledges, flat bars, stairs, and trannies, an intermediate course with rails down stairs and banks, and an advanced course with a cloverleaf bowl and a large full pipe. With 6,968 sq. m (75,000 sq. ft.) of skate-able surface, basketball courts, and four sand volleyball courts, it's one of the largest skateboard parks in North America and draws skaters of all ages from all over the continent.

1220 9 Ave SW. Free admission. Open 24 hours. C-TRAIN: 10th St SW.

South of Downtown

Heritage Park ★★ ☺ In the city's southwest, on the banks of the man-made Glenmore Reservoir—which is also Calgary's water supply—sits one of the liveliest historical re-creations to be found in Alberta. The largest historical village in all of Canada, Heritage Park, as the name suggests, offers visitors a taste of Calgary's frontier past, from its settler days in the early 19th century through its fur-trading roots in the 1860s all the way through to the construction of the railway in 1910, which linked what was, until then, an outpost to the rest of the country. Steam engines, horse-drawn carriages, and a paddlewheel on the Reservoir are all part of the attraction. The park offers costumed interpreters, street theater, and over 150 buildings and exhibits.

1900 Heritage Dr. SW. ℰ **403/268-8500.** www.heritagepark.ca. C$19 adults, C$14 children. May 22 to Labour Day daily 9am–5pm. C-TRAIN: Heritage station.

East of Downtown

Calgary Zoo, Botanical Garden & Prehistoric Park ★ ☺
Calgary's large and thoughtfully designed zoo resides on St. George's Island in the Bow River. The Calgary Zoo comes as close to providing natural habitats for its denizens as is technically possible. You'll particularly want to see the troop of majestic lowland gorillas and the African warthogs. The flora and fauna of western and northern Canada are on display in the Botanical Garden, and there's an amazing year-round tropical butterfly enclosure, as well. If you're there at 10am, you can take in the official welcome and meet with a zoo professional. Call to inquire about special summer events, such as Thursday Jazz Nights and free interpretive talks called "Nature Tales."

1300 Zoo Rd. NE. ℰ **403/232-9300.** www.calgaryzoo.ab.ca. C$19 adults, C$17 seniors, C$11 children 3–12, free for children under 2. Daily 9am–5pm. C-TRAIN: Zoo station.

Telus World of Science Calgary ☺
In the fall of 2011, Telus World of Science will reopen in a sleek and modern new 6-hectare (15-acre) location close to the Calgary Zoo, with ecologically inspired architecture and design. In the meantime, there's the Creative Kids Museum and a revolving door of exhibits at the old location, which was originally built as a planetarium in 1967. The new World of Science, the first new science center in Canada in more than 25 years, will have permanent exhibits covering topics from the human body to Earth and space. For updates, check the website (www.calgaryscience.ca).

New location: St. George's Dr. NE. Old location: 701-11St. SW. ℰ **403/268-8300.** www.calgaryscience. ca. General admission C$19.75 adults, C$16.75 youth aged 13 to 17 and seniors, C$12.25 children 3 to 12. Telus Sun–Thurs 9am–6pm, Fri & Sat 9am–10pm.

West of Downtown

Canada Olympic Park ☺
The lasting memento of Calgary's role as host of the 1988 Winter Olympics stands in Olympic Park, which was the site for ski jumping, luge, and bobsledding during the Games. The Olympic Hall of Fame and Museum features the world's largest collection of Olympic artifacts, including the torch used to bring the flame from Greece; costumes and equipment used by the athletes; superb photographs; and a gallery of all medal winners. The reason why the park is still an exciting destination is the availability of activities and lessons. In winter, both adults and children can take downhill and cross-country ski lessons, learn to ski jump or snowboard, or get an introduction to snow skating. More exciting are the opportunities to ride a luge or bobsled. In winter, for C$165 adults, you can experience the twists and turns of the Olympic Track in a bobsled. In summer, there's mountain biking, a kid-friendly Eurobungy (a trampoline-like bungee jump), ziplining, minigolf, and a climbing wall.

88 Canada Olympic Park Rd. SW. ℰ **403/247-5452.** www.coda.ab.ca. Daily lift ticket C$42 adults, C$36 students, C$28 seniors, C$33 children 13–17, C$26 children 5–12, C$2 children under 5; C$99 families (separate fees for activities & lessons). Museum C$6.20 adults. Tour venues year-round Fri–Mon 10am–4pm, Tues–Thurs 10am–9pm; ski hill Nov 14 to Mar 29 Mon–Fri 9am–9pm, Sat & Sun 9am–5pm

Calaway Park ★ ☺
On the western fringes of the city, just off the Trans-Canada Highway on the way to Banff, Calgary's Calaway Park is the largest outdoor

amusement park in western Canada. The park contains everything from roller coasters to the log ride and bumper cars, as well as daily live entertainment, western-themed minigolf, and a whole host of rides designed specifically for younger kids. It also regularly holds a variety of events to entice the visitor, such as the fantastically named Rad Dad day. *Note:* At the beginning and end of the season, the park is open only on the weekend and on public holidays.

245033 Range Rd. 33. ✆ **403/240-3822.** www.calawaypark.com. C$32 adults, C$23 seniors, C$25 children 3-6. May 17 to June 27 Sat & Sun 10am-7pm; Sept 6 to Oct 13 Sat & Sun 11am-6pm; June 28 to Sept 1 daily 10am-7pm.

OUTDOOR ACTIVITIES & SPECTATOR SPORTS

Nestled as it is in the foothills of the Rocky Mountains, the city of Calgary is a sporty, active place that embraces its professional teams with passion and takes to the great outdoors with equal enthusiasm. Much of that outdoor ambition is spent in the nearby magnificence of Banff, but in-city, a comprehensive network of cycling paths and abundant park space make urban outdoorsmanship a readily available option. With its two rivers, the Bow and the Elbow, urban angling is popular here, especially on the Bow, the larger of the two, where it's not uncommon to hook a 907g (2-lb.) trout within the city limits. So, be sure to bring some hiking boots, or at least some sturdy runners; if the constant bustle of boomtown starts to exhaust, natural refuge abounds. For rental of all sorts of outdoor gear, the best place in town is the **University of Calgary's Outdoor Centre** (✆ 403/228-5038; www.calgary outdoorcentre.ca). They rent more than 10,000 items, from tents and sleeping bags to skis and bikes. They also have year-round courses open to all in subjects like bike maintenance and avalanche safety, and weekend workshops in things like whitewater kayaking and backcountry ski mountaineering.

Parks & Natural Areas

Bowmont Park   Wildlife and rare plant species abound in this 155-hectare (383-acre) park in the city's northwest. Running along the bank of the Bow River, between Home Road and Nose Hill Drive, Bowmont is cleaved by three major ravines with deep forestation, as well as grassy slopes. You can access the park from Silver Valley Boulevard NW or Silver Crescent Drive NW.

Bowness Park   The riverside Bowness (8900 8th Ave. NW) became a civic park well over a century ago, and families still flock to it as a favorite picnic spot. A lagoon offers the opportunity to rent canoes and paddleboats; in winter, it's an ice rink (boat and skate rentals are available at the **Parkside Café** [✆ 403/286-8668] in the park).

Carburn Park and Beaverdam Flats   Along the east shoreline of the Bow River, on either side of the loud, multilane Glenmore Trail, are lagoons, hiking paths, and picnic facilities. Great blue heron, osprey, and kingfishers can all be found filling up on fish here. The paved pathway around the lagoon, at 3km (1.9 miles), is a favorite for in-line skaters. It's at 62nd Avenue and 16th Street SE.

Edworthy Park   Just west of downtown, Edworthy was once part of the expansive (and now defunct) Cochrane Ranch. It sits on the south shore of the Bow River and is a popular spot for kids. Inside the park is the Douglas Fir Trail, a short (4km/2.5-mile), delightfully un-urban hike just outside the city's heart. Here, you'll find a forested trail that winds along cliffs above the river to a stand of Douglas fir trees—some of them more than 400 years old. Coyote, rabbits, and woodpeckers all make their home here, and deer pass through on occasion, as well. Edworthy is also brimming with history: variously serving over the past few centuries as a buffalo kill site and tipi camp for Native Canadians, a commercial market garden, and a brick factory and a sandstone quarry that supplied the material for downtown's many sandstone buildings. Four playgrounds, covered cooking areas, and open-pit barbecues make modern Edworthy an ideal spot for family outings. It's at Bow Trail (9th Ave.) and Spruce Drive SW.

Fish Creek Provincial Park ★ Fish Creek (℡ **403/297-5293;** tpr.alberta.ca/parks/fishcreek/default.asp), at the city's southern end, is the only urban provincial park in Alberta. At 1,400 hectares (3,459 acres), it's also among the largest urban parks in all of North America. Fish Creek hosts about 2 million visitors every year, many of them drawn to the 50km (31 miles) of trails for hiking, biking, and horseback riding. Simone Lake offers swimming, and the park contains an historic site, as well: the restored 1800s **The Ranche,** now a restaurant (see "Where to Dine," earlier in this chapter).

Two river valleys—the Bow and Fish Creek—intersect here, making the park abundant in bird life. Mule and whitetail deer roam free, as well; muskrat, beaver, weasels, and coyotes are also abundant. The park's varied habitat explains why: West

Sandstone

Calgary is a very new city, by most measures. In 1951, only 127,000 people lived here. In 2007, it broke a million; 400,000 of them arrived in the past 25 years. That's a lot of people in a relatively short period of time, and much of the cityscape sparkles with a disarming newness: Skyscrapers glint in the near-perpetual sunshine, and suburbs sprawl far in every direction. As such, Calgary often gets knocked for its ever-forward-looking mindset—at the expense, some say, of not looking back. But look around the city's compact, sky-scraping downtown, and you'll see evidence of an architectural history well respected. Early Calgary was built of sandstone, much of it from the nearby Bow Valley (Edworthy Park, just west of downtown, comprises the old quarry where much of it came from). One of the most stunning examples is Old City Hall, complete with

a clock tower, across a public square from the gleaming all-glass New City Hall on Macleod Trail and 7th Avenue SE, built in 1907. But there are sandstone gems aplenty, including the venerable Grain Exchange Building, just south of Stephen Avenue Mall on 1st Street SW, built in 1910, or the Memorial Park Library, built in 1912 as the Carnegie Library by the Pittsburgh steel magnate Andrew Carnegie. It sits in Memorial Park, between 12th and 13th avenues SW and 2nd and 4th streets SW.

In the early part of the 20th century, it all came to earn Calgary the natural moniker "The Sandstone City." Why? Well, it was close by, it was plentiful, but most importantly, perhaps, it was fireproof: In 1886, a rampant fire burnt much of Calgary to the ground. Sandstone, city fathers reasoned, stood a better chance.

of Macleod Trail, the valley walls are heavily forested with spruce and balsam trees; East of Macleod, the valley broadens into the open basin of the Bow Valley. Fish Creek itself is a spawning stream for rainbow trout.

The park's cultural resources run deep, particularly regarding the history of the Aboriginal peoples in the region and the ranchers who came to displace them. You'll find ancient tipi rings and buffalo-jump sites at the western end of the park. **Shaw's Woolen Mill** site is near the center, and ranch sites are at either end. An archaeological interpretive center provides a wealth of information dating back 8,000 years.

The park opens every day at 8am and closes at dusk. The Bow Valley Ranche visitor center (open Mon–Fri 8:15am–4:30pm) provides maps and information on various sites in the park. Here, you can also join walking tours or see slide presentations from park-staff interpreters. Maps and information can also be found at the **Fish Creek Environmental Learning Centre** (© 403/297-7827; open Mon–Fri 8:15am–4pm). Bow Bottom Trail will take you to the east entrance, and the Bow Valley Ranche visitor center, at 37th Street SW at 146th Avenue SW, will take you to the park's west entrance and the Fish Creek Environmental Learning Centre.

Glenmore Park, Glenmore Reservoir, and Weaselhead Flats The Glenmore Reservoir is the source of many Calgarians' drinking water, and a strict no-swimming law is closely observed. However, there are still many opportunities for recreation on or around the water. Glenmore Park, at the south end of Crowchild Trail SW, surrounds the reservoir on the north and south shores. It has cycling paths and tennis courts, as well as ample green space. On the north shore, you'll find the members-only **Calgary Rowing Club** (© 403/249-2880; www.calgaryrowing. com), which has some lessons and public programs, and the **Calgary Canoe Club** (© 403/246-5757; www.calgarycanoeclub.com), which rents canoes on the reservoir for C$35 per day (C$25 for a half-day). On the south side of the reservoir is the **Glenmore Sailing Club** (© 403/238-2044; www.glenmoresailingclub.com), which operates a sailing school. It's also members-only, but some public programming is available.

At the south end of the reservoir is **Weaselhead Flats** (http://blog.talkaboutwild-life.ca), a mostly untouched expanse of foothills wilderness abutting the Sarcee Indian Reservation to the south. A favorite for birdwatchers, there are more than 70 species to be found here. A paved bicycle path winds down into the region on its way around the reservoir, which is one of the best ways to spend an active day in the city. Glenmore Park is reached by taking Crowchild Trail S until it ends at the park entrance.

Nose Hill Park Just off 14th Street NW, between John Laurie and Berkshire boulevards, this is Canada's biggest chunk of protected urban natural prairie grassland—1,092 hectares (2,698 acres). Created in 1973, it's been left in its natural state. Native people used this for hundreds of years as a vantage point to watch the meanderings of the buffalo. Look for old tipi rings or hunt for large, smooth boulders called glacial erratics. The city skyline looms in the valley below—a majestic urban view.

Prince's Island Park Food fairs, music festivals, cultural events, outdoor theater—Prince's Island functions almost as Calgary's communal backyard. You can run, walk, or cycle here, dine at the River Café (see p. 90), or just lounge in the grass under the shade trees and watch the world go by. The river burbles by on both sides for a relaxing audio backdrop. You can reach the park via a footbridge either from Eau Claire Market from the south or Memorial Drive near Kensington from the north.

Stanley Park   This park is close to downtown, nestled along the Elbow River at 42nd Avenue SW, just west of Macleod Trail. Picnic tables and barbecue pits are set in a lovely, riverfront setting. Wade in the river, cycle along the paved paths, or just lounge in the sun.

Cycling Tours

With its huge network of paved pathways, Calgary is a great city to get around by bike. The options are almost endless. Here are a few popular routes to explore.

CYCLING TOUR 1: **BOW RIVER PARKS**

START:	**Prince's Island Park**
FINISH:	**Prince's Island Park**
DISTANCE:	**About 40km (25 miles), if you follow the entire route; 3 to 4 hours**
BEST TIME:	**Mid-morning, so you can take a picnic lunch to Bowness Park.**
WORST TIME:	**Morning and afternoon rush hours, when this route is well traveled by cycling commuters.**

This loop follows the north bank of the Bow River from Prince's Island Park to the Stoney Trail Bridge, west of downtown, and returns along the south side of the river. The tour largely follows the course of Calgary's annual Stampede Marathon, held in July. You'll cycle past the Kensington district and through Edworthy, Bowmont, and Bowness parks. While you'll need at least 3 hours for the whole tour, various bridges along the route make convenient turnaround points for shorter trips.

This tour starts at Prince's Island Park. If you're driving, park at Eau Claire on the south side of the Bow River and follow the pedestrian bridge to the north side. Or park on the north side near the curling club on Memorial Drive and take the pedestrian overpass across Memorial Drive to the paved pathway. Cycle along the north bank of the river toward Kensington at 10th Street NW.

1 Pathway Hub

At the corner of Memorial Drive and 10th Street, this is information central for Calgary's parks and pathways. You'll find a public information center and concession area on the main floor. The Calgary Area Outdoor Council is located on the second floor. Continue cycling west past Crowchild Trail toward Edworthy Park, about 7km (4¼ miles) from Prince's Island Park.

2 Edworthy Park

Here, you'll find washrooms, a water fountain, and a coffee and ice cream stand. If you're ready to turn back, you can cross the footbridge here and return to Prince's Island Park along the south side of the river. Otherwise, continue traveling along the westbound pathway.

3 Shouldice Athletic Park

You're likely to find a baseball or soccer game in progress here. Named after southern Alberta rancher James Shouldice, the park is also a popular gathering spot for Canada geese. (Don't expect them to yield to cyclists—they stand their ground assertively and get downright belligerent in the spring when they're parading around with flocks of goslings.)

When you reach Bowness Road, the path crosses under the John Hextall footbridge. When you emerge—this is where you'll link up with the pathway on the return leg of the tour—go left for 1 block. At 52nd Street, take a left and cycle to the top of the hill, where you'll reconnect with the pathway (beside a church).

4 Bowmont Park

The pathway climbs through a hilly stretch of poplars and open fields in Bowmont Park, a haven for wildlife. If you're ready to turn back, you can cross to the south side of the river (via two footbridges), and cycle along the pathway to Bow Crescent. Follow the pathway under 85th Street and through Baker Park, which is the site of a former sanatorium, and cross over to the south side of the river when you reach the Stoney Trail Bridge.

5 Bowness Park

This is one of Calgary's most popular family picnic areas. With washrooms, water fountains, picnic tables, and a concession stand, it's an ideal spot to take a break. Leave the park through the main gates and follow 48th Avenue E to 79th Street, where you'll re-connect with the pathway.

6 Douglas Fir Trail

Here, the pathway winds along the river bank at the base of the Douglas Fir Trail. You may be lucky enough to spot a coyote, beaver, or deer. This out-of-the-way stretch of riverfront is also a popular area for bird-watching.

 TREE-LOVING bridge **BUILDERS**

How do you build a major highway bridge across a river without damage to trees in the valley below? Builders who engineered Calgary's longest bridge across the Bow River solved the problem with a novel approach to construction. They didn't erect the bridge—they launched it. The 476m-long (1,562-ft.), four-lane Stoney Trail Bridge, which curves across the Bow at heights of up to 36m (118 ft.), was built with an innovative technology imported from Germany.

The south shore of the Bow River has the most easterly stand of old-growth Douglas fir in Canada. Conventional bridge construction would have involved clearing trees in the river valley to bring in cranes and move sections of the bridge into place. Instead, the Stoney Trail Bridge was precast in 19 concrete sections at a site on the north side of the river, then pushed—by hydraulic jacks—across to the south side, one 1,100-ton piece at a time.

Continue traveling west, past the Crowchild Trail Bridge. You'll pass the Pump Hill Theatre, Nat Christie Park (just east of 14th St.), and the Shaw Millennium Skateboard Park, on your right.

7 Eau Claire

The pathway takes you back to Eau Claire, where you'll find cafes and pubs with inviting outdoor patios.

CYCLING TOUR 2: **FISH CREEK PROVINCIAL PARK**

START:	**Mallard Point, at the northeast end of the park.**
FINISH:	**Shannon Terrace Environmental Education Centre, at the west end of the park.**
DISTANCE:	**38km (24 miles); 3 to 4 hours.**
BEST TIMES:	**Any morning or afternoon when the weather is fine. Picnic areas are located throughout the park.**
WORST TIMES:	**After 4pm, when the visitor center is closed. Note that Fish Creek Provincial Park is open only during the day. Closing times vary throughout the year, but generally coincide with darkness.**

This tour follows mostly paved trails through Fish Creek Provincial Park, from east to west. If you're ambitious and have the time, the park is easy to reach by bicycle from virtually anywhere in the city. Or you can drive or take public transit. If you're driving, you can access the north end of the park via Canyon Meadows Drive SE. Park at Mallard Point. By transit, take the C-Train to the Fish Creek/Lacombe station. Bikes are allowed on C-Trains at all times except morning and afternoon rush hours on weekdays.

---

1 Mallard Point

The tour starts at Mallard Point, a picnic area in a stand of cottonwood trees at the northeast end of the park. This section of the park is popular with anglers.

Follow the paved pathway through a hay field to the picnic area at Burnsmead. Continuing on, you'll cross Bow Bottom Trail. To detour to Sikome Lake, turn left. This is the only public lake with a beach within 90 minutes of the city. Needless to say, it's packed on hot days. Otherwise, take the right branch and head west to the Bow Valley Ranche Visitor's Centre, located about 6km (3¾ miles) from Mallard Point.

2 Bow Valley Ranche Visitor's Centre

This is the main visitor center for the park, and you can pick up trail maps and park information. You'll also find the Ranche restaurant, which specializes in contemporary Alberta cuisine. The small wooden house next door is Annie's Bakery Café, popular with cyclists and in-line skaters.

Helmet Law

In Alberta, helmets are required by law for all cyclists under age 18 and recommended for all cyclists.

FAMILY-friendly ROUTES

If you're traveling with young children, the pathways near Eau Claire and Prince's Island Park downtown feature easy terrain along with bathrooms and water stops. South of downtown, Carburn Park is a good bet for beginner cyclists. The paved path around the perimeter of the lagoon on 18th Street SE, south of Glenmore Trail, is an easy 3km (1.9-mile) loop. Or head for Pearce Estate, just off Blackfoot Trail at the north end of 17A Street, and cycle to the Inglewood Bird Sanctuary at the east end of 19th Avenue. You'll find picnic areas and washrooms at both ends.

A 4km (2½-mile) cycle through hay fields takes you to the Glenfield picnic area, which has lots of washrooms, along with three picnic shelters equipped with wood stoves. Continue traveling west, under Macleod Trail, through cottonwood and spruce trees to Voltier's Flats. The paved pathway ends here—it's gravel and shale to the west end of the park.

3 Shannon Terrace Environmental Education Centre

This center, near the western edge of the park, is the turnaround point for this tour. Don't be surprised to meet a group of school kids investigating the spruce forest and wetlands near the center. Fish Creek is just a quick stroll to the south.

Follow the pathway past the footbridge and under the train bridge. You'll emerge on Crescent Road NW. Cycle along Crescent Road east to the John Hextall Bridge (see Bow River Parks Cycling Tour, Stop 3, above) and return to Edworthy Park on the same stretch of pathway you traveled earlier. At Edworthy Park, take the foot bridge to the south side of the river, and cycle through the park and across the train tracks. You'll find washrooms and water fountains in the park.

Other Sports

CLIMBING   To warm up for your Rockies summit quest, head to the **Calgary Climbing Centre** (© **403/276-6484;** www.calgaryclimbing.com), which has two locations in the city for indoor climbing and bouldering. They also have courses year-round.

CROSS-COUNTRY SKIING   They may not be as picturesque as the trails at, say, Lake Louise, but urban Nordic ski trails in Calgary proper abound. Try the **municipal golf courses** Confederation (3204 Collingwood Dr. NW; © **403/974-1800**) or Shaganappi (1200-26 St. SW; © **403/974-1810**). See www.calgary.ca/golf for more information. City parks like Bowness and Fish Creek also have great trails. Call © **403/268-3888** for updated trail conditions in the city parks.

FLY-FISHING   Urban angling doesn't get much better than this. Walk a few blocks from an office building, tie on a fly, and cast to your heart's content on the mighty Bow River, home to 60cm (24-inch) rainbow and brown trout. Contact the guides at **Fish Tales Fly Shop** (© **403/640-1273;** www.fishtalesflyshop.com) for a quick lesson. They have 1-day courses for beginners for C$95, as well as full-day guided excursions from C$550.

GOLFING   Not surprisingly, Calgarians are nuts about golf. There are dozens of courses within a 45-minute drive of downtown. Some of the best courses open to the public are **RiverSpirit Golf Club** (© **403/246-4776;** www.riverspiritgolf.com), just to the west of Calgary; **Heritage Pointe** (© **403/256-4494;** www.heritagepointe.com), in the far southeast; and **Silverwing Golf Course** (© **403/269-8005;** www.silverwinggolf.com), close to the airport. Greens fees from C$45 to C$63.

MOUNTAIN BIKING   **Nose Hill Park** and **Bowmont Park** (see "Parks & Natural Areas," earlier in this chapter) have trails designated for mountain biking. **Canada Olympic Park** (see p. 102) has lift-access downhill mountain biking, with a terrain park, dirt-jump stunts, and lessons.

Spectator Sports

Calgary Flames   True to its Canadian-ness, Calgary loves its Flames, the city's entry in the big-league National Hockey League, with almost religious passion. The Flames moved to Calgary from Atlanta in 1980, and the intervening decades have seen a lot of ups and downs. The undoubted high point came in 1989, when the Flames won their one-and-only Stanley Cup, the NHL's championship. Big things were expected in the years that followed—fans spoke shamelessly about a "dynasty" regarding this powerhouse team—but it wasn't to be. The '90s saw the once-mighty Flames dwindle in power to the point where, by 2003, they had missed the playoffs for seven straight seasons. An improbable turnaround in 2004 saw the Flames make a Cinderella run all the way to the Stanley Cup finals, only to lose to the Tampa Bay Lightning in seven games. But the city's love affair with the team had been re-kindled; it was expressed most mightily on 17th Avenue SW—re-dubbed "The Red Mile"—during the 2004 playoffs, where thousands of fans would crowd the streets, immobilizing traffic as they celebrated (police took to closing the street to vehicles on game nights). Recent years have not been as kind to the Flames, who have tended to make the playoffs only to lose in the first round, if they even make it. But hope springs eternal, and the passion for a generation of fans has been renewed; after many years of church-silent crowds, the Saddledome is now one of the loudest in the league.

Pengrowth Saddledome, 555 Saddledome Rise SE. © **403/777-4646** for tickets. www.calgaryflames.com. Regular season runs Oct–Apr.

Calgary Stampeders   The Stamps, as they're known, marked their 65th year of competition in 2010. The venerable Canadian Football League team has won the Grey Cup, the league championship, five times. The CFL game—Canada's top pro football league—has subtle differences to the one played in the National Football League, such as a larger field (110 yards long vs. 100 yards, and 65 yards wide vs. 53½ yards) and only three downs rather than four. But aficionados argue that the extra room only serves to make the game more exciting. Some players who flourished in the NFL were CFL stars first, and the Stampeders boast two marquee quarterbacks in Doug Flutie, who starred later with the Buffalo Bills, and Jeff Garcia, who played for San Francisco, Philadelphia, Detroit, and Tampa Bay in the NFL. The Stamps, as they're known, play at McMahon Stadium, a gloriously open outdoor stadium on the campus of the University of Calgary, during a season that runs the breadth of the Canadian summer and fall.

McMahon Stadium, 1817 Crowchild Trail NW. ℂ **403/777-0000** Ticketmaster or **403/289-0258** team's ticket office. www.stampeders.com. Regular season runs June–Oct.

Calgary Hitmen Calgary's entry in the world of major junior hockey—an amateur feeder league for the NHL, where top players spend 3 or 4 years, from the age of 16 onward, in hopes of pro glory—is a well-attended, well-liked, and inexpensive option for the bona fide hockey fan. Unless you're an ice hockey aficionado, don't bet on name recognition, as most of the teams in the Western Hockey League are from significantly smaller centers (the Kamloops Blazers, the Spokane Chiefs), but the product on the ice is fast, spirited, and the best hockey under the age of 19 you're bound to find anywhere. Walk-up tickets on game day are almost always available at the Saddledome box office.

Pengrowth Saddledome, 555 Saddledome Rise SE. ℂ **403/777-0000** Ticketmaster. Regular season runs Oct–Apr.

The Calgary Roughnecks The Roughnecks arrived in Calgary in 2000 and, just 4 years later, claimed their first National Lacrosse League (NLL) championship. Not a sport for everyone, but the rough-and-tumble aspects of lacrosse will likely appeal to the football fans in the crowd.

206 11th Ave. SE. ℂ **403/294-9244.** www.calgaryroughnecks.com.

The Calgary Vipers The Vipers are Calgary's entry in the minor pro Northern Baseball League and the only professional baseball team in Southern Alberta. The Vipers joined the league in the spring of 2005, along with their provincial rivals, the Edmonton Cracker-Cats.

2255 Crowchild Trail NW. ℂ **403/277-2255.** www.calgaryvipers.com.

ORGANIZED TOURS

A guided tour can help you get your bearings in Calgary and scout out spots you might want to come back to on your own. Several tour operators will help you on your way, on wheels or on foot.

On Wheels

Brewster Group Travel The 4-hour City Sights Tour departs from downtown Calgary every morning in the summer. You can catch the bus at the Sandman Inn (8:15am), the Palliser Hotel (8:20am), or the Calgary Marriot (8:30am). You need to be present 5 minutes before departure to board. The tour gives you a good overview of downtown, with stops at Fort Calgary and Canada Olympic Park. Admission to both is included in the ticket price.

ℂ **800/760-6934.** www.explorerockies.com. C$49 adults, C$25 children 14 & under. June through September only.

Hammerhead Tours This city tour takes 3½ hours and stops at Fort Calgary, Devonion Gardens, Heritage Park, Scotsman's Hill, and the Chinese Cultural Centre, as well as Eau Claire Market and Canada Olympic Park. Tickets are C$45, and the tours operate year round but run more often in the summer, with morning, afternoon, and evening options.

© **403/590-6930.** www.hammerheadtours.com. C$45 adults.

Time Out for Touring   City tours begin at 8am on Mondays, Wednesdays, and Fridays at the base of the Calgary Tower, pass through Eau Claire Market and Chinatown, and visit Stampede Park, the Pengrowth Saddledome, Fort Calgary, and the Olympic Speed Skating Oval. Reservations are required. Other tours will stop at Canada Olympic Park and Lougheed House. Customized tours for groups are also available, as are day trips outside the city. Pickup is available at most major downtown hotels, or you can meet at the Calgary Tower. Tours run about 4 hours and are C$65 per person.

© **403/217-4699.** www.tour-time.com. C$65 adults. June through September only.

On Foot

Guided walking tours of the city typically trot out all the old chestnuts: the Palliser, Stephen Avenue, Olympic Plaza, Chinatown, and Eau Claire. **Time Out for Touring** (*©* **403/217-4699;** www.tour-time.com) offers walking tours at C$25 per person.

A Calgary seniors' group leads informal walks through downtown Thursdays from June to September. Tours begin in the lobby of the Glenbow Museum at 130 9th Ave. SE. There is no contact number for this group, so you're taking your chances, but it's free.

Free walking tours of **Union Cemetery,** Calgary's oldest civic burial ground, are conducted Sunday afternoons in the summer. The 90-minute tours are led by Parks Department volunteers. Heroes, villains, and other colorful characters abound. For information, call City of Calgary Cemeteries at *©* **403/221-3660.**

A walking tour for gourmands is the **Urban Safari** (*©* **403/283-3158;** www.urbansafaritours.com). Starting at C$75 per person and going up to C$120 per person (which includes wine), the Urban Safari walks you to no fewer than five downtown dining hotspots for samples of fine cuisine and flights of wine.

Another offbeat walking tour is the **Calgary Ghost Tour** (*©* **403/472-1989;** www.calgaryghosttours.com), which simply is what it says it is: a wander through Calgary's haunted past (and present!). Tours depart on a number of different days and from several different locations from May to October—best to call or check the website for current information. Rates are C$15 to C$20 adults. Private tours for groups of 10 or more can also be arranged.

SHOPPING

Calgary is a retail Mecca, with virtually all of the world's top luxury brands well-represented—a reflection of the moneyed population that's riding high at the moment with the upward-spiraling price of oil. People here like to buy stuff, and a vast array of retail opportunities have sprung up to accommodate them. The avant-garde is in short supply, and mega-mall chain fare is the order of the day. But there are a handful of unique experiences to be had, if you want to put a dent in your wallet.

Downtown

Here, you'll find a network of multi-level malls tucked into the bases of the office towers, the majority of them with entrances on the Stephen Avenue Mall. This is where much of Calgary's high-end retail resides, anchored by swish department store **Holt Renfrew** at the eastern end of Stephen Avenue Mall in the newly-refurbished Eaton Centre (751 3rd St. SW; ☎ **403/269-7341**; www.holtrenfrew. com). Think Neiman Marcus, and you've more or less got it: high-priced brands like Jil Sander, Giorgio Armani, Hugo Boss, and Paul Smith, arrayed in luxurious, if somewhat cramped, environs. For Calgary's many executives, this is also power-suit central, with a made-to-measure shop, as well.

The Eaton Centre also sports a **Sears** (☎ **403/298-4311**; www.sears.ca), which can be handy for lost or forgotten essentials. The Eaton Centre is compact but four stories high, and is connected to the east via the Plus 15 walkway system to the TD Centre, another venue for high-end shopping. Many of the major chain-brand stores are to be found between these two malls, like **Club Monaco, Banana Republic, Eddie Bauer, Roots, Lacoste,** and **Gap.** There's also a **Birk's** store here, which is probably Canada's most venerable independent jeweler and silverware dealer.

Famed Canadian menswear dealer **Harry Rosen** occupies two levels of the TD Centre, on floors 2 and 3. Notable women's fashion dealers include **BCBG by Max Azria, Jacob,** and **Esprit.** Street level, you'll find a **Sport Mart,** a discount sporting goods store.

South of the TD Centre—once again, reachable by the Plus 15 walkway—you'll find the less-occupied but still quite swanky **Banker's Hall** (335 8th Ave. SW; ☎ **403/770-7145**; www.bankershall.ca). The **Brass Monocle** (☎ **403/228-9191**; www.brassmonocle.com), perhaps the city's most fashion-forward optician, is found here, along with pricey German leather goods maker **Taschen!** (☎ **403/262-5422**) and a local mainstay for high-end men's fashion, **Henry Singer** (☎ **403/234-8585**; www.henrysinger.com).

Continuing along Stephen Avenue on the Plus 15 level, you'll eventually reach **Scotia Fashion Centre,** a drab, empty-feeling portion of the downtown shopping area that nonetheless leads to multi-storied **The Bay** (200 8th Ave. SW; ☎ **403/262-0345**; www.thebay.ca), a venerable Canadian department store formerly known as the Hudson's Bay Company; it's a cut above Sears in terms of being a little more up-market. They have high end labels like Calvin Klein, as well as lingerie, linens, electronics, sporting goods, and furniture. It's more modest than, say, Holt's, but it's always good value and a good place to replace essentials—bathing suits, underwear, socks—forgotten or lost along the way.

The density of second-level mall shopping downtown has done much to blunt the actual retail opportunities on the streets themselves, but Stephen Avenue holds at least a couple of options. **Riley and McCormick** (220 8th Ave. SW; ☎ **800/661-1585** or 403/262-1556; www.realcowboys.com) is an authentic western-wear shop at the stroll's eastern end, while the **Arnold Churgin** store (227 8th Ave. SW; ☎ **403/262-3366**; www.arnoldchurgin.com) is a mainstay for any women's shoe fashionista. Housed in a glossy black Art Deco building since 1964, Churgin's has flourished in good times and weathered the bad; it's a Calgary institution.

New to the downtown area are **Fashion Central** (corner of Stephen Ave. and 1st St.; ☎ **403/543-9900**), a sleek new retail complex that houses small boutiques by creative and independent fashion designers in a beautiful refurbished heritage building, and **Art Central** (corner of Centre St. and 7th Ave.; ✆ **403/543-9600**), a visual art complex that houses studios, art galleries, and funky shops. This is a great spot to find truly unique souvenirs.

A bit further north, on the shores of the river is **Eau Claire Market** (200 Barclay Parade SW; ✆ **403/264-6450;** www.eauclairemarket.com). Envisioned as a fresh-food market modeled after Granville Island in Vancouver, the market never really took off as such. The intervening years have seen it morph into a warehouse for amusing *tchotchkes* and crafts, which, depending on your taste, could consume an entire afternoon or annoy within minutes. Still, some of the stalls and stands here feature imported fabrics and objects from Asia and South America, as well as local artisan-made goods.

Design District

From 10th Avenue to 12th Avenue SW, and 4th Street to 14th Street SW, Calgary's Design District—so named in 2006 to draw more people to the area—includes dozens of furniture and home-decor stores, restaurants, art galleries, architects, and home builders.

Flooring, hardware, bedding, dishes, lighting, and furniture can all be found here. Design District shops showcase everything from antiques (**The French Connection,** 1222 11th Ave. SW; ✆ **403/283-4344;** www.frenchconnectionantiques. com) to sleek modern design (**Koolhaus,** 724A 11th Ave. SW, ✆ **403/731-5665,** www.koolhausdesign,com; **Robert Sweep**, 739 11th Ave. SW, ✆ **403/262-8525,** www.robertsweep.com).

This is the neighborhood to find everything from 18th-century French armoires to Mies van der Rohe Barcelona chairs to cutesy *objets,* like Alessi clocks and utensils. Walking west down 11th Avenue SW from 4th Street SW, a casual stroll (without stopping) would cover almost the entire area in about 20 minutes.

17th Avenue/Mission District

This lively zone just south of downtown, from 10th Street to 4th Street SW, and 25th Avenue to 16th Avenue SW, contains much of the city's most eclectic and interesting fashion. A surfeit of vintage shops are to be found here, like **Divine** (720 17th Ave. SW; ✆ **403/228-2540;** www.divineplanet.com), a basement-level warehouse of vintage wear that includes a piercing and tattoo parlor, **Blue Light Special** (601 17th Ave. SW; ✆ **403/245-5338**), or **Junk Star Vintage** (718 17th Ave. SW; ✆ **403/245-0222**).

Eclectic, of-the-moment fashion options abound here, as well, at shops like **Purr** (919 17th Ave. SW; ✆ **403/244-7877**), which carries trendy brands like Ben Sherman, and **Goodfoot** (736 17th Ave. SW; ✆ **403/245-5414;** www.getonthegoodfoot. ca), a sneaker store/gallery that prides itself in the most avant-garde and hard-to-find sneaker design. **Worth** (119-1013 17th Ave. SW; ✆ **403/228-1003;** www.astore calledworth.com) provides fashion-forward design for men and women, while **Gravity Pope** (524 17th Ave. SW; ✆ **403/209-0961;** www.gravitypope.ca) is one of the premiere hip shoe stores in all of western Canada.

South from 17th Avenue SW on 4th Street SW you'll find mostly restaurants, many of them great (see "Where to Dine," earlier in this chapter), but there's at least one fashion find: **Henry** (2115A 4th St. SW; ✆ **403/209-5030**), a men's outlet for high-fashion jeans, with some interesting and eclectic avant-garde women's choices, as well.

The Mega Malls

A lot of Calgary shopping is relegated to the suburban malls, the largest of which, **Chinook Centre** (6455 Macleod Trail SW; ℂ **403/255-2161**; www.chinook centre.ca), is a burgeoning center of commerce, replete with every major label and chain store you could possibly think of (the only Williams-Sonoma in town is here). More than 200 stores await within, giving the shopaholic potential days of diversion in its climate-controlled comfort.

In the northwest, near the University of Calgary, **Market Mall** (3625 Shaganappi Trail NW; ℂ **403/288-5466;** www.marketmall.ca) covers a lot of the same ground, with chains galore and acres of climate-controlled comfort, while farther south, **SouthCentre** (100 Anderson Rd. SE; ℂ **403/271-7670;** www.southcentremall. com) completes Calgary's triumvirate of massive malls. The content varies only slightly, with Chinook being the most complete; expect much of the same content you'd find in the suburban malls of any major North American city.

Bargains

A couple of outlet malls exist on the city's fringes, where you'll find out-of-date but pleasantly inexpensive fare. **Deerfoot Mall** (901 64th Ave. NE; ℂ **403/274-7024;** http://deerfootmall.shopping.ca) in the city's northwest, near the airport just off Deerfoot Trail, offers the ubiquitous Canadian clearance chain **Winners** (www.winners.ca), as well as second-chance goods from major retailers such as Liz Claiborne, Fairweather, and Smart Set. Generally drab—its tag line is "Western Canada's only enclosed outlet mall"—but if you're willing to dig a bit, there are bargains to be found.

On the western edge of the city, where the foothills start to roll, is the aptly named **Westhills Towne Centre.** All big box chain stores, Westhills features the requisite Winners, as well as some better outlets than at Deerfoot, such as Roots, Mexx, Jacob, and Le Château.

The new **Cross Iron Mills** (ℂ **403/984-6888;** www.crossironmills.com) just north of the airport has plenty of (200+) outlet and regular stores, as well as 17 big-box stores and 20 stores that have no other location in Alberta. It's the largest single-level shopping center in the province.

CALGARY AFTER DARK

To get a read on Calgary's vibrant cultural scene, pick up a copy of *FFWD*, the local free arts and entertainment weekly. There, you'll find listings for movies, art openings, upcoming concerts, clubs, and theater.

The **Calgary Centre for the Performing Arts** (205 8th Ave. SE; ℂ **403/294-7455**)—now called the Epcor Centre, after its corporate sponsor—is the catch-all venue for live theater, symphony, and opera. Calgary has a vibrant theater scene, with three major companies: **Alberta Theatre Projects** (ℂ **403/294-7402**; www. atplive.com), **Theatre Calgary** (ℂ **403/294-7440;** www.theatrecalgary.com), and the avant-garde, internationally celebrated **One Yellow Rabbit** (ℂ **403/264-3224;** www.oyr.org), all working out of the Epcor Centre. Epcor is also home to the excellent **Calgary Philharmonic Orchestra** (✆ **403/571-0270;** www.cpo-live. com), an international-class ensemble.

A little farther afield is the **Loose Moose Theatre** (1235 26th Ave. SE, in the Crossroads Farmer's Market; ✆ **403/265-5682;** www.loosemoose.com), the originator of a kind of improvisational comedy called Theatre Sports (think *Whose Line Is It Anyway?*). Improv is a weekly event; children's shows surface occasionally, as well. Tickets range from C$10 to C$12.

Calgary has several legitimate casinos whose proceeds go wholly to charities. None impose a cover. Located across from the Stampede grounds, the **Elbow River Inn Casino** (1919 Macleod Trail S; ✆ **403/266-4355;** www.elbowrivercasino. com) is the largest and most central; it offers Las Vegas–style gaming, plus a poker variation called Red Dog. It has a 24-hour poker room.

Calgarians, as a group, are young (more than half are under 35), moneyed, and thirsty. The popular cocktail strips, which reach critical mass around the 17th Avenue SW/4th Street SW axis, are always busy, and on the weekend, jammed full to near-overflowing. The area is more focused on cocktail lounges and pubs than nightclubs, and downtown, which bustles during the day, still suffers from a lack of people at night.

Larger clubs are sprinkled outside the central zone and away from the downtown core, particularly since, in development-mad Calgary, one of the biggest, most popular—and craziest—clubs, **Cowboys,** fell victim to the wrecking ball in 2008 to make way for yet another skyscraping tower, first moving to a new location and then closing permanently in 2010. Rapid redevelopment can make Calgary nightlife hard to follow; once a vibrant live-music zone, 1st Street SW at 11th Avenue has, like Cowboys, since faced the wrecking ball to make way for condominium development. Keep an eye on *FFWD* if live music is your thing; Calgary has it in spades.

Downtown

Barley Mill Neighbourhood Pub   A number of pubs and late-night watering holes are just outside the Eau Claire Market on the Barclay Parade plaza. The Barley Mill Neighbourhood Pub is an old-school pub with a great patio and second-story deck plunked down in the plaza across from the market. This is better-than-average pub grub served in a relatively refined, woodsy pub atmosphere. The nearby park makes it even better. 201 Barclay Parade SW. ✆ **403/290-1500.** www.barleymill.net.

Broken City   Broken City is a hipster hangout with a strong cast of local music several times a week. Expect to see live local bands on Tuesdays, Thursdays, and Saturdays. At press time, Broken City offered a Tuesday night special of Wing Night and "punk rock" Bingo, which it affectionately dubbed "Wingo." 613 11th Ave. SW. ✆ **403/262-9976.** www.brokencity.ca. Cover charge varies.

The Garage   Eau Claire Market is the home of the Garage, a hip warehouse-of-a-bar/restaurant with an emphasis on playing billiards and listening to loud alternative rock. It's a guy's place through and through. Watch sports, eat nachos, and play some stick, if you like—but never forget, with happy hour and cocktail specials a-plenty, the main sport here is drinking. A lot. Summer is particularly nice when the Garage, near the river, opens its doors almost entirely to the outside. 200 Barclay Parade SW. ✆ **403/262-6762.** www.the-garage.ca.

Hi-Fi Club   The Hi-Fi, a popular hipster hangout, is an electronic- and dance-music destination, with occasional live performances but largely a rotating cast of DJs. 219 10th Ave. SW. ⓒ **403/263-5222.** www.hificlub.ca.

Roadhouse   Since the venerable Cowboys Bar was shut down in early 2010, the Roadhouse has become the top Calgary destination for raunchy, honky-tonking good times. There are five big bars, a huge dance floor, and scantily clad ladies. The entire city misses the unique western schwag of Cowboys, but this is a close a replacement as you'll find. Keep a handle on your partner. 840-9th Ave SW. ⓒ **403/398-7623.** www. roadhousecalgary.com.

West   If you're in a suit and want to meet others in similar suits for an after-work drink (that may turn into many after-work drinks), this new three-story lounge on the top floor of the Scotia Centre is your place. Relaxed enough that you can let down your hair, expect to see stylish execs and worker bees sipping on martinis and uncorking $100 vintages. The heated rooftop patio stays open 8 months of the year. 225 7th Ave. SW. ⓒ **403/237-5556.** www.westrestaurantandbar.com.

17th Avenue SW/4th Street SW

Bungalow   A half-block east of the Mercury Lounge (see below) is its sister property, Bungalow, a well-named (it's a single-story), modern-rustic resto-bar with warm wood accents and sleek contemporary style. A small front patio is thrust up to the sidewalk and slightly elevated—the better to watch the weekend crowds go by. Packed on the weekend and, like the Mercury, a haven for the beautiful people. A nice long bar allows for discreet see-and-be-seen activities. 524 17th Ave. SW. ⓒ **403/209-5005.** www.bungalow524.com.

Melrose   Formerly a cavernous sports bar with more massive-screen TVs than you could count on both hands, Melrose has morphed into a more stylish lounge. The party on 17th Avenue almost always centers on Melrose, especially on nights when the Calgary Flames are playing. Food and service have improved with the funky new look. 730 17th Ave. SW. ⓒ **403/228-3566.** www.melrosecalgary.com.

The Mercury Lounge ★★★   A Calgary staple, the Mercury, as it's known, is a dark wood–and–black leather *boîte* that favors complex cocktails and ambient-heavy candlelight. The walls are lined with large-scale classic boxing photos, like George Chuvalo versus Muhammad Ali. This is where young, stylish Calgarians go for a night out, though if quiet is your bag, you might want to move on around 10pm. That's when the DJ starts, and the tiny bar becomes a heaving, impromptu dance floor. Around the corner, the Merc's dining room—connected by a door in the back—is a little quieter, and the food is great; its patio is a perfect place to enjoy a cocktail and a summer sunset. 1530 5th St. SW. ⓒ **403/229-0222.** www.themercury.ca.

The Metropolitan Grill   This resto-bar on the second floor of the Mount Royal Village shopping center (ⓒ 403/245-8171) boasts an extensive menu, but let's face facts: No one's here for the grill. As the evening wears on, a glut of the young and aggressively single let their eyes wander freely, surveying what's available. Most nights, most everything is; the Met is probably the most popular—and most bald-faced—pickup joint in town. 880 16th Ave. SW. ⓒ **403/802-2393.** www.themetropolitangrill.ca.

Ming ★★   A small and unassuming spot just below street level, Ming is a refuge in the often-frenzied swirl of revelry on 17th. With its rich red walls, the club is sophisticated, edgy, and fashionable, and a welcome respite from throbbing music and drunken teens. The cocktail menu focuses on unique martinis with political inspirations: the Mother Teresa has Bombay gin, after the Indian city, while others are named for Napoleon, Gandhi, and Buddha. Ming's late-might menu is small but inventive, if the urge to nosh strikes. Very civilized, indeed, Ming is the place for deep, cocktail-infused conversation. And in case you miss the swirl, a handful of ringside seats at street level let you observe from a safe distance. 520 17th Ave. SW. *©* **403/229-1986.**

The Ship and Anchor ★★   The mother of all alt-pubs—that is, pubs committed to Calgary's long-standing and lively alternative music scene—the Ship, as locals call it, is a dark cave inside, but boasts a patio nearly twice its interior size right on the prime 17th Avenue strip. The pub fare—nachos, chicken wings—is more than passable, and the frosty pitchers of draught—usually filled with product from local-hero microbrewery Big Rock—keep the outdoor throngs content as long afternoons turn into even longer evenings. A Calgary tradition. 534 17th Ave. SW. *©* **403/245-3333.** www.shipandanchor.com.

Elsewhere

Ranchman's Cookhouse and Dance Hall   Ranchman's is "Canada's Greatest Honky Tonk!" Or so it claims. But it's hard to argue with the venerable institution. Camped out since 1972 on Macleod Trail S, well outside the core, Ranchman's has long been a magnet for real-life cowboys (not the kind that used to go to Cowboys) and the city slickers who love them. Live entertainment—country only, of course—line-dancing, two-step lessons, and a menu that boasts such staples as ribs, chili, and barbecued chicken means that Ranchman's knows its clientele. During Stampede, it's no surprise to find the real cowboys—the ones in actual competition—hanging out here. In increasingly urban Calgary, Ranchman's is home on the range. Another slogan: "If it ain't Ranchman's, it ain't real!" Too right. 9615 Macleod Trail SW. *©* **403/253-1100.** www.ranchmans.com.

Gay Calgary

Fab Bar   Laid back and stylish, this used to be the top lesbian bar in Calgary when it was known as Money-Pennies, but it now appeals to all sorts of folks. They have a pretty decent menu, as well, and a pool table that's a good place to mingle. 1742 10th Ave SW. *©* **403/263-7411.** www.fab-bar.com.

Texas Lounge at Goliaths   Also known as "the Bunker," this lounge is tucked next to Calgary's gay bath house, below ground off 17th Avenue. It's a small space, so be prepared to rub shoulders. It's also definitely a spot for drinking (and notorious, often, for people who drink *a lot*). 308-17th Ave SW. *©* **403/229-0911.** www.goliaths.ca/texaslounge.html.

Twisted Element   Twisted Element calls itself "the largest gay club west of Montreal"—a tall claim, given the large-scale clubs in Vancouver—but it mostly lives up to it. The bar, in the city's northwest, not far from Kensington or the University of Calgary, features a cocktail lounge in the basement and a jam-packed dance club on the main floor. 1006 11th Ave. NW. *©* **403/802-0230.** www.twistedelement.ca.

SOUTHERN ALBERTA

Alberta narrows south of Calgary, where the Rocky Mountains pinch in from the west and cut south and east into Montana. In the southwestern corner of the province, the result is an abrupt shift in terrain; trademark foothills, which run along most of the Rockies' eastern slope, are noticeably absent here, as the prairie simply buckles and rears up into rocky slopes.

That's the main feature of Waterton Lakes National Park, the least populated of the three national mountain parks in Alberta. As a result, though, virtually everything east of the park is resoundingly flat—the great plains, with their vast horizons and giant skies. They say you can see a car driving away from you all day out here, and they're only half kidding; the Canadian prairies have to them an eerie emptiness you have to see to believe.

But this is also a place of ancient intrigue. Millions of years ago, it was the site of a massive inland sea where marine dinosaurs from the Cretaceous period cruised the waters in search of prey and the lush surrounding lands supported massive herbivores and carnivores alike. It's not uncommon to come across bone-fossil fragments when you're just wandering the canyons near Drumheller and certainly in the aptly named Dinosaur Provincial Park, one of the richest fossil sites in the world.

The start—or end, depending how you look at it—of the Cowboy Trail, Alberta's famed ranchland path (now highway) along the Rocky Mountain fringe, is in Southern Alberta, at Cardston. If you didn't know, you wouldn't need to be told: This is cowboy country, and all the horses, pickup trucks, and honky-tonks go along with it. For more information on the Cowboy Trail, see chapter 8.

DRUMHELLER

Located 130km (81 miles) northeast of Calgary in Alberta's badlands, the **Drumheller Valley** is one of the premier dinosaur-fossil hunting places on Earth. It wasn't always so, though. In the 1930s, Drumheller was a boomtown of a different sort. Rich in coal deposits throughout the surrounding badlands, it swelled to more than 30,000 people. But after a few fruitful decades, the coal was all but mined out, and the town was dying. Desperate for a new anchor industry, in 1967, a large federal prison became the town's largest employer.

But the town was overlooking something else, buried in the ground. Seventy-five million years before, an extraordinary range of dinosaurs roamed the badlands—so named for its rough, difficult-to-farm soil, though at the time it was largely an inland sea. The first discovery, by James B. Tyrrell in 1884, was an enormous skull of a predator, the Albertosaurus. The rich prehistoric resource hovered in the background for decades, though, as industry took hold, even though paleontologists from all over the world had made Drumheller a center of study. Then, in 1985, the **Royal Tyrrell Museum of Paleontology** opened, and Drumheller was truly open for the dinosaur business. About half a million visitors make their way here each year now, drawn largely to the museum and such sites as **Horsethief** and **Horseshoe canyons**—where, until recently, a casual meander along one of its hiking trails would yield pocketfuls of dinosaur-bone fragments. The fossils are still there, but be warned: The province states that "all fossils in or on the ground are owned by the province." Taking them constitutes theft. So look, touch, but leave them in peace.

Essentials

GETTING THERE

BY CAR   From Calgary to Drumheller (130km/81 miles), take Highway 2 North to Route 72 East. Take Route 72 through Beiseiker, a Hutterite community, where it becomes Route 9, which takes you into central Drumheller. It'll take about 90 minutes.

BY BUS   Greyhound Canada (© **800/661-8747** or 403/218-3000; www.greyhound.ca) runs a daily bus from Calgary to Drumheller. The trip takes about 2 hours, and the cost is C$76 round-trip.

VISITOR INFORMATION

The very helpful **Drumheller Visitor Information Centre and Chamber of Commerce** (60 1st Ave. W; © **866/823-8100** or 403/823-7703; www.traveldrumheller.com) is located in the same complex as the **World's Largest Dinosaur,** a giant sculpture of a Tyrannosaurus Rex that towers over the north part of town. Literally, you can't miss it—it's visible from everywhere, its menacing scowl the dominant feature of Drumheller's modest skyline. Here, you'll find information on absolutely everything, from hiking to museums to tours to accommodation. Staff members are even willing to make calls on your behalf if you're stuck for a place to stay. You can climb the dinosaur, as well (see "The World's Biggest Dinosaur," below).

The World's Biggest Dinosaur

It's a pretty easy claim, given that the giant T-Rex statue straddling the Drumheller Tourism office is about four times the size the real McCoy ever was, but kids will still love climbing up the gigantic beast's innards to reach the observation deck in his mouth. Stare out at Drumheller and the badlands beyond through the massive, pointy teeth. The cost is C$3 per person; it's open in the summer daily 9am to 9pm. For more information, call ℂ **866/823-8100.**

Exploring the Area

The badlands that surround Drumheller are a fascinating mix of arid prairie and deep, dramatic canyon carved over the millennia by the **Red Deer River.** Two canyons, Horsethief Canyon and Horseshoe Canyon, drop dramatically downward into the bald prairie; the land is so seamless at the canyons' edges that you can hardly see into them unless you're right on top. This is great road-tripping land.

A road called the **Dinosaur Trail** is a 55km (34-mile) loop that starts west from town along the northern edge of the Red Deer River, crosses the river on the tiny **Bleriot car ferry** (free), and continues along the south side of the river and back through town.

Along the northern leg of the Trail, you'll pass the Royal Tyrrell Museum (see "Attractions," below) and a spectacular viewpoint from which you can see deep into Horsethief Canyon and the badlands beyond, to the west. The name is come by fairly, according to local legend: In the late 19th century, a rancher left his horses in the canyon only to see them disappear. The following season, the horses had returned, sporting a different brand. Horsethief Canyon trails are steep and rugged, and unforgiving for those not in decent shape or wearing proper footwear, so be warned.

The southern leg of the Dinosaur Trail passes by Horseshoe Canyon, the more dramatic of the two and the easier to hike. A network of pathways leads through the spectacular buttes and plateaus carved over millennia by the river, and the badlands stratification is clear to see. You can almost see the history melting away before your eyes.

The Hoodoo Trail heads down the Red Deer River to the historic **Atlas Coal Mine** in the sweet town of East Coulee, where an excellent little bakery serves fresh goods inside the **East Coulee School Museum** (ℂ **403/822-3970;** www.ecsmuseum.ca).

Just south off Highway 10 is the strange little village of Wayne, which is part ghost-town and part hideout for fascinating modern characters. You'll cross 11 bridges in only 6.5km (4 miles) en route. It's the home of the century-old **Last Chance Saloon** and the **Rosedeer Hotel** (ℂ **403/823-9089** for both), a haven for travelers. Come for a buffalo burger and fries at lunch and drift into the past.

A guided tour of the region is a good idea, and the best of them is **Wild West Badlands Tours** (ℂ **403/823-3118;** www.wildwestbadlandstours.com). Your

Southern Alberta

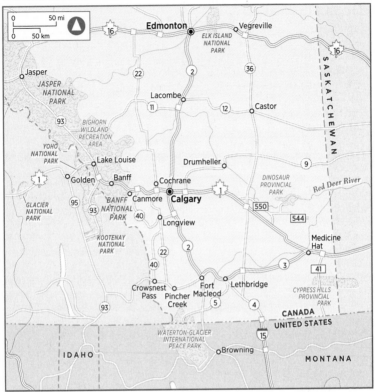

Hoodoos

Formed by natural erosion of Alberta's sandstone landscape, there are formations called "hoodoos" all over the province. But none are as haunting—or as bizarre—as the hoodoos that lie outside Drumheller. Three to six meters (10–20 ft.) tall and mushroom-like, they were believed by the local native bands to be petrified giants who came to life at night. Their thick, rounded pillars are capped with an odd brim. They seem like an assembly of close-together mesas in miniature, except for their protruding caps, called capstones. These formations take millions of years to form and are thus protected by the provincial government; the examples outside Drumheller aren't guarded full-time, however, and occasionally bear footprints on their capstone—which, if dislodged, would surely mean their quickly-eroded end. The hoodoos site is located 16km (10 miles) south of Drumheller on Hoodoo Trail (Hwy. 10).

BLACKFOOT CROSSING: EXPLORING first nations HISTORY

Located an hour west of Calgary on the Trans-Canada Highway and about 90 minutes from Drumheller, the Blackfoot Crossing Historical Park (© **888/654-6274** or 403/734-5171; www.blackfoot crossing.ca) tells the many stories of the First Nations. It's situated on an historically important bend of the Bow River, where Treaty 7 was signed in 1877 between Queen Victoria and the First Nations group of the western prairies. Today, it is part of the broad Siksika Reserve, and it's an interesting, welcoming, and beautiful place to explore the culture, history, and contemporary issues facing First Nations groups. You can also spend a night in a tipi and follow outdoor interpretive trails.

guide, Pat Mulgrew, is a long-time badlands resident and a font of knowledge on the region's prehistoric past. Different tours cover the museums, the canyons, a cluster of bizarre sandstone formations called the hoodoos, and a couple of authentic western ghost towns (still with a few inhabitants). Tours range from 4 to 8 hours; full-day tours are C$40 adults, C$27 children 7 to 17, or C$110 for families of four.

Another interesting option is the badlands from above: **Mountainview Helicopters** (© **403/334-4354;** www.mvheli.com) offers badlands helicopter tours that explore Horseshoe Canyon. No reservations are required; tours are between 5 and 12 minutes long, and they run from mid-June to early September. Tickets are C$52 adults, with a minimum of 2 people.

Hammer Head Scenic Tours (© **403/590-6930;** www.hammerheadtours. com) has 9-hour tours to the Drumheller badlands and the Royal Tyrrell Museum out of Calgary for C$90 per person. Once weekly, the company also runs its van to Head-Smashed-In Buffalo Jump for C$97 per person (see p. 152).

Attractions

Royal Tyrrell Museum ★★ ☺ Just north of Drumheller, and about 145km (90 miles) northeast of Calgary, this is one of the world's best paleontology museums and educational facilities. It is also the main event here: Of the half-million visitors that come to Drumheller each year, the Tyrrell draws almost 400,000 of them.

And it offers far more than just impressive skeletons and life-size models, though it has dozens of them. The entire fossil record of the Earth is explained, era by era, with an impressive variety of media and educational tools. You can walk through a prehistoric garden, watch numerous videos, use computers to "design" dinosaurs for specific habitats, watch plate tectonics at work, and see museum technicians preparing fossils. The museum is also a renowned research facility where scientists study all forms of ancient life and give visitors a window into their work.

Kids will go crazy for the interactive displays, to say nothing of the hands-on experiences, like a bucket of fossilized T-Rex teeth there for the handling. Multiple programs for kids age 7 and up can be found here, with the Badlands Science Camp being the best: Kids from 9 to 15 can overnight in the badlands with museum staff and explore the realm of the dinosaurs for themselves. Give yourself at least 2 hours for the inside part and at least 30 minutes to walk the interpretive trail just in front.

Hwy. 838, Midland Provincial Park, Drumheller, AB T0J 0Y0. © **888/440-4240** or 403/823-7707. www. tyrrellmuseum.com. Admission C$10 adults, C$8 seniors, C$6 children 7-17; free for children under 7. C$30 families. Mid-May to Sept daily 9am–9pm; Oct to mid-May Tues–Sun 10am–5pm.

Where to Stay

While Drumheller is a well-served tourist destination, quality accommodations are still sparse. If you plan to go in the summer, book well ahead, as the major chain hotels can fill up fast.

Drumheller Ramada Inn & Suites   There is little to distinguish this hotel from its neighbors, or from any hotel anywhere, for that matter. But families will be grateful for the indoor pool and waterslide in summertime, when it can be very hot outside. The rooms are decorated in the same colors as the badlands: ochre, beige, and rust. Even the standard rooms have simple kitchenettes. Other freebies include a simple continental breakfast, local calls, parking, newspapers, and wireless internet.

680 2nd St. SE, Drumheller, T0J 0Y0. © **403/823-2028.** www.ramada.com. 74 units. C$214–C$224 double; C$236 suite. Rates include continental breakfast. AE, DC, DISC, MC, V. **Amenities:** Fitness center; pool w/waterslide. *In room:* A/C, hair dryer, minibar, free Wi-Fi.

Heartwood Inn and Spa ★★   Surely there's no place in Drumheller with more warmth and heart than this lovely inn close to downtown. The rooms are all large and comfortable, with a perhaps over-stuffed country style. Each has a jetted tub, flat-screen TV, and big fluffy beds. There's a nice garden with the ubiquitous dinosaur bones and other dino statues. But the friendly staff are the real stars. They'll take care of everything for you, from dinner reservations to golf tee times, and make sure you get the most out of your Drumheller time. For C$10, the breakfast is the best in town. They also have the only spa in town.

320 North Railway Ave., Drumheller T0J 0Y4. © **888/823-6495** or 403/823-6496. Fax 403/823-4935. www.innsatheartwood.com. 10 units. C$105–C$260 double. AE, MC, V. **Amenities:** Spa. In room: A/C, TV, hair dryer, Wi-Fi.

Super 8   The Super 8 is a clean, no-nonsense option right on the highway in central Drumheller. Some rooms have kitchens, and across the parking lot is a 24-hour IGA grocery store—a blessing amid the town's meager dining options.

800-680 2nd St. SE (Hwy. 10 & 2nd St.), Drumheller T0J 0Y0. © **888/823-8882** or 403/823-8887. www.super8.com. 72 units. C$202 double; C$260 suite. Rates include continental breakfast & access to

---

 MOVIE magic

The badlands have provided the backdrop for plenty of Hollywood movies over the years, from the ghost town of Rowley in the Canadian production *Bye Bye Blues* to the Oscar-winning Clint Eastwood film *Unforgiven.* Canadian auteur Atom Egoyan filmed large portions of his film *Ararat* nearby, using the badlands to double for the Armenian landscape. All is not so serious, though; Jackie Chan's comic romp through the west, *Shanghai Noon,* was shot here, as was the Seth Green comedy *Knockaround Guys.*

Rosebud

A tiny prairie gem cradled in a river valley on a provincial byway, Rosebud is a thriving arts center just off the map. The main draw is the superb theater, which is connected to an art school and surrounded by galleries. Theater packages include lunch or dinner pre-show at the historic **Mercantile Dining Room** (℗ **403/677-2001**) and then an uplifting show in the Opera House. The town has just over 100 residents, most of whom are involved in the theater. You can stay at any of the many bed and breakfasts to be found here, or at the **Rosebud Country Inn** (℗ **403/677-2211**; www.rosebud.ca/country_inn.htm). Details on accommodation and attractions can be found at www.rosebud.ca. Take provincial Route 9 West from Drumheller and keep your eyes peeled for Route 840 South. It's about a half-hour's drive from Drumheller.

all-day coffee, tea & treats. AE, DC, DISC, MC, V. **Amenities:** Fitness center; Jacuzzi; pool. *In room:* TV, fridge, hair dryer, high-speed Internet.

CAMPING

There are several campgrounds along the Dinosaur Trail, which can be found at www.traveldrumheller.com/campgrounds.html. The oldest and best established of these—not to mention the closest to the Royal Tyrrell—is the **Dinosaur Trail RV Resort** (℗ **403/823-9333;** www.holidaytrailsresorts.com/dinosaurtrail; C$50 full RV hookup; C$40 RV, power only; C$35 tent). Just a few minutes west of the museum entrance, the campground sits on the banks of the Red Deer River. A choice of 200 hook-ups provides ample space. Tenting is also available. Amenities include pool, shower, laundry, canoe rentals, and a convenience store. Open May 1 to September 30. Reservations strongly recommended.

Where to Dine

Drumheller isn't known for its culinary options. There are a few surprises, though. **Athens** (71 Bridge St.; ℗ **403/823-3225**) has excellent Greek food and hospitality. The **Vietnamese Noodle House** (202-2nd St. W; ℗ **403/823-2000**) has hearty pho soups and salad rolls, as well as Western favorites like burgers. For a coffee and treat, drop into Main Street's **Café Italiano** (35-3rd Ave. W; ℗ **403/823-4443**).

Dinosaur Provincial Park

In Red Deer River Valley near **Brooks,** about 225km (140 miles) east of Calgary and 193km (120 miles) southeast of Drumheller, you'll find perhaps the greatest concentration of fossils from the late Cretaceous period in the world. The park is one of the planet's most important paleontological sites; more than 300 complete dinosaur skeletons have been found here, earning it UNESCO World Heritage Site status.

Park excavations continue from early June to late August, based out of the Field Station of the Royal Tyrrell Museum. Much of the park is a natural preserve, with access restricted to guided interpretive bus tours and hikes ranging from 2¾ to 4 hours. Space on these tours is limited, so be prepared to be flexible with your

FOSSILS WERE NOT always FIRST

While recent decades have seen a lot of international paleontological attention paid to Alberta's badlands, it wasn't always the case. In the height of the coal boom, the fossils weren't just ignored—they were a nuisance. As miners extracted the coal from underground, they had to sort through the minerals looking for fossils to remove them, as any that made it to a coal-fired oven had a tendency to explode and foul the good coal—a disaster for quality control. Needless to say, the fossils they removed weren't kept for posterity, but disposed of, or crushed; as a result, it's hard to say how many potentially important discoveries were thrown out with the trash.

choices. "Rush" tickets are sold at 8:30am for that day's events; maximum four tickets per person. Reservations are strongly encouraged in July and August. From May to August, lab tours are given so that you can view fossil preparation.

But you don't need a lab to see fossils. The ground here is littered with them. Most are fragments, but you should be able to identify teeth, if not larger portions of dinosaur anatomy. Be warned: These are not souvenirs, and the Alberta government considers removing them from the park akin to stealing. So look and touch, but don't keep.

Five self-guided trails and two outdoor fossil displays are also available. Your best bet is to camp (reserve a campsite by calling © **877/537-2757** or visiting www. reserve.albertaparks.ca) and start your visit at the Visitor Center (open summer Sun–Thurs 8:30am–5pm, Fri and Sat 8:30am–7pm).

Fees for advance tickets for bus tours and hikes are C$12 adults, C$8 children 7 to 17, C$34 families; all tickets are free for children under 7. Lab tours are C$12 adults, C$8 children. Maps of the hiking trails can be found on the park's website, www.tpr.alberta.ca/parks/dinosaur.

MEDICINE HAT

The Hat, as locals like to call it, lies 291km (181 miles) southeast of Calgary on the Trans-Canada Highway, close to the Saskatchewan border, and sits at the center of Alberta's vast natural-gas fields (Rudyard Kipling famously described it as the city with "all hell for a basement.") And in case you're wondering where the name came from (who wouldn't?), it's drawn from the Native Canadian word *saamis,* which means "medicine man's hat."

A lot of modern industry has moved to Medicine Hat to be near the gas, making this an unlikely factory town surrounded by grain fields. There's not much to recommend for the tourist here: The Hat is a whistle-stop for truckers and travelers making the long trek across the prairies. Consequently, the Trans-Canada Highway is lined with the requisite fast-food joints and motels you'd expect.

Though your time in the province is probably best spent elsewhere, Medicine Hat does have some charms. In the early 1900s, the primary industry was fashioning brick and china from the local clay deposits. Consequently, the town's old downtown is a showcase of handsome frontier-era brick buildings. It's worth an hour to explore the historic city center, flanked by the South Saskatchewan River. Together, the buildings, many of them restored, form a quaint picture of frontier life on the prairie.

The Hat is also home to the **Medicine Hat Clay Industries National Historic District** (713 Medalta Ave. SE; ✆ **403/529-1070;** www.medalta.org). Two natural features, abundant prairie clay and the natural gas to fire the ovens, coalesced in the early part of the 20th century to make Medicine Hat the ceramics capital of Canada. The site has a new interactive museum where you can enter a rare circular kiln and learn about the history of clay products. The Hat, however, remains a place that most people pass through, not go to. But those hot summer drives across an unforgiving prairie can leave one needing a break—especially the little ones—and Medicine Hat can offer that, too. **The Riverside Waterslide and Amusement Park** (1401 Powerhouse Rd. SW; ✆ **403/529-6218**) can be a welcome cool-off from a hot car. A whirlpool, river ride, go carts, and minigolf are all on offer, as well. It's open daily all summer, from 10am to 8pm.

All that aside, as you drive through, notice the deep river valley the Hat sits in—a lovely feature carved out of the bald, flat prairie. Visitor information can be found at the **Tourism Medicine Hat** office (8 Gehring Rd. SW; ✆ **403/527-6422;** www. tourismmedicinehat.com).

About 81km (50 miles) south of Medicine Hat lies **Cypress Hills Provincial Park**, 316 sq. km (122 sq. miles) of highlands—outliers of the Rockies—that rise 450m (1,476 ft.) above the flat prairie grasslands. In this preserve live many species of plants and animals, including elk and moose, usually found farther west in more mountainous regions.

Medicine Hat offers little to the gastronome. There is the requisite **Earl's** (3215 Dunmore Rd. SE; ✆ **403/528-3275**), always a reliable option, and a selection of pubs and roadhouses. **DeVine** (579 3rd St. SE; ✆ **403/580-5510**) is a nice spot for contemporary fare in the historic downtown.

LETHBRIDGE

East of Fort Macleod, 105km (65 miles) north of the U.S. border and 216km (134 miles) southeast of Calgary, Lethbridge is a delightful garden city set in the deep, beautiful Old Man River Valley and a popular convention site (it gets more annual hours of sunshine than most places in Canada). Lethbridge started out as Fort Whoop-Up, a notorious trading post that bartered whiskey to the Plains Indians in return for buffalo hides and horses. The post boomed during the 1870s, until the Mounties arrived to bring order. Today, Lethbridge is a pleasant prairie city and Alberta's third largest, with a population of 66,000. For details, contact the **Lethbridge Visitor Centre** (2805 Scenic Dr.; ✆ **800/661-1222** or 403/320-1222; www.visitlethbridge.com), open daily 9am to 5pm.

Though downtown is slightly disappointing in its lack of activity (many of the storefronts are vacant), the city has much to offer. Lethbridge has two good art centers that display regional and touring art. The **Southern Alberta Art Gallery** (601 3rd Ave. S; ✆ **403/327-8770;** www.saag.ca) has a number of changing art shows throughout the year; the gift shop is a good place to go for local crafts. It's open Tuesday to Saturday from 10am to 5pm and Sunday from 1 to 5pm. The **Bowman Arts Centre** (811 5th Ave.; ✆ **403/327-2813**) is housed in an old school and is the fine-arts hub of Lethbridge, with studios, classes, offices for arts organizations, and two galleries featuring the works of area artists; it's open Monday to Friday 9am to 9pm and Saturday 10am to 4pm.

The **Sir Alexander Galt Museum and Archives,** at the west end of 5th Ave. (502 1st St. S, *©* **403/320-4258;** www.galtmuseum.com), is an excellent regional museum located in an historic former hospital. Exhibit galleries focus on the local Native culture, the city's coal-mining past, and the role of immigrants in the region's growth. Two galleries are devoted to the works of regional artists. The back windows of the museum overlook the impressive Oldman River Valley, with its natural park systems. It's open daily 10am to 5pm; admission is C$5 adults, C$4 seniors and students, C$3 children 7 to 17, and free for children 6 and under.

The city's heritage as a frontier whiskey-trading center is commemorated at the **Fort Whoop-Up Interpretive Centre** (*©* **403/329-0444;** www.fortwhoopup. com) in **Indian Battle Park** (follow 3rd Ave. S toward the river). A replica of the fort—the original was built by Montana-based traders of buffalo skins and whiskey in the 1870s—stands in the park, with costumed guides providing horse-drawn carriage tours, interpretive programs, and historic reenactments. During July and August, it's open daily 10am to 5pm; the rest of the year, it's open Wednesday to Sunday 10am to 4pm. Admission is C$7 adults, C$6 seniors, C$5 students, and free for children 5 and under.

The pride of Lethbridge is the **Nikka Yuko Japanese Garden** (*©* **403/328-3511;** www.nikkayuko.com) in Henderson Lake Park on Mayor Magrath Drive, east of downtown. Built for the Canadian centennial in 1967, the garden was championed by Cleo Mowers, publisher of the *Lethbridge Herald,* as a tribute to the many Japanese-Canadians who endured a dark period of Canadian history: During the Second World War, thousands of Japanese-Canadians were placed in internment camps, often thousands of miles from their homes, for fear of enemy collaboration. Mowers teamed with Reverend Yutetsu Kawamura, a Canadian Buddhist priest, and his wife Yoneko, to make the garden a reality. Remarkably, perhaps, a large number of Japanese interned near Lethbridge stayed in the area; almost 2% of the population is of Japanese descent. The garden represents unity between two cultures that, in the not so distant past, were deeply estranged.

The garden is extraordinarily tranquil. Its pavilion and dainty bell tower were built by Japanese artisans without nails or bolts. The garden is one of the largest Japanese gardens in North America; Japanese-Canadian women in kimonos give tours and explain the philosophical concepts involved in Japanese garden design. From late June to Labour Day, the garden is open daily 9am to 8pm; mid-May to late June and after Labour Day to early October, it's open daily 9am to 5pm. Admission is C$7 adults, C$5 seniors, C$4 children 6 to 17, and free for children 5 and under.

Birds of Prey Centre ☺   Canada's largest interpretive center devoted to hunting birds is here on 28 hectares (70 acres) of wetland just outside Lethbridge. You can begin in the interpretive center, to familiarize yourself with the birds you're about to see, and move on to the various options—an interactive experience, with a burrowing owl nestling on your shoulder; a "hawk walk" where you can watch these agile predators, like golden eagles, at close range; or flying demonstrations, as the magnificent beasts are put out to their daily exercise right in front of you. It's fascinating for kids and enthralling overall.

2124 16th Ave., Coaldale (18km/11 miles east of Lethbridge on Hwy. 3). © **403/345-4262.** www. burrowingowl.com. Admission C$8.50 adults, C$7.50 seniors, C$5.50 children 6–18, C$4.50 children 3–5, free for children 2 & under. Daily May 10 to Sept 10 9:30am–5pm.

Where to Stay

Ramada Lethbridge
Along the city's aptly named Scenic Drive, which curls south and west from downtown along the Old Man River Valley, you'll eventually reach a cluster of commercial activity (big-box stores and chain restaurants) at the intersection with Mayor Magrath Drive S. Here, you'll find the Ramada, a pleasant, off-the-rack mid-range hotel made slightly exceptional by its excellent service. Breakfast is included here, as is access to its giant indoor waterslide—not a bad way to keep kids happy after a long day in the car.

2375 Mayor Magrath Dr. S., Lethbridge, T1K 7M1. © **403/380-5050.** www.ramadalethbridge.ca. 119 units. C$95 double; C$225 suite. Rates include continental breakfast & access to all-day coffee, tea & treats. AE, DC, DISC, MC, V. **Amenities:** Restaurant; fitness center; pool w/waterslide. *In room:* TV, hair dryer, high-speed Internet.

Sandman Inn
Another budget staple, the Sandman sits on a busy stretch of Mayor Magrath Drive, just south of downtown. Surrounded by fast-food joints and gas stations, it's hardly picturesque, but it is convenient. Across the street from Nikko Yuko Japanese Garden and a few blocks from Highway 3, it's a good spot from which to access what the town has to offer and then easily move on. Rooms are large, pleasant, and unremarkable; a 24-hour Denny's downstairs offers cheap and easy fare.

421 Mayor Magrath Dr. S., Lethbridge, T1J 3L8 © **403/328-1111.** www.sandmanhotels.com/hotel/ alberta/lethbridge.php. 139 units. C$159 double; $179 suite. AE, DC, DISC, MC, V. **Amenities:** Restaurant; fitness center; pool w/waterslide. *In room:* TV, hair dryer, high-speed Internet.

Where to Dine

Dono Sushi JAPANESE
World War II internment camps gave Lethbridge a relatively high Japanese population, and most agree the new Dono Sushi is the best place for Japanese fare in town. Sushi, sashimi, *maki, donburi*—Dono covers all the bases, and amply so. The C$42 dinner special set for two, with sushi, tempura, chicken *katsu,* beef teriyaki, house salad, and two bowls of rice, could easily feed three.

1009 Mayor Magrath Dr. S. © **403-380-3308.** Main courses C$10–C$15. AE, MC, V. Mon–Sat 11:30am– 2pm, 5–9pm. Closed Sun & holidays.

Ric's Grill NORTH AMERICAN/STEAKHOUSE
The Lethbridge branch of this popular chain is certainly unique in its location, atop what was once a 30,000-gallon water tank. Ric's rises at the axis of Mayor Magrath Drive and Highway 3, just south of downtown, and offers a commanding view of downtown and the river valley beyond. Fare here is uncomplicated, hearty, and good quality: Lots of steaks and ribs, rack of lamb, and a grilled ahi tuna steak with wasabi lime butter. Pastas, sandwiches, and stir-fries round out the extensive menu.

103 Mayor Magrath Dr. S. © **403/317-7427.** www.ricsgrill.com. Main courses C$15–C$38. AE, MC, V. Daily 11am–11pm.

VULCAN

The folks in Vulcan, Alberta, 120km (75 miles) southeast of Calgary on Highway 23, have a motto you've likely heard before: "Live long and prosper." Granted, the town was named well before Leonard Nimoy's pointed-eared alter-ego, Mr. Spock, became a cult legend. But never let it be said that an Albertan would let an opportunity to make a few bucks go to waste. The tourist bureau features a miniature *Starship Enterprise* as a welcoming sign, and the building itself looks lifted from the set of the late-60s *Star Trek* set itself. Every June, Vulcan, a small farming community, celebrates Spock Days/GalaxyFest and brings in whatever tangentially Trek-related celebrity they can get (in 2010, it was Tim Russ, who played Tuvok on *Star Trek: Voyager*).

Fort Museum of the Northwest Mounted Police

Forty-four kilometers (27 miles) west of Lethbridge in Fort Macleod stands what was in 1873 the western headquarters of the Northwest Mounted Police (219 25th St.; ✆ **403/553-4703;** www.nwmpmuseum.com). Named after Colonel Macleod, the redcoat commander who brought peace to Canada's West, the reconstructed Fort Mcleod is now a provincial park and is still patrolled by Mounties in their traditional uniforms.

The fort is filled with fascinating material on the frontier period. Among its treasured documents is the rule sheet of the old Macleod Hotel, written in 1882: "All guests are requested to rise at 6am. This is imperative as the sheets are needed for tablecloths. Assaults on the cook are prohibited. Boarders who get killed will not be allowed to remain in the house." A highlight of visiting the fort in summer is the Mounted Patrol Musical Ride (at 10, 11:30am, 2, and 3:30pm), with eight horseback Mounties performing a choreographed equestrian program to music. Admission is C$8.50 adults, C$7.50 seniors, C$6 children 12 to 17, C$5 children 6 to 11, and free for children 5 and under. Open from July 1 to Labour Day daily 9am to 6pm, and May 4 to June 30 and Labor Day to Thanksgiving daily from 9am to 5pm.

A short distance west of Fort Macleod is the remarkable **Head-Smashed-In Buffalo Jump Historic Site.** See p. 152 for a full review.

On the way west on provincial Route 5 from Lethbridge, you pass through the tiny town of **Cardston,** which is notable for two things: Being the southernmost point of Alberta's **Cowboy Trail** (see p. 150) and having the **Remington Carriage Museum** (Hwy. 2, Cardston; ✆ **403/653-5160;** www.remingtoncarriagemuseum. com). It's special interest, to be sure, but this private museum has been voted the "best indoor attraction in Canada" by Attractions Canada. It's a thorough survey of transportation before the combustion engine ruled the roads. Every manner of carriage is present in the collection, along with a healthy dose of history; interpreters are also passionate and frighteningly knowledgeable about the subject. A guided tour can take anywhere from 45 minutes to 2 hours; opt for the shorter version unless you're a carriage devotee. The museum also has one of the only carriage-restoration shops in North America. A popular attraction for kids is the carriage rides, with real live horses pulling you around the museum grounds. Museum summer hours are 9am to 6pm; for the remainder of the year, 10am to 5pm. Admission is C$9 adults, C$8 seniors, C$5 children 7 to 17, and free for kids 6 and under. Carriage rides are C$4 adults, C$2.50 children 4 to 17; free for kids 3 and under.

Just before you reach Waterton, you pass through the aptly named hamlet of **Mountain View,** from which the Rockies loom in the near distance. Here, you'll find not much more than gas and a general store, but just off Route 5 is the Nelson Ranch, home of **Mountain Meadow Trail Rides** (© **866/653-2413** or 403/653-2413; www.mountainmeadowtrailrides.com). An 809-hectare (2,000-acre) spread tucked into the province's southwest corner, the Nelson family has owned this ranch since 1898. Lately, they've turned to welcoming visitors, their 50 horses leading trail rides through spectacular scenery. Rides range from hourly to week-long. Rest your bones in the hot tub next to their cozy cabins. The Nelsons love sharing their family history and western heritage with visitors, and you'll be glad they do: Bordering Waterton Lakes National Park to the west, the ranch nestles up against the Montana border to the south.

Basic rides range from C$38 to C$125 per person, for adults and youth over 12 years of age. Check the website for more details. True adventurers—and usually those with riding experience—can ride range with the Nelsons on a 3- or 4-day cattle drive as they move their herd of 200.

WATERTON LAKES NATIONAL PARK

Of the province's mountain parks—the others being Banff and Jasper—**Waterton Lakes** (© **403/859-2252;** www.watertonpark.com), tucked in the province's southwest corner, is the most remote and therefore least traveled. Therein lies its charm: While Banff teems with international tourist buses and a surfeit of tacky souvenir shops, Waterton enjoys a quiet remove. Deer lounge on the front lawns of the few homes in Waterton Township, while bighorn sheep wander the main street. The occasional bear or cougar wanders through, too, the town folk say, but they're equally comfortable with—or oblivious to—the human presence. If there was ever a town at one with nature, this is it in that nature hardly seems to notice it at all. There's also a free-roaming herd of buffalo near the park's entrance that seem equally unaffected by the cars that meander into their paddock.

There's not a lot to notice. A handful of hotels, even fewer restaurants, and a store or two in which to indulge your urge to splurge on outdoorsy gear and mountaineering equipment. But then, you don't come to Waterton to go shopping. Waterton—not even that remote, at a mere 2½ hours from Calgary—is one of the province's two true wilderness parks (the other being Wood Buffalo, in the north), and it draws vacationers looking for a taste of that unspoiled world.

They won't be disappointed. Waterton was designated a UNESCO World Heritage site in 1995. Waterton Lake, the icy-blue, glacier-fed body of water at Waterton's heart, connects to **Glacier National Park** across the U.S. border in Montana, and all around it are a network of hiking paths that take adventurers deep into the wilderness. There are 200km (124 miles) of trails in Waterton Lakes National Park, ranging in difficulty from short strolls to steep treks of several days' duration. A

WATERTON-GLACIER INTERNATIONAL
peace PARK

Waterton Lakes and Glacier National Park, in Montana, straddle either side of the U.S.-Canada border and, while distinct, together they make up the Waterton-Glacier International Peace Park. Created in 1932, the intention was to symbolize not only cooperation between the two countries, but also the common priority of preserving the wilderness areas they shared. As of 1979, both parks became biosphere reserves, and both enjoy UNESCO World Heritage Site status, which they received jointly in 1995.

variety of people make use of them, including hikers, horse riders, and bicyclists. One such hike can take you all the way into Glacier Park in the U.S.—to a remote ranger station and, since 9/11, a Customs house, so be sure to bring identification and proof of citizenship. Cougars; grizzly and black bears; and deer, sheep, and mountain goats are all active in the area, and hikers are asked to use caution on the paths.

Waterton has the unique geographical feature of transitioning quickly from prairie in the east to mountains in the west, without the transitional phase of foothills. The sudden shift in landscape is jarring and dramatic, and unlike anywhere else in the Rocky Mountain range. While striking, it also provides the less outdoorsy among us certain comforts—a golf course just inside the park gates, for one. Waterton may be a wilderness park, but it's not without its creature comforts. High tea at the Prince of Wales Hotel is another—a touch of British civility in the shadow of mountains as rugged as any you'll see.

Essentials

There is a fee to enter Waterton, as with most Canadian national parks: C$7.80 adults, C$6.80 seniors, C$3.90 children 6 to 16, free for children 5 an under; C$20 families. Purchase your pass at the Waterton Lakes Visitor Information Centre (✆ 403/859-2252; www.pc.gc.ca/pn-np/ab/waterton/index.aspx).

GETTING THERE

Waterton is not well-served by public transportation lines, so a car is near-essential just to get there. Consider renting at the Calgary airport and driving down. It's your best bet not only to get there, but also to get around.

BY PLANE The closest international airport is Calgary, 2½ hours away, which is served by any number of major airlines: Air Canada, WestJet, United Airlines, Continental, American (see chapter 6 for more information). Lethbridge County Airport is closer (1½ hours), so you can connect from Calgary on **Air Canada's** regional service (✆ 888/247-2262; www.aircanada.ca).

BY CAR Waterton lies at the end of provincial Route 5, which meets provincial Route 6 (aka the Cowboy Trail) at the park gates. At Cardston, Route 5 meets Highway 2, which is the fastest way south from Calgary, 262km (163 miles) away. If coming from Lethbridge, just take Route 5 123km (76 miles) west and south until you reach the park gates.

BY BUS **Greyhound Canada** (☎ 800/661-8747 or 403/218-3000; www. greyhound.ca) runs buses from Calgary to Pincher Creek, about 45 minutes away. Once there, your best bet is to take a taxi, which should cost about C$65. **Crystal Taxi** (☎ 403/627-4262) is a good bet.

GETTING AROUND

It's most handy to have your own car. However, if you don't, you can take advantage of a few shuttle services offered within Waterton. A free hourly shuttle takes you to Red Rock Canyon from **Tamarack Outfitters** (214 Mountain View Rd.; ☎ 403/859-2378). They can also take you to the trail head for the Carthew-Alderson Summit hike at Cameron Lake for C$20 per person; it stops at other trail heads en route. Then, you can hike back into town.

VISITOR INFORMATION

Just across from the Prince of Wales Hotel on the way into Waterton Township is the **Parks Canada office** (☎ 403/859-2252; www.pc.gc.ca/pn-np/ab/waterton/index.aspx). Here, you'll find all the park information you need, from maps of hiking trails to conditions and weather warnings. This is where you can purchase your park pass (see "Essentials," above). They'll also let you know if there's been a bear or cougar sighting recently—handy info if you plan to venture forth on foot.

For more information, contact the **Waterton Chamber of Commerce and Visitor's Association** (P.O. Box 55, Waterton Lakes National Park, AB, T0K 2M0; ☎ 403/859-2224; www.mywaterton.ca).

Exploring the Park

The park's main entrance road leads to Waterton townsite, the only commercial center, with a number of hotels, restaurants, and tourist facilities. Other roads lead to more remote lakes and trail heads. Akamina Parkway leads from the townsite to Cameron Lake, glimmering beneath the crags of the Continental Divide. Red Rock Parkway follows Blackiston Creek past the park's highest peaks to Red Rock Canyon. From here, three trails lead up deep canyons to waterfalls.

The most popular activity in the park is the **Waterton Inter-Nation Shoreline Cruise** (☎ 403/859-2362; www.watertoncruise.com), which leaves from the townsite and sails Upper Waterton Lake past looming peaks to the ranger station at Goat Haunt, Montana, in Glacier Park. The tour boat operates from June through early October. In the high season, from the last weekend of June through August, there are four tour boat departures daily, including a nice evening one at 7pm that promises the best wildlife viewing, with two or three daily in the shoulder seasons (check the website for exact schedules). Only during the high season does the boat land in Montana for a 15-minute stop. The cruise usually takes just over 2 hours, including the stop in Montana. The price is C$38 adults, C$18 children 13 to 17, and C$12 children 4 to 12.

Outdoor Activities

HIKING/BIKING

The parks authority offers a comprehensive description of all hiking trails in the park, including their length, difficulty rating, and maps, on their excellent website (www.pc.gc.ca/waterton). Most walks are day hikes, climaxing at small alpine lakes cradled in spectacular mountain vistas, though longer routes exist. Both hikers and bikers populate the trails. Bikes can be rented from **Pat's**, in town (② **403/859-2266;** www.watertoninfo.com/m/pats.html), for C$34 per day.

Families and those looking for a simple leg-stretcher will like the short Cameron Lake Trail. The lake itself is the attraction—an icy bowl cradled by a mountain bowl to the south, Cameron Lake sits below tons of snow and ice held tight in the bowl in the early spring. Just next door, the short Akimina Lake trail takes no more than half an hour. For a fast workout, head up the Bear's Hump Trail right above the Visitors Center. You'll climb 200m (656 ft.) in just under 3km (1.9 miles) and have a spectacular view of both Waterton lakes and the valleys around them. The most famous day hike is to Crypt Lake. This 17km (11-mile) round-trip hike is strenuous, but well worth it for those in shape—experienced hikers consider it one of the top 10 in Canada. A water taxi from Waterton townsite takes you across the lake to the trail head, where you'll begin a 700m (2,297-ft.) ascent past a towering 170m (558-ft.) waterfall, through a natural tunnel and over a heart-fluttering traverse along the edge of a cliff. At the top, the aquamarine waters of Crypt Lake signal a welcome respite before the return trip down.

BOATING

While you can bring your own canoe, rowboat, or windsurfer to Waterton Lake itself, you won't find rentals here (possibly because of liability; winds come up fast on Upper Waterton, and the icy water can be deadly for neophytes). If you want to paddle around a more gentle lake nearby, **Cameron Lake Boat Rentals** (② **403/859-2396**) offers canoes, rowboats, paddle boats, and kayaks during the summer.

GOLF

The **Waterton Park Golf Course** (P.O. Box 2000, Waterton Lakes National Park, AB, T0K 2M0; ② **403/859-2114**) is one of the oldest in Alberta. An original Stanley Thompson design (he designed the famed courses in Banff and Jasper), hazards include staggering mountain views and errant deer and elk. Greens fees are C$47 for 18 holes.

HORSEBACK RIDING

Alpine Stables (② **403/859-2462**), across from the golf course on the way to the townsite on Entrance Road, offers guided rides on more than 250km (155 miles) of trails.

No Swimming!

The crystal-blue waters of Waterton Lake may look inviting, but be sure to dip your toe in before you dive—chances are it'll come back with icicles on it. Even in high summer, the lake rarely warms up past 60°F (16°C), and even that is only the top 6 inches or so. Just below the surface, the water drops well into the 40s (about 4°–8°C), making a refreshing dip more likely to be a hypothermic experience.

Waterton Is for Families!

From the safe and clean streets of the small townsite, where kids can roam, bike, scooter, or skateboard to their hearts' content, to the well-located campsite and friendly locals, this is a great place for families. Simpler and more compact than Banff or Jasper, Waterton has some great short and flat hikes, many of which lead to lakes.

The town has a playground, wading pool, and beaches, and little traffic. Many of the hotels sleep four or more in a room, and the townsite's campground is not bad either. Throughout the summer, there are family-friendly theater programs at the townsite's Falls Theatre most evenings.

Where to Stay

Like most national parks, the accommodation range is disproportionate to the size of the town. The same is true in Waterton, but in miniature: The permanent population of the park is 279, which swells to over 2,000 in the summer. You'll see a handful of cottages in town, but many more hotels. Still, most are unassuming and modest, and impinge little on the natural surroundings. Remember, in the parks prices for virtually everything are seasonal, with summer rates, starting in June, being the most expensive. Prices tend to drop after Labour Day.

Bayshore Inn   Located right on the waterfront, this sprawling motel-styled hotel now has a long list of amenities (spa, bistro, gift shop) and the best views in town after the Prince of Wales. All the rooms have patios, almost all of them overlooking the lake. Inside, the rooms have some dated fixtures and styles, but they are spacious and comfortable. Renovated bathrooms are a bit hospital-esque, but bright and clean. They also have the only spa in town.

111 Waterton Ave., Waterton Lakes, AB T0K 2M0. © **888/527-9555** or 403/859-2211. www.bayshoreinn. com. 70 units. C$199 non-lakefront double; C$229 lakefront double; C$259 suite. AE, DC, DISC, MC, V. Closed mid-Oct to Apr. **Amenities:** 3 restaurants; lounge; spa. *In room:* A/C, TV, hair dryer.

Crandell Mountain Lodge   A Tudor-like inn a few blocks from the lake, this lodge has rooms in all sorts of configurations. The country decor is consistent throughout, but there's charm in the old country style. Some deluxe rooms have tubs, but most have only stand-up showers in tight bathrooms. Most rooms have fireplaces. The doubles with two queen beds are the most modern. The three-room suite with one bathroom and full kitchen sleeps up to six. Ask for a quieter top-floor room.

102 Mountview Rd., Waterton Park, AB T0K 2M0. © **866/859-2288** or 403/859-2288. www.crandell mountainlodge.com. 17 units. C$140–C$170 double; from C$195 suites. AE, DC, DISC, MC, V. **Amenities:** Concierge. *In room:* TV, minibar, no phone.

Prince of Wales Hotel   Situated on a hillock that rises above the north end of Waterton Lake, the Prince, a National Historic Site built in 1927, is surely one of the most dramatically placed hotels in the world. From the atrium-style lobby, windows stretch from the floor to several stories above, giving visitors the entire vista to drink in. As a hotel, the Prince just barely passes muster and is much in need of a makeover. Rooms are a little weary, with a strange layout that will remind you of a cruise ship (sinks across from the bed, small windows). The beds all have new soft-top mattresses, so you'll likely get a good night's sleep. If you have mobility issues, be warned, there are a lot of stairs to climb and only one elevator that works only some of the time. But then there's that view . . . which is what you're paying for. It's not a bad investment when in one of the most beautiful places on Earth. The Prince serves high tea on Royal Doulton china every day at 2pm in the lobby. Another investment, at C$29 per person, but well worth it.

Waterton Lakes National Park, Waterton, AB T0K 2M0. © **403/236-3400.** www.princeofwales waterton.com. 86 units. June 27 to Sept 21 from C$234 double; C$799 suite. AE, DC, DISC, MC, V. Closed mid-Sept to early June. **Amenities:** Restaurant; lounge; Wi-Fi. *In room:* Minibar (in some rooms).

Waterton Lakes Resort   A new-ish property located right in the middle of town, the resort boasts many of the creature comforts more rustic accommodations in town lack: a fitness center, pool, and whirlpool. It models itself after a chalet, with 11 different buildings in the complex. What it lacks in character it makes up for in comfort: accommodations are spacious, many have kitchens, and particular atten-tion has been paid to view-lines to the surrounding mountains. A good bet for those seeking the comforts of home. It's one of the few hotels open year-round.

101 Clematis Ave., Waterton Lakes National Park, AB T0K 2M0. © **888/985-6343** or 403/859-2150. www.watertonlakeslodge.com. 80 units. May to June 15 and Sept 5 to Oct 15 C$134 double, C$174 suite; June 16 to Sept 4 C$185 double, C$245 suite. AE, MC, V. **Amenities:** Restaurant; fitness center; pool w/ waterslide. *In room:* TV, hair dryer, high-speed Internet.

CAMPING

There are three campgrounds in Waterton operated by Parks Canada (www.pc.gc. ca/pn-np/ab/waterton/activ/activ3_e.asp), all with different fees and amenities. Some have full hook-up service; others are more for those roughing it. Reserva-tions are recommended, especially in high season. Fire permits, at C$8.80 per day, are in addition to camp site fees, which are in addition to regular park admittance fees.

The **Townsite Campground** (© **403/859-5133**) is open mid-April to mid-October and has 238 sites, 95 of which are fully serviced. The best spot for large RVs, it has hot showers, flush toilets, food storage, and kitchen shelters. Campsites range from C$38 for full hookup to C$23 for unserviced walk-in sites. You can reserve any of them (© **877/737-3783;** www.pccamping.ca); you must book ahead of time!

Crandell Campground (© **403/859-5133**) is open mid-May to early Septem-ber, and the 129 unserviced sites are first-come, first-served—no reservations. The campground sits along the Red Rock Parkway in Blakiston Valley in a mountain for-est. Flush toilets, piped water, kitchen shelters, some fire rings and firewood, food storage, recycling bins, and a dump station are all available. Crandell Lake is a short 2km (1¼-mile) hike from the campground. Fees are C$22 per night. In 2010, Parks Canada added five traditional tipis for campers, sleeping six each. The rate is C$55 per night, plus a C$11 reservation fee.

Belly River Campground (© **403/859-5133**) is open mid-May to mid-September, and the parks service describes it as "primitive." Campsites are available only on a first-come, first-served basis. The site, on Chief Mountain Highway, is

26km (16 miles) from Waterton townsite. It has 24 unserviced sites with well water, flush and dry privies, food storage, kitchen shelters, fire rings, and firewood. Set in an aspen forest next to the Belly River, it's a secluded site with a good degree of privacy. Foxes, bear, and deer often wander through. Fees are C$16 per night.

Where to Dine

Dining in Waterton is fairly basic, with a predictable amount of tourist fare and pub grub. But from counter service to high end, there are some gems.

Bayshore Lakeside Chophouse ★★ CANADIAN   The only restaurant in Waterton that's directly on the lake, the view alone is worth a visit. The dining room has seen some hard use, but the food's still a solid bet. The menu is centered on Alberta beef (tenderloin, New York strip loin, boneless rib eye) and local game. There are also a few fish dishes, such as grilled salmon with dill and grilled tilapia with mango. This is the most upscale place in a low-key town. The same building also contains the Glacier Café (same ✆), a more casual spot serving up soup, salads, sandwiches and burgers

111 Waterton Ave. ✆ **403/859-2211.** Main courses C$20–C$36; breakfast buffet C$16. AE, DISC, MC, V. Apr to Oct 15 daily 7am–10pm. Closed Oct 16 to Mar.

Bel Lago Ristorante ★ ITALIAN   Waterton's only committed Italian restaurant, the dining experience is taken as seriously here as anywhere in town. The Italian-trained chef offers a 10-course antipasti menu based on what is fresh. Fresh salads and cheeses, homemade pastas, and a nice selection of *secondi*—lamb *osso buco* or salmon in a lemon basil sauce, for example—offer respite from the rusticity, if you need it. There are daily panini specials for lunch, including one with prosciutto, cherry tomatoes, smoked cheese, and onion. Their patio is also one of the most peaceful places in town, a bit more adult-friendly than the other places so popular with families.

110 Waterton Ave. ✆ **403/859-2213.** Main courses C$15–C$32. MC, V. Daily 11:30am–10pm.

Pearl's Café CAFE   Pick up a quick breakfast or a hiker's lunch to go at this classic cafe in the heart of town. For breakfast, there's a famous French toast—cinnamon-scented, with vanilla sour cream sauce and toasted pecans. They make bagged lunches, complete with Pearl's rollups (Greek chicken, fiesta club, or sundried tomato chicken with gorgonzola) and homemade energy bars. The dinner menu is the same as the lunch menu, light and healthy. After hiking, drop in for a hot chocolate and scone. There's live music most Sunday evenings during the summer.

305 Windflower Ave. ✆ **403/859-2498.** Main courses C$8–C$15. AE, MC, V. Daily 7am–7pm.

The Waterton Bagel and Coffee Company BAKERY   A cute, congenial bagel joint just off the main strip, next to the movie theater, that serves up fresh, tasty fare like prosciutto, arugula, smoked chicken, and—a breakfast favorite—steamed eggs and chive with cheddar on a variety of bagels (which are generally not made in-house). At C$5 a bagel, it's also a deal and great hiking fuel to start your day. Also the best espresso in town.

309 Windflower Ave. ✆ **403/859-2466.** Bagels from C$5. No credit cards. Daily 7am–8pm.

KANANASKIS COUNTRY & THE COWBOY TRAIL

Kananaskis Country is the name given to a cluster of Alberta provincial parks on the Rocky Mountains' eastern slope, southeast of Banff National Park, including Peter Lougheed Provincial Park, Spray Valley Provincial Park, and Elbow-Sheep Wildland Provincial Park. Together, they make up 4,250 sq. km (1,641 sq. miles) of protected Rocky Mountain wilderness.

Once considered only a gateway region to more glamorous Banff, Kananaskis has come into its own and is now a recreation destination on par with more famous brand-name resorts in the Rockies in terms of offerings, and it's quieter in terms of crowds. Kananaskis—or "K-Country," as it's called by locals—has an air of the untouched about it, especially compared to the well-trodden streets and highly maintained trails of Banff. This can be both a good and bad thing because, while it feels much less busy and picked over, Kananaskis lacks some of the amenities that a more veteran tourist region like Banff possesses. Still, it's equally spectacular in terms of its surroundings, and that's why you're here.

Wildlife abounds here, from deer and moose to bighorn sheep, mountain goats, black bears, and grizzlies.

Located just west of K-Country and just outside the eastern boundary of Banff National Park, the town of Canmore is an old mining village that's grown into a resort town a la Whistler or Aspen, with real estate developments and golf courses in a dramatic location beneath the soaring peaks of Three Sisters Mountain. Only 20 minutes from Banff, the scenery here is magnificent and the accommodations generally much less expensive and less busy than those in Banff. Dining and shopping are equal to the offerings in Banff, and Canmore has a more authentic small-town feel than tourist-trodden Banff.

Weather is usually warmer and sunnier here than in Banff, which is conducive to great golf: Stewart Creek and SilverTip at Canmore, along with the championship course at Kananaskis Village, are among the best in North America.

When the 1988 Olympics were held in Calgary, Parks Canada wouldn't allow the alpine ski events to be held inside the Banff National Park. Nakiska, in Kananaskis, became the venue instead, vaulting this ski area to international prominence.

Also, because Kananaskis Country isn't governed by national-park restrictions, there's better road access to out-of-the-way lakeside campgrounds and trail heads, which makes this a more convenient destination for family getaways (there are more than 3,000 campsites in the area!). This provincial parkland also allows "mixed use," including some traditional (though heavily regulated) ranching. Some of the best guest ranches in Alberta operate here.

The main road through Kananaskis Country is Highway 40, which cuts south from Highway 1 at the gateway to the Rockies and follows the Kananaskis River. Kananaskis Village—a small collection of resort hotels, a golf course, and shops—is the center of activities in Kananaskis Country, with Canmore serving as the main hub, about 30 minutes from the village. Highway 40 eventually climbs up to 2,206m (7,238 ft.) at Highwood Pass, the highest pass in Alberta, before looping around to meet Highway 22 south of Calgary. Highway 40 is open only in summer, from mid-June to November, so be sure to check closures before you attempt it.

CANMORE & KANANASKIS

You could almost drive right past Canmore, distracted by the stunning scenery high above both sides of the Trans-Canada Highway. Don't make that mistake. A few blocks from the highway (and a few blocks from the "hotel run" along Bow Valley Trail, which runs parallel to Hwy. 1) is one of the most charming, active, artistic, and upscale little mountain towns anywhere. You won't be the first to stop here, though. The population of Canmore is booming, including a large percentage of weekenders and vacation-home owners who have bought up condos and townhouses like hot cakes. Today, there are 12,000 folks who call this place home. Canmore is very strategically located, just kilometers from the east gate of Banff National Park and a little less than an hour from Calgary.

For all the booming, Canmore's old town center is still quite pleasant to explore. Canmore has actually been around since the 1880s, when it was the headquarters for the coal mines that fueled the Canadian Pacific Railroad's transcontinental trains as they climbed up over the Rockies. The old downtown area is next to the Bow River and is reached by turning onto Main Street off Railway Avenue. Downtown is undeveloped and quiet by Banff standards, but three pleasant, pedestrian-friendly blocks are lined with shops, brewpubs, cafes, galleries, restaurants, and boutiques.

The Canmore Geoscience Museum (902b 7th Ave., inside the Civic Centre; ℂ **403/678-2462;** www.cmags.org), tells the story of the community from its days as a coal-mining camp to its pinnacle as Olympic host.

Essentials

GETTING THERE

Canmore is an hour west of Calgary on the Trans-Canada Highway, just east of the Banff National Park gates, and is served by **Greyhound Canada** (© **800/661-8747** or 403/260-0877; www.greyhound.ca) and **Brewster** (© **403/762-6767;** www.brewster.ca) buses. **Banff Airporter** (© **888/449-2901** or 403/762-3330; www.banffairporter.com) has private shuttles to Canmore from the Calgary Airport for C$105 return. Kananaskis Village, which is reached directly by car by exiting onto Highway 40 south from the Trans-Canada Highway (about 15 minutes east of Canmore), can be reached via numerous tour operators from Canmore, as well.

VISITOR INFORMATION

For information on Kananaskis and Canmore, contact **Kananaskis Country** (© **866/432-4322;** www.kananaskisvalley.com) or the **Barrier Lake Visitor Information Centre** (© **403/673-3985**). In Canmore, your best bet is the very good **Canmore Tourism Office** (907A 7th Ave.; © **403/678-1295;** www.tourism canmore.com). The province-wide **Travel Alberta Visitor Information Centre,** at the Bow Valley Trail exit off Highway 1 (© **403/678-5277**; www.travel alberta.com), also has lots of information on Canmore.

Where to Stay

KANANASKIS VILLAGE

The lodgings in Kananaskis Village were built for the Olympics, and in fact, Kananaskis was the site of the G8 Summit in 2002, so you may well stay in a room once graced by a world leader. There's no more than a stone's throw between the hotels, and to a high degree, public facilities are shared among all the hotels.

Delta Lodge at Kananaskis This resort hotel, built for the Olympics and more recently the site of a G8 Summit in 2002, consists of two separate buildings that face each other across a pond at the center of Kananaskis Village. The Lodge includes a shopping arcade and a number of drinking and dining choices. Its guest rooms are large and well furnished; many have balconies, and some have fireplaces. The hotel hosts many conferences and has a bit of an impersonal, corporate feel, as well as a slightly dated look. The Signature Club service rooms are more private and include breakfast. The Summit Spa and Fitness Centre provides health and beauty treatments for both men and women. Golf courses, bike paths, and hiking trails are right at your doorstep.

1 Centennial Dr., Kananaskis Village, AB T0L 2H0. © **866/432-4322** or 403/591-7711. www.deltalodgeat kananaskis.ca. 412 units. C$249–C$319 double. Ski/golf package rates & discounts available. AE, DC, MC, V. Self-parking C$11; valet parking C$15. **Amenities:** 4 restaurants; bar; babysitting; bike rental; concierge; concierge-level rooms; golf courses nearby; health club; whirlpool; 2 pools (saltwater & indoor); room service (7am–1am); spa; tennis courts. *In room:* A/C (in Signature Club), TV/VCR w/pay movies, fridge, hair dryer, Internet, minibar.

Kananaskis Wilderness Hostel This is a great place for a recreation-loving traveler on a budget. The hostel is located at the Nakiska Ski Area, within walking distance of Kananaskis Village, and is close to 60 mountain biking, hiking, and cross-country ski trails. Area outfitters offer special discounts to hostel guests. The hostel has a common room with a fireplace and four private family rooms. Families are welcome.

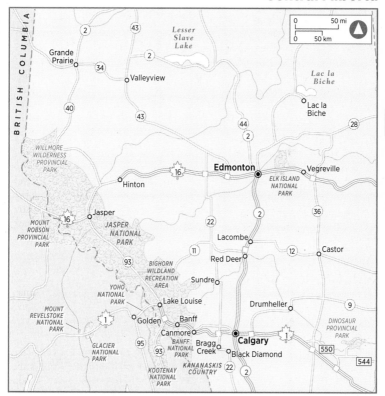

1 Ribbon Creek Rd., at Nakiska Ski Area. ☎ **866/762-4122** or 403/670-7580 for reservations, or 403/591-7333 for the hostel. www.hihostels.ca. 38 beds. C$23 (members), C$27 (nonmembers) bed; C$60 (members), C$68 (nonmembers) private room. MC, V. Free parking. *In room:* No phone.

Sundance Lodges and Camp ☺   Part wilderness campground, part Tipi-lodge, this complex in Kananaskis is family-friendly and a great way to immerse yourself in the outdoors without giving up simple luxuries like hot water. Painted canvas tipis sleep four and have simple wooden-framed beds and a small kerosene heater; "trapper's tents" are more rustic but still cozy. Both have private picnic areas and fire pits. There's also laundry, hot showers, a small store, and room for RVs and personal tents. Best of all, the Kananaskis River is just steps away.

Hwy. 40 (22km/14 miles south of the Trans-Canada Hwy. in Kananaskis); Kananaskis Village, AB T0L 2H0. ☎ **403/591-7122.** www.sundancelodges.com. 60 units (18 trapper's tents, 12 tipis & 30 camp-sites). Trapper's tent C$79; tipi C$57–C$77; unserviced campsite C$28. Closed Sept 18 to May 23. **Amenities:** Camping equipment rental.

CANMORE

About half of the hotel development in Canmore dates from the 1988 Olympics, and the rest dates from—oh, last week or so. That said, Canmore's steam-rolling growth slowed somewhat in the last couple of years; many buildings originally set up as private condominiums have been shifted to vacation rentals and hotel-type lodging options.

To a large degree, this is due to the restrictions on development within the national parks to the west: Hoteliers, outfitters, developers, larger stores, and other businesses designed to serve the needs of park visitors find Canmore, right on the park boundary, a much easier place to locate than Banff. As a result, Canmore is now a destination in its own right.

The main reason to stay in Canmore is the price of hotel rooms. Rates here are between a half and a third lower than in Banff, and the small downtown area is blossoming with interesting shops and good restaurants. Canmore hotels can represent especially good deals on discount hotel websites.

For a complete list of B&Bs, contact the **Canmore-Bow Valley B&B Association** (P.O. Box 8005, Canmore, AB T1W 2T8; www.bbcanmore.com).

Blackstone Mountain Lodge Spend a night or two here and pretend you have your own home in beautiful Canmore. Rooms are all suite-style condominiums. The decor is urban chic, but the views are all natural. Units have one or two bedrooms; all have at least two spa-inspired bathrooms, patios with barbecues, kitchens with granite countertops, flat-screen TVs, and fireplaces. It's about a 15-minute walk from downtown, so a car will be necessary.

Riding Herd at a Guest Ranch

Brewster's Kananaskis Guest Ranch, 30 minutes east of Banff on Highway 1 (P.O. Box 340, Exshaw, AB, T0L 0C0; ✆ 800/691-5085 or 403/673-3737; www.kananaskisguestranch.com), the original family homestead from the 1880s, was transformed into a guest ranch in 1923. The 33 fully modern guest rooms, in chalets and cabins, have full bathrooms. Doubles are C$114 to C$144 per person, with breakfast and dinner included. Activities include horseback riding, rafting, canoeing, hiking, golfing, and more.

Long-distance backcountry horseback rides are a specialty—a 2-day trip costs around C$450—and backcountry campsites have newly constructed sleeping cabins.

Another old-time guest ranch with a long pedigree, **Rafter Six Ranch Resort**

(P.O. Box 100, Exshaw, AB, T0L 0C0; ✆ 888/26-RANCH [888/267-2624] or 403/673-3622; www.raftersix.com), is located in a meadow right on the banks of the Kananaskis River. This full-service resort is open year-round and accommodates guests in an especially inviting old log lodge (with restaurant, barbecue deck, and lounge), various sizes of log cabins, and large chalets that sleep up to six and have full kitchens. All units have private bathrooms. Lodge rooms are C$179 for standard and C$215 for superior, and double cabins and chalets go for C$253 to C$449, including all meals and activities. Casual horseback and longer pack rides are offered, as well as raft and canoe trips. Seasonal special events might include rodeos, country dances, and hay or sleigh rides.

170 Kananaskis Way, Canmore, AB T1W 2A8. © **888/830-8883** or 403/609-8098. Fax 403/679-7098. www.blackstonecanmore.ca. 123 units. From C$240 one-bedroom; from C$300 two-bedroom; June 26 to Sept 7 weekly rates C$1,200 one-bedroom, C$1,500 two-bedroom. AE, DC, DISC, MC, V. Free parking. **Amenities:** Babysitting; fitness center; hot tub. *In room:* Kitchen, free Wi-Fi.

Chateau Canmore ★

You can't miss this enormous red-roofed complex along the hotel strip. Like a series of 10 four-story conjoined chalets, the all-suite Chateau Canmore offers some of the largest rooms in the area. The accommodations are very nicely decorated in a comfortable rustic style, while the lobby and common rooms look like they belong in a log-style lodge. Each standard suite has a fireplace and separate bedroom, while the deluxe one- or two-bedroom suites add a living room and dining area. Just like home, but with a better view. The best rates are available on their website.

1718 Bow Valley Trail, Canmore, AB T1W 2X3. © **800/261-8551** or 403/678-6699. Fax 403/678-6954. www.chateaucanmore.com. 120 units. From C$124 standard suite; from C$149 deluxe suite. AE, DC, DISC, MC, V. Free parking. **Amenities:** Dining room; lounge; health club; indoor pool; limited room service; spa. *In room:* AC, TV, fridge, hair dryer, Wi-Fi.

Grande Rockies Resort

The newest and largest place in town was opened in the summer of 2010 by the luxury hotel chain Metropolitan Hotels. The design is thoroughly modern and user-friendly. You can squeeze a whole crowd into a single unit. Rooms are all suites, with one or two bedrooms (some with additional pull-out couches), and they're all equipped with full kitchens and stream showers. They're mostly decorated in creams with brown linen fabrics and contemporary Western art. Other luxury bonuses include barbecues, flat-screen TVs with Blu-Ray players, and digital safes. There's also a family-friendly indoor pool area. It's right on the highway, so ask for a south-facing unit.

901 Mountain St., Canmore, AB T1W 0C9. © **877/223-3398** or 403/678-8880. www.granderockies. com. 150 units. From C$215 one-bedroom; from C$295 two-bedroom. AE, DC, MC, V. Free parking. **Amenities:** Restaurant; lounge; concierge; fitness center; hot tub; pool; Wi-Fi. *In room:* A/C, TV w/ Blu-Ray player, hair dryer, kitchen.

Mount Engadine Lodge ★★★

While not in Canmore proper, this rustic lodge—set in pristine wilderness along the Spray Lakes Parkway in Kananaskis Country, where the pavement turns to gravel—is a great candidate for a true mountain getaway. It takes about half an hour to reach the lodge, but it's worth the trip. Small and cozy, the lodge is perched at 1,844m (6,050 ft.) above sea level, surrounded by the majesty of the Rockies. Just below the bluff where it sits is Moose Meadows—so named for the many moose that wander through, among countless other wildlife, as you sip wine on the deck—an expanse of mountain meadow wetland. The sense here is of a place unstuck in time, the mountains as they were before the ranchers, settlers, or tour buses ever came close. Of course, when you go back inside and enjoy home-cooked meals with some of the best fresh, local ingredients, it's hardly roughing it. Simply one of the best options to be found in the Rockies.

South of Canmore, on the Spray Lakes Pkwy., Rte. 742; P.O. Box 40025, Canmore, AB T1W 3H9. © **403/678-4080.** www.mountengadine.com. 8 units. From C$390 double. Rates include breakfast and dinner. Children 6–12 C$100; children under 5 stay free in parent's room. AE, MC, V. **Amenities:** Restaurant. *In room:* No phone.

Highway 40 isn't open half the year, and even the half that it is (between June and Nov) still sees a fair complement of snow. That's because Highway 40 runs through the Highwood Pass, the highest-elevation roadway in Alberta at 2,206m (7,238 ft.). This is spectacular, rugged territory, the truest backcountry you can reach by road—made all the more so because of its half-year closure. Wildlife abounds here, so keep your eyes peeled—if you can unglue them from the jaw-dropping scenery that surrounds you, that is.

Paintbox Lodge ★ One of the few lodgings in Canmore's charming town center, the Paintbox Lodge is a cozy, small, and luxurious boutique inn that mingles rustic mountain charm and refined sophistication. The lodge offers seven guest rooms in the main building and a two-bedroom suite with a full kitchen in a separate lodge. Run by two former Olympians, the service is relaxed and friendly. Best of all, you'll be just steps from the Bow River and the lively cafes and shops of Canmore.

629 10th St., Canmore, AB T1W 2A2. ℂ **888/678-6100** or 403/609-0482. Fax 403/609-0481. www. paintboxlodge.com. 8 units. C$179–C$229 double. Rates include full breakfast. MC, V. Free parking. *In room:* TV w/movie channels, CD player, fridge, minibar, Wi-Fi.

CAMPING

Kananaskis is a major camping destination for families, and the choice of campgrounds is wide. Of the major parks that comprise Kananaskis, Peter Lougheed Provincial Park has six campgrounds, Kananaskis Valley has one, Spray Valley Provincial Park has two, Highwood/Cataract Creek (farther south, near Mountain View) has five, Elbow River Valley has six, and Sheep River Valley has seven.

There's a concentration of campgrounds at Upper and Lower Kananaskis Lakes in Peter Lougheed Park, some 32km (20 miles) south of Kananaskis Village. A few campgrounds are scattered nearer to Kananaskis Village, around Barrier Lake and Ribbon Creek. For the more intrepid wilderness seekers, the Lougheed Park campgrounds feel significantly more remote, surrounded by peaks and centered on a long, gorgeous mountain lake; closer to the village, campgrounds feel more civilized—and, therefore, usually are more crowded.

For a full-service campground with RV hook-ups, go to **Mount Kidd RV Park** (ℂ **403/591-7700;** www.mountkiddrv.com), just south of the Kananaskis golf course.

For comprehensive listings of all campgrounds and their specific amenities, go to www.kananaskiscountrycampgrounds.com.

Where to Dine

Communitea Café ★★ CAFE/VEGETARIAN It's all about healthy choice at this funky corner cafe. Choose from more than 80 blends of tea; build your own lunch bowl (rice, noodles or salad; soy-ginger, curry, or peanut satay). Breakfast panini and great nibbles, like *edamame* and salad rolls, make it a good choice throughout the day. Regular evening concerts are almost always surprisingly pleasant. Don't miss the lattes either; they're probably the best in town.

#117-1001 6th Ave. (at the corner of 10th St.). © **403/678-6818.** www.thecommunitea.com. Main courses C$8–C$12. AE, MC, V. Mon–Sat 9am–5pm; Sun 10am–5pm.

Crazyweed Kitchen ★ FUSION   You can't talk about food in Alberta without mentioning the ground-breaking, ever-innovative Crazyweed in Canmore. For a decade, foodies have flocked here for the cool vibe, hip wine list, and general enthusiasm for great food. They'll take a predictable Alberta rib-eye and add a chile crust. Short ribs are served with curry, lemongrass, and peanuts. A more affordable option is a flatbread pizza; try the pesto, pear, stilton, and spinach pie. Both the menu and the service are unpredictable and provocative, meaning there are occasional errors and misses. But, generally, it's worth the risk.

1600 Railway Ave. © **403/609-2530.** www.crazyweed.ca. Main courses C$24–C$38. AE, MC, V. Mon–Fri 11:30am–3pm, Sat & Sun 10:30am–3pm; daily 5–10pm.

The Drake Inn and Pub ★ GASTRO PUB   As the slogan goes, "If it's happening in Canmore, it's happening at the Drake." Definitely the most active pub in town, there's also hearty meals to be had here. The food is reasonable, simple, and very good, and the service friendly and familiar. Stick with staples like homemade burgers (which are excellent and can be beef or bison) and fish and chips. The Drake also has a rather stunning patio with views of the Three Sisters Mountain. The Drake also offers clean, bright, motel-style accommodations for reasonable rates, from C$129 for a basic double.

909 Railway Ave. © **403/678-5131.** www.thedrakeinn.com. Main courses C$12–C$19. AE, MC, V. Mon–Fri 11am–11pm; Sat & Sun 10am–12am.

Harvest ★ 🎁 CAFE   Just off Main Street in downtown Canmore is one of the Bow Valley's best-kept secrets. Cafeteria-style counter service yields fresh, flavorful, and very reasonable foods like quiches, croque-monsieurs and mesdames, and soups. The sandwiches are a big draw, with fillings like curried chicken and pineapple, and *capicolli* ham with artichoke. The shady front patio, off the main drag, is a peaceful place to survey the gorgeous scenery. On Sunday mornings, locals line up for cinnamon buns.

718 10th St. © **403/678-3747.** Sandwiches C$7–C$9. No credit cards. Mon–Fri 8am–4pm; Sun 10am–3pm. Closed Saturdays.

Iron Goat Pub and Grill PUB   If a view is your priority, you can't do better than this new pub-style restaurant in the Canmore suburb of Cougar Creek. The cathedral ceilings and massive patio do their best to showcase the peaks around town; on a summer afternoon, it's the best patio in town. The food inside is, well, so-so, with usual suspects like pizza, nachos, wings, and fajitas. A better bet would be the Alberta baby back half rack of ribs with apple-butter barbecue sauce or a maple-glazed venison strip. There's also a kids menu.

703 Benchlands Trail. © **403/609-0222.** www.irongoat.ca. Main courses C$13–C$32. AE, MC, V. Mon–Sat 11am–11pm; Sun 9am–11pm.

Mountain Mercato ★ ITALIAN/CAFE   This little gem of a cafe on Main Street will transport you from the Rockies to a chic corner of Europe. It's part gourmet shop, chock full of upscale and imported ingredients, and part snack bar. The food is mostly to go, but you can opt to stay in (or eat out on the street-side patio) and enjoy their specialty, grilled panini sandwiches. The espresso is pricey but superb.

Canmore and Kananaskis haven't always been tourist Meccas. In fact, as the cluster of hotels on Railway Avenue sometimes painfully reminds visitors, Canmore was a railway town—the hotels back onto the still-active tracks—before it was anything like a holiday destination. While Banff was a tourist destination from the get-go, Canmore, founded in 1884, was a blue-collar coal-mining town. At the turn of the 20th century, Canmore was part of Banff National Park and remained so until the 1930 National Park Act deemed mining inappropriate for a national park. Rather than removing the mine, they moved the park boundary. Bankhead, a coal-mining town near Banff at the base of Cascade Mountain, was shut down, and many of its houses were moved to Banff and Canmore.

102-817 Main St. ℂ **403/609-6631.** www.mountainmercato.com. Sandwiches & salads C$7–C$10. AE, MC, V. Daily 11am–6pm.

The Trough ★★ CONTEMPORARY   Don't let the name fool you: This is no feedbag joint. Chosen as Canada's seventh-best restaurant by *enRoute* magazine in 2007, the Trough is a gastronome's delight. At only 10 tables, it's exceptionally intimate, and the menu offers powerful and intense flavors in inventive choices, from a Lebanese rack of lamb and jerk-spiced back ribs to wild BC halibut with orange coconut curry. The Trough is especially suited to the oenophile, as the sommelier goes out of his way to find small and limited releases, especially from the Canadian and American West.

725B 9th St. ℂ **403/678-2820.** www.thetrough.ca. Reservations recommended. Main courses C$22–C$38. AE, MC, V. Wed–Sun 5:30–11pm.

The Wood Steakhouse & Lounge CONTEMPORARY   Set in the old Sherwood family homestead, the Wood is well-named: The expansive log-cabin environs set the stage for a dining experience that's at once rustic and urbane, with vaulted log ceilings, log walls, and sleek black leather seating throughout. This is a steakhouse, pure and simple, with simple preparations of grilled AAA Alberta beef being the dominant feature of the menu. But there are plenty of non-beef options, as well, such as pork chops with charred jalapeno relish and a seared ahi tuna with a crust of three peppers and acacia honey. During hockey season, come to the bar for a pint and to catch the game. During summer, the expansive and sunny patio is the place to people-watch in Canmore.

838 Main St. ℂ **403/678-3404.** www.thewood.ca. Reservations recommended. Main courses C$18–C$42. AE, MC, V. Daily 7:30am–11pm.

Exploring Canmore & Kananaskis

It's the excellent access to outdoor activities that makes Canmore and Kananaskis Country such a prime destination. But don't discount Canmore's casual sophistication in town, either. A handful of stylish boutiques like **Gingerella** (106–721 Main St.; ℂ **403/609-3144**) carry brand names like Fly London, Kenneth Cole, and

John Fluevog, as well as handmade Canadian jewelry; **Indigo Bay** (100–817 Main St.; ☏ **403/678-8808**) has youthful, upbeat, and fun women's clothing from unique international designers. There's a wealth of galleries, most of them in the 3-block stretch of Main Street, and most of them dedicated to images of the mountains that loom above; for more eclectic interests and contemporary works, check out the **Elevation Gallery** (100–729 Main St.; ☏ **403/609-3324**).

However, the big reason to be in Canmore is to enjoy the glorious outdoors in all its myriad forms. For the outdoors-minded, from its offices in Kananaskis Village and in Canmore (at 999 Bow Valley Trail), **Inside Out Experience Tours** (☏ **877/999-7238;** www.insideoutexperience.com) represents most local outfitters. You'll find bike trips, trail rides, rafting, hiking, and sightseeing tours on offer. **Canadian Rockies Adventure Centre** (701 Bow Valley Trail; ☏ **877/226-7625** or 403/678-6535; www.canadianrockies.ca) also will help you book anything and everything.

CROSS-COUNTRY SKIING & MOUNTAIN BIKING

The **Canmore Nordic Centre Provincial Park,** just south of town off Spray Lakes Road (1988 Olympic Way, Canmore; ☏ **403/678-2400;** http://tpr.alberta.ca/parks/kananaskis/parks_canmore.asp), was developed for the Olympics' cross-country skiing competition, though the facility is now open year-round. In winter, the center offers 70km (43 miles) of scenic cross-country trails, plus the on-site **Trail Sports** shop (☏ **403/678-6764**) for rentals, repairs, and sales. In summer, hikers and mountain bikers take over the trails, and Trail Sports offers bike rentals, skill-building courses, and guided rides.

DOWNHILL SKIING

Kananaskis gained worldwide attention when it hosted the alpine ski events for the Winter Olympics in 1988, and skiing remains a primary attraction in the area. At **Nakiska** (☏ **800/258-7669** or 403/591-7777; www.skinakiska.com), skiers can follow in the tracks of past Winter Olympians. Very family-friendly, it offers terrain for every age and ability, and is open from early December to mid-April. Adult lift tickets cost C$52.

HA LING peak

Ha Ling, a cook for the Canadian Pacific Railway, took on a bet: Some put C$50 on the chance that he couldn't climb a local mountain, plant a red flag on the summit, and come back down in less than 10 hours. According to the *Medicine Hat News* of October 24, 1896, Ha Ling had started his climb at 7am one day the previous week and was back in time for lunch. Unfortunately, nobody believed him. So he did it again. Taking a crowd of doubters with him as witnesses, he scrambled up the mountainside and planted a second, larger red flag beside the first. Locally, the peak became known as Chinaman's Peak, in his honor. In 1997, as a nod to both the famous climber and its less-than-politically-correct colloquial moniker, the peak was renamed for its famous climber. Ha Ling Peak is now marked with a plaque at a park across from the Canmore Nordic Centre on the Spray Lakes Parkway, just south of Canmore's main street. You can still climb Ha Ling Peak via a relatively easy path on its south side.

HIKING, CAVING, DOG-SLEDDING, HELICOPTERS & MORE

Canmore is surrounded by mountains and, being on the doorstep of Kananaskis Country, it's an ideal base from which to explore the many, many hiking trails to be found here. You can set out for days or just a few hours, depending on your level of ambition. **Canadian Rockies Adventure Centre** (701 Bow Valley Trail; ✆ **877/226-7625** or 403/678-6535; www.canadianrockies.ca) or **Inside Out Experience** (✆ **888/999-7238;** www.insideoutexperience.com) can help set you on your way, with maps and/or guides, as you prefer; so can **Canmore's Tourism Office** (907 7th Ave., Canmore; ✆ **403/678-1295;** www.tourismcanmore.com).

A number of tour operators are happy to take you on interpretive hikes in the area. **Mahikan Trails** (✆ **403/609-2489;** www.mahikan.ca) leads half- and full-day hikes into the mountains all year long, through significant Aboriginal sites with a mind to teaching guests about the natural history of the area and its first peoples.

Yamnuska Mountain Adventures (✆ **403/678-4164;** www.canadianrockies hiking.com) leads cross-country skiing, mountaineering, and hiking programs in Kananaskis Country, as well as beginner classes for rock and ice climbing. All guides and instructors are certified with the Association of Canadian Mountain Guides.

If you pass through Canmore in winter, you could contact **Snowy Owl Sled Dog Tours** (✆ **403/678-4369;** www.snowyowltours.com) and head out with a pack of huskies to mush across the frozen Spray Lakes. A 2-hour tour starts at C$149 per person.

If you'd like to see the beautiful scenery of the Canadian Rockies from the air, contact **Alpine Helicopters** (✆ **403/678-4802;** www.alpinehelicopter.com), which operates out of Canmore. A 12-minute flight over the Rockies start at C$109 per person, with a minimum of three passengers. For a 30-minute flight, the price is C$249 per person. To add some activity to your flight, contact **Martha's Heli Hikes** (✆ **403/609-0824**). An unforgettable full-day guided hike starts with a 6-minute helicopter ride up into the higher elevation. Rates are C$469 per person, including lunch. There's also plenty of hiking in and near Canmore and Kananaskis that doesn't require guides, all with the same signature Rocky Mountain experience. **Heart Creek Trail,** an easy 4km (2.5-mile) stroll, can be found east of Canmore, just off the Trans-Canada Highway at the Lac des Arcs exit. Signs will point to the trail head. On your journey, take the right fork at the first major junction and follow the wide gravel path along the creek bed. Seven log bridges traverse the creek, offering breathtaking views of Mount McGillivray and Heart Mountain.

The **Grassi Lakes hiking trail** is one of the region's signature hikes. Rated as a moderately difficult hike, it's 3.8km (2.4 miles) round trip—a half-day outing. You reach it by driving up the Spray Lakes Road past the Nordic Centre; the trail head is just beyond where the pavement turns to gravel. You'll climb 250m (820 ft.) through thick forest to two lovely mountain spring–fed lakes. Here, you'll find rock paintings left by Aboriginals centuries before and a panoramic view of the townsite below. On the way down, be sure to look back up over your shoulder to catch the waterfalls behind you.

Grotto Canyon is another easy one, at 4km (2.5 miles). The trail head is a 10-minute drive east of Canmore along Highway 1A to Grotto Pond. You'll see a sign here for the Grotto Canyon hike. Keep to the main trail—there are several side trails here—across a dry gulch and past an industrial plant, which might seem odd, but keep going, as the best is yet to come. You'll reach a bench overlooking a riverbed, with a spectacular view of Gap Lake, just before the entrance to Grotto Canyon, with its tall, steep walls. Keep your eyes peeled for Aboriginal pictographs, but look, don't touch—your hands will help weather away these important artifacts.

Spray Lakes in Kananaskis Country also offers some of the most iconic scenery to be found in the Rockies. Some of the best include Burstall Pass, Rummel Lake, and Chester Lake. All trails are accessed from the **Smith Dorrien Trail/Spray Lakes Road.** The road climbs sharply south of Canmore and turns to gravel not far past the Nordic Centre. You'll see trail heads every 10 minutes or so. These are the access points to genuine alpine terrain, many of them leading to alpine meadows and mountain lakes.

As you get deeper into Kananaskis Country, you'll find yourself at Peter Lougheed Provincial Park, which is centered around the Upper and Lower Kananaskis Lakes, about 30km (19 miles) south of town along Route 742, the Spray Lakes Parkway. This is as gorgeous as Kananaskis gets. There's almost no end to trails in and around the lakes to be found here for hiking, biking, and horseback riding; try the **Kananaskis Canyon interpretive hike** at the north end of the lower lake or the **Upper Kananaskis Lake circuit,** about 10km (6¼ miles) that takes you around this gorgeous mountain lake. Those seeking altitude might choose the **Rawson Lake Trail**, a fast 4km (2.5-mile) climb up to a lovely lake beneath the cliffs of Mt. Sarrail.

GOLF

The Kananaskis area features four championship golf courses and one of Canada's premier golf resorts. **Kananaskis Country Golf Course** boasts two 18-hole, par-72 courses set among alpine forests and streams, and featuring water hazards on 20 holes, 140 sand traps, and four tee positions. It's rated among the top courses in Canada. For information, contact Golf Kananaskis (Kananaskis Country Golf

Bear Country

You're not in Banff yet, so you'll not have been handed the pamphlet at the park gates warning you that "you're in bear country." But you are—Kananaskis is as wilderness-oriented, if not more so, than anything Banff has to offer, and that means the big omnivores are likely on the prowl. They don't want to run into you any more than you do them, but still, it's best to be prepared. So, follow some simple rules: Try to avoid surprise encounters by traveling in groups. Make noise—talk loudly, sing songs, or clap your hands to let the bears know you're coming. Keep your eyes peeled for tell-tale signs you might not be alone, like tracks, droppings, or freshly clawed tree trunks marking the bear's territory. If you see a bear, don't approach it and definitely don't offer it food. Don't run. Don't turn your back on the bear; rather, back away slowly. Appear as passive as possible; you don't want the bear to see you as a threat to his or her territory. Keep your voice down, and don't make eye contact. Remember, the chances of this happening are extremely remote; bears are generally tolerant of humans. Your best bet is to make sure you don't surprise it.

Course, P.O. Box 1710, Kananaskis Village, AB T0L 2H0; © **877/591-2525** or 403/591-7272; www.kananaskisgolf.com). Greens fees are C$90.

Near Canmore, the low-key 18-hole **Canmore Golf Course** is right along the Bow River, at 2000 Eighth Ave. (© **403/678-4785**; www.canmoregolf.net). Greens fees are C$80. Their clubhouse has a great patio.

The Les Furber–designed **Silver Tip Golf Course** (© **403/678-1600**; www.silvertipresort.com) is an 18-hole, par-72 course high above Canmore that calls itself "extreme mountain golf." You'll be eye-to-eye with the Canadian Rockies here and perhaps look wildlife in the eye, too—grizzly bears have been known to roam on the course. Boasting a length of 7,300 yards, the course has sand bunkers on all holes and water on eight. Greens fees range from C$105 to C$175. Also at Canmore is the **Stewart Creek Golf Club** (© **877/993-4653**; www.stewartcreekgolf.com), with 18 holes, 32 bunkers, and a beautiful location below the Three Sisters peaks. The course measures 7,150 yards and incorporates natural lakes, streams, and even historic mine entrances. Greens fees range from C$150 to C$195, including use of a golf cart.

HORSEBACK TRIPS

The Kananaskis is noted for its dude ranches (see "Riding Herd at a Guest Ranch," p. 142), which offer a variety of horseback adventures from short trail rides to multiday pack trips. A 2-hour guided ride will generally cost about C$60 per person. In addition, **Boundary Ranch,** just south of Kananaskis Village on Highway 40 (© **877/591-7177** or 403/591-7171; www.boundaryranch.com), offers a variety of trail rides, including a horseback lunch excursion.

RAFTING

Then there's always an old classic, white-water rafting. The Kananaskis and Bow rivers are the main draw here. In addition to a range of half-day (C$75) and full-day (C$125) white-water trips, there are excursions that combine a half-day of horseback riding with an afternoon of rafting (C$144). Inside Out Experience (see above) can provide more information. All prices are per person.

The **Canadian Rockies Rafting Company** (© **877/226-7625**; www.rafting.ca) is among the most established rafting tour companies in the area, with a range of different trips—the more gentle ride along the Kananaskis River, to the whitewater rush of British Columbia's Kicking Horse River (with rapids as high as Class IV). These are mountain rivers, so bear in mind, it's cold.

THE COWBOY TRAIL

Running all along the eastern fringe of the Rockies in Alberta is the famed 700km (435-mile) Cowboy Trail, transitional lands between the vast prairies to the east and spectacular mountain terrain to the west. Here, the climate is moderate, the scenery is rugged and spectacular, and Alberta's western heritage is on full display. The string of small towns here are linked by Highway 22, from Cardston (on Hwy. 6; Hwy. 22 starts at Pincher Creek) to the south and Mayerthorpe in the far north. It skirts the southern and western edge of Calgary and passes through Rocky Mountain House on the way north. All along the way, the rolling fields and mixed forests and plains are some of the best ranchland to be found anywhere. This is also Bible country, with a handful of "cowboy churches"—to say nothing of several Christian camps—along the way.

The best thing about the Cowboy Trail, though, isn't so much what's on it as what isn't: It's a gorgeous and peaceful drive through not much at all, with the majesty of the Rockies looming close by to the west. It's one of the most serene, beautiful journeys you can take in the province—or anywhere else, for that matter—with a little cowboy culture thrown in at the various towns just to spice things up. Rodeos aren't annual events out here—they're weekly, at least in the summer. Regular "ranch rodeos"—rodeos for working ranch hands at the large-scale local ranches, whose work blends with their play—pop up frequently.

At times, the Cowboy Trail can feel like a step back in time—not a bad thing in a province where oil wealth has most of its residents rushing forward as quickly as possible. Here, on the fringes of the Rockies, things slow down enough for a look back. If you have only a day, do the drive south from the Trans-Canada Highway to Pincher Creek, looping back up to Calgary. The northern part isn't as quaint, and the mountains are more distant. Many services (like ranches and campgrounds) are open late May to early September only. For more information, visit www.thecowboy trail.com. This section starts at the south and makes its way north.

Cardston

The town of Cardston is the official starting point (or ending point, depending which way you're traveling) of the Cowboy Trail on Highway 22, and the ranchland that surrounds it certainly attests to that. Cardston was settled in 1887 by Mormons who traveled north from Utah in one the West's last wagon migrations. It's perhaps fitting, then, that Cardston's main attraction is the **Remington Carriage Museum** (© **403/653-5139;** www.remingtoncarriagemuseum.com), the largest collection of horse-drawn vehicles to be found anywhere in North America. It has 5,853 sq. m (63,000 sq. ft.) of video displays, installations, and a carriage-restoration shop—one of the only ones in North America—and represents the private collection of local tycoon Don Remington, who donated his collection of 49 carriages to the province in 1985. He died 2 years later, too soon to see his dream of a carriage museum become a reality, but his legacy lives on, with more than 200 carriages and a site that was voted "the best indoor attraction in Canada." It's for a particular crowd, to be sure—how much time can you spend talking about carriages, anyway?—but well worth a look. Kids will love the carriage rides in the summer, pulled by real, live horses.

In Cardston, you'll also find the **Cardston Alberta Temple,** built by the Mormon pioneers who settled Cardston in 1887. The temple was the second built by the church outside of the continental U.S.

From Cardston, you'll pass through the aptly named **Mountain View** to the west, a flyspeck of just a few buildings just a few minutes from Waterton Lakes National Park. The Rockies loom large here, as the rolling prairie gives way to mountains in an alarmingly short run-up. Nearby, **Mountain Meadow Trail Rides** (© **403/653-2413;** www.mountainmeadowtrailrides.com) offers half-day, day-long, and overnight horseback riding on the Nelson ranch, run by a fourth-generation ranching family whose gorgeous spread bumps up against the Waterton park boundary.

Veer off the trail for a moment before heading north, though. Turn west along Highway 3 toward Crowsnest Pass, a pass through the Alberta Rockies and into British Columbia. It's a worthy diversion to stop in at the **Frank Slide Interpretive Centre** (✆ **403/562-7388;** www.frankslide.com), a truly chilling historic site just off the trail to the west. One day in the early morning hours of 1903, a significant portion of Turtle Mountain simply fell off, crushing the town of Frank and most of its inhabitants. The rubble field, which stretches for at least a mile, is an extraordinary site, with boulders the size of houses hurled in every direction. The interpretive center, which completed a major renovation in 2008, is a must-see.

Not far north of Mountain View, you'll pass the **Twin Butte General Store** ★★ (✆ **403/627-4035;** www.twinbuttestore.ca), which has a very good Tex-Mex restaurant, and you can also pitch a tent for C$5 a night.

Near to Twin Butte is the **Great Canadian Barn Dance** (✆ **866/626-3407** or 403/626-3407; www.gcbd.ca), in the hamlet of Hillspring. This is a great family weekend get-away with real Albertan hospitality. There's a barn (with B&B rooms on-site), a campground, and live music and line-dancing lessons every Friday and Saturday night. This is good, clean fun—no alcohol allowed.

Pincher Creek

The next town of any size along the trail is Pincher Creek, a bustling community of about 3,500 people in the heart of Alberta ranching territory. The town's claim to fame is probably its annual festival of **Cowboy Poetry** (www.pcgathering.com). Founded in 1986, it's a gathering for some of the best country bards to be found here or abroad—and an excuse for a 2-day barbecue of Alberta beef, of course. It takes place each June. Here, you'll find the **Bloomin' Inn** (✆ **403/627-5829;** www. bloomin-inn.com), a traditional guest ranch with great food and an emphasis on making countrified crafts, run by Colleen and Francis Cyr. Rates start at C$109 for B&B accommodation.

North of Pincher Creek, along the Porcupine Hills and the Mountain Forest Reserve, towns become few, save for tiny **Lundbreck** (pop. 600) and **Cowley** (pop. 230). Sparse forests and rolling hills abound here, near **Chain Lakes Provincial Park,** which has camping in the gorgeous foothills for C$15 a night. If camping's not your style, you can try the **Chimney Rock B&B** (✆ **403/646-0151;** www. bbcanada.com/chimneyrock.html), a spectacularly remote spot in the Livingstone Range, at the foot of the Rockies. Rates start at C$120 for a double. A naturalist offers a tour of wild edibles in season; local cuisine and sustainable ranching are priorities.

Head east of Pincher Creek towards Fort Macleod: It's worth the side trip to take in the fascinating **Head-Smashed-In Buffalo Jump Historic Site** ★★ (✆ **403/553-2731;** www.head-smashed-in.com). A UNESCO World Heritage Site, this is one of the oldest and best-preserved buffalo jumps on Earth. With a deep understanding of both the local landscape and the behavior of bison, native peoples would use this precipice as a place to chase stampeding bison off a cliff. They'd subsequently use the carcasses of killed bison for food, clothing, shelter, and utensils. Come here to contemplate a custom that has more than 6,000 years of history. There's also a campground on-site with tipi camping.

Highway 22 North

Just south of aptly named Longview is the **Bar U Ranch ★★** (*©* 403/395-2212; www.pc.gc.ca/lhn-nhs/ab/baru/index.aspx), a national historic site. This is definitely a must-stop on the Cowboy Trail! Some say this is where corporate ranching was born: The Bar U ran a big operation, employing thousands of cowboys and running hundreds of thousands of cattle from 1882 to 1950. Bar U outlasted virtually everyone, but it couldn't outlast time: As ranches modernized and herds grew, Bar U owner Patrick Burns sold off parts of the vast ranch in 1950, bringing its dominance to a close. But the original Bar U site, with its horse barns, bunkhouses, mess hall, and office, remain intact. Thirty-five buildings, all told—a slice of Alberta history, perfectly preserved.

Longview (pop. 300) is a place where old and new Alberta meet: It's an oil-and-gas staging center for nearby wells but also undeniably cowboy country, with a reputation for some of the best grass-fed beef in the province. It's also the hometown of Ian Tyson, Alberta's cowboy balladeer. Think of Canada's Johnny Cash, and you've almost got it. Tyson gives voice to the entire cowboy culture of the province; his best-known song, "Four Strong Winds," performed with wife Sylvia, is an iconic international hit. His mournful, sensitive songs can be heard in almost every bar, restaurant, and saloon in cowboy country. Tyson maintains a ranch in the area, as well as a cafe: **Ian Tyson's Navajo Mug** (*©* 403/558-2272; www.thenavajomug.com) may be the only place this side of Calgary to get a decent cappuccino.

Longview is also where, in season, you'd turn off to head up Highway 40 into Kananaskis Country via the Highwood Pass, the highest pass in Alberta (see p. 144)

 ## Ian Tyson, Alberta's Country Bard

There's probably not a more loved Albertan songwriter than Ian Tyson. Tyson is the real deal: Though he was born in Victoria, BC, he spent his formative years working ranches in eastern BC and western Alberta, and is pure cowboy, through and through.

Though his career took off after hitchhiking to Toronto in 1957, where he formed the folk duo Ian and Sylvia with his soon-to-be-wife Sylvia Fricker—the pair hosted a national television show between 1970 and 1975—his heart never left Alberta. Eventually, Tyson became disillusioned with both the country-music scene and his marriage to Sylvia, so he headed home to Alberta to take up cattle ranching again.

But the music didn't end. After a few years of dabbling, Tyson had put together enough material for an album, and at a music festival in Nevada in 1983, he performed to raves. Ian Tyson, songwriter, was back in the saddle. He's since never looked back: awards, albums, tours, and decades later, he's the undisputed bard of Alberta.

Tyson is not prolific, and that's where the Longview Ranch, on the Cowboy Trail, comes in. There's a gravel path that Tyson will spend hours meandering along, where, he says, 80% of his songwriting is done in his head. So, as much as Alberta needs Ian Tyson, it's fair to see he needs Alberta, too. It's one marriage that will never end.

at 2,206m (7,238 ft.). Highway 40 is open only from mid-June to November, so be sure to check closures before you attempt it.

About an hour south of Longview is the **Sierra West Ranch and Cabins ★★** (𝒞 **403/628-2431;** www.sierrawestcabins.com), a beautiful and authentic working cattle ranch tucked up against the Livingston Mountains. Guests seeking a place for horseback riding, ranch-handling, cowboy-ing, or just peace and quiet can stay in cozy log cabins (from C$125) that have kitchenettes. Your hosts, Randy and Ginny Donahue, also offer daily horseback rides and an annual 2-day cattle drive each August.

Black Diamond/Turner Valley

On from Longview lie the sister cities of **Black Diamond** and **Turner Valley,** slightly larger towns which are linked by a road called the Friendship Trail that has a handful of motels and, in Black Diamond, the unexpected **Marv's Classic Soda Shop** (121 Centre Ave. W.; 𝒞 **403/933-7001;** www.marvsclassics.ca), where '50s-era rock and roll is alive in the heart of cowboy country. They serve up burgers and fries, shakes, and a whole lot of memories. Ask Marv to sing you a song. Both towns have charming little Main Streets.

In Turner Valley, you'll find the **Turner Valley Gas Plant National and Provincial Historic Site** (𝒞 **403/933-7738;** www.culture.alberta.ca/tvgp). The oil and gas is gone from here now, but when Dingman Well No. 1 blew in, Alberta's oil and gas industry was born. Ranchers and oilmen shared the foothills for a time; during World War II, this was the largest-producing gas field in the British Commonwealth. A C$2-million refurbishment project has tours closed as of 2010; check before visiting.

Priddis/Bragg Creek

Up through **Millarville** and on to **Priddis,** which these days barely skirts the rapidly swelling suburbs of Calgary, you'll find more ranchland with more dramatic roll to the landscape as the trail veers west. The Cowboy Trail follows Highway 22X at this point, and there's a curious confluence of old and new here, as family ranches share fences with nouveau-riche estates. One of the best golf courses in Alberta, **Priddis Greens** (www.priddisgreens.com), is here, but it's fully private—so don't plan on playing unless you know a member or have a spare C$42,000 for the membership fee.

East of Priddis is the renowned **Spruce Meadows** (𝒞 **403/974-4200;** www.sprucemeadows.com) equestrian center, one of Canada's top horsemanship venues. Privately owned, North America's best show jumpers are here throughout the summer, competing for more than C$6 million in prizes in events open to the public. The Ascott-esque style make this a must in the Calgary social scene.

A little west of the course and a little south off Highway 22X is the **Homeplace Ranch** (𝒞 **877/931-3245** or 403/931-3245; www.homeplaceranch.com), a guest ranch run by the McKinney family in the glorious environs of the high foothills. The McKinney family homesteaded here in 1912 and still run a cattle ranch on their vast property; they welcome guests for riding tours and lessons. Rustic—don't expect to find wireless Internet here—but comfortable, it's one of the best ways to see Alberta as it was. Packages start at C$350 a night and include all meals, accommodations, and riding.

Following Highway 22X farther west would take you back into Kananaskis Country and **Elbow Falls** on the Elbow River, a popular spot for day hikes and picnics. But to follow the trail, you need to go north on Highway 22 into **Bragg Creek,** a pleasant mountain town that's evolved into something of a nearby rural retreat for moneyed Calgarians. There's not much to do here—a strip mall done up in rustic wooden clapboard is the "town center"—but that's part of the point. As an access point to the mountains and Kananaskis, it's a quiet refuge, though a couple of urbane amenities have sprung up, like **Madrina's Ristorante** (© **403/949-2750;** www. madrinasristorante.com), a simple and classic Italian restaurant set in a wooded area off the main road, and **Infusion** (© **403/949-3898;** www.infusionbraggcreek. com), a stylish, contemporary French-Asian fusion restaurant with great local fare. For a coffee and a scrumptious snack, you can't beat the bear claws at the **Buttercup Country Bakery** (© **403/949-2253;** www.buttercupcountrybakery.com) in the village square. If you are short of time, this is your chance to turn either west to Canmore and Banff, or east to pop back into Calgary.

Cochrane

On the north side of the Trans-Canada Highway, the trail continues to **Cochrane,** a fast-growing Calgary bedroom community with deep roots in cowboy culture. Just a half-hour from downtown Calgary in good traffic, Cochrane is rapidly expanding, and it's easy to see why: The spectacular location in the foothills next to the Bow River is drawing city slickers with a taste for country living in droves. Calgary's boom has the city limits pushing ever-closer to Cochrane's boundaries, but the town retains its commitment to western heritage, with sites like the **Cochrane Ranche-House** (© **403/668-0484;** www.cochraneranchehouse.ca), which was built in 2004 to recognize ranching and rodeo as twin pillars of rural Albertan culture, with exhibitions and permanent collections of artifacts, photography, and art on display. You'll find major fast-food chains, chain motels, and big box retail all over the place; whether it's a pillaging of Western culture or just an update is a matter of some debate. But Cochrane's tidy main street is still quaint and well kept. It also has some of the best ice cream in Alberta: **MacKay's** (© **403/932-2455;** www.mackays icecream.com) has been drawing folks for miles around for more than 60 years for their selection of dozens of homemade pies, served a la mode, of course.

North of Cochrane, the mountains seem a little less close, though still prominent, as they veer north and west. The great plains dominate as you skirt the edge of Rocky Mountain Forest Reserve. You'll pass by the tiny hamlets of **Cremona** and **Water Valley;** there's hardly any other signs of habitation—just the rolling fields and the mountains looming in the west.

Sundre

Next on the Trail is **Sundre.** You're starting to push into the northern oil-producing region now, and while agriculture is still the dominant economic force here, you'll see wells amid the ranchlands, and less and less charm. In Sundre, you can visit the **Pioneer Museum** (© **403/638-3233;** www.museum.sundre.com), 1.6 hectares

(4 acres), complete with blacksmith shop, school, ranger station, and pioneer cabins. It's open May to September.

A little north of Sundre is the hamlet of **Caroline,** population around 600. It's a real one-horse town, but Caroline grabbed headlines courtesy of its best-known native son, Kurt Browning. Browning, a Canadian and world figure-skating champion, is honored at the local rink here. Inside the Kurt Browning Arena (*C* **403/722-3022**), you'll find **Kurt's Korner,** full of objects and memorabilia from his skating career.

Rocky Mountain House

Next stop on the trail is Rocky Mountain House, a national historic site in its own right. David Thompson, the celebrated cartographer, explorer, and fur trader, is credited with mapping as much as 20% of North America. Rocky Mountain House was his base for charting a pass through the Rocky Mountains. But that's not the only history in this small, high-plains town. The rival Hudson's Bay Company and North West Company both operated out of Rocky Mountain House for 76 years, making it a central point of commerce and trade. The **Rocky Mountain House National Historic Site** (*C* **403/845-2412;** www.pc.gc.ca/lhn-nhs/ab/rockymountain/index_e.asp) is a cluster of four important trading posts, complete with tipi and wooden fortress. Every August, the town celebrates the David Thompson Days festival in his honor.

Rocky Mountain House rose to prominence as a trading post due to its strategic location, at the confluence of two rivers (the North Saskatchewan and Clearwater) and the mouth of a mountain pass. That pass now contains the **David Thompson Parkway,** one of the most gorgeous drives in a province laden with them, which connects with the **Icefields Parkway** farther west in Banff.

Modern Rocky Mountain House positions itself as a jumping-off point for nature tourism to the mountains in the west. The local tourism authority can be found online at www.whereadventurebegins.com. They're able to provide comprehensive trail and campground listings, tour operators, and maps.

North of Rocky Mountain House, the trail's population grows ever more sparse, and the concentration of oil development denser. The town of **Drayton Valley** (pop. 7,000) is a dusty oil town on a broad expanse of plain with little to recommend, though the North Saskatchewan River does pass through here—and at full spring run-off flow, it's a sight to behold. Drayton Valley also hosts important rodeos throughout the summer (www.albertarodeo.ca/draytonvalley.htm). The Cowboy Trail technically ends at the town of Mayerthorpe, north of the Yellowhead Highway (Highway 11), which connects Edmonton and Jasper. The Pembina River runs through Mayerthorpe; the longest wooden trestle bridge in Western Canada is here.

BANFF & JASPER

I f you're a tourist in Alberta, either Banff or Jasper—and likely both—is probably why you're here. Along with Waterton to the south, and Yoho and Kootenay to the west (in British Columbia), Banff and Jasper complete a network of federal parkland that protects the majestic peaks of the Canadian Rockies in a continuous flow of staggering size and beauty. A UNESCO World Heritage site reaching more than 20,000 sq. km (7,722 sq. miles), it's rightly one of the most famous, and most successful, nature preserves on Earth.

But if you've come here to see Banff, don't think you're alone in that idea. More than 3 million tourists pass through Banff National Park each year, meaning that that lovely, protected natural zone all along the Rockies can some-times have the hectic feel of being in a city—albeit a par-ticularly beautiful one. Visitors tend to cluster in a few key areas: the Banff townsite, the shores of Lake Louise, and the Columbia Icefield.

The crowds flock here for good reason: You'll rarely, if ever, see such jaw-dropping mountain splendor. But the town of Banff, plunked down in a stunningly beautiful valley, has, at times, the air of a high-priced mall or theme park; Jasper, while significantly more subdued, still draws its throngs, with ample ways to separate you from your money.

Still, both places have so much more to offer than luxury shopping and dining in a mountain setting. So, get out of the car and get into the mountains. Hiking, biking, rafting, canoeing, kayaking, and fishing, as well as pack trips on horseback, are great ways to leave the crowds behind and experience the parks as nature (and the government) intended. Many of these adventures are just steps away from your hotel. Skiing here is also world-class: the resorts of Mount Norquay, Sunshine

Village, and the jewel of the parks, Lake Louise (the site of annual World Cup races), are among the largest ski areas in the world; also not to be missed is the excellent but largely under-the-radar (and thus much less crowded) Marmot Basin in Jasper.

One of the principal beauties of these two parks is how you can have one foot in two worlds, almost simultaneously. Set out on one of the hiking trails, and you can quickly find yourself in a preternatural setting that suggests a world that man has yet to discover; crave some creature comforts, and some of the most opulent hotels on Earth are here to serve you—particularly the early railway hotels now owned by the Fairmont chain, the Chateau Lake Louise, the Jasper Park Lodge, and the iconic Banff Springs Hotel. All built by the Canadian Pacific Railway, starting in the late 19th century, as a way to kick-start tourism, these three hotels are the last word in luxury. The effect has snowballed so that Banff and Jasper parks have an array of luxury options, from hotels and live music to shopping and dining, which play off the surrounding wilderness with an urbane, sophisticated feel.

Getting around here is easy if you have your own vehicle. The network of paved roads is excellent, but in high season, sheer volume can make it slow going. A major project will turn the main artery, the Trans-Canada Highway 1, into a four-lane superhighway through the park by early 2011. The main goals are to improve traffic flow, but also to include fences, overpasses, and underpasses to improve wildlife movement through the area and reduce human-wildlife accidents. From Calgary, it's a stunning 1-hour drive up the Bow River to Banff on Highway 1, and driving from Edmonton to Jasper on the Yellowhead Highway (Hwy. 16) takes from 3 to 4 hours. Both these roads (which continue over the Rockies into British Columbia), along with the Icefields Parkway between Lake Louise and Jasper, remain open year-round.

ESSENTIALS OF BANFF & JASPER

The Banff and Jasper parks regions are among the most rugged and wild in the world. The natural splendor is almost beyond belief: Jagged peaks soar above burbling mountain streams that link icy, emerald alpine lakes; summertime brings colorful wildflowers dotting expansive alpine meadows, walled in by mountains all around; preternatural glaciers are cradled in massive mountain bowls; and all this is populated by wildlife particular to its alpine ruggedness—cougars, grizzlies and the like. Between them, Banff and Jasper, along with Waterton to the south, and Yoho and Kootenay National Parks to the west, preserve the entire spine of the Rockies from the U.S. border stretching north for 1,127km (700 miles).

All that being the case, you can't expect to have it all to yourself. And you won't—millions of tourists pass through both of these parks each year, so if you're looking for peace and quiet in the wilderness, note that these two parks offer a lot less of it than you might expect (though Banff, with its proximity to Calgary, is worse than Jasper this way). Still, a little bit of effort will whisk you into a private alpine paradise.

It's best to visit the parks in the off-season if you can—September and October, or May and June for hiking; December or April for skiing. If not, be sure to plan well ahead, or you may find it difficult to secure the accommodation you want. The parks can handle only so many people, and they're usually full all summer long.

Orientation

Taken together, Jasper and Banff cover 17,519 sq. km (6,764 sq. miles) of rugged alpine wilderness. Even so, they're wonderfully easy to navigate. Well-maintained highways link the major centers, making car travel between them a breeze, although extreme weather can occasionally make driving in the parks a trial. In particular, watch the weather reports in winter for snow squalls and white-outs, as these can obliterate visibility and transform the highways into long, black skating rinks.

The townsites of Banff and Jasper—the main accommodation and dining hubs of the respective parks, as well as the staging areas for tours and information—are 287km (178 miles) apart, connected by Highway 1 and Highway 93, the Icefields Parkway, one of the world's most beautiful drives. Banff is 128km (80 miles) from Calgary via Highway 1; Jasper is 375km (233 miles) from Edmonton on Route 16, the famous Yellowhead Highway.

Entry to the Banff, Jasper, Yoho, and Kootenay network of parks, per day, costs C$9.80 adults, C$8.30 seniors, C$4.90 children, and C$20 families. An annual pass to the National Parks of Canada—which gives entry to 27 of the country's national parks for an entire year from the date of issue—costs C$68 adults, C$58 seniors, C$33 children, and C$136 families.

Visitor Information

Travel Alberta (*©* **800/661-8888;** www.travelalberta.com) can provide accommodations and visitors' guides, as well as the excellent Traveler's Guide and a road map. There's a separate guide for campers, as well.

Tours & Excursions

The Brewster family has long been a fixture in Banff, and as such, they've become one of the titans of the local tourist trade. Brewster operates the park system's principal tour bus operation, as well as the specialized vehicles that clamber up the mountainside to the Athabasca Glacier along the Icefields Parkway.

Brewster Transportation and Tours (100 Gopher St., Banff; *©* **866/606-6700** or 403/762-6767; www.brewster.ca) can take you to most of the main attractions in both parks, either as a package tour or one-off trios to single attractions. Their local Rockies-based adventures are operated under the brand **Explore Rockies** (*©* **800/ 760-6934;** www.explorerockies.com). Call for a full brochure or ask the concierge at your hotel to arrange a trip. Sample packages include

o **Banff to Jasper (or vice versa):** Some 9½ hours through unrivaled scenery, this tour takes in Lake Louise and a view of the ice field along the parkway. (The return trip requires an overnight stay, not included in the price.) In summer, the one-way fare is C$172 adults, C$82 children. If you don't want the tour, there's also a daily express bus between Banff and Jasper for C$79 one-way; kids under 15 pay half price.

Banff & Jasper

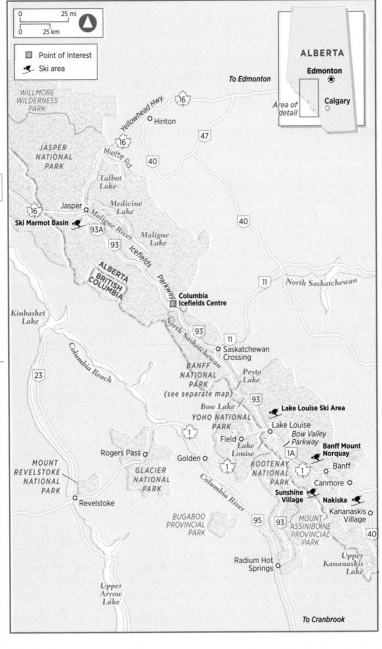

0 25 mi
0 25 km

■ Point of Interest
⛷ Ski area

ALBERTA

Edmonton
⊛

Area of
detail

Calgary
○

To Edmonton

WILLMORE
WILDERNESS
PARK

Yellowhead Hwy.

16

Hinton

47

16

Miette Rd.

40

JASPER
NATIONAL
PARK

Talbot
Lake

Medicine
Lake

40

16

Jasper

Ski Marmot Basin ⛷

93A

Maligne River

Maligne
Lake

93

Icefields

ALBERTA
BRITISH
COLUMBIA

Parkway

11

North Saskatchewan

Columbia
Icefields Centre

Kinbasket
Lake

North Saskatchewan

93

11

23

Columbia Reach

Saskatchewan
Crossing

BANFF
NATIONAL
PARK

Peyto
Lake

(see separate map)

93

Bow Lake

Lake Louise Ski Area

YOHO NATIONAL
PARK

Lake Louise

Bow Valley
Parkway

1

Field

Lake
Louise

1A

Banff Mount
Norquay

Rogers Pass

Golden

1

KOOTENAY
NATIONAL
PARK

1

Banff

MOUNT
REVELSTOKE
NATIONAL
PARK

GLACIER
NATIONAL
PARK

Columbia River

Sunshine
Village ⛷

Canmore

Nakiska ⛷

Revelstoke

BUGABOO
PROVINCIAL
PARK

95

93

MOUNT
ASSINIBOINE
PROVINCIAL
PARK

Kananaskis
Village

40

Radium Hot
Springs

Upper
Kananaskis
Lake

Upper
Arrow
Lake

To Cranbrook

○ **Columbia Icefields:** On this 9-hour tour from Banff, you stop at the Icefields Centre and get time off for lunch and a Snocoach ride up the glacier. Adults pay C$151 children pay C$75; tour prices include a trip up onto the glacier in the massive Explorer—essentially a bus on steroids with wheels the height of a pickup truck. It's open from mid-April through mid-October only.

Another local tour company offering smaller-sized tours is **Discover Banff Tours** (© **877/565-9372** or 403/760-5007; www.banfftours.com). They'll help you set up a self-guided driving tour with a personalized GPS, and they also have excellent wildlife-viewing safaris in the evenings.

Seasons

In peak season, hotels charge top rates and restaurants are jammed. Banff and Jasper have two peaks: summer (late June to late Aug), when it rarely climbs above 77°F (25°C), making it ideal for hikers and backpackers; and winter (Dec–Feb), when skiers flock to what is probably the finest skiing terrain in all of Canada.

March to May is decidedly off-season: Hotels cut rates significantly, and you can choose the best table in any eatery. However, it's often too warm for skiing, and too cold and wet for hiking. There's plenty of rain in the warmer months, so don't forget to bring some suitable raingear.

Lodging in the Parks

If you're in the parks in high season, you almost have to think of it as a competition or musical chairs. Both Banff and Jasper could easily add a few thousand hotel rooms and fill them without much trouble, but they can't; due to conservation regulations, development is severely restricted in the parks.

Although there are more than 5,000 tourist beds in Banff, rates can be expensive and are often under the control of big tour-bus companies that reserve huge amounts of rooms well ahead of the season. It's important to plan ahead. If you're flexible, last-minute-deal travel websites are a great alternative—try Priceline, Travelocity, or Expedia, all of which may turn last-minute cancellations into savings of as much as 50% for you. Demand in neighboring Canmore (see chapter 8), while high, isn't quite at Banff levels, so the 20-minute drive can often pay off.

For the most part, hotels are well-kept-up in the parks, but few would justify these high prices anywhere else in the world. Knowing that, you have some decisions to make. You can choose to splurge on one of the world-class hotels here, which are often only a bit more expensive than the midrange competition. The only real way to keep lodging costs low is to camp. For information on camping, see p. 183–185.

If you are have trouble finding a room or simply don't want to deal with the hassle, contact **Banff Accommodation Reservations** (© **877/226-3348;** www. banffinfo.com). They'll help you find available rooms and also happily give advice to help you make the most of your trip.

In the off-season, prices drop dramatically—often as much as 50%. Most hotels offer ski packages in winter, as well as other attractive getaway incentives. Ask about any special rates, especially at the larger hotels.

While it's thrilling to see wildlife here, the parklands are no zoos! Here, animals roam free, and the natural rhythms of the wilderness are maintained. There are 53 species of wild mammals here, 13 of which are on Parks Canada's "Species at Risk" list. Some animals meander along and across highways and hiking trails, within easy camera range. However tempting, never feed the animals and don't touch them. You can be fined up to C$500 for feeding any wildlife, for one thing. For another, it's extremely dangerous.

As docile as some of these animals may seem, remember: These are wild creatures for whom the first rule is survival. If they feel threatened, they will either run or attack. And while they can seriously hurt you, you might be doing the same to them. Bighorn sheep, for one, get accustomed to summer handouts of bread, candy, potato chips, and marshmallows when they should be grazing on the high-protein vegetation that'll help them survive through the winter. Moose have taken a kindly offered snack as an invitation to join a picnic, and once a moose has decided that's what he or she wants, you won't be able to say no: They sometimes weigh well over a ton.

During elk calving season, some trails will be closed to hikers for their own safety. A new mother elk is quick to take any nearby activity, however innocent, as an imminent threat to her newborn calf. Surprising a mother and calf could also result in a panic that separates them, sometimes for good.

Then there are bears. Both black and grizzly bears call the parks home; grizzlies, at up to 2m (6½ ft.) on their hind legs, are the more threatening of the two, but don't underestimate the grizzly's smaller cousin, the black bear, which is relatively small at 1.5m (5 ft.) long. Both can be very dangerous when startled or threatened; your best bet is

HOTEL ALTERNATIVES

If you're looking for a B&B, there are many options; check out www.banffbedand breakfast.org for a complete listing.

Hostels are probably the most affordable option in Alberta's Rocky Mountain parks—at least, if you want a roof over your head and running water. **Hostelling International** runs a large network of hostels throughout the parks; to find out more about Alberta hostels, check out www.hihostels.ca.

There is a wide variety of campgrounds in Banff National Park, and you can now reserve a spot online at some of them via telephone at ⓒ 877/737-3783 or online at www.pccamping.ca. Many, though, remain first-come, first-served—don't expect to be able to arrive any day of the summer and find availability at your choice campground. You must plan ahead, especially if you want to be near the town of Banff. Check with Parks Canada at the **Banff Information Centre** (224 Banff Ave.; ⓒ **403/762-1550**) for updated campsite availabilities.

The Great Outdoors

Since the Canadian Pacific Railway built its famous mountain lodges and started drawing Eastern tourists to the West in the 1920s, these two parks have been at the center of alpine outdoorsmanship in North America.

to make plenty of noise on the trails as you walk (singing and clapping your hands work well) to let them know you're coming.

The grizzly spends most of the summer in high alpine ranges, well away from tourist haunts. As one of North America's largest carnivores, its appearance and reputation are awesome enough to make you beat a retreat on sight. But the cuddly looks and circus antics of the black bear tend to obscure the fact that these, too, are wild animals: powerful, faster than a horse, and completely unpredictable.

Hiking in bear country (and virtually all parkland is bear country) necessitates certain precautions; ignore them at your peril. Never hike alone and never take a dog along. Dogs often yap at bears, then when the animal charges, they run toward their owners for protection, bringing the pursuer with them. Above all, never go near

a cub. The mother is usually close by, and a female defending her young is the most ferocious creature you'll ever face—and possibly the last. In the Canadian Rockies, there are more "bear jams" than "traffic jams" as tourists pile up in their vehicles to snap photos of grizzlies or black bears, creating chaos on the roads. Whistling, yelling, running about . . . tourists behave strangely in the presence of a magnificent mammal, causing problems that can turn fatal for the bear and for other drivers. If you see a bear and want a closer look, slow down safely but do not stop. Give the bear space. No matter the circumstances, stay in your vehicle and do not approach the bear. Once alerted to the sighting of a bear, Parks Canada staff and often the police will appear at the scene and urge travelers to keep moving. Remember to call in a bear sighting to © **403/762-1470.**

With decades to cultivate the industry, it's now exceptionally professional, well-developed, and full of abundant choices. If you're staying in Banff, Jasper, or Lake Louise, you'll find that outfitters, guides, and rental operations are sophisticated and make it easy and convenient to get outdoors. Most hotels offer a concierge service that can arrange activities for you; for many, you need little or no advance registration.

If you're hesitant about heading into the wilderness, fear not: You don't even have to break a sweat to enjoy the magnificent scenery. Short interpretive trails often have little climbing and take 30 blissful minutes. Hire a horse and ride to the backcountry, or take an afternoon trail ride. Jasper, Banff, and Lake Louise each have gondolas to lift travelers from valley floor to mountaintop. Bring a picnic and soak up the view. If you're not ready for white water, the scenic cruises on Lake Minnewanka and Maligne Lake offer a more relaxed waterborne adventure.

BIKING Both parks provide free maps of local mountain-bike trails; the Bow Valley Parkway, between Banff and Lake Louise, and Highway 93A in Jasper Park are both good, less trafficked—and staggeringly beautiful—roads for road biking. Bike rentals are easily available nearly everywhere in the parks.

ROCK CLIMBING, ICE CLIMBING & MOUNTAINEERING The sheer rock faces on Mount Rundle near Banff and the Palisades near Jasper are popular with rock climbers, and the area's many waterfalls become frozen ascents for ice climbers in winter. Instruction in mountaineering skills is offered by **Yamnuska Inc. Mountain School,** based in Canmore (© **866/678-4164** or 403/678-4164; www.yamnuska.com).

SKIING Banff and Jasper offer some of the best skiing in the world; in Banff, Sunshine Village and Lake Louise are two huge ski areas, with Louise being the larger of the two, and arguably the most scenic. Sunshine, still huge, has less skiable terrain, but it's above the tree line and tends to have more snow that lasts deeper into the season—usually into mid-May. Mount Norquay, just above the town of Banff, is much smaller, but steep and challenging; it's also the only one to offer night skiing. Jasper, meanwhile, has Marmot Basin, a lovely mid-size ski area that doesn't get anywhere near the traffic of the Banff resorts—a plus for that alone.

Wherever you go, skiing here can be superb: The snowpack is copious, the scenery beautiful, après-ski festivities vibrant and occasionally wild, and accommodations world-class. Lift tickets are generally cheaper than at comparable resorts in the United States.

Heli-skiing isn't allowed in the national parks but is popular in the adjacent mountain ranges near Golden in British Columbia. **CMH Heli-Skiing** (217 Bear St., Banff; © **800/661-0252** or 402/762-7100; www.cmhski.com) is the leader in this increasingly popular sport, which uses helicopters to deposit skiers on virgin slopes far from the lift lines and runs of ski resorts. CMH offers trips that last anywhere from 5 to 10 days, to 11 locations; prices begin at C$3,800 per person, including lodging, food, and transport from Calgary. Skiers must be 19 years of age or older.

WHITE-WATER RAFTING & CANOEING The Rockies' many glaciers and snowfields are the source of mighty rivers like the Bow, Kicking Horse, and Athabasca. Outfitters throughout the region offer white-water rafting and canoe trips of varying lengths and difficulty—you can spend a single morning on the river or plan a 3-day expedition. Jasper is central to a number of good white-water rivers. **Maligne Rafting Adventures Ltd.** (© **780/852-3370**; www.mra.ab.ca) offers packages for rafters of all experience levels.

WILDLIFE-VIEWING Banff and Jasper are great places to see alpine animals in the wild, from hundreds of species of birds to large mammals. Both parks teem with wildlife—bighorn sheep, grizzly and black bears, deer, elk, mountain goats, moose, coyotes, lynxes, wolves, and more. See "Park Wildlife & You," below, for important warnings on how to handle wildlife encounters in the parks responsibly and safely.

BANFF NATIONAL PARK

Having celebrated its 125th birthday in 2010, Banff is Canada's oldest and most famous national park, its fabulous and dramatic landscapes the first, best argument that Canada's abundant, spectacular wilderness was worthy of federal protection. Its 6,641 sq. km (2,564 sq. miles) of incredibly dramatic mountain landscape, glaciers,

- **Size of Banff National Park:** 6,641 sq. km (2,564 sq. miles)
- **Established:** 1885
- **Highest elevation:** Mount Forbes, 3,612m (11,850 ft.)
- **Naturally occurring species of mammals:** 69
- **Roads:** 320km (199 miles)
- **Hiking trails:** 1,500km (932 miles)
- **Campsites:** More than 2,800

- **Park employees:** 400 in summer, 225 in winter
- **Visitors:** 3.8 million per year
- **Banff townsite year-round population:** 8,721
- **Elevation of Banff townsite:** 1,384m (4,541 ft.)
- **Lake Louise year-round population:** 1,041
- **Elevation of Lake Louise Village:** 1,731m (5,679 ft.)

high moraine lakes, and rushing rivers make it clear no argument was to be made at all; this is one of the most gorgeous places on Earth.

If there's a downside, it's that everybody knows it. In the towns of Banff and nearby Lake Louise (though much less so in Louise), a walk on main street can give you the odd sensation of walking in midtown New York City at rush hour, and it's not because of the urbane sophistication the towns have cultivated; it's crowded, and the sidewalks can be shoulder to shoulder.

Happily, the wilderness is just steps away. Thanks to outstanding infrastructure, and professional guides and outfitters, it's easy in Banff National Park to get on a raft, bike, or horse and find a little solitude. Alternatively, consider visiting the park off-season, when prices are lower, the locals are friendlier, and the scenery is just as stunning.

For more information on the park, contact Banff National Park (P.O. Box 900, Banff, AB T1L 1K2; ✆ **403/762-1550;** www.pc.gc.ca).

Outdoor Pursuits in the Park

The town of Banff may tempt you with high-end shopping, impressive restaurants, and a seemingly endless array of fudge shops, but you owe it to yourself to step out into the park's well-tended wild. From easy to extreme, there are plenty of options for everyone. If you don't know where to start, don't worry; there are many outfitters here, but the recommendations below are typical of what's available.

BIKING The most popular cycling adventure in the Canadian Rockies is the 287km (178-mile) trip between Banff and Jasper along the Icefields Parkway, possibly the most spectacular mountain drive on Earth.

You can do this on your own (bear in mind that this is a not a route for the inexperienced or out of shape, as at high elevation, your lungs will be challenged to get enough oxygen out of the thin air to feed your starving muscles), but it doesn't hurt to have an experienced bike-touring outfitter to squire you around. Give yourself at least 3 long days. Try **Rocky Mountain Cycle Tours** (✆ **800/661-2453** or 604/898-8488; www.rockymountaincycle.com) for 6-day supported trips starting at C$2,350 per person.

If you'd prefer a self-guided tour, simply rent a bike in Banff or Lake Louise, and pedal along the Bow Valley Parkway—Highway 1A—between Banff and Lake

Louise; running parallel to the much busier Highway 1, the Bow Valley Parkway runs along the skirt of Castle Mountain, one of the most impressive peaks in all of Banff. It's a solid day trip for an average cyclist, with a few ups and downs.

There are more than 190km (118 miles) of mountain-biking trails in Banff National Park. Be aware that mountain biking is permitted on only a select number of trails. Families and beginners can ride the Spray River Loop. Those looking for a rush ought to try the Stoney Squaw epic downhill trail near Mt. Norquay.

FISHING You need a permit to fish in Banff National Park. Pick one up at the **Banff Information Centre** (224 Banff Ave., ℂ 403/762-1550). Vermillion Lakes is a popular spot with a limited supply of fish. Better for lake fishing is Lake Minnewanka. The Bow River is one of the finest fly-fishing rivers in the world. For the more personal touch, Big Jim Dykstra (a fair name; he's 65) of **Hawgwild Flyfishing** (ℂ **403/678-7980;** www.flyfishingbanff.com) specializes in fly fishing, and he'll pick you up in his vintage blue Suburban at your hotel and squire you to his rivers in the area. A catch is guaranteed, or your money back! Tours start at C$479 for two people for a full day.

Banff Fishing Unlimited (ℂ **403/762-4936;** www.banff-fishing.com) offers a number of fly-fishing expeditions on the Bow River, as well as lake fishing at Lake Minnewanka. All levels of anglers are accommodated, and packages include part- or whole-day trips.

GOLF The **Fairmont Banff Springs Golf Course** (ℂ **403/762-6801;** www.fairmont.com/banffsprings/recreation/golf) rolls out along the Bow River beneath towering Mt. Rundle. One of the most venerable courses in Canada, and one of the most expensive, it offers 27 holes of excellent golf. Although associated with the resort hotel, the course is open to the public. Greens fees for 18 holes are C$219 in summer and drop down to C$149 in spring and fall.

HIKING Banff is a hiker's dream come true. The trails are incredibly varied and rewarding, ranging from easy 1-hour strolls to demanding full-day outings. For a good listing of popular hikes, pick up the free *Banff/Lake Louise Drives and Walks* brochure from the national park information center at 224 Banff Ave. Here are a few of my favorites.

Cory Pass, at 5.8km (3.6 miles) each way and climbing 915m (3,002 ft.), is one of the most strenuous and challenging hikes in Banff, but it's also by far the most spectacular one near the town of Banff. The highlight is the 2,300m (7,546-ft.) monolithic limestone cliffs of the Sawback Range. It'll take you about 6 hours.

Johnston Canyon, 24km (15 miles) north of Banff on Highway 1A, is one of the best day hikes and also among the most popular. It starts with a gentle incline into a narrow limestone canyon; the walls are more than 30m (98 ft.) high, but only 5m (16 ft.) across, and the path skirts the cliff face, tunnels through walls, and winds across wooden footbridges for more than a mile.

The hike to the lower falls, which takes about half an hour, is a gentle breeze, but the vertical starts to increase after that, and the crowds start to fall away. An hour later, as you reach the upper falls, where black swifts dive in the waterfall's spray, the number of people will likely have thinned considerably. Another hour, over increasingly steep terrain, will take you to the Inkpots, a wide-open high-alpine meadow where you'll find a collection of small, deep pools fed by underground springs (the varying depths of the pools result in different hues of deep green, hence the name). Round trip to the Inkpots is a good 4 hours; but budget for longer—the meadow, with a swift-running creel, is as scenic a spot as you'll find anywhere and relatively untraveled.

Lake Agnes/Beehives is a classic hike above Lake Louise into a picturesque hanging valley with a treasure-like emerald lake. An historic teahouse awaits after hiking 5.1km (3.2 miles) up a moderate and wide trail. Connect to the Beehive trail down, looping along the shores of Lake Louise. This hike is good for families.

Nigel Pass (Icefields Pkwy., Hwy. 93) is a 15km (9.3-mile) round-trip trek that's a favorite day hike in the part of the Icefield area where Banff and Jasper national parks meet. You'll have superb views of the Columbia Icefield. Look behind you to see the looming forms of Parker Ridge, Mount Saskatchewan, and the Hilda Glacier. Give yourself at least 5 hours to complete this hike.

Paradise Valley/Larch Valley, near Lake Louise, is a 17km (11-mile) hike that runs the gamut of alpine terrain, from high meadow and steep cliffs to the fringe of towering peaks, beside thundering falls, and over a majestic pass before ending at spectacular Moraine Lake. This is a difficult hike that will take you 7 or 8 hours to complete; you might not want to attempt it if you're not in good physical condition. Parks Canada often requires hikers to stay in groups of six or more due to bear activity in the area. Often, small groups of less than six gather at the trail head to join forces.

Parker Ridge is a fantastic 5km (3.1-mile) trail that takes you up to a ridge top with expansive views of the Columbia Icefield and Saskatchewan Glacier, one of the largest alpine valley glaciers in the Rockies. Keep an eye on the lower slopes for grizzly bears and mountain goats. Be prepared for cold and windy weather. Budget a couple of hours' round trip.

Peyto Lake/Bow Summit is a short, 20-minute stroll heading out from the Icefields Parkway (Hwy. 93); this trail takes you to a jaw-dropping viewpoint of Peyto Lake, Peyto Glacier, and the Mistaya Valley. Interpretive displays along the 1.2km (.7-mile) loop explain the basics of the subalpine and alpine landscape.

Plain of the Six Glaciers is beautiful but busy; you'll want to leave early to avoid the crowds on this glorious hike. The trail begins at the far end of Lake Louise (the lake itself, not the town) and ascends to an exposed moraine below Victoria Glacier. It offers an exceptional view of six other glaciers (hence the name). You can have lunch or just a warming cup of tea at the historic Plain of the Six Glaciers Teahouse; if you're suitably fortified, you can hike the last half hour to the Victoria Glacier Viewpoint.

To reach **Sulphur Mountain Boardwalk,** take the Sulphur Mountain Gondola, in the town of Banff, to the top, where this gentle stroll begins. Wander along an elevated boardwalk for about 1km (.6 mile) that takes you to the top of Sanson Peak, where you'll find an historical weather-monitoring station. Along the way, interpretive plaques will tell you all about the stunning vista that lies below the ridge you're now skirting from the comfort of a steady, level surface.

Naming Banff

The town of Banff, established in 1886, began its life as a stop on the trans-continental railroad as the somewhat-less-than-romantic "Siding 29"—not exactly a catchy marketing tag. The Canadian Pacific Railway, which built such icons as the Banff Springs and the Chateau Lake Louise, knew their plans for mineral hot springs and luxury hotels in the gorgeous Rockies provided an unparalleled opportunity to kick-start a tourism industry in the West, but they needed something a little more capable of capturing the imagination of potential travelers than a nondescript number. So they looked to George Stephen, the first president of the CPR. Stephen and CPR vice-president Donald Smith were both born in the Scottish county of Banff-shire; and so the town of Banff came to be named. Obscure though it was at the time, Banff has taken on new meaning; to millions of tourists who have passed through its extraordinary landscapes, Banff will always mean pristine alpine experience, with all the comforts.

When the skiers go home for the season up at Sunshine Village near Banff (usually late June), a spectacular guided-tour season begins, featuring lush and colorful alpine meadows. **White Mountain Adventures** (© 800/408-0005 or 403/760-4403; www.sunshinemeadowsbanff.com) will take you via school bus up a ski run into the alpine zone and the Continental Divide for C$26 per person from the Sunshine parking lot or C$55 per person from the town of Banff. This is an extraordinary area to wander, hike, and stroll. A highly sensitive wilderness area, the crest of the ski hill, well above the tree line, gives way to an astonishing alpine meadow sprinkled with wildflowers. Beyond, to the west, the Rockies unfurl in all their majesty.

In town, it's easy to strike out from the townsite and find any number of good, short hikes. There are paths in town along both sides of the Bow River; from the west end of the Bow River Bridge, trails lead east to Bow Falls, past the Fairmont Banff Springs, and then back around and up to the Upper Hot Springs. Just beyond town, the Fenlands Trail begins just past the train station and makes a loop through marshland wildlife habitat near the Vermillion Lakes.

From the Cave and Basin Centennial Centre, you'll find the trail head for the Sundance Trail, which tracks alongside the Bow River to Sundance Canyon, 5km (3.1 miles) further on; another 2.5km (1.6 miles) will take you up and past Sundance Falls.

If you're not keen on setting out on your own, Parks Canada offers several guided hikes daily in the summer months. The Banff Information Centre has a chalkboard outside that lists the hikes and their departures daily; there may also be upcoming options not listed, so feel free to ask if you don't see anything that suits.

Some routes are free, while others (like the popular evening Wildlife Research Walks) charge a small fee; all require preregistration. For information and preregistration, call © **403/762-9818.**

[Fast FACTS] BANFF NATIONAL PARK

ATMs   **Alberta Treasury's** Banff branch is at 317 Banff Ave., in the town of Banff (✆ **403/762-8505**). In Lake Louise, there is an ATM in **Samson Mall** (✆ **403/522-3678**). The **Bank of Montreal** is at 107 Banff Ave. (✆ **403/762-2275**), and the **Canadian Imperial Bank of Commerce (CIBC)** is at 98 Banff Ave. (✆ **403/762-3317**). Exchange foreign currency at these banks or, for better rates, try the **Custom House Global Foreign Exchange** at 211 Banff Ave. (✆ **403/760-6630**). The **Royal Bank,** at 117 Banff Ave., has an ATM but does not offer other banking services.

Car Trouble & Towing Services   In Banff, try **Standish Towing and Recovery** (162 Eagle Crescent; ✆ **403/762-4869**). In Lake Louise, **Rocky Mountain Towing** (✆ **403/522-3534**) will pick you up as far north as the Icefield Information Centre, Jasper National Park, and as far west as Yoho National Park. Both of these towing services have the capacity to tow RVs. And both are open 24 hours.

Drug Stores   **Rexall Drug Store,** on the lower level of Cascade Plaza (317 Banff Ave.;

✆ **403/762-2245**), or **Gourlay's Pharmacy** (229 Bear St.; ✆ **403/762-2516**).

Emergencies   Call ✆ **911** for fire, ambulance, police, hospital, or Parks Canada assistance. Call ✆ **800/332-1414** for poison control.

Gas Stations   At the end of Banff Avenue, there is a **Husky Service** (601 Banff Ave.; ✆ **403/762-3341**). Closer to the heart of town, both **Banff Shell** (230 Lynx St.; ✆ **403/760-6675**) and **Petro-Canada** (302 Lynx St.; ✆ **403/762-4434**) are at the corner of Lynx and Wolf streets. There's a gas station about 30km (19 miles) north of the Banff townsite at Castle Mountain Village, just east off the Trans-Canada Highway on Highway 1A (✆ **403/522-2783**). In the village of Lake Louise, 30 minutes northeast of the town of Banff, fill up at **Lake Louise Esso** (200 Village Rd.; ✆ **403/522-3578**) or at **Lake Louise Petro-Canada** (Hector and Whitehorn rds.; ✆ **403/522-3755**). There is also a gas station at Saskatchewan Crossing, about 81km (50 miles) north of Lake Louise (✆ **403/761-7000**), but

be warned: Fill up in Lake Louise or Jasper so you can avoid it. This isolated station knows it's the only game in town, with prices as much as 50% higher than in Banff or Jasper.

Grocery Stores   Banff's largest grocery store is **Safeway** (318 Marten St.; ✆ **403/762-5378**). Smaller **Nestor's Market** (122 Bear St.; ✆ **403/762-3663**) has everything. There's a small grocery store on Tunnel Mountain called **Chalet Grocery,** in the Douglas Fir Resort (✆ **403/762-5447**). In Lake Louise, head to the **Village Market,** in Samson Mall (101 Lake Louise Dr.; ✆ **403/522-3894**).

Laundry   In the Town of Banff, try **Cascade Coin Laundry,** in the Cascade Plaza (317 Banff Ave.; ✆ **403/762-3444**). On Tunnel Mountain Road at the Douglas Fir Resort, **Chalet Coin Laundry** has a playground in front (✆ **403/762-5447**).

Medical Services   Banff's Mineral Springs Hospital is located at 301 Lynx St. (✆ **403/762-2222**).

Permits   Pick up your park permit at the **Banff East Gate,** on the Trans-Canada Highway 1 coming west from Calgary, or at the **Banff Information Centre** (224 Banff Ave.; ℂ 403/762-1550), where you can also get back-country permits and fishing permits. You can also get permits in Lake Louise at the **Lake Louise Visitor Centre**, in Samson Mall (101 Lake Louise Dr.; ℂ 403/522-3833).

Photo Supplies **Banff Camera Shop,** at the corner of Banff Avenue and Buffalo Street (ℂ 403/762-8386). One-hour developing is available at the **Film Lab** at 120 Banff Ave. (ℂ 403/762-2126). In Lake Louise, **Pipestone Photo** is in Samson Mall (101 Lake Louise Dr.; ℂ 403/522-3617).

Post Offices **Canada Post** (204 Buffalo St., Banff; ℂ 403/762-2586). In Lake Louise, send mail from **The Depot,** at the Samson Mall (101 Lake Louise Dr.; ℂ 403/522-3870).

Taxis Banff Taxi (ℂ 403/762-4444), Legion Taxi (ℂ 403/762-3353), Mountain Taxi and Tours (ℂ 403/762-3351).

Weather Updates Call ℂ 403/762-2088 for the latest forecast. For road conditions, call **Rocky Mountain National Parks** (ℂ 403/762-1450). For avalanche reports, call **Banff National Park** (ℂ 403/762-1460).

HORSEBACK RIDING Riding a horse in the Canadian Rockies is a classic, fun way to explore the area. The area has a rich cowboy heritage and plenty of backcountry to ride. **Warner Guiding and Outfitting** (ℂ 800/661-8352 or 403/762-4551; www.horseback.com) offers short day trips with a meal (breakfast in the morning or evening dinner rides) from the town of Banff for C$151 per rider. Multiday trail rides start at C$825 per person for 3 days. Minimum age is 18.

In Lake Louise, **Timberline Tours** (ℂ 888/858-3388 or 403/522-3743; www.timberlinetours.ca) offers day trips to some of the most spectacular nearby spots, such as a 3-hour ride to Big Beehive, above the lake (C$105) or a 4-hour ride to the Plain of Six Glaciers (C$125). Three day trips start at C$705 per rider; you can go as long as 10 days in the back country for C$2,350 per rider.

RAFTING & CANOEING Rafting can be as easy and gentle as a 2-hour family float trip on the Bow River, just below Banff Townsite; **Canadian Rockies Rafting Company** (ℂ 877/226-7625 or 403/678-6535; www.rafting.ca) offers trips from C$55 adults, C$45 children under 16 (the company allows children as young as 3 on the float). On its website, Canadian Rockies Rafting rates its various trips the way ski hills do: Green circle for beginner, blue square for intermediate, and black diamond for the rough stuff.

The gnarliest rapids in the area are just across the border on British Columbia's **Kicking Horse River,** with Class IV rapids. Canadian Rockies Rafting offers trips to Kicking Horse for C$125 adults or C$115 children 12 to 15 (children under 12 not permitted), lunch included. You can do a half-day, but it's only C$15 or C$10 less, respectively, and doesn't include lunch.

It seems only natural that you'd want to paddle a canoe on these glorious Canadian lakes. Canoe rentals are available at Moraine Lake (ℂ 403/522-3733) or at the Fairmont Chateau Lake Louise (ℂ 403/522-3511). Rates are C$50 per hour. In the town of Banff, head to **Blue Canoe Rentals** (at the end of Wolf St.; ℂ 403/762-5465). Rates are C$35 for the first hour and then C$21 for every hour after that.

SKIING   Skiers will feel close to heaven in Banff, with so much great terrain, variety, and choice. The park has three principal ski areas (Mount Norquay, Sunshine Village, and Lake Louise), two of them huge, offering an incredible mix of terrain; as an added bonus, all are within about 45 minutes of each other and of the town of Banff along Highway 1. Their proximity has resulted in an alliance for booking and promotional purposes, which makes exploring their options a single stop online, at www.skibig3. com. You can also contact the **Ski Banff Lake Louise Sunshine** office (P.O. Box 1085, Banff, AB T0l 0C0; ✆ **403/762-4561**). Passes are 3 out of 4 days C$240 adults, 4 out of 5 days C$320 adults, and the like. Children 13 to 17 and seniors 65 and over pay C$71 per day. Kids 6 to 12 pay C$26 per day.

The smallest of the three, Banff Mount Norquay (✆ **403/762-4421;** www. banffnorquay.com), is just above the Town of Banff, across the highway; you can see the shops and restaurants of Banff Avenue from its chairlifts. It's small, but steep, and can be challenging; its signature run, the North American, is one of the steepest runs on the continent. Norquay tends to emphasize family skiing; the resort offers day care and instruction, and is the only ski area in the region to offer night skiing. They also have afternoon-only and hourly ski passes. Full-day lift tickets are C$55 adults, C$43 children 13 to 17 and seniors, and C$17 children 12 and under.

To get to **Sunshine Village's** (✆ **403/762-6500**; www.skibanff.com) vast skiable area, well above the tree line, you'll take a long ride on an alpine gondola just to get to the ski area's base. There, you'll find the main lodge (an old log cabin–cum–pub), a ski and snowboard school, and the recently renovated Sunshine Mountain Lodge.

Just 15 minutes west of Banff off Highway 1, Sunshine gets more snow than any ski area in the Canadian Rockies (more than 9m/30 ft. per year!). Skiing often continues into late May. Lift tickets here are C$76 adults, C$62 seniors, C$54 for children 13 to 17, and C$26 children 12 and under. Just riding the gondola is C$26 per person.

Lake Louise Ski Area (✆ **800/258-SNOW** [800/258-7669] in North America or 403/552-3555; www.skilouise.com) is the largest of the three, with both the front and back sides of one mountain and the front of another. It is massive, gorgeous, and at times, extremely challenging. In addition to the main lodge at the base, there are two other lodges, one halfway up the front side and another at the bottom of the back side. The one on the back side, Temple Lodge, has a big deck for BBQing burgers; on a sunny, warm spring day, it's packed with sun-worshipers working on their goggle tans.

Lake Louise has 1,680 skiable hectares (4,151 acres) and 113 runs, making it among the largest ski resorts in North America. Lift tickets are C$78 adults, C$63 seniors, C$55 children 13 to 17, and C$27 children 12 and under.

Cross-country or Nordic skiing is also a favorite winter activity in Banff. It can be relaxing, strenuous, and peaceful. There are more than 80km (50 miles) of managed ski trails in the park. Get updated trail reports at www.pc.gc.ca/banff. Beginners can try the Golf Course Loop near the Fairmont Banff Springs Hotel. More experienced skiers shouldn't miss the Pipestone Loops and track-set trails at Moraine Lake near Lake Louise.

Banff Arts Festivals

One of Banff's non-natural wonders is **The Banff Centre,** an outstanding international cultural-development facility that hosts world-class artists, dancers, writers, and thinkers throughout the year. Some of the Banff Centre's most outstanding arts events include

o The Banff Summer Arts Festival, which runs from June to August and includes live outdoor theater, art displays, and jazz workshops.

o The Banff International String Quartet Competition, held annually in late August.

o The Playbill Series, which runs through the summer and includes live performances by well-known pop, jazz, and world-music musicians.

o The Banff Centre Festival of Mountain Films and Books, held each November.

For tickets to any of these events, call the Banff Centre box office at (✆ **800/ 413-8368** or 403/762-6301, or visit www.banffcentre.com.

Banff Townsite

So gorgeous is Banff townsite, it can sometimes seem surreal: quaint buildings, some of them historic, line a bustling main street, over which loom the peaks of the Rockies so close you feel like you could reach out and touch them. Mt. Rundle, the town's signature peak, towers over Banff Avenue from the south; its appearance lends support to the tectonic-plate theory of mountain creation, as one side, smooth as the plains, crests at a point and gives way to a jagged underside. To the south, the Bow River Bridge traverses the fast-rushing Bow in the shadow of massive Mt. Cascade.

It's postcard perfect—exactly why the Banff Springs Hotel was built by the Canadian Pacific Railway company in 1888 (it's now owned by the luxurious Fairmont hotel chain), to draw tourists to the rugged beauty of the Rockies, providing all the comforts, including geothermally heated hot springs. The plan worked: Visitors flocked, and the town grew rapidly to accommodate.

The setting may be unreal, but in some cases, so is the town; in between the remaining historic buildings are high-end contemporary shopping malls, with luxury international brands and inflated prices. Banff also has an alarming surfeit of fudge shops—the international symbol for "tourist trap." Banff is vibrant and cosmopolitan, its sidewalks crowded with people from all over the world year-round; what it isn't, though, is peaceful—especially in summer.

ESSENTIALS

GETTING THERE If you're flying into Calgary and heading straight to Banff, call and reserve a seat on the **Banff Airporter** (✆ **403/762-3330;** www.banff airporter.com). Vans depart from Calgary Airport roughly every 2 hours; a one-way ticket costs C$53.

The closest VIA Rail train service is at Jasper, 287km (178 miles) north. **Brewster Transport** (✆ **403/762-6767**) offers an express bus between the two park centers five times weekly for C$79 one-way.

Greyhound (✆ **800/661-8747** or 403/260-0877; www.greyhound.ca) operates buses that pass through Banff on the way from Calgary to Vancouver. One-way fare between Banff and Calgary is C$26. The depot is at 100 Gopher St. (☏ **403/762-6767**).

If you're driving, the Trans-Canada Highway takes you right to Banff's main street, Banff Avenue; the town is 129km (80 miles) west of Calgary.

VISITOR INFORMATION   The **Banff Information Centre,** at 224 Banff Ave. (P.O. Box 1298, Banff, AB T0L 0C0; ☏ **403/762-0270;** www.banfflakelouise. com), houses both the Banff Lake Louise Tourism Bureau and a handy and helpful national-park information center. The center is open daily June 15 to October 15 from 9am to 9pm and the rest of the year from 9am to 5pm. Ask for the Official Visitors Guide, which is packed with information about local businesses and recreation. For information on the park, go to www.pc.gc.ca.

ORIENTATION   Banff's townsite is a simple place to understand; Banff Avenue is the main drag running north-south, with the Bow River Bridge at the south end. Bear Street, which has become increasingly developed as Banff has grown in recent years, parallels Banff Avenue 1 block west.

Just over the river stands the park administration building, an historical landmark, in the midst of well-kept grounds. Banff Avenue ends on the south side of the bridge, splitting into a T; to the left are **the Fairmont Banff Springs Hotel,** the **Upper Hot Springs** and the **Banff Gondola;** turn right, and you'll be on your way to Cave and Basin Historic Site, where the park was born.

At the northwestern edge of town is the old railroad station, and a little farther northwest, the road meets the Trans-Canada Highway again, branching off to Lake Louise and Jasper. In the opposite direction, northeast, is the highway going to Canmore and Calgary.

The **Greyhound and Brewster Bus Depot** (☏ **403/760-8294**) is located at the corner of Gopher and Lynx streets, at the north end of town, about a block west of Banff Avenue.

GETTING AROUND   Banff's new **ROAM** (☏ **403/760-8294**) public bus system has hybrid buses zipping all over town, with stops at all the attractions and near most hotels. One route runs from the Fairmont Banff Springs down Banff Avenue and on to Tunnel Mountain; the other runs between the north end of Banff Avenue and the Sulphur Mountain Gondola and Upper Hot Springs. The bus operates year-round. Fares are $2 adults, $1 seniors and children 6 to 12, and free for children under 6. An unlimited day pass costs $5 per person. For a taxi, call **Mountain Taxi and Tours** (☏ **403/762-3351**).

For a rental car, contact **National** at Caribou and Lynx streets (☏ **403/762-2688**) or **Budget** at the corner of Banff Avenue and Caribou Street (☏ **403/762-4565**). Reserve well in advance, as cars are frequently sold out.

ATTRACTIONS

Sulphur Mountain Gondola ★★ ☺   It takes 8 minutes from where you board a gondola to the top of Sulphur Mountain, the easiest summit in Banff by far. Below you, the Bow River Valley spreads out in a glorious vista of rushing water and jagged mountain peaks below. Your altitude gain from the valley floor to the summit is 698m (2,290 ft.); once you arrive, you're at 2,281m (7,484 ft.) above sea level. The summit offers a new perspective on the peaks you've been straining your neck to gawk upward at; on Sulphur Mountain, you're at their level, so you can

Banff

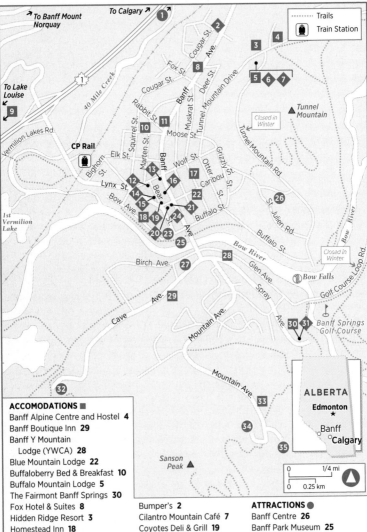

To Calgary ↗ **1**

To Banff Mount Norquay ↗

2

Cougar St.

3

4

Ave.

Fox St.

8

Deer St.

Tunnel Mountain Drive

Closed in Winter

5 **6** **7**

Cougar St.

Banff

▲ Tunnel Mountain

To Lake Louise

9

40 Mile Creek

Rabbit St.

Muskrat St.

Squirrel St.

11

10

Moose St.

Tunnel Mountain Rd.

Vermilion Lakes Rd.

CP Rail

Marten St.

Elk St.

Bighorn St.

Banff

Wolf St.

Otter St.

Grizzly St.

Caribou St.

St. Julien Rd.

26

Bow River

13

12 **14**

16

17

Lynx St.

Bear St.

15

Bow Ave.

18 **19**

22

21

Buffalo St.

Buffalo St.

Bow River

1st Vermilion Lake

20 **23**

24

25

Ave.

Closed in Winter

Bow River

Golf Course Loop Rd.

Birch Ave.

27

28

Glen Ave.

Spray

🏌 Bow Falls

Ave.

Ave.

29

33

Cave

Mountain Ave.

30 **31**

Banff Springs Golf Course

Mountain Ave.

Sanson Peak ▲

32

33

34

35

Sanson Peak

ALBERTA

Edmonton ★

Banff ○
●**Calgary**

········ Trails

🚂 Train Station

0 ———— 1/4 mi
0 ———— 0.25 km

ACCOMODATIONS ■
Banff Alpine Centre and Hostel **4**
Banff Boutique Inn **29**
Banff Y Mountain
    Lodge (YWCA) **28**
Blue Mountain Lodge **22**
Buffaloberry Bed & Breakfast **10**
Buffalo Mountain Lodge **5**
The Fairmont Banff Springs **30**
Fox Hotel & Suites **8**
Hidden Ridge Resort **3**
Homestead Inn **18**
Red Carpet Inn **11**
Rimrock Resort Hotel **33**
Rocky Mountain B&B **17**
Storm Mountain Lodge **9**

DINING ◆
Barpa Bill's **12**
The Bison Mountain Bistro **14**
Bow Valley Grill **31**

Bumper's **2**
Cilantro Mountain Café **7**
Coyotes Deli & Grill **19**
Eddie's Burger Bar **20**
Elk and Oarsmen **24**
Giorgio's **13**
Grizzly House **16**
Maple Leaf Grille & Spirits **21**
Sleeping Buffalo at
    Buffalo Mountain Lodge **6**
Wild Flour Bakery **15**

ATTRACTIONS ●
Banff Centre **26**
Banff Park Museum **25**
Buffalo National
    Luxton Museum **27**
Cave and Basin
    National Historic Site **32**
Lake Minnewanka Boat Tours **1**
Sulphur Mountain Gondola **35**
Upper Hot Springs Pool **34**
Whyte Museum of the
    Canadian Rockies **23**

look not only straight at them, but also beyond—to more distant peaks and valleys in almost every direction.

Follow a boardwalk along the mountain ridge as far as neighboring Sanson Peak, where you'll find an historical weather station. Just like anywhere in Banff, even at an alpine summit, there are ways to spend money: a mediocre restaurant, a pricey snack bar, and a gift shop with very typical fare are all willing to lighten your wallet. Don't bother; it's all the same stuff you'll get in town. A coffee in the snack bar is cheap rent for the amazing view, though. ·

The lower terminal is 2.5km (1½ miles) southeast of town on Mountain Ave. ℂ **403/762-2523.** www. explorerockies.com/banff-gondola. C$29 adults, C$14 children 6-15. May 1 to Labour Day 8:30am–9pm; check website for off-season schedule.

Banff Centre ★★   A center for arts, culture, leadership, and education, this institution is known around the world as a breeding ground for creativity and innovation. Built in 1933 as a theater school, it now hosts courses, workshops, festivals, and concerts with some of the most acclaimed performing artists in the world. They come to Banff to expand their artistic horizons amid inspirational surroundings, and visitors lucky enough to nab tickets are the richer for it. Throughout the summer, there are regular events, from literary readings to jazz concerts to outdoor theater performances. There's also a great indoor pool and fabulous rooftop restaurant open to visitors, all within walking distance of Banff Avenue. Check the schedule as soon as you get to Banff and drop by the new box office in a tiny heritage cabin downtown (211a Bear St.) for more information.

107 Tunnel Mountain Dr. ℂ **403/762-6100** or 403/762-6301 Summer Arts Festival hotline. Pay-what-you-can to C$40. Main box office Tues–Sat noon–5pm; downtown box office Tues–Sat noon–3pm & 3:30–6pm.

Banff Park Museum ★   Built in 1903 by the Natural History Branch of the Geological Survey of Canada, the museum is a showcase of its growing stock of creatures preserved by taxidermy, a must for wildlife fans. Its original tally of mounted specimens was eight mammals, 259 birds, a turtle, 57 specimens of wood, 814 plants, and 201 mineral samples. John Macoun of the Natural History Branch described these as "an almost complete representation of the birds and flowering plants found within the limits of the park." The building that houses the specimens might be the best thing about the museum; the largest and most elaborate example of the early phase of park design that used decorative cross-log construction, it's a National Historic Site.

91 Banff Ave. ℂ **403/762-1558.** C$4 adults, C$3.50 seniors, C$3 children 6-16. Summer daily 10am–6pm; fall-spring daily 1–5pm.

Buffalo Nations Luxton Museum   Housed in a log fort just west of the Bow River Bridge, this interesting museum is devoted to the history of the First Nations peoples of the Canadian Rockies and Northern Plains. It offers realistic dioramas, tipis, artifacts, ornaments, and exhibits on daily life of the local First Nations.

1 Birch Ave. ℂ **403/762-2388.** C$8 adults, C$6 seniors & students, C$2.50 children 6-12. May-October daily 11am–6pm; Nov-April daily 1–5pm.

Cave and Basin National Historic Site   This little hole in the ground was the birthplace of Banff National Park. Warm natural hot springs discovered by two railway workers on their day off were soon pumped into a large pool, where dozens of people would gather to soak. The number of travelers hoping to find solace in its apparently curative waters grew. The CPR saw the opportunity for tourism and built the Banff Springs Hotel, providing a luxury destination to go along with the healing springs.

The original springs and pools haven't held up well to the heavy traffic they've received over the decades and are no longer open to the public (the Upper Springs, further up the slope of Sulphur Mountain, serve that purpose now). But the site offers a surfeit of historical background as to how and why Banff came to be, complete with interpretive displays and historical videos.

1.5km (1 mile) west of Banff (turn right at the west end of the Bow River Bridge).© **403/762-1566.** C$4 adults, C$3.50 seniors, C$3 children 6-18. May 15 to Sept daily 9am-6pm; Oct to May 14 Mon–Fri 11am-4pm, Sat & Sun 9:30am-5pm.

Lake Minnewanka Boat Tours   Even though some call it a giant bathtub, there's no denying the beauty of Lake Minnewanka, an aquamarine glacial lake cradled by massive peaks all around that is the largest lake in Banff National Park. It used to be called "Lake of the Water Spirits" by the Stoney Nation. Early Europeans found it equally intimidating, calling it "Devil's Lake." A 2-hour cruise is relaxing and a nice way to come to your own conclusion on the pros and cons of Minnewanka. Your boat offers 360 degrees of windows for appropriate wilderness gawking, but your boat will also likely be packed to claustrophobia-inducing capacity. Be sure to make reservations, especially in high season. There are five sailings a day in summer; buses leave from Banff every day specifically for this purpose, from the bus station and major hotels.

24km (15 miles) north of Banff. © **403/762-3473.** www.minnewankaboattours.com. Tickets C$44 adults, C$19 children 5-11. Mid-May to early Oct.

Upper Hot Springs Pool   For more than a century, visitors have been coming to Banff to "take to the waters." Unlike the Cave and Basin (see above), the outdoor pool here is large, hygienic, warm (usually 90°F/32°C), and pleasant. It can also be very crowded. Come when it's chilly outside; it's particularly lovely on a winter's evening. A bench runs all around the pool's edge, allowing you to sit comfortably in the soothing waters. And while the pool is updated, the building, built in 1931, is actually a perfectly preserved example of mountain architecture of the era. Inside, though, it's contemporary and where you'll find the **Pleaidas Spa** (© **403/760-2500**), complete with steam room, massage, and aromatherapy.

At the top of Mountain Ave. (4km/2½ miles south of Banff). © **403/762-1515.** Pool C$7.30 adults, C$6.30 seniors & children; C$23 families. Swimsuit & towel rentals C$1.90 each. Spring-fall daily 9am-11pm; reduced hours in winter.

Whyte Museum of the Canadian Rockies   Named for its benefactors Peter and Catharine Whyte—a local boy and the high-born Massachusetts girl he met at the Boston Museum School of Fine Art in 1927—the museum is the only one of its kind, dedicated to the art, history, and culture of the Rockies. Tireless philanthropists, the couple lived in Banff from 1930 onward and set about enhancing its cultural life, and collecting artifacts and art about Banff's uniqueness; the foundation they started to fund the museum is still its principal source of funding.

The museum, now housed in a lovely modern building, serves many needs—art gallery, history museum, and keeper of local lore. The museum curates exhibitions of landscape painting—the Whytes' main love—both contemporary and historical, but is largely devoted to the history and culture of the Rocky Mountains. This is the place to learn about the characters that made Banff what is today.

111 Bear St. ⓒ **403/762-2291.** www.whyte.org. C$8 adults, C$5 seniors & students, free for children 6 & under; C$15 families. Daily 10am–5pm.

SHOPPING

Alongside skiing and hiking, shopping vies for the title of Banff's most popular sport. Most shops have clerks who speak Japanese and Chinese to serve the large contingent of Asian tourists, and a handful of these stores are actually Japanese-run. There's also a large crowd of young Australians manning the shops, thanks mainly to a diplomatic agreement between the two Commonwealth countries which offers work visas to people under 30, and to the Aussie desire to live and breathe winter during their Canadian "walkabout."

Banff shopping also offers mountain gear shops in spades; every mall (and there are at least three) has a good-sized outdoor outfitter. There's a glut of places to buy T-shirts and other tourist *tchotchkes,* but you can also buy a Rolex here or flesh out your collection of Vuittons at exclusive Banff boutiques. It's enthralling enough for some that Banff Avenue is as much of Banff as they ever see. While it's good fun, don't squander all your time here—there are malls everywhere, but there's only one Banff National Park.

Where to Stay

All accommodation prices listed are for high season, normally mid-June to mid-September and over the Christmas and New Year's holidays; nearly all hotels have discounts for late fall, late winter, and spring lodging. If you're having trouble finding affordable lodgings in Banff, try properties in Canmore, located 20 minutes away (see chapter 8). If you want to camp, Banff National Park offers hundreds of campsites. See "Camping," later in this chapter, for more information.

VERY EXPENSIVE

Buffalo Mountain Lodge   On a hillside just above the bustling main drag of Banff, this lodge aims to be an upscale mountain retreat. Both the impressive main building (where meals are served) and the lodge rooms dotted across the property have peeled log-framed walls, cathedral ceilings, fieldstone fireplaces, and a casually elegant cottage feel. All rooms are spacious, with claw-foot tubs and contemporary detailing with natural materials, like slate. Guest rooms 900 through 1100 are the farthest removed from Tunnel Mountain and, therefore, the most private. They look out onto a peaceful forest. Between the guest accommodations and the lodge itself is Buffalo Mountain's "hot tub"—more a hot pool because it accommodates up to 25 people. It's close enough to town (there's bus stop right in front) to keep you close to the action, but still feels miles away.

1.6km (1 mile) northeast of Banff on Tunnel Mountain Rd. (follow Otter St. from downtown); Banff, AB T1L 1B3. ⓒ **800/661-1367** or 403/762-2400. Fax 403/760-4492. www.buffalomountainlodge.com. 108 units. C$174–C$344 double; C$204–C$334 suite. AE, MC, V. Free parking. **Amenities:** 2 restaurants; lounge; exercise room; Jacuzzi; steam room. *In room:* TV, hair dryer, free Internet.

The Banff Springs Hotel

In the name of national unity the Government of Canada pitched in on building the trans-Canada railway back in the 1880s, but it wasn't enough to save the Canadian Pacific Railway from floundering in massive debt at the project's end. In today's lingo, the CPR needed to *diversify*—both its business and its asset base—and it happened upon the relatively new industry of tourism as a possible salvation.

CPR vice-president William Van Horne summed up the business strategy at the time thusly: "Since we can't export the scenery, we'll have to import the tourists." They already had the railway and the trains; they just needed to provide them with the destination.

That destination was to become the Banff Springs Hotel, the grandest and finest of the network of CPR hotels to come. Van Horne hired a famous architect, Bruce Price, to design the building. And by 1886, the plans were finalized and construction began. Opening June 1, 1888, the Springs had cost the debt-plagued company C$250,000; it was then the largest hotel in the world, but would pay off the debt it incurred at a typical room rate of C$3.50 per night.

The Springs, as the locals call it, was a smashing success. Instantly a favorite destination, it also kick-started the town of Banff's development, bringing hordes of people west to discover the endless beauty to be found within the park; having escaped the filth of the cities, many of them never went back, starting businesses (and families) and fostering the town's early growth.

The hotel that stands today isn't much like the one Price designed; fires, subsequent repairs, and more extensive renovations by Fairmont, which included adding a huge conference center and additional buildings, have taken away some of the original charm. But make no mistake, the Springs remains one of the world's premiere hotels, with views, amenities, and a level of service few can match.

The addition of the award-winning multi-million-dollar Willow Stream Spa has kept the place on the top of the "best hotels in the world" lists. The hotel is a national historic site with at least a handful of photo opportunities and deserves a short tour.

The Fairmont Banff Springs Banff wouldn't be Banff without the Springs. Literally. Credited with kick-starting the modern local tourist trade, the stately stone building, looking like the mountain retreat of some opulent monarch, was the magnet that drew tourists west in the early part of the 20th century to discover the majesty of the Canadian Rockies for themselves. When the Canadian Pacific Railway opened its crown jewel property in 1888, it was an instant hit, and it has gone on to become an iconic building. The Springs has been added to, renovated, and reconstructed more times than anyone can count, but nothing dents its majestic air; it is still the signature hotel of the Rockies, and the level of service—not to mention the prices—reflect it. The rooms aren't huge, but expect sumptuous linens, fancy soaps and lotions, real art, and quality furniture. Bathrooms are generally small. The Gold Floor rooms are by far the nicest. With the views, the spa, the history, and the near-pageantry of service (the Springs maintains a staff of 1,200), this is an amazing testament to a bygone era of luxury.

405 Spray Ave. Banff, AB T1L 1J4.© **800/441-1414** or 403/762-2211. Fax 403/762-5755. www.fairmont. com. 768 units. C$469–C$739 double; C$719–C$769 suite. Rates include full breakfast & service charges. AE, DC, DISC, MC, V. Valet parking C$33; self-parking C$25. **Amenities:** 9 restaurants; 2 lounges; babysitting; bike rental; concierge; Banff Springs golf course (considered one of the most scenic in the world); Jacuzzi; Olympic-size pool; 24-hr. room service; spa; 4 tennis courts. *In room:* A/C, TV/VCR w/pay movies & video games, hair dryer, Wi-Fi for minimal fee.

Rimrock Resort Hotel   The sleek and modern Rimrock sits perched on the edge of Sulphur Mountain, removed from town. The views are outstanding. Nearly every room has a commanding view of the stunning landscape, but the main lounge—with its towering ceilings and windows that run all the way from ceiling to floor—is an extraordinary place from which to drink it all in, especially given the huge fireplace that anchors the room in the center. Everything about it suggests understated opulence, from its unpolished marble floors to the traditional—though still plump and comfortable—sofas and chairs, and excellent service. Suites offer room to roam and have wet bars and balconies. Request a room on the east face of the south wing for the choicest views (all rooms are priced according to their views—Standard, Deluxe, Premium, and Grandview). The Rimrock is peaceful and elegant, with more seclusion than its competitor the Springs. In the winter, there's also an outdoor ice rink with a fire pit. Hot chocolate and cider are served during the winter at the rink.

300 Mountain Ave. (5km/3 miles south of Banff), Banff, AB T1L 1J2.© **800/661-1587** or 403/762-3356. Fax 403/762-1842. www.rimrockresort.com. 346 units. C$220–C$680 double; C$800–C$950 suite. AE, DC, DISC, MC, V. Valet parking C$10; free self-parking in heated garage. **Amenities:** 2 restaurants; 2 bars; babysitting; concierge; health club; hot tub; pool; 24-hr.room service. *In room:* A/C, TV w/pay movies & video games, hair dryer, Internet, minibar.

EXPENSIVE

Banff Boutique Inn ★   A local couple with a passion for inn-keeping have turned an old-fashioned building (original built as a European-style *pension* in the 1943 and known as Pension Tannenhof) into a lovely inn, with modern decor and mountain hospitality. It's a breath of fresh air in Banff. Rooms have strange layouts, some with very small bathrooms and others with fireplaces and jetted tubs. But the vibe is relaxing and stylish. The excellent breakfast spread includes a wide variety of home-baked goodies and is served in a cozy room with contemporary works by local artists. The kitchen is available to guests for snacks and picnic preparation, although there is a permanent coffee and tea station.

121 Cave Ave., Banff, AB T1L 1B7.© **403/762-4636.** www.banffboutiqueinn.com. 10 units. C$150–$310 double. Rates include breakfast. MC, V. Free parking. *In room:* TV (in most rooms), hair dryer, Wi-Fi.

Fox Hotel and Suites   Not dead-center in the town of Banff, but rather a pleasant, though still walkable, remove from the hubbub, the Fox—and its sister properties the Banff Lodging Company, the Banff Caribou Lodge, the Banff Ptarmigan Inn, and Rundle Manor, among others—offer pleasant, contemporary accommodations with a good complement of amenities. The rooms are mostly suites with kitchenettes and one or two bedrooms. Loft-style second floor units have mountain views. And while the facilities qualify as luxury, it's nowhere near the price. A man-made replica "hot springs" completes the package in the basement; the faux rock walls are kind of corny, but the hot water still sooths ski-weary bones very nicely.

461 Banff Ave., Banff, AB T1L 1H8. ☎ **800/661-8310** or 403/760-8500. www.bestofbanff.com. 117 units. C$199 double; C$279–C$379 1-bedroom suite; C$404–C$429 2-bedroom suite. AE, MC, V. Free parking. **Amenities:** Restaurant; lounge; exercise room; hot pool; steam room. *In room:* TV, hair dryer, Wi-Fi.

Hidden Ridge Resort ☺

If you'd like lots of personal space, to be able to pre-pare your own meals, and to be away from the bustle of Banff Avenue, this collection of stylish cabins along Tunnel Mountain Road provide privacy in townhouse-style apartments. All units have full kitchens and wood-burning fireplaces, and two new outdoor hot pools with fabulous views above Banff. You can fit up to 10 people in the premier two-bedroom lofts, great for families and groups. Besides the kitchen, there are outdoor barbecue and picnic tables for those unforgettable Rocky Mountain summer evenings. Two giant new outdoor hot pools make for easy living, as well. Kids will like the wildlife that wander by and all the hiking trails at your doorstep.

901 Hidden Ridge Way, Banff, AB T1L 1H8 ☎ **800/661-1372** or 403/762-3544. www.bestofbanff.com/hrr. 107 units. C$179–C$429 suite. AE, DISC, MC, V. *In room:* TV, hair dryer, kitchen, Wi-Fi.

Storm Mountain Lodge ★★

If you're weary of the relative sameness of most of the hotels in the park, Storm Mountain Lodge is a welcome respite. Built in 1922 halfway between the town of Banff and Lake Louise by the CPR as one of eight bungalow camps to encourage tourism, the lodge doesn't just feign elegant rusticity—it *is* rustic. The main building, a log structure lined with windows and a lovely outdoor veranda, is open and cozy with its thick wood walls; most of the accommodation is in a collection of old-fashioned log cabins on the property, all of them with big stone fireplaces and large, comfy tubs. Units 9 and 10 are furthest away from the often noisy Highway 93, while units 11 and 14 have great views of Castle Mountain. On the border with British Columbia and Kootenay National Park, you'll be far from any of the decent restaurants in Banff or Lake Louise (although they do have a pretty standard restaurant on-site), but close to hiking trail heads and wildlife; if you've come here to experience the wilderness, it's right outside your door.

On Hwy. 93 (just west of Castle Junction); Banff, AB T1L 1C8. ☎ **403/762-4155.** Fax 403/762-4151. www.stormmountainlodge.com. 16 units. C$239 double; C$199 pine cabin; C$289 log cabin (sleeps up to 4). Rates include breakfast. Additional adult C$20. Children under 8 stay free in parent's room. MC, V. Closed Oct 9 to Nov 9. **Amenities:** Restaurant; concierge. *In room:* Hair dryer, kitchenette (in cabins), no phone.

MODERATE

Blue Mountain Lodge Just steps from Banff Avenue, this is a good choice for travelers on a budget who don't want to miss a single second of all the action. Offering simple, clean, and pleasant rooms, the owners at this little place go the extra mile, from a superb breakfast to afternoon home-baked snacks and free wireless. Rooms are decorated in local-inspired motifs, with characters like beaver trappers and cowboys. Light meals and snacks can be prepared any time of the day in the guest kitchen. It's also family-friendly.

327 Caribou St., Banff, AB. T1L 1C4. ☎ **403/762-5134.** www.bluemtnlodge.com. 10 units. C$119–C$179 double. MC, V. Rates include breakfast. Additional adult C$15. *In room:* TV, Wi-Fi.

Buffaloberry Bed and Breakfast ★ The unpretentious owners of this little inn love the outdoors, and their B&B, in a building nestled in one of downtown Banff's quieter areas, may be the best sleep in town, thanks to soundproof rooms, blackout curtains, solid-core doors, and luxurious natural linens. Bathrooms are spacious, and each room has its own heat control. Breakfasts include homemade pastries. But the best part of staying here is the chance it gives you to slip into the "real" Banff, where people actually live and work. It's a Banff that can be hard to find amidst the rows and rows of hotels and parking stalls.

417 Marten St. Banff, AB T1L 1G5.© **403/762-3750.** www.buffaloberry.com. 4 units. $325 double. MC, V. No children under 10 allowed. *In room:* TV.

Homestead Inn ♦
The decor may be a little outdated, and the polyester bed-spreads aren't exactly the last word in comfort, but it's clean, spacious, comfortable, and well-located in the center of town—all you can ask for in one of the best lodging deals in Banff. Factor in the free downtown parking and free wireless Internet, and this well-maintained older motel is a real winner in the budget class.

217 Lynx St., Banff, AB T1L 1A7 © **800/661-1021** or 403/762-4471. www.homesteadinnbanff.com. 27 units. C$147 double. Additional adult C$10. Children under 12 stay free in parent's room. AE, MC, V. Free parking. **Amenities:** Family restaurant. *In room:* TV, hair dryer, minibar.

Red Carpet Inn ♦
Run by a long-time innkeeper family, this classic hotel is one of the best deals in Banff. Simple guest rooms are furnished with easy chairs and desks. There's an excellent restaurant right next door. The biggest rooms have a king bed and a fireplace for very reasonable prices. Freebies include free local calling, free parking, free wireless Internet, and a complimentary continental breakfast. The entire facility is very well-maintained and very clean—just the thing if you don't want to spend a fortune.

425 Banff Ave., Banff, AB T1L 1B6 © **800/563-4609** or 403/762-4184. www.banffredcarpet.com. 52 units. C$140–C$150 double; C$174 double w/king bed & fireplace. Rates include continental breakfast. AE, MC, V. Free parking. **Amenities:** Jacuzzi (in winter only). *In room:* A/C, TV, fridge, hair dryer, Wi-Fi.

Rocky Mountain B&B ☺
A former boarding house converted into a B&B, this pleasant and rambling inn offers comfortable, clean, and cozy rooms, and a location just a few minutes from downtown. Accommodations have a mix of private and shared bathrooms. Four units have kitchenettes. Full breakfasts go beyond coffee and toast; guests choose between French toast, crepes, breakfast burritos, and the like. Families are welcome.

223 Otter St., Banff, AB T1L 1C3. © **403/762-4811.** www.rockymtnbb.com. 10 units. From C$100 double. Rates include breakfast. Additional adult C$15, additional child C$10. MC, V. Free parking. *In room:* TV.

INEXPENSIVE

Banff Alpine Centre and Hostel
This well-known establishment is beloved by travelers and backpackers around the world. It's a fun place to stay and very reason-ably priced. Dorm rooms sleep four to six people, and there are five double rooms with private baths that are a good bargain. The atmosphere here is casual yet full of energy, as so many of the guests are keen outdoors types. The pub downstairs is always lively, and the restaurant has reasonable prices for mediocre food. A good option for younger travelers and active families.

801 Hidden Ridge Way (at Tunnel Mountain Dr.), Banff, AB T1L 1B3.© **403/762-4123.** Fax 403/762-3441. www.hihostels.ca/alberta. 52 units; 216 beds. Members C$36 bed, nonmembers C$40 bed; members C$120 double, nonmembers C$128 double. Children under 12 stay half-price w/parent. MC, V. **Amenities:** Restaurant; 2 lounges; Wi-Fi. *In room:* No phone.

Banff Y Mountain Lodge (YWCA) The YWCA is a bright, modern building with good amenities, just across the Bow River bridge from downtown. The Y welcomes men, women, singles, couples, and family groups, with accommodations in private or dorm rooms. Some units have private bathrooms.

102 Spray Ave., Banff, AB T1L 1C2. ℰ **800/813-4138** or 403/760-3207. www.ymountainlodge.com. 43 units; 80 beds. C$33 bunk in dorm room (bedding included); C$88–C$120 double; C$135 family room w/private bath. MC, V. Free parking. **Amenities:** Restaurant; Internet. In room: No phone.

BACKCOUNTRY LODGES

If you aren't up for carrying a tent and gear on your back, but still want a true wilderness experience and excellent hiking, consider spending a night or two at one of Banff's historic backcountry lodges. Banff has three rustic private lodges operating in its backcountry (meaning there is no road access; they're all ski-, hike-, or bike-in). And this is not "rustic" in the sense of luxuriously appointed log cabins with private fireplaces and stone bathrooms; no, the rusticity is not a decor choice, but is utterly authentic—meaning some lack such things as electricity, phones, and (alas) indoor plumbing.

For that level of rusticity, you might expect them to be easy on the budget. They're not. But they operate on the principle that some things are worth more than a Jacuzzi tub. Like, say, a night or two in the untouched alpine wilderness, where no car will ever go. This is peace beyond peace—places where you truly realize how tiny we are in the churn of natural history.

Most include all meals, have at least at a 2-night minimum stay, and are open to hikers in July and August and skiers from January through March.

A few hours' hike from the Lake Louise ski area, the revered **Skoki Lodge** (ℰ **877/956-8473** or 403/522-1347; www.skoki.com) is a National Historic Site nestled next to wildflower-dotted alpine meadows. The first ski lodge in Western Canada, the building itself is a gorgeous log structure. It is rustic—there's no running water or electricity. But there is serene beauty and warm hospitality, not to mention a soothing wood-fired sauna and gourmet meals (all included), served buffet-style. Candles and kerosene lamps light up the lodge at night, giving the lodge that unstuck-in-time sense of apartness in the wilderness. It's open to cross-country skiers in winter and hikers in summer. Rates are C$109 to C$263 per person, depending on dates.

Brewster's Shadow Lake Lodge (ℰ **866/762-0114**; www.shadowlakelodge. com), on the shore of Shadow Lake in the Egypt Lakes area about four hours hike in from the highway northwest of the Town of Banff, has heated washrooms with running water, showers, and solar-powered lighting—for the backcountry, luxury indeed. Its rates are C$215 per person per night, based on double occupancy.

Just outside the park is another historic and charming gem, **Mt. Assiniboine Lodge** (ℰ **403/678-2883**; www.canadianrockies.net/assiniboine). Rooms start at C$260 per person per night, including meals, guides, and lodging. For those not keen on hiking or skiing the 28km (17 miles) into the lodge, it can be accessed by helicopter for an extra $130 per person each way.

Sundance Lodge (ℰ **800/661-8352**; www.xcskisundance.com) is a heritage building deep in the woods, but only a 16km (10-mile) hike or ski from the town of Banff. It's a great choice for families looking for a true wilderness experience, with the creature comfort bonus of hot showers and fresh-cooked meals. Rates are

There are three registration methods for front-country campgrounds in Banff and Jasper national parks.

An online **Parks Canada** reservation system allows campers to reserve a site in advance at a limited number of their campsites in the Rockies via a website (www.pccamping.ca) or via telephone (*(C)* **877/737-3783**). There is an C$11 fee to make a reservation, but that's a small price to pay in high season, when the stress of wondering where you're going to lay your head tonight can offset the therapeutic relaxation you came out here to find in the first place.

You can't pick a specific site within a campground; the reservation just guarantees a spot on a first-come, first-served basis. Tunnel Mountain and Lake Louise Trailer campgrounds are the only ones you can make a reservation for online.

You can also use the regular registration method, which applies to campsites that are set aside for first-come, first-served campers who prefer not to reserve ahead of time. You register with a Parks Canada attendant at the campground when you first arrive (there's usually a building staffed 24 hr. a day).

The third method is to self-register, and it applies to many of the more remote campgrounds in both parks. Unlike the more accessible campgrounds, there's no building at the entrance to these campgrounds. It's more of a "self-serve" approach. You simply drive in to the campground and find an empty campsite. There's a small kiosk near the entrance, which will take your money (it doesn't accept credit or debit cards, and it doesn't give change).

Put your money in one of the envelopes provided and drop it in the slot, remembering to tear off the end of the envelope and mark the date that you're staying until on it. Take it back to your campsite and fasten it to the sign with your site's number on it. A Parks Canada staff member making daily rounds will pick it up first thing in the morning.

C$166 per person for the first night, with lower rates for additional nights; children 6 to 12 are welcome here, at C$85 a night (children under 6 not allowed).

CAMPING

There are a wide variety of campgrounds in Banff National Park, and you can reserve a spot online for many of them at www.pccamping.ca or via telephone at *(C)* **877/737-3783**. Very few last-minute spots are available; you must plan ahead, especially if you want to be near the town of Banff. Summer is especially crowded, for obvious reasons, so don't expect a lot of privacy at any of them from June to August.

Camping Near Banff Townsite

Castle Mountain Campground   This is a small, remote campground located on the Bow Valley Parkway (Hwy. 1A) about 20 minutes from the town of Banff, half way to Lake Louise. It's a good base for exploring the trails below the fabled walls of Castle Mountain, which towers just above it. It qualifies as a "rustic" campground; not many frills to be found here (i.e., no RV hook-ups and therefore no running water) but the shop at Castle Mountain Village is just a short walk away. A good family campground.

34km (21 miles) west of Banff townsite on the Bow Valley Pkwy. (Hwy.1A). 43 sites. C$22 site. Open May 18 to Sept 4.

Johnston Canyon Campground   Johnston Canyon is one of the most popular day hikes in Banff, which is good news in that most of the foot traffic is gone by late afternoon. The campsite is surprisingly peaceful, nestled in the forest here just 20 minutes from Banff townsite. The best sites back onto Johnston Creek.

25km (16 miles) west of Banff townsite on the Bow Valley Pkwy. (Hwy.1A). 132 sites. C$27 site. Open June to Sept 18.

Tunnel Mountain Village Campground   This is Banff's biggest campground. It's also the closest one to the townsite—walking distance to Banff Avenue, making it also one of the busiest and, at times, rowdiest. Adding to this, perhaps, is its size, with more than 1,000 sites. It's divided into three sections: a mixed tent and RV camp 2.5km (1½ miles) east of town; an RV Mecca 4km (2½ miles) east of town; and a trailer- and tenter-friendly section to the east of the RV area. Clearly, this is not the way to get away from it all, but RVers love it; tenters wanting to walk to Banff Avenue like it, too. But this is as far from Banff wilderness as camping gets.

4km (2½ miles) east of Banff townsite on Tunnel Mountain Rd. Tunnel Mountain Village I: 618 sites; C$27 site; May 4 to Sept. Tunnel Mountain Village II: 188 sites; C$32 site w/electrical hook-up; open year-round. Tunnel Mountain Trailer Court: 321 sites; C$38 site w/full hook-up; May 4 to Sept.

Two Jack Campground   On the Minnewanka Loop, Two Jack is split into two: a main, densely wooded, relatively private larger campground, and a smaller one (Lakeside). It's about 13km (8 miles) northeast of Banff townsite. The small lakeshore area is popular, with good reason: It's the most scenic and peaceful campground near the town of Banff.

12km (7½ miles) from Banff townsite on Minnewanka Loop Rd. Two Jack Main: 380 sites; C$22 site; May 18 to Sept 4. Two Jack Lakeside: 74 sites; C$27 site; May 18 to Sept 18.

The Continental Divide

The Continental Divide is the dividing line of the North American continent between two major watersheds. East of the Divide, which cleaves its way from Northern Canada all the way into the Gulf of Mexico, rivers and streams build into tributaries and flow into Hudson's Bay or the Atlantic Ocean; on the west side of the divide, the water flows the opposite direction, rushing toward the Pacific. Running along the jagged path of the Rockies, it's also the dividing line between the provinces of Alberta and British Columbia; you'll come across trail markers on various hikes, as well as on the Continental Divide Express chairlift at Sunshine Village; one of the support poles has a sign that says "Welcome to British Columbia" as it skirts along the divide; just a few poles later, where the line has zagged back west, there's a sign welcoming you back to "Sunny Alberta."

If you want to see where the water flow splits, there's a sign marking the provincial border in Kootenay National Park, where you can actually observe the divergent water flow.

Backcountry Camping

There are 50 designated backcountry campsites in Banff; their access varies greatly. Some are just a couple of hours from the trail head; others take a full day (20km/12 miles) just to reach. **Remember:** Most mountain hikes demand significant altitude gain, so don't budget your time and pace thinking this is a level stroll. Hiking up into Egypt Lake, for example, the first day is almost entirely uphill and strenuous until you reach the high alpine plains.

Remember: You must have a Wilderness Pass (C$9.80 per day or C$69 for an annual pass) and a campsite reserved before you hit the trail. Some campsites are legendary among hikers all over the world, and the demand is great; campsites can be booked up to 3 months prior to your dates, and the most popular ones are booked for the season within a day or two. Contact the Banff National Park backcountry reservation line (© **403/762-1556**). Don't expect much from these sites except a fire pit, an outhouse (maybe), and somewhere to hoist your food up out of reach of animals (an essential in the backcountry). Don't drink the stream or lake water to avoid Giardiasis. You'll need to either boil the water or use a water-treatment system. And you will certainly want to bring toilet paper.

Some sites can be reached from Banff townsite, by following the Spray Valley Trail. Sites at Egypt Lake, Shadow Lake, and Fish Lakes have their trail heads about a half-hour drive from town. There are also campsites along the shores of Lake Minnewanka, northeast of the townsite, which are accessible only by canoe. Families may like sites at Taylor Lake or Glacier Lake, which are accessed by relatively easy trails.

Farther up the Icefields Parkway, there are trail heads to more sites still in Banff (not yet Jasper). Consult the Banff website for full listings and maps at www.pc. gc.ca/eng/pn-np/ab/banff/activ/activ33.aspx. The Banff Information Center, listed in "Hotel Alternatives," earlier in this chapter, will also be able to help you out. A backcountry campsite costs C$10 per person per night, and there is a C$12 reservation fee. You cannot reserve backcountry sites online.

Backcountry Huts

There is a significant amount of luck involved in reaching the backcountry huts in Banff National Park, operated by the Alpine Club of Canada (ACC), as they are few (there are six), small (most accommodate about a half-dozen people, max), and very, very popular. If you get a spot reserved at one, though, you'll quickly see what all the fuss is about. These are remote places, often along a towering bluff above a remote valley, or face-on to a glacier—places you probably won't see any other way. Almost all are a good full-day hike or ski into the backcountry; as such, they're most often used by hikers on treks lasting several days or mountain climbers making an ascent of a nearby summit. And you must reserve ahead of time. If you show up without a reservation, you'll not be given a bed unless it is an emergency.

Some of the huts are comfortable cabins (the Castle Mountain Shelter, perched on a cliff called Goat Plateau, halfway up Castle Mountain, accommodates six people comfortably and has a propane stove; it's accessed by a challenging scramble up the mountain face and is closed in winter due to extreme avalanche hazard);

others are just shacks. None have running water or power, and few are close to a water source—so plan to bring that with you, too.

Bow Hut, by measure of remoteness, is the "easiest" to access, though it's far from easy by anyone's measure. It's a 6-hour hike from the trail head at Bow Lake and a steady climb.

If you aren't a member of the ACC, rates are C$36 per person per night for a simple bunk and access to the facilities: some huts are subject to peak-rate pricing at certain times of the year. Rates for members are substantially lower. For more information on backcountry huts or on ACC membership, contact the **Alpine Club of Canada** (© **403/678-3200;** www.alpineclubofcanada.ca). The site also lists what you should bring to a hut to make your experience as comfortable as possible. Remember, you must contact the ACC before you arrive. You can't just show up at a hut and expect to find sleeping room. You'll also need a valid Wilderness Pass from Parks Canada (see "Backcountry Camping," above).

Where to Dine

Going out to eat in Banff can be surprisingly entertaining. Some complain that prices are high, waiting times long, service indifferent, and entrees smallish. But if you stick to the places listed below, you'll find charm, variety, and refreshingly good food for a little mountain town of only 8,000 people. Banff Avenue has all types of restaurants, and the crowd has spilled over to neighboring Bear Street, 1 block to the north.

If you're nonplussed by the options, you can always fall back on the Banff franchise of the Earl's chain (229 Banff Ave.; © **403/762-4414;** www.earls.ca), with the same menu, quality, and pricing of other Earl's listings in this guide. For those with a modicum of curiosity, however, there are at least a couple of great options offering unique takes on local cuisine that also deliver value.

EXPENSIVE

The Bison Mountain Bistro ★★★ CANADIAN Casually rustic, the Bison simply is the best of Banff. It calls itself "Rocky Mountain Comfort Food," but it manages to be innovative and elegant. Try the pizza with house-made venison pepperoni, wild mushrooms, and crisped leeks, and you'll see what I mean. With a huge emphasis on local and seasonal ingredients and as much made in-house as possible (the bread here is fantastic all by itself), the Bison is casual enough that you can stop in for a snack and not break the bank (the pizzas, a trail mix and baby spinach salad, and shrimp and crab mini tacos are all outstanding), or have a full blown multi-course meal (of grilled bison tenderloin, venison, or organic chive gnocchi, to name a few) and feel like you're in a major cosmopolitan center. The decor is as adaptable and enticing as the menu; wholly contemporary—yet with its vaulted wood ceilings and floors, still cozy and homey—it's a great respite from the touristy offerings in much of the town.

Bison Courtyard, 211 Bear St. © **403/762-5550.** Reservations recommended on weekends. Main courses C$19–C$45. AE, MC, V. Sat & Sun 10am–2pm; daily 5–11pm.

Bow Valley Grill ★ CANADIAN The Banffshire Club is the fanciest dining room at the Banff Springs, but the more low-key Bow Valley Grill ranks right up there with the best in town. First, it takes in the famous hotel's multi-million-dollar views of the Fairholme Mountain Range and the Bow Valley. It also offers the hotel's almost equally famous pricing—the cocktail menu lists single drinks for as much as C$25—but the food here is excellent, and if you're into scenic dining, it's worth the premium. The open kitchen delivers such lovely local fare as pan-fried Bow River trout—that's the river you can see from your table—and, of course, top-grade Alberta beef. While the cuisine isn't overly ambitious—baked potatoes remain a standard accompaniment with beef—it's hard to argue with fresh, seasonal meats and fish grilled rotisserie style, and a perfect preparation to boot. If it lacks originality, it makes up for it in quality; this is one of Banff's most-loved, consistent restaurants for just that reason. Their brunch buffet is a classic for any special Sunday morning.

In the Fairmont Banff Springs Hotel, 405 Spray Ave. ℭ **403/762-6860.** Reservations recommended June–Aug (only on weekends the rest of the year). Brunch buffet C$27; main courses C$24–C$46. AE, DC, DISC, MC, V. Daily 6:30am–2pm & 6–9pm.

Cilantro Mountain Café ★ CALIFORNIAN Part of the sprawling Buffalo Mountain Lodge complex, this is the casual choice set in the equally peaceful location of Sleeping Buffalo. An offshoot of the original Cilantro on Calgary's 17th Avenue (see chapter 6), the Banff Cilantro has many of the same priorities: a casual, California-style cuisine—here, inflected with a mountain flair, like the wild game meats—with a wide selection of apple-wood–fired oven pizzas, the item on which the original Cilantro's enduring reputation was based. It's cozy and rustic here, with raw-log walls and everything a rough, warm wood. There's also a great patio from which to survey the lodge's private, tranquil grounds.

In the Buffalo Mountain Lodge, 700 Tunnel Mountain Rd. ℭ **403/760-2400.** Reservations recommended on weekends. Main courses C$15–C$28. AE, MC, V. June 6 to Sept 9 Wed–Sun 5–10pm; Dec 19 to June 5 Fri–Sun 5–10pm. Closed Sept 10–Dec 18.

Giorgio's Trattoria ITALIAN This has long be the top Italian restaurant in the Canadian Rockies. And since a new chef took over, Giorgio's is more relaxed, fresher, and simpler. Dine Italian family–style by sharing dishes like an antipasto platter, risotto, and a wood-fired pizza. Don't want to share? Then you can't miss the Tuscan Caesar salad and veal scaloppini.

219 Banff Ave. ℭ **403/762-5114.** Reservations recommended. Main courses $15–$40. AE, MC, V. Daily 5–10pm.

Grizzly House FONDUE This is old-school tourist Banff. A pervasive veneer of the faux-rustic is the Grizzly House's shtick, and what a shtick it is. Goofy fonts, clapboard set deliberately askew, this is Banff at its theme-park best (or worst, depending on your perspective). Grizzly House is all about fondue—cheese, chocolate, seafood, rattlesnake, frogs' legs, alligator, and buffalo. Steaks and game dishes are the Grizzly's other specialties. It's noisy and sometimes hard to focus here, so it's not for everybody, but for the been-there-done-that-got-the-T-shirt set (the Grizzly House sells those—and mugs and an array of other tourist *tchothkes*— all emblazoned with its goofy font) it's not a bad option, as the food is actually quite good.

207 Banff Ave. ℭ **403/762-4055.** Reservations recommended. A la carte fondue C$26–C$63. AE, MC, V. Daily 11:30am–midnight.

Maple Leaf Grille & Spirits NEW CANADIAN   A less-inventive version of the Bison Mountain Bistro—and, given its sprawling upstairs dining room, intended for a much larger crowd—the Maple Leaf nonetheless provides nicely prepared casual fare—bison, elk, caribou—but with some creative flair, like a seafood tower of oysters, mussels, prawns, scallops, smoked salmon, and grilled squid, among others (available in one, two, or three tiers); local roasted duck and BC salmon; and, of course, a vast array of Alberta beef, from tenderloin to prime rib to quite excellent burgers. It really is a sampling of Canadiana cuisine, coast to coast.

137 Banff Ave. © **403/760-7680.** Reservations recommended. Main courses C$18–C$48. AE, MC, V. Daily 10am–11pm; limited menu 11pm–2am.

Sleeping Buffalo at Buffalo Mountain Lodge ★ CANADIAN   Just outside town, the Buffalo Mountain Lodge occupies a peaceful, treed area that provides some escape from bustling Banff. The restaurant here, Sleeping Buffalo, reflects the chilled-out vibe; set in the hotel's spectacular log cabin–style main lodge, with a huge stone fireplace at its heart, the dining room is rustic, cozy, and posh all at once. The BML reflects the major food trend in Banff (and all of Alberta, really), with its commitment to regional ingredients and reliance on incorporating game animals (though all are farmed) like venison, caribou, and bison. The chef's fusion of the trend to a bygone era of fine dining (though the menu changes seasonally, you'll always find lamb, quail, and/or pheasant somewhere) makes the BML's take on it all its own—especially when you consider many of the sauces and seasonings are spiced with herbs from the lodge's very own extensive garden.

In the Buffalo Mountain Lodge, 700 Tunnel Mountain Rd. © **403/760-4484.** www.buffalomountain lodge.com. Reservations recommended on weekends. Main courses C$19–C$44. AE, DC, MC, V. Daily noon–10pm.

MODERATE

Bumper's STEAKHOUSE   If a place has been serving visitors Alberta beef at affordable prices since 1975, it's got to be on to something good. Simple meals star Alberta beef: Prime rib, a half-dozen cuts of steak, and baby back ribs are the usual go-to choices. They also have the best salad bar in town. While it's nothing fancy, Bumper's is a classic. As their slogan says, "If you haven't been to Bumper's, you haven't been to Banff!"

603 Banff Ave. © **403/762-2622.** Main courses $10–$40. AE, MC, V. Daily 5–10pm.

Coyotes Deli & Grill ★ SOUTHWEST/MEDITERRANEAN   Fresh, healthy, relaxed (when there isn't a lineup of people waiting for a table), and very popular with locals, Coyotes is one of the few places in town where you'll find more than the standard one or two options, but rather a broad array, like a spicy black bean burrito or a southwestern polenta with ratatouille. There's something for everybody here, including a healthy baked salmon and grilled meats. They also have an excellent breakfast menu. Coyotes is popular, so make a reservation.

206 Caribou St. © **403/762-3963.** Reservations recommended. Main courses C$16–C$28. AE, DC, MC, V. Daily 7:30am–11pm.

Eddie's Burger Bar ★ BURGERS   Build your own gourmet burgers well into the evening at this fun bar–cum–burger shop. The bison burger comes with sautéed mushrooms, double-smoked bacon, and roasted garlic aioli on an English muffin. The Red White Blue has hot buffalo sauce, bacon, and blue cheese. Kobe, Kiwi, Aussie, veggie, and chicken burgers are also options. Beef burgers are organic and pure Albertan, and a great value. Add sweet potato fries or *poutine*. Eddie also has a large cocktail menu and the best milkshakes in the Rockies, made with Mackay's ice cream.

137C Banff Ave (at Caribou St.).© **403/762-2230.** Main courses $8–$16. MC, V. Daily 11:30am–3am.

Elk & Oarsmen PUB Settle in with some locals to watch the game and dig into the best pub food in Banff at this upstairs pub right on the main drag. Recommended choices are the Black Angus steaks or a burger (you have elk, bison, beef, salmon, or chorizo to choose from!). There's a great patio on the rooftop, regular happy-hour specials, and big-screen TVs.

119 Banff Ave. (upstairs).© **403/762-4616.** Main courses $10–$27. AE, MC, V. Kitchen open daily 11am–11pm (pub stays open until 1am).

Wild Flour Bakery CAFE/BAKERY The Wild Flour is a hearty organic bakery on the burgeoning culinary strip of Bear Street (just a few doors down the street from where the Bison Mountain Bistro (see above) is located); you'll find great treats and snacks here (fantastic brownies and cinnamon buns), as well as artisanal breads. The granola bars are handy to have in pocket for a day of hiking. The cafe serves up local Kicking Horse espresso, and they also do more meal-sized fare; a breakfast sandwich of herbed egg frittata and old cheddar is a great day-starter; grilled panini like Valbella ham and gruyere with hazelnut pesto is a great lunch, especially in combo with a soup, coffee, and a cookie of your choice.

Bison Courtyard, 101-211 Bear St.© **403/760-5074.** Lunches C$6–C$10; lunch combo C$11. MC, V. Daily 7am–7pm.

INEXPENSIVE

Banff isn't really the place for the frugal traveler, unless you want to resort to the grocery stores. Thankfully, they're readily available; a full-sized Safeway can be found at Martin and Elk streets, and if you're in a hostel, there will almost surely be a common kitchen.

The **Cascade Plaza Mall,** on Banff Avenue, has a food court, and if you get really desperate, there's always **McDonald's,** at 116 Banff Ave. But don't do that—for just a bit more, you can go to one of the three locations of the local coffee shop **Evelyn's** (201 Banff Ave., 229 Bear St., or in the Town Centre Mall). They're all crowded by folks needing a coffee fix. There's home baking, though you're not likely to make a meal of their muffins. Your best bet to stay out of the tourist-food trap is to prepare meals yourself.

Barpa Bills GREEK For something "to go," you can't beat a souvlaki in a warm pita, hot off the grill at this little Bear Street joint. It's topped with fresh *tzatziki* sauce and cooked to order. There are also gyros, burgers, and *poutine* (a French-Canadian specialty). Grab a stool at the counter if you want to eat in, but don't expect friendly chatter with the staff!

233 Bear St.© 403/762-0377. Main courses $6–$14. No credit cards. Daily 11am–9pm.

Banff after Dark

Banff's magnetic draw for young people from all over the world, most of them working in the resorts, gives Banff nightlife an overwhelming college-town feel. Almost all the hotels have bars or lounges, but they are more sedate; all along Banff Avenue in-season, you'll find something going on in the many, many pubs.

One of the old standbys is the **Rose & Crown** (202 Banff Ave.; ✆ **403/762-2121**). It's been around long enough to establish its reputation as a rowdy, fun beer-swilling joint. On a summer night, the rooftop patio is hard to beat—all big sky and stars above, and the hustle and bustle of Banff Avenue right below. Inspired by the birthplace of Guinness, selecting a draught at the **St. James's Gate** (205 Wolf St.; ✆ **403/762-9355**) is just about the toughest challenge in Banff—there are 33 beers on tap, as well as 50 single-malt scotches and 10 Irish whiskeys. Live music is almost always Celtic, and a blast. Oenophiles will do best at **The Bison Lounge** (213 Bear St.; ✆ **403/762-5550**), which has a great list of wines by the glass and snacks from the outstanding bistro upstairs. It's the most cosmopolitan hangout in town. Grab a spot at the communal table to make new friends. At **Wild Bill's Saloon** (201 Banff Ave.; ✆ **403/762-0333**), you can embrace Alberta's western heritage whole-heartedly. Wild Bill's lets the rock bands play on its least-important nights, Monday and Tuesday, but starting Wednesday and all through the weekend, the hootin' hollerin' Western pride comes to the fore. It's non-stop line dancing and hurtin' tunes, mostly by Albertan country bands passing through.

Banff also has its own urbane cocktail lounge called **Aurora** (110 Banff Ave., downstairs; ✆ **403/760-5300**), complete with an array of DJs and martinis. Its sister club, the **Hoodoo Lounge** (137 Banff Ave.; ✆ **403/760-8636**), offers nightly events ("Throw Your Panties" being one of them) and dancing to DJs, as well.

But that's nothing compared to **Outabounds** (137 Banff Ave.; ✆ **403/762-8434**), Banff's most popular dance bar. Located in a dingy basement, the four bars serve up beers and sloppily made cocktails to young patrons—most of them resort employees—while the packed dance floor is obscured in a shroud of dry-ice fog.

LAKE LOUISE

Lake Louise is probably most famous not for the lake itself, but for the hotel named after it, the Chateau Lake Louise. One of the same family of Canadian Pacific Railway hotels that gave us the Banff Springs, the Chateau, as the name suggests, was modeled after the French building style; some find it beautiful, others not so much. The lake, though, is undeniably stunning. At the far end of the lake (perhaps an hour's hike on the Lakeshore Trail), the Victoria Glacier hangs above the blue-green waters, preternatural and spectacular.

Lake Louise, the village, is 56km (35 miles) northwest of Banff, but leaves behind the crowded, touristy feel of its neighbor. It's small, for one thing, centered around a shopping plaza nestled in trees next to the Bow River. There is no main street, and it is an overall perfectly peaceful place. It also sits next to one of the largest ski areas in North America and offers easy access to some of the most amazing trekking to be found in the park.

When you get to the Chateau, though, expect to fight for parking in summer and brave the crowds (this might be the only place in Louise you find them) heading out to take a stroll (or just take a photo) along the Lakeshore Trail.

You can reach the back of the lake quickly and easily via a flat trail. Then, decide if you want to continue up toward the Plain of Six Glaciers Trail to a teahouse with a beautiful view. The location is deeply rewarding and otherworldly.

What to See

In the summer, the ski lifts at the Lake Louise Ski Area become a sightseeing gondola (www.lakelouisegondola.com), taking you for a 14-minute ride to an elevation of 2,088m (6,850 ft.) at the top of Mount Whitehorn, across the wide Bow Valley from the lake. There's a Wildlife Interpretive Centre, as well as guided nature walks. From May to September (in between ski seasons), gondola fees for adults are C$26; children 6 to 15 C$13. Kids under 6 can ride for free.

On the way up the long, winding road from Lake Louise Village to the Chateau and the lake is a left turnoff to **Moraine Lake.** Don't miss this rough, windy road because the end of it is spectacular! Lake Louise may be on the top of the marquee, but this supporting act is equally stunning—and much less traveled. Wild and dramatic, Moraine Lake is walled in by a chain of 10 peaks 3,000m (9,843 ft.) high.

The lake is smaller than Louise but has an oddly intimate air, closed in as it is by the mountains on one side and a massive rock slide on another. You can hike a short stretch of lakeside path to the foot of the mountains in about 10 minutes or up a rock pile in about 15 minutes to a lookout for good view. Some of the premiere hikes in Banff begin here, as well. The serenity of this place is amazing, especially if you are here before noon. The lodge also has a lovely restaurant for lakeside dining in this very special place.

Where to Stay

Lake Louise, being small as it is, has few options, most of them expensive. The local HI here, the **Lake Louise Alpine Centre**, 203 Village Road, Lake Louise, AB T0L 1E0; ℂ **866/762-4122** or 403/522-2202; www.hihostels.ca), is jointly owned and run by HI and the Alpine Club of Canada, and is a very reasonable option. It's huge, modern, comfortable, and conveniently located. The hostel also offers guide-led hikes daily. Linens are included in the rates: Dorm-room beds C$28 for members, C$42 for nonmembers; private rooms C$110 members, C$118 non-members.

Baker Creek Chalets ★ Off the beaten track on the gloriously scenic Bow Valley Parkway, just east of Lake Louise, Baker Creek Chalets sit on babbling Baker Creek, apart from much of the tourist bustle. The red-roofed complex is wonderfully secluded and private; as such, Baker Creek offers the Banff wilderness that many come looking for but few find. Bears, elk, and deer routinely stroll by. Cabins mainly sleep four to six and have kitchenettes and wood-burning fireplaces. It's the kind of place you want to settle in and spend an entire week exploring. It's well worth a night away if you've been mainly centered in the town of Banff. The train runs sporadically throughout the day and night right next to the property; if you are a light sleeper, ask for a quiet cabin. There are several room configurations, so call Baker Creek to find something that best suits your needs and budget. Also, the on-site Baker Creek Bistro (see below) is one of the top places to dine in this part of Alberta.

11km (6¾ miles) east of Lake Louise on Hwy. 1A; Lake Louise, AB T0L 1E0. © **403/522-3761.** www. bakercreek.com. 35 units. C$290–C$335 double. AE, MC, V. Free parking. **Amenities:** Restaurant; lounge; gym; steam room; sauna. *In room:* Kitchen, no phone.

Deer Lodge   Just before reaching the lake and the Chateau, you'll pass Deer Lodge, a heritage lodge with more affordable rates in a very good location, just a short stroll from the lake (and the Chateau) itself. Plus, where the Chateau often feels overrun, Deer Lodge remains oddly tranquil. Its rustic log structure is a homey, cozy option with real mountain authenticity: Built in the 1920s, the original Lodge was a teahouse for the early mountaineers who came to the area to hike (the original tearoom is now the Mount Fairview Dining Room and Bar, offering Northwest cuisine). Now owned by the same company that owns Buffalo Mountain Lodge (see above) in Banff, like there, there's an emphasis on serenity. There are rooms from three eras: small, basic rooms in the original lodge; larger rooms in the newer Tower Wing; and Heritage Rooms, the largest rooms in the newest wing, which have been completely renovated and have sunny balconies. Comfortable but not posh, this is mountain vacationing the way your grandfather might have done it, with old-fashioned plumbing and heating issues to go with it.

109 Lake Louise Dr., Lake Louise, AB T0L 1E0. © **800/661-1595** or 403/522-3747. www.deerlodgelake louise.com. 73 units. C$105–C$200 double (lodge rooms); C$190–C$300 double (Heritage Rooms). AE, MC, V. Free parking. **Amenities:** Restaurant; lounge; rooftop Jacuzzi; sauna.

The Fairmont Chateau Lake Louise ★★★   Should you decide to forget you have a budget, the Chateau Lake Louise is one of two places where you should do it (Fairmont Jasper Park Lodge (see below) is the other). The Chateau, on the shores of the emerald waters of spectacular Lake Louise, has perhaps the most picturesque location of any hotel in the country. Ancient ice hangs suspended above the lake at the far end in the Victoria Glacier; the frigid waters, just down the steps from the dining room and lounge, are plied by canoes and kayaks in warm weather and ice-skaters in winter. The massive, formal structure, blue-roofed and turreted, is furnished with Alpine-styled sumptuousness and charm.

The guest rooms, while quite modest in size, are nevertheless very elegant, warm, and comfortable, with pine and oak furniture, walls done in soft tones, and luxurious feather duvets. Each guest room has a different heritage photo of a local pioneer and a botany sketch—unique touches. Having said this, there is a large variety in size and decor, depending on which of the three wings you stay in. Rooms with lake views cost much more than those on the other side of the hall (which still have nice mountain views). None of the rooms (save the Royal and Belvedere suites) have balconies or patios, though. The new Gold Floor has superior service. The pool is nothing special, but the hotel's rich heritage, coupled with access to amazing hiking and skiing, is unmatched on the planet. This is not a peaceful place, given the throngs of visitors that storm the Chateau every day, but the guest rooms are truly sumptuous and the service top notch. Truly the best of high-end Banff.

111 Lake Louise Dr., Lake Louise, AB T0L 1E0. ℰ **800/441-1414** or 403/522-3511. www.fairmont.com. 554 units. C$399–C$599 double. Children under 17 stay free in parent's room. Off-season rates & packages available. AE, DC, DISC, MC, V. Valet parking C$35; self-parking C$25. **Amenities:** 5 restaurants; 2 bars; babysitting; bike rental; concierge; concierge-level rooms; health club; exercise room; Jacuzzi; indoor pool; 24-hr. room service; sauna; canoe rental. *In room:* A/C, TV, hair dryer, minibar, Wi-Fi.

Lake Louise Inn   With limited options in Lake Louise for mid-range budgets, this inn stands out. You'll pay less than at the other places listed here (except for the hostel), but don't expect anything special. It's dated and a bit stuffy, with only mediocre service. There are five different buildings in the Lake Louise Inn complex, which keeps the social space—restaurant, bar, lounge, pool, Jacuzzi, steam room—separate from the accommodations, spread out among four other buildings. There's a wide range of accommodations, starting with a simple room with double beds and moving up to superior lofts—great for families, as they sleep as many as eight. The lofts are more airy, with two bedrooms, two bathrooms, and a full kitchen.

210 Village Rd., Lake Louise, AB T0L 1E0. ℰ **800/661-9237** or 403/522-3791. www.lakelouiseinn.com. 247 units. C$199–C$289 double. AE, DC, MC, V. Free parking. **Amenities:** Restaurant; bar; Jacuzzi; indoor pool; sauna. *In room:* TV, fridge, hair dryer, Wi-Fi.

Moraine Lake Lodge ★   Understated and lovely, the Moraine Lake Lodge has the feeling of being apart from the world in the wilderness—even though it's only a 15-minute drive from the Fairmont Chateau Lake Louise, and the parking lot can feel like a zoo during peak hours. When the day-trippers leave, though, this lodge becomes secluded, private, and gorgeous. There are eight modern but basic rooms in the original building and six in a separate wing next door, with frills such as fireplaces. Along the shore of the lake, private cabins with fireplaces and beautiful lake-view balconies sit in seclusion. No attempt at old-world opulence is made here; the focus is on the outside, where it should rightly be. There's really no need to go anywhere else; the restaurant is top-notch, serving inventive local cuisine like game meats and fish. Room rates include continental breakfast, afternoon tea, use of canoes on the lake, and naturalist presentations and hikes.

13km (8 miles) south of Lake Louise, at Moraine Lake, Lake Louise, AB T0L 1E0. ℰ **877/522-2777** or 403/522-3733. www.morainelake.com. 33 units. C$227–C$449 double; C$599 cabin. Rates include continental breakfast. AE, MC, V. Free parking. Closed early Oct to May. **Amenities:** 2 restaurants; bar; concierge; canoe rental; Wi-Fi. *In room:* Hair dryer, no phone.

Post Hotel ★★★   This is almost as much a Lake Louise landmark as the Chateau—albeit ¹⁄₂₀ₜₕ the size. But while you may sacrifice the lakeside setting, you'll miss none of the crowds. The Post, though understated, is quietly one of very few properties in all of Western Canada that is part of the exclusive Relais & Chateaux network, a French hospitality industry designation extended to only the best of the best. The Post is certainly that: quintessential mountain style with traditional log post-and-beam construction, but the rustic structure is tricked out in pure luxurious comfort. The service is Swiss-style (exquisite and professional). Most rooms have stone fireplaces, heated slate bathroom floors, and private balconies, while the common areas, like the lobby and library, often boast a roaring fire and comfortable overstuffed sofas and chairs. The spa is the best in Lake Louise. But the real feature of the Post Hotel is the dining room (see below), which is simply one of the best anywhere in Canada. The Post has come a long way in the past 25 years; it used to be little more than a motel, though the dining room was always special—an international destination in the backwoods of old-time Lake Louise. The current Swiss-Canadian owners built around the restaurant's reputation (and structure; it still occupies its original building) and brought the entire Post Hotel up to the dining room's standard. The result is simply one of the best mountain retreats you'll find anywhere.

200 Pipestone Rd., Lake Louise, AB TOL 1E0. ⓒ **800/661-1586** or 403/522-3989. www.posthotel.com. 92 units. C$345–C$455 double; from C$585 suite; C$465–C$1,400 cabin. AE, MC, V. Free parking. Closed Nov. **Amenities:** Restaurant; 2 bars; babysitting; Jacuzzi; indoor pool; sauna. *In room:* TV/VCR, hair dryer, Wi-Fi.

CAMPING
Lake Louise Area

Lake Louise Campground Downhill from the extravagant Fairmont Chateau Lake Louise, this campground is a hive of activity, even if it's more low-key than the very crowded Tunnel Mountain facility. It does offer the same close-to-town convenience. A 10-minute stroll takes you into Lake Louise's village; a little farther uphill (4km/2½ miles) is the Chateau and the lakeshore (if, say, you want to break up your rustic camping experience with high tea). The tent and the trailer areas are separated, with the tent area in the trees near the river; the trailer area is more open and closer to the highway and railway line. Overall, a relatively relaxed camping experience in jam-packed Banff.

58km (36 miles) northwest of Banff townsite on Trans-Canada Hwy. 1. Lake Louise tent area: 210 sites; C$28 site; May 11 to Sept. Lake Louise trailer area: 189 sites; C$32 site w/electrical hook-up; open year-round. Exit at Lake Louise & turn left after passing under the railway bridge onto Fairview Rd.

Protection Mountain Campground The closest campground to Lake Louise that isn't the complex above, this makes a good base for exploring both the park's east and west territories. It's rustic with few amenities, though. A good choice for tenters and trailers, but not ideal if you're traveling by RV.

48km (30 miles) west of the Banff townsite on the Bow Valley Pkwy. (Hwy. 1A); 10km (6¼ miles) west of Castle Junction. 89 sites. C$22 site. June 22 to Sept 3.

North of Lake Louise

Mosquito Creek Campground Along the Icefields Parkway 24km (15 miles) north of Lake Louise, Mosquito Creek is not for the casual camper (though it's not as unpleasant as the name might suggest; it's actually quite beautiful, tucked in a small valley above which massive peaks loom). Still, with no showers, sinks, or flush toilets (outhouses only), it's not ideal accommodation for everyone. There are two different areas: one a gravel-strewn field, the other a wooded space. Stick to the field if you can; the woods are buggy at night.

24km (15 miles) north of Lake Louise on the Icefields Pkwy. (Hwy. 93). 32 sites. C$16 site.

Waterfowl Lake Campground This is my favorite campground in the park because of its peacefulness and scenery, 57km (35 miles) north of Lake Louise. It's scenic and tranquil, and it has amazing views of the surrounding mountains and glaciers. On the lake is a small recreation area (though swimming would be foolhardy; this is glacier water), which is also a popular spot to launch a canoe or kayak, and paddle around the icy-blue waters.

57km (35 miles) north of Lake Louise on the Icefields Pkwy. (Hwy. 93). 116 sites. C$22 site. June 15 to Sept 9.

BACKCOUNTRY HOSTELS

These are rustic choices, to be sure (read: no indoor plumbing), but they're a small step up, comfort-wise, from sleeping in a tent, and they're full of like-minded out-door adventurers from all over the globe. Run by Hostelling International, they're a good choice for larger groups or if you're looking for hiking and backpacking companions.

Reservations are highly recommended, particularly in the summer months; because of their relative inexpensiveness and popularity, they tend to be packed. Though there's usually not a bathroom, shower, or toilet to be found, each has a shared kitchen.

You can make a reservation by calling **Hostelling International** at ℂ **403/670-7580**, or by logging on to www.hihostels.ca/alberta. None of the hostels listed below have direct phones. All are highway accessible.

Castle Mountain Wilderness Hostel, on the Bow Valley Parkway (Hwy. 1A) 1.5km (1 mile) east of the Trans-Canada Highway (Hwy. 1) and Highway 93 junction, is open year-round and has hot water and flush toilets. Though its environs are definite wilderness, it's also convenient to the creature comforts of downhill skiing, as Lake Louise is only 20 minutes west and Sunshine is 20 minutes east. But if that's not why you came, the hostel is in close proximity to a web of hiking and cross-country ski trails, all at the foot of the Rockies. The common room has a big wood-burning fireplace; family rooms are not available. Rates are C$23 per person per night for Hostelling International members, C$27 per person per night for nonmembers. There are no private rooms, only shared dorms.

Just 26km (16 miles) north of Lake Louise on the Icefields Parkway 93 is the **Mosquito Creek Wilderness Hostel,** also run by Hostelling International. This is probably the most comfortable of these "off the grid" type of hostels, with private/family rooms available, a sauna, and a fireplace. It's a cluster of rustic cabins along a fast-rushing creek, close to scenic Bow Lake and a number of glorious hiking trails. There's also a lovely sauna. Rates are C$23 per person per night for HI members, C$26 per person per night for nonmembers. Private rooms are available for C$60 for members and $68 for nonmembers.

The **Rampart Creek Hostel** sits near the northern border of Banff National Park, 95km (59 miles) north of Lake Louise on the Icefields Parkway. It's a popular mid-point for cyclists making the Icefields Parkway trek between Banff and Jasper; it's also well-traveled by rock and ice climbers looking to scale the spectacular nearby faces. Rates are C$23 per person per night for members and C$26 per person per night for nonmembers. There are no private rooms.

Where to Dine

Baker Creek Bistro ★★ CANADIAN Fresh and modern food is served by warm and friendly folks inside a cozy heritage cabin about 10 minutes south of Lake Louise. It's definitely worth the drive and makes a great pit-stop on your way to the Icefields Parkway from Banff. It focuses on local ingredients simply but inventively prepared—recent menu items included blue crab and prawn cakes in coconut, curry and lime ginger aioli, aromatic smoke-roasted game hen, cedar plank wild salmon, and bison short ribs. Chef Shelley Robinson is also an expert pastry chef, so save room for dessert.

15km (9¼ miles) east of Lake Louise on Hwy. 1A. © **403/522-2182.** Reservations suggested. Main courses C$25–C$32. MC, V. Daily noon–3pm & 5–9pm.

Laggan's Mountain Bakery and Deli ★ DELI/BAKERY Laggan's is old-school Louise. Wonderfully hippie—and accordingly disorganized—you'll forgive the chaos for the lovingly prepared muffins, cookies, artisanal breads, soups, and wonderful take-out sandwiches that will sustain you on a day trek. A Nanaimo bar and coffee-to-go are de rigueur for après skiers. Beat the lineups by entering the alternative door on the left side and heading for the second cashier. The quiches and the tofu vegetarian rolls are affordable and delicious. Sandwiches are made on Laggan's home-made breads.

101 Lake Louise Dr. (in Samson Mall). © **403/522-2017.** Main courses C$5–C$12. MC, V. June–Sept daily 6am–8pm; Oct–May daily 6am–6pm.

Lake Louise Station STEAKS/SEAFOOD A throwback to Banff's whistle-stop past, the Station, as it's known, is really a station—it was the train stop in town until VIA Rail pulled the plug on its Calgary–Vancouver run in the '80s. With the building lying fallow, some enterprising entrepreneurs got the bright idea to turn this lovely old log building into a restaurant. It's been a real hit: Guests now dine in the old waiting room or enjoy a quiet drink in the old ticketing lobby. The menu is constantly being revamped, with a new focus on fresh ingredients and inspired combinations of retro classics with modern twists. Start with an organic baby spinach salad with goat cheese and candied pecans. Main courses include simple items like burgers, pasta, and pork tenderloin, or something more exotic like vegetable curry and duck confit. Of course, there's AAA Alberta beef, such as a New York strip with green peppercorn Cognac sauce. In the summer, barbecues are held in the Station garden, and the dining car is open for dinner on Friday and Saturday evenings. It's very popular with tour groups.

200 Sentinel Rd. © **403/522-2600.** Reservations recommended on weekends. Main courses C$15–C$34. AE, MC, V. Daily 11:30am–10pm. Closed fall–spring.

Post Hotel Dining Room ★★★ INTERNATIONAL This is the priciest place in Lake Louise by far, but it's up there with the top restaurants in North America, so your money is well spent. *Wine Spectator* magazine made it one of only four restaurants in Canada to win its Grand Award for its exhaustively fantastic 32,000-bottle wine cellar (1,800 are on the wine list at any given time); *Gourmet* magazine recently called the dining room the "third best" rustic culinary retreat on Earth. A meal here, in the hotel's original log building, is an experience hard to match: It's cozy, with a roaring fireplace; the service is unbeatable; and the food, well, hardly needs my endorsement—Google the Post's dining room, and let your mouth water at the praise handed out by taste buds far more practiced and sophisticated than mine. The menu focuses on flavorful meat and seafood, with impressive desserts a worthy follow-up. The service is first-class; diners are expected to dress appropriately (no hiking shorts, please!). Suffice it to say that, for the true foodie in the crowd, the Post simply shouldn't be missed. If there's a restaurant in the Rockies you'll regret passing up, this is the one.

200 Pipestone Rd., Lake Louise.© **403/522-3989.** www.posthotel.com. Reservations required. Main courses C$36–C$52. AE, MC, V. Daily 11:30am–2pm & 6–10pm.

Walliser Stube Wine Bar ★ SWISS   The Swiss have had a legendary influence on Lake Louise, mostly as mountain guides. Their cuisine and culture live on inside the Fairmont Chateau Lake Louise's Walliser Stube. A *stube* is a parlor, and this restaurant's dark wooden walls and library-sized wine cellar balances out the deep green and blue scene out the window. The Swiss invented cheese fondue, and the version you'll have here would put most of what you'd find in Switzerland to shame—it's simply excellent. Even if the Walliser Stube were just a place for a meal, it would be fantastic; an incredibly comfortable space, in one of the best hotels in the world, in one of the most majestic settings on the planet, is hard to beat.

In the Fairmont Chateau Lake Louise, 111 Lake Louise Rd., Lake Louise.© **403/522-1818.** Reservations required. Main courses C$30–C$47; fondues for 2 C$35–C$47. AE, DISC, MC, V. Daily 6–9pm.

THE ICEFIELDS PARKWAY

The 278km (173-mile) stretch of road that winds its way along the Rockies' spine from Lake Louise to Jasper is easily one of the most awe-inspiring drives you'll ever encounter. In good traffic, you could do the drive in 3 hours, but why would you? Along Highway 93 here, it's as much about the journey as the destination.

As you wind your way through mountain bowls cradling ancient glaciers high above, you can't help but be taken by a sense of the infinite; this thin ribbon of tarmac seems so insignificant next to these looming giants that you may feel like a visitor on another planet.

Above your sightline, midway between Banff and Jasper, glaciers spill down into bowls that are fragments from the Columbia Icefields, which cover these peaks for kilometers in a massive dome of prehistoric ice. This is one of the biggest non-polar ice fields in the world, and life has depended on its bounty for thousands of years. The ice fields are the source of some of the most significant rivers in the west, including the Columbia, the Athabasca, and the North Saskatchewan, all of which have nurtured the development of complex ecosystems over millennia and helped make human settlement of the West possible.

If it took the planet millions of years to sculpt this tableau, you can spare a little more than 3 hours to check it out. There are dozens of turn-outs along the way—picnic areas and viewpoints alongside fascinating rock formations and aquamarine lakes—to allow you a slightly deeper drink into the abundant planetary history to be found here. This is also the domain of wildlife such as the usually elusive mountain goat (often found traversing the valley from one set of peaks to the other; you'll see them frequently on the road, so watch out); bighorn sheep are common as squirrels, and you might even catch sight of a bear.

A popular and breathtaking experience is an excursion up onto the Athabasca Glacier at the Columbia Icefields in a giant purpose-built bus with wheels 6m (20 ft.) in diameter. This is as close as you can get to the ice fields themselves. The **Columbia Icefields Centre** (© **780/852-7032**), a giant complex with a museum, cafeteria, gift shop, restaurant, and lodge, sits across Highway 93 from the Athabasca Glacier; an excursion up onto the ice (operated by **Brewster Sno-coach Tours;** (C) **403/762-6735;** www.columbiaicefield.com) costs C$49 adults and C$24 kids. It takes about 90 minutes. You'll be warned on-site, but it's worth understanding that walking on a glacier can be very dangerous, as fissures and breakaway chunks of ice can happen any time. Implicit with buying a ticket is that you do so at your own risk.

The **Glacier View Inn** ((C) **877/423-7433**), with a restaurant featuring mostly overpriced cafeteria food, is part of the Icefields Centre; it has double rooms starting at C$235.

The **Icefields Centre** also has a Parks Canada office ((C) **780/852-7030**) that answers questions about the area. It stands beside the lodge and is open May to June 14 daily from 9am to 5pm; June 15 to September 7 daily from 9am to 6pm; and September 8 to October 15 daily from 9am to 5pm. It is closed October 16 to April.

The Icefields Parkway starts just northwest of Lake Louise, where Highway 1 continues west toward Golden, British Columbia; and Highway 93 (the Icefields Pkwy.) curls north along the Bow River towards Jasper. Bow Lake, the river's source, pools at the base of Crowfoot Glacier, a worthy stop-off point. **Num-Ti-Jah Lodge** (see "Where to Stay," below), on the shores of Bow Lake, is a good place to stop for lunch (and one of the only ones). This venerable lodge sits in a spectacular spot in the valley and also offers simple accommodations.

From Bow Summit, the parkway descends into the North Saskatchewan River drainage, where you'll find the Peyto Lake Viewpoint. You can get to it only on foot, but the brief (if steep) path pays off nicely when you reach the aquamarine lake's stunning shores.

The North Saskatchewan River turns west at the junction of highways 93 and 11. Here, there's a complex with a gas station, a basic motel, a gift shop and cafeteria called "the Crossing" ((C) **403/761-7000;** www.thecrossingresort.com), with a sub-par cafeteria and a tacky gift shop. Standard rooms are C$159 a night. This is the only gas station between Lake Louise and Jasper, so be sure to fuel up.

Just off the parkway, on the David Thompson Parkway (Hwy. 11) heading east, is the landing site for **Icefield Helicopter Tours** ((C) **888-844-3514;** www.icefield heli.com), which leave from the Cline River Heliport. One of the most breathtaking sights you'll ever see is the Columbia Icefields from above. As you hover not 12m (39 ft.) above the thick ice caps that stretch for dozens of kilometers in all directions, splayed across the mountaintops like a thick blanket, your mind will struggle to grasp what you're seeing. Tours start at C$189 adults; you can add a stopover—and a glass of champagne in a remote mountain valley—for an additional C$69.

Out of the North Saskatchewan drainage, you'll climb up into Sunwapta Pass. You'll feel like the ascent will never end, and the surrounding terrain is awesome and a little bit frightening. But the scenery is the perfect balm for anxiety.

Here, in the shadows of 3,490m (11,450-ft.) Mount Athabasca, the icy tendrils of the Columbia Icefields come into view. You've been surveying the glaciers from

What is a glacier?

A glacier forms in an area where more snow falls in winter than melts in summer. In the Rockies, glaciers are usually found at high elevations, where the average temperature is below freezing. Most of the snow sticks around throughout the year, although some is lost to wind, direct evaporation from ice to water vapor, and summer melting. Glaciers are also formed at lower elevations, in the shady slopes of steep mountains.

Why is glacial ice so blue?

Unlike the stunning color of many lakes and rivers in the Canadian Rockies, the beautiful color of the Athabasca Glacier has nothing to do with minerals. It's because the ice is so pure. Air and other impurities that reflect white and gray have been squeezed out of the crystals deep within the glacier; thus, wavelengths of light reflect only the blue spectrum.

What is an ice field?

An ice field is a body of ice from which glaciers flow outward in more than one direction. The Columbia Icefield, for example, flows in three separate directions.

How many glaciers flow from the Columbia Icefield?

Six named glacier valleys have outlets from the Columbia Icefield: Athabasca, Dome, Stutfield (these are the ones you can see from the Icefields Pkwy.), Columbia, Castle-Guard, and Saskatchewan.

What is the highest peak in the Columbia Icefield?

Mount Columbia is the highest peak in the Columbia Icefield, measuring 3,747m (12,293 ft.). It is second only to Mount Robson, the highest peak in the whole of the Canadian Rocky Mountains, at 3,954m (12,972 ft.). It is not visible from either the Icefields Parkway or the ridge behind the Icefield Information Centre.

below; if you took the Icefields tour, you saw the lip of the fields themselves at the top of the Athabasca Glacier. But up here, you'll see that they're tiny fragments of a colossal surface. The Columbia Icefields cover nearly 518 sq. km (200 sq. miles) and are more than 760m (2,493 ft.) thick.

From the Columbia Icefields, the parkway descends steeply into the Athabasca River drainage. From the parking area for Sunwapta Falls, travelers can choose to crowd around the chain-link fence and peer at the turbulent falls or take the half-hour hike to equally impressive but less crowded Lower Sunwapta Falls. Athabasca Falls, farther north along the parkway, is another must-see. Here, the wide and powerful Athabasca River constricts into a roaring torrent before dropping 25m (82 ft.) into a narrow canyon. The parkway continues along the Atha-basca River, through a landscape of meadows and lakes, before entering the Jasper townsite.

Where to Stay

Hotels are scant along the parkway, but rustic hostels that are ideal for cyclists, hikers, climbers, and other rugged sightseers can be found at Mosquito Creek,

Rampart Creek, Hilda Creek, Beauty Creek, Athabasca Falls, and Mount Edith Cavell (see "Backcountry Hostels" above). Reservations for all Icefields Parkway hostels can be made by calling ✆ **866/762-4122**.

Num-Ti-Jah Lodge ★ 🎁   This rustic and secluded red-roofed lodge on the shores of Bow Lake sports the most scenic location of any lodging in Banff National Park. Built in 1937 by trapper and guide Jimmy Simpson, the building is pretty much as it was then, with every detail preserved. (Simpson, who left England and came to Canada at age 19, became a legendary eccentric and much-admired Banff pioneer.)

There's nothing overly fancy here, just simple comforts, an incredible view, and the pleasure of being a half-hour's drive from the next-closest accommodations—it's one of the few secluded lodges in Banff National Park, even though it's located right off the Icefields Parkway. You'll be paying for the location, not the amenities. The stairs creak as you climb them, and the walls are thin; guest rooms are furnished in a modest style, and the light flickers a bit when you switch it on. Bathrooms in all guest rooms are clean, though quite basic and small, with stand-up showers. All-inclusive packages take away any worrying about meals. The setting is full of rustic mountain ambience. Drawing an outdoor-loving crowd of people who aren't necessarily looking for luxury amenities, guests here prefer a lodge with heaps of character and history. Sometimes, that just leaves you imagining the possibilities an upgrade could do, but to love Num-Ti-Jah is to love it as it is.

40km (25 miles) north of Lake Louise on Hwy. 93, Lake Louise, AB T0L 1E0.✆ **403/522-2167.** www.num-ti-jah.com. 25 units. C$318–C$365 double. AE, MC, V. Rates include breakfast. Additional adult C$15. Free parking. Closed mid-Oct to early Dec. **Amenities:** Restaurant; lounge w/pool table. *In room:* No phone.

JASPER NATIONAL PARK

Jasper's earliest incarnation, in the 1840s, sounded less than inviting. It was described by a visiting painter as "composed of two rooms of about 14 and 15 feet square. One of them is used by all comers and goers, Indians, voyageurs and traders, men, women, and children being huddled together indiscriminately."

An inauspicious beginning. But that's hardly the Jasper of today. Established as a park in 1907, in the intervening 170 years, Jasper has expanded from such humble beginnings to become Canada's largest mountain park, with crowds flocking there for its hiking, biking, climbing, horseback riding, and rafting. Visitors will also be able to find shopping and fine dining in Jasper, but such urbane attractions are not the focus, as in Banff; Jasper's tourists seem more interested in what lies outside of town than what's in it. The result is a charming alpine village with a few fancy frills, but nothing approaching the commercial theme park vibe that has befallen Banff. For more information on the park's attractions, contact **Jasper National Park** (P.O. Box 10, Jasper, AB T0E 1E0; ✆ **780/852-6176**; www.pc.gc.ca).

[Fast FACTS] JASPER NATIONAL PARK

ATMs & Banks
Canadian Imperial Bank of Commerce (CIBC; 416 Connaught Dr.; ☏ **780/852-3391**) and **TD Canada Trust** (606 Patricia St.; ☏ **780/852-6270**). There is a currency exchange house in the **Jasper Marketplace Inn** (616 Patricia St.; ☏ **780/852-3370**). All of these locations have ATMs.

Car Trouble & Towing
Services Jasper Towing has 24-hour service and trucks capable of towing your RV (☏ **780/852- 3849**).

Drugstore Jasper Park
Rexall Drugs has a pharmacist on duty (602 Patricia St.; ☏ **780/852-4441**).

Emergencies For fire,
ambulance, or police, dial ☏ **911.** There are emergency call boxes located sporadically along major park highways. For park-related emergencies, contact the **Warden Service** (☏ **780/852-6155**).

Gas Stations There are
a handful of gas stations in the town of Jasper,

including **Avalanche Esso** (702 Connaught Dr.; ☏ **780/ 852-4721**) and Jasper Shell (638 Connaught Dr.; ☏ **780/852-3022**). There is another gas station at Saskatchewan Crossing, just south of the border between Banff and Jasper national parks on Highway 93 (the Icefields Pkwy.; ☏ **403/761-7000**). It is usually closed from mid-November to mid-March.

Groceries Stock up at
Super A Foods (601 Patricia St.; ☏ **780/852-3200**) or **Nutter's Bulk Foods** (622 Patricia St.; ☏ **780/852-5844**). **Robinson's Good Food Naturally** (218 Connaught Dr.; ☏ **780/852-3195**) has a deli and bakery.

Internet Access Log
on to check your e-mail at **More Than Mail** (620 Connaught Dr., Square Mall; ☏ **780/852-3151**) or the **Soft Rock Café** (632 Connaught Dr.; ☏ **780/852-5850**).

Laundry Get your
camping clothes clean at

Coin Clean (607 Patricia St.; ☏ **780/852-3852**).

Medical Services
Seton Hospital, in the **Town of Jasper** (518 Robson St.; ☏ **780/852-3344**).

Permits You can pur-
chase all park permits at the **Jasper National Park Information Centre** (500 Connaught Dr.; ☏ **780/ 852-6716**).

Photo Supplies Get
your digital photos printed at the **Tekarra Color Lab** (600 Patricia St., below Earl's Restaurant; ☏ **780/ 852- 5525**) or head to **Jasper Camera & Gift Ltd.** (412 Connaught Dr.; ☏ **780/852-3165**).

Post Offices You can
mail letters and packages from **Canada Post** (502 Patricia St.; ☏ **780/852-3041**).

Taxis Try Heritage Cabs
(☏ **780/852-5558**) or Jasper Taxi (☏ **780/852-3600**).

Weather Updates For
weather updates in Jasper National Park, call ☏ **780/ 852-3185.** The service is available 24 hours.

Outdoor Pursuits

You can find much of the gear you'll need for everything from fishing to rafting at a number of local stores. **On-Line Sport and Tackle** (600 Patricia St.; ☏ **780/852-3630**) has an assortment of mountain bikes, tents, fishing gear, skis, canoes, and rafts available for rent, and the shop can also provide guides for rafting and fishing trips. At **Freewheel Cycle** (618 Patricia St.; ✆ 780/852-3898), you'll be able to find snowboards, cross-country ski equipment, and lots of bikes. For a full selection of local guides and outfitters, a visit to the **Jasper Adventure Centre** is a must. White-water rafting and canoeing trips, horseback rides, guided hikes, and other activities can be arranged out of the center, located at 604 Connaught Dr. (✆ 800/565-7547 in western Canada or 780/852-5595; www.jasperadventure centre.com), open June 1 to October 1 daily from 9am to 9pm.

FISHING   Jasper-based anglers who try their luck at trout fishing tend to favor the convenience of Patricia and Pyramid lakes, located just north of the city. Visitors, on the other hand, can visit **Currie's Guiding** (✆ 780/852-5650; www. curriesguidingjasper.com) to arrange fishing trips to beautiful Maligne Lake. The cost is C$225 per person for an 8-hour day, with tackle, bait, boat, and lunch included (a minimum of two people is required—ask about special single and group rates). If you fish on your own, a permit is C$9.80 a day, available at outfitters in town.

GOLF   Golf addicts know to play a round at the 18-hole course at **Jasper Park Lodge** (✆ 780/852-6090), east of the Jasper townsite, ranked by *Score Magazine* as the best golf course in the province. Despite being one of the most popular courses in the Rockies, it has plenty of obstacles, with 73 sand traps and even the occasional visit from curious wildlife. In high season, a round of 18 holes will cost you C$225 per person.

HIKING   When selecting a day hike in Jasper, think about the weather, your own fitness level, and the trail conditions. Trails here generally involve a lot of climbing and descending. Most are open from late June to late September. Check the latest trail conditions at the **Jasper Information Centre trail conditions hotline** (✆ 780/852-6176). The brochure *Day Hikers' Guide to Jasper National Park,* C$1 at the information center, details dozens of hikes throughout the park. For those who prefer to hike with a guide, contact **Jasper Park Lodge Mountaineering and Interpretive Hiking** (✆ 780/852-3301) or **Walks and Talks Jasper** (✆ 780/ 852-4945; www.walksntalks.com) for a selection of half- and full-day guided hikes. In general, hikers looking to spend a single, lovely day in the woods will find excellent backcountry trails around the park. For hikes that treat you to a glimpse of the most sublime scenery in the Canadian Rockies, however, multi-day and long-distance backpacking adventurers have far more numerous options if you're willing to go the distance.

The **Jasper Discovery Trail** makes a good first jaunt, a prelude to more serious hikes and a chance to explore the edge of town. One option is to start at the parking lot between the Jasper Yellowhead Museum and the Catholic Church, then follow the trail markings west in a counterclockwise loop, where you can get the best views. The route goes in an 8km (5-mile) loop around the townsite, which will take you 2½ hours to walk in its entirety; however, beginners will be happy to note that it is easy to leave the trail and return to it at various points on the town's perimeter.

Near the Fairmont Jasper Park Lodge, other trails ring Beauvert and Annette lakes (the latter being wheelchair accessible). For more of a rugged hike, Pyramid and Patricia lakes just north of town also have looping trails. **Pyramid Lake** is the best of the trails that wind from the Jasper townsite up through the Pyramid Bench; a complete round-trip runs 17km (11 miles). Kids over 8 can take it on. Due to its low elevation, this trail has less snowfall than others and is often ready to be trammeled on early in spring and well into the first throes of winter. The beginning elevation is 1,020m (3,346 ft.), and the elevation gain is 300m (984 ft.). Begin your hike at the Jasper Activity Centre, keeping to the right when you cross Pyramid Lake Road; after ascending a quick but somewhat challenging path, you'll end up on a wide bluff that boasts picturesque views of the Athabasca River. Keep an eye out for the fluffy bighorn sheep that are often seen grazing in the area and the wildflowers that carpet the sloping meadows along the benchland in the late summer months. Bird-watchers will especially enjoy Cottonwood Slough, a pleasant marshy area the route passes that is home to many beautiful, colorful species. Before reaching Pyramid Lake, you will pass through a forest, peaceful and cool; after the lake, a variety of trails will lead you back to town.

Cavell Meadows is a hike designed for those who enjoy alpine wildflowers, with a cornucopia of the blooms thriving in its cool, marshy environment along the path as you make your descent. It is thus rather popular, so it's best to make the trip either in the early morning or the late afternoon to avoid the crowds. Be prepared for early season closures of the 8km (5-mile) round-trip trail due to wet conditions and erosion. The elevation is 1,738m (5,702 ft.) to begin with, and the elevation gain is 400m (1,312 ft.). The first part of the trail follows the same route as the **Path of the Glacier ★★** trail, but shortly branches off to the east. The trail gets steeper as it climbs up over a moraine—a small hill made up of glacial rock and debris—but then levels out. After passing through a well-graded—and very pretty—upper subalpine forest, the trail comes to a junction; keep right for a more gradual ascent of the two loop sides, and left for a steeper one. The trail then enters sparse, tree-lined vegetation before proceeding to the alpine region beyond. At its higher elevation points, you may find many lovely views of Angel Glacier and Mount Edith Cavell. On the descent, you return to the trail head via the aforementioned Path of the Glacier trail.

There is a little-known secret about **Maligne Canyon's** breathtaking view of the most impressive gorge in the Canadian Rockies, but we'll let you in on it: The view is at its most spectacular when you look up from the depths of the gorge itself. It is therefore a shame that so many visit the canyon's highest mounts but so few venture down very far. It is rewarding to start at the bottom, which, of course, has the added bonus of allowing you to hike downhill on your return. The complex of different paths around the canyon makes a good choice for a group, as there are a number of access points across six different footbridges, allowing the less keen to make the loop back and meet fellow hikers by car farther down the pit. Stay to the right at all crossroads. The elevation at the beginning is 1,030m (3,379 ft.), and you lose and then later regain 100m (328 ft.). The hike is 3.7km (2.3 miles) one-way.

For a stunning view of the entire Maligne Valley, head up from beside the Maligne Lake Lodge to an old fire lookout atop the **Bald Hills.** The trail goes through a lodgepole pine forest up a gradual climb, eventually opening into a subalpine meadow. It continues to the foot of a small, rounded mountain (or a "bald hill"). From here, there are a variety of trails past the lookout to more impressive viewpoints. In late July, this is a great place to see wildflowers in the high alpine terrain. At the trail head, the elevation is 1,680m (5,512 ft.), and the trail climbs 480m (1,575 ft.). The hike is 10km (6.2 miles) round-trip.

One of Jasper's best longer day hikes is **Saturday Night Lake,** one of the first trails to have its snow melt in the spring. Because it is available so early in the year, you can hike for just half a day if you choose to go only as far as the Marjorie or Caledonia lakes—or turn it into an overnight trip by camping at High Lake or Minnow Lake, the two backcountry campsites found along the route. The trail begins right from the townsite, which is nice for those wanting to start out quickly. From there, you'll walk through a verdant, treed valley west of the townsite, passing several small, glistening lakes along the way.

Valley of the Five Lakes is a rather mellow hike, well maintained and mostly flat. It leads to a series of small woodland lakes that are perfect for having a picnic and even doing some fishing, making it a preferred spot for families. Follow the route from the trail head through a lodgepole pine forest, then cross a boardwalk over Wabasso Creek, where you can point out a beaver or two to the children. After that there is a short climb that leads to an open meadow, from which point the trail splits into a variety of numbered loops. If you take the #9a up and return via the #9b, you'll be rewarded with a panoramic view of the breathtakingly mountainous terrain that rings the trail—highly recommended. The beginning elevation is 1,070m (3,510 ft.), and the elevation gain is 30m (98 ft.). It's a 6km (3.7-mile) round-trip.

The **Lower Sunwapta Falls** is something of a misnomer, as it is really three separate waterfalls along the Sunwapta River, but few hikers ever venture to the lower falls, which lie just below the main one. Together, the falls make a sublime natural scene, but the main falls is attraction enough by itself. Sunwapta Falls is on every tour-bus route, and the parking lot, just off the west side of the Icefields Parkway, is often jammed full of tourists eager to see it. To hike around the falls, start out from the parking lot and follow the main upper-falls viewing trail to where the pavement ends. From there, descend by degrees through a lodgepole pine forest. You'll be treated to lovely views of the falls, as well as the Sunwapta River, the upper Athabasca Valley, and the glaciers atop Mount Quincy. The beginning elevation is 1,320m (4,331 ft.), and the total elevation drop to the falls is 80m (262 ft.). It's 2km (1.2 miles) one-way.

For another magnificent waterfall route, try quiet **Stanley Falls/Beauty Creek,** which passes no fewer than eight waterfalls as it stretches up from the Icefields Parkway alongside Beauty Creek. The beginning elevation is 1,570m (5,151 ft.), and the elevation gain is 110m (361 ft.), with the round-trip being 6.4km (4 miles). The hike is best in early summer, when the water level is high and the falls are at their most explosive. The trail crawls up a low dam wall across a marsh and up to the disused, dismantled Banff-Jasper Highway; once you cross it, you finally reach the trail's end—the spectacular Stanley Falls.

The best hike in the eastern reaches of Jasper is the **Sulphur Skyline,** a must for all keen hikers not intimidated by quick climbs. After 2.4km (1.5 miles), the trail heads over Shuey Pass, switchbacking across a series of avalanche slopes. The true summit is just beyond here, bare and rocky. From here, you can see the front ranges of the Canadian Rockies. From the trail head at 1,370m (4,495 ft.), the trail climbs 700m (2,297 ft.). The hike is 9.6km (6 miles) round-trip.

Be Weather Wary

The weather in the Canadian Rockies is incredibly variable, and a day that begins warm and pleasant might not stay that way. A sunny winter day with temperatures hovering around the freezing mark can easily become bitterly cold, with whiteout storms, strong winds, and clouds, and snow sometimes arriving in just a matter of hours. Dress warmly and wear layers so that you can adjust to conditions as they happen. Call ℂ **780/852-3185** for weather updates.

If you're already taking a tour of the Columbia Icefield or you are camping near the ice fields, consider a hike up on the lovely **Wilcox Pass,** where you can get a panoramic view of the natural wonder that feeds eight major glaciers. Wilcox Pass lies on the edge of a large alpine valley, just east of the Athabasca Glacier; it makes a good day hike, but avoid the trail until July, when the snow melts and the route is far more pleasant. The hike begins with an ascent through a forest of stunted Engelmann spruce and subalpine fir. Look around; you'll be dazzled by how much the views of the Columbia Icefield outdo any that you can get from the highway. Work your way up to the ridge, passing through fragrant meadows of alpine wildflowers; watch out for bighorn sheep on the trail. Once at the ridge, you have the choice of continuing on to Wilcox Pass or turning around and heading back—you don't have to make it to the top of the pass to enjoy this trail and its dazzling vistas. The beginning elevation is 2,042m (6,699 ft.), and the elevation gain is 335m (1,099 ft.). It's 8km (5 miles) round-trip to the pass; 11km (6.8 miles) one-way to Tangle Falls.

HORSEBACK RIDING For a short horseback ride, **Pyramid Stables** (ℂ **780/852-7433;** www.mpljasper.com) offers 1- to 3-hour trips (as well as a day trip) that provide a stunning vista of the Athabasca River Valley. For long-distance trail rides that will take you into the backcountry, call **Skyline Trail Rides** (ℂ **888/582-7787** or 780/852-4215; www.skylinetrail.com), with 3-day trips to a far-off but well-appointed lodge that include accommodation, meals, horses, and licensed guides for C$650. From early May to mid-October 1½- to 4½-hour guided rides are conducted daily, starting at C$43 for 90 minutes from both companies. Long or short, trail horseback riding is a fantastic park experience that allows you to take in views of the natural scenery. Trained guides respond to your level of riding experience in choosing the trail and use only animals that are tame, steady, and not easily spooked.

RAFTING Jasper is a good place to find float and whitewater trips down several rivers, including the Athabasca, Fraser, and Sunwapta, and the city is loaded with rafting outfitters. The mild rapids of the Athabasca River are nice for beginners and kids, with a 2-hour trip starting at C$59 adults, C$25 children under 13. Hairier trips down the Sunwapta River will appeal to those with a little more experience—or who just want a thrill. Ask your hotel concierge for assistance to find outfitters or contact **Maligne River Adventures** (ℂ **780/852-3370;** www.mra.ab.ca), which offers trips down both rivers, as well as a 3-day wilderness trip on the riotous Kakwa River (Class IV).

9

BANFF & JASPER | Jasper National Park

Jasper's first superintendent was one Maynard S. Rogers, who served from 1913 to 1914 and again from 1917 to 1929. When it came time to build the structure that would house his and various other administrative offices in 1914—now a National Historic Site that houses the Jasper National Park Information Centre—he had the idea that it should reflect the landscape in form and substance. At his direction, builders used natural materials such as cobblestone, river rock, and timber, and architects strove to emulate the asymmetrical balance of the surrounding Rockies. Rogers had good reason to be motivated about how the building was constructed—he had to live there since that was where superintendent's quarters were located until 1931. The building is still one of the most influential examples of the lovely, rustic architecture in Canada's national parks.

SKIING   For the fun of Banff without the crowds, visit Marmot Basin, Jasper's exciting, underrated downhill ski region, located just 19km (12 miles) west of Jasper on Highway 93. The resort offers a chance to ski the national park's deep valleys, with their diverse wildlife, waterfalls, and carpets of thick, lush forest. Marmot has 52 runs, seven lifts, rarely any lines, and slopes with few wind gusts. Lift tickets start at C$72 during the regular season; contact ✆ **780/852-3816** or www.skimarmot.com.

Jasper Townsite

Born as a railroad division point, Jasper Townsite lacks its southern neighbor's fame, but locals—and many tourists—prefer its unpretentious air and smaller, outdoor sports–crazy crowd. Compared to Banff's amusement-park idea of alpine adventure, Jasper provides an authentic, friendly atmosphere that is refreshingly rough around the edges. Although new development can be seen on boutique strips such as Patricia Street, with shopping malls and nightspots jostling for space, Jasper retains its small-town, lived-in charm: You can sense that real people live here.

Essentials

GETTING THERE   Jasper is a significant transportation hub, with rail, highway, and bus routes all running through the town, connecting it to most major cities in western Canada. Jasper lies 287km (178 miles) northwest of Banff, on the Yellowhead Highway system that links it with Vancouver, Prince George, and Edmonton. Also connecting it to Vancouver and Edmonton are three VIA Rail trains that run weekly. At the **train station** (✆ **780/852-4102**) at the town center, along Connaught Street, you can also catch the Skeena line west to Prince George and Prince Rupert. The station is also where you can find **Greyhound buses** (✆ **780/852-3926**) and **Brewster Transportation** (✆ **780/852-3332**), which offer express service to Banff, as well as a large number of sightseeing excursions. **Sundog Tours** (✆ **888/786-3641**; www.sundogtours.com) has daily shuttles from Edmonton and Banff to Jasper. They also have various sightseeing tours, including a half-day train journey across the border into British Columbia's Mt. Robson Provincial Park.

VISITOR INFORMATION For information on the townsite, contact **Jasper Tourism and Commerce** (P.O. Box 98, Jasper, AB T0E 1E0; © **780/852-3858;** www.jaspercanadianrockies.com). They can help with lodging and outfitting options, and their office is at 500 Connaught Dr. The **Jasper National Park Information Centre** (© **780/852-6176**) is in the same place, a heritage building in the heart of town. Get all the updates on everything Jasper here.

ORIENTATION Jasper townsite's main street, Connaught Drive, runs alongside the Canadian National Railway tracks. It plays home to many of Jasper's hotels, with another handful located at the northern end of Connaught and Geike streets, a half kilometer (¼ mile) from downtown. A block west of Connaught is Patricia Street, the center of much new development in the city, with new shops and cafes appearing each season. The post office is at the corner of Patricia and Elm streets.

GETTING AROUND For a taxi, call © **780/852-5558** or 780/852-3600. For a rental car, contact **National** (607 Connaught Dr.; © **780/852-1117**).

Exploring the Area

Travel just northeast of Jasper, off the Jasper Park Lodge access road, and you'll find the **Maligne River Valley,** which drops from a gorgeous alpine lake down to meet the Athabasca River, cutting a spectacular canyon into the limestone on its way. The chasm of Maligne Canyon gets up to 46m (151 ft.) deep at points, yet only 3m (9¾ ft.) across. Hikers may follow a trail down the mountainside that bridges the gorge six times and even rest in a teahouse at the top of the canyon in the summer months.

According to First Nations beliefs, spirits were responsible for the way **Medicine Lake**—a natural wonder that lies downstream from Maligne Lake—appeared and disappeared regularly every year. The Maligne River flows into Medicine Lake, which comes into existence every spring, grows 8km (5 miles) long and 18m (59 ft.) deep, and then vanishes in fall, leaving only a dry gravel bed through the winter—a magic trick accomplished through a system of underground drainage caves.

Next, you'll come to the cerulean blue, alpine waters of **Maligne Lake,** ringed by towering, white-capped peaks—one of the park's great beauty spots. The glassy waters are fed by the glaciers in the mountains that surround it like icy guards; it is the second-largest lake in the world to get its water that way. Maligne is known as the "hidden lake," but that doesn't keep the tour buses away, many of them taking the wildly popular 90-minute boat cruise to **Spirit Island** in the middle of the lake. During high season, the scenic, guided tours leave every hour on the hour from below the Maligne Lake Lodge, an attractive summer-only facility with a restaurant and bar (but no lodging). Tickets for the cruise are C$55 adults and C$28 children. The site is also a popular attraction for hikers, anglers, trail riders, and rafters. All facilities at Maligne Lake—including lake cruises, fishing, trail rides, a white-water raft outfitter that offers trips down three Jasper Park rivers, and even a shuttle bus between Jasper and the lake—are operated by **Maligne Tours** (www.malignelake. com). Offices are located at the lake, as well as a second location in Jasper, at 626 Connaught Dr. (© **780/852-3370**). They'll also organize a shuttle to the lake from the townsite for C$20 one way.

The chilly Maligne Lake waters are too cold for swimming, but you can rent a boat, canoe, or sea kayak. The lake is also chock full of "nothin' but trout"—the

Jasper

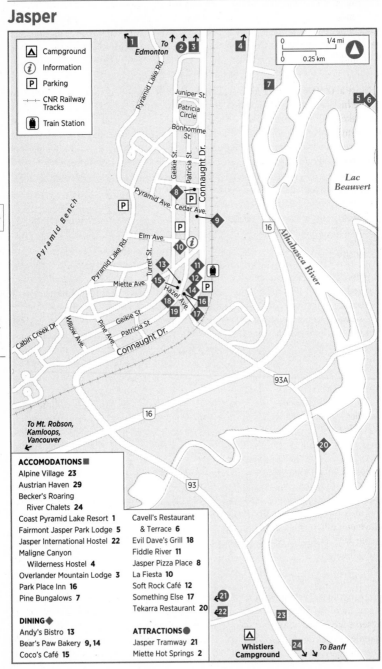

Legend

- ◭ Campground
- ⓘ Information
- P Parking
- ┼┼ CNR Railway Tracks
- 🚂 Train Station

To Edmonton

To Mt. Robson, Kamloops, Vancouver

To Banff

Juniper St.
Patricia Circle
Bonhomme St.
Geikie St.
Patricia St.
Connaught Dr.
Pyramid Ave.
Cedar Ave.
Elm Ave.
Turret St.
Miette Ave.
Hazel Ave.
Geikie St.
Patricia St.
Connaught Dr.
Cabin Creek Dr.
Willow Ave.
Pine Ave.
Pyramid Lake Rd.
Pyramid Bench

Lac Beauvert
Athabasca River

Whistlers Campground

ACCOMODATIONS ■
Alpine Village **23**
Austrian Haven **29**
Becker's Roaring River Chalets **24**
Coast Pyramid Lake Resort **1**
Fairmont Jasper Park Lodge **5**
Jasper International Hostel **22**
Maligne Canyon Wilderness Hostel **4**
Overlander Mountain Lodge **3**
Park Place Inn **16**
Pine Bungalows **7**

DINING ◆
Andy's Bistro **13**
Bear's Paw Bakery **9, 14**
Coco's Café **15**

Cavell's Restaurant & Terrace **6**
Evil Dave's Grill **18**
Fiddle River **11**
Jasper Pizza Place **8**
La Fiesta **10**
Soft Rock Café **12**
Something Else **17**
Tekarra Restaurant **20**

ATTRACTIONS ●
Jasper Tramway **21**
Miette Hot Springs **2**

rainbow and eastern brook variety. Guided fishing trips are available that include equipment, lunch, and hotel transportation, with half-day excursions starting at C$199 per person when at least two people are going (prices rise steeply for single fishers). Stop by the Maligne Lake Boathouse to purchase fishing licenses, tackle, bait, and boats.

Jasper Tramway   South of Jasper, off Highway 93, lies Canada's longest and highest aerial tramway tour, Jasper Tramway. It's the fastest and easiest way to get to the high alpine environment. Starting at the foot of Whistler's Mountain, each car takes 30 passengers and hoists them 2km (1¼ miles) up to the peak (2,220m/7,283 ft.)—a beautiful, scenic midair ride. But you won't want to go back down right away. At the summit, you'll step out into an alpine tundra picnic area carpeted with mountain grass. Views of the Athabasca and Miette valleys are stunning. You can hike 45 minutes uphill to the summit of Whistler's Mountain. Dress warmly and bring good shoes. Combo tickets that include meals at the upper terminal's Treeline Restaurant are available.

Off Hwy. 93, south of Jasper. ✆ **780/852-3093.** www.jaspertramway.com. Tickets C$29 adults, C$15 children X-5, free for children 4 & under. Lifts operate Apr 24 to May 20 & Aug 29 to Oct 11 daily 10am–5pm; May 21 to June 25 9:30am–6:30pm; June 26 to Aug 28 9am–8pm. Cars depart every 10-15 min. Call for off-season rates. Closed mid-Oct to Apr.

Miette Hot Springs   The hot mineral-water pools—cooled before they are allowed to touch your skin—can be enjoyed in an expansive swimming pool or in two soaker pools, surrounded by trees and a sublime mountain skyline with a view of Ashlar Ridge. Campgrounds and a cozy lodge with food and drink are nearby. But the hot springs are only one reason to make this enjoyable side trip: There are also the elk, deer, coyotes, and moose that populate the driving route to Miette, making it one of the best places in the park to view wildlife. And the trail head for one of the best hikes in Jasper, the Sulphur Skyline, is right next door, so you can earn your soak.

Drive 60km (37 miles) northeast of Jasper off Hwy. 16. ✆ **780/866-3939.** C$6.05 adults, C$5.15 seniors & children; C$18 families. June 22 to Sept 9 daily 8:30am–10:30pm; May 11 to June 21 & Sept 10 to Oct 8 daily 10:30am–9pm.

Shopping

Shopping in Jasper is very particular to this mountain town. A number of galleries in the town of Jasper feature Inuit and Native arts and crafts, such as **Our Native Land** (601 Patricia St.; ✆ **780/852-5592**). Jasper's shops and boutiques are chock full of high-end outdoor and recreation gear, with Patricia Street and Connaught Drive containing most of the quality brands such as North Face. The arcade at the Jasper Park Lodge, called the **Beauvert Promenade,** has some excellent clothing and gift shops.

Where to Stay

All prices listed below are for the high season, which are typically 50% higher (or more) than the rest of the year—book before June or after September, if possible. Reserve well in advance. For off-season rates, be sure to call—they usually follow a complex structure. Lodging in Jasper can be difficult; most of the mid-range hotels were built in the same era (early 1980s) and are all owned by a single chain. If you

Jasper Hotel Goes Down with the *Titanic*

The Banff Springs Hotel would have had a counterpart in Jasper, if not for the sinking of the *Titanic*. In 1910, Charles Melville Hays, president of the Grand Trunk Railway, was making big plans for a resort at Miette Hot Springs called Chateau Miette. Its elaborate design called for the water from the springs to be piped to a luxury hotel situated at the mouth of the Fiddle River. Fate had other plans for Melville, however: Melville died on the HMS *Titanic* in 1912, and his big-hotel dreams went down with him.

can't find a room, contact **Rocky Mountain Reservations** (© 877/902-9455 or 780/852-9455; www.rockymountainreservations.com), which offers a free booking service for Jasper accommodations and activities.

VERY EXPENSIVE

Fairmont Jasper Park Lodge ★★★   From the 364 hectares (900 acres) of Jasper Park Lodge's wooded, elk-inhabited grounds along Lac Beauvert to the central lodge's lofty ceilings and huge, cozy fireplaces, Jasper's most exclusive lodging lives up to its name. The Jasper Park Lodge, located about 8km (5 miles) east of Jasper proper, was built by the Canadian Pacific Railroad in 1923 and still retains a feel of woodsy gentility, a pampered wilderness experience. It's like an upscale summer camp for adults (and their kids) spread over the largest commercial property in the Canadian Rockies. There's a revered golf course, a gorgeous lake for paddling, bike trails, tennis courts, a spectacular outdoor pool, and bend-over-backward service. The decor is something of a puzzle, but an enjoyable one, as accommodations are a mix of cabins, lodge rooms, chalets, and cottages—all chosen from different eras and styles. In 2010, they finally added a full-service spa. Call and let the staff walk you through the room that will suit your budget and needs; you're certainly paying enough for the privilege. Ask about promotions and packages.

Old Lodge Road, Jasper, AB T0E 1E0. © **800/441-1414** or 780/852-3301. www.fairmont.com. 446 units. C$199–C$599 double; C$399–C$829 lakefront suite; from C$1,197 cabin. AE, DC, DISC, MC, V. Free parking. **Amenities:** 8 restaurants; 2 lounges; babysitting; bike rentals; children's center; concierge; golf course; health club; heated outdoor pool; 24-hr. room service; full service spa; tennis courts; canoe & paddle-boat rentals. *In room:* TV w/pay movies, hair dryer, Wi-Fi (free).

EXPENSIVE

Alpine Village   On the banks of the rushing Athabasca River, these rustic yet stylish red-roofed log cottages make a cozy, romantic base, good for keeping things quiet and simply enjoying the natural beauty of the park. They range from brand-new deluxe bedrooms suites to quaint cabins that date to 1941. Most have some form of a kitchenette. Cabins furthest from the road are quieter, but those along the river (next to the road) have the best views. The Deluxe Bedroom Suites have sweet little balconies. The one-room cabins make for great honeymooning, and the larger ones can house a large family that wants to cook its own meals. Sunshine pours into the kitchens.

2.5km (1½ miles) south of Jasper townsite (on Hwy. 93, at the junction w/Hwy. 93A); Jasper, AB. T0E 1E0. © **780/852-3285.** Fax 780/852-1955. www.alpinevillagejasper.com. 41 units. C$180–C$300 double; C$210–C$230 1-bedroom cabin; C$360 family cabin. Children 6 & under stay free in parent's room. MC, V. Closed mid-Oct to mid-May. **Amenities:** Jacuzzi. *In room:* Hair dryer, kitchenette (in some).

Coast Pyramid Lake Resort   With a picturesque lakeside setting in a valley above the townsite, this small resort offers plenty of activities, solitude, and lovely new rooms. The main lodge building—where the restaurant has a stunning view of the lake—sits atop the boat rentals, gift shop, and small spa facility. Guest rooms are decorated in earth tones with plenty of plaid as an accent, and all have pull-out sofas. Walls are thin in the older wing. The top-floor Cavell Rooms, built in the late 1990s, are the largest and most modern guest rooms, perfect for families planning on staying a few days. It's slow-paced up here, and you'll need a car.

6km (3¾ miles) north from Jasper townsite on Pyramid Lake Rd.; Jasper, AB T0E 1E0.ⓒ **800/663-1144** or 780/852-4900. www.coasthotels.com. 62 units. C$265–C$320 double; from C$430 suite. Children 17 & under stay free in parent's room. AE, MC, V. **Amenities:** Restaurant; bike rental; fitness room; hot tub; canoe & fishing-rod rental; Wi-Fi. *In room:* TV, hair dryer, minibar.

Park Place Inn ★   Urban and friendly, this is the only place in town one could call an upscale boutique inn—with reasonable rates, to boot. The 12 spacious rooms have a cowboy heritage theme, with beautiful linens, goose-down duvets, hardwood floors, and plenty of space. Bathrooms are particularly luxurious, with huge jetted tubs (many that are claw-foot style), jetted showers, and fancy amenities. Located upstairs on Jasper's bustling Patricia Street, it feels downtown, if that's possible in Jasper.

623 Patricia St.ⓒ **866/852-9770** or 780/852-9770. www.parkplaceinn.com. 14 units. C$229–C$269 double. Children 13 & under stay free in parent's room. AE, MC, V. *In room:* A/C, TV, hair dryer, minibar.

Pine Bungalows   A good choice if you don't need to be pampered, but want some privacy and have your own car. Cabins along the Athabasca River here are nostalgic and family-friendly. Some have been pretty much the same for 50 years, aside from a few upgrades in plumbing and heating, so it's a place that keeps families returning for generations. Most of the cabins now have fireplaces, and nearly all of them have kitchenettes. The best cabins are nos. 1 through 12, right on the river. Themed weekends, from birding to history, are offered throughout the summer.

#2 Cottonwood Creek Road, Jasper.ⓒ **780/852-3491.** www.pinebungalows.com. 72 units. C$140–C$160 double, C$185–C$220 2-bedroom cabin. *In room:* No phone.

MODERATE

Big hotels aren't your only option for staying in Jasper. In the high season, dozens of area homes become B&Bs. While they are by no means luxurious—especially compared to the classier home-stay options in Banff—they are often good value, most ranging from C$60 to C$85 for double occupancy, usually paid in cash. Get a complete list by contacting the **Jasper Home Accommodation Association** (P.O. Box 758, Jasper, AB T0E 1E0; www.stayinjasper.com). It's not a booking agency, so you'll have to contact the association's members directly to reserve.

If you're not the B&B type, Jasper also has a few motor lodges. Try the friendly but basic **Maligne Lodge** (900 Connaught Dr.; ⓒ **800/661-1315** or 780/852-3143; www.malignelodge.com), a two-story motel wrapped around a kidney-shaped pool. It also has a family restaurant and bar. Rooms start at C$199 for a double.

Austrian Haven   A good choice for those wishing to get away from Jasper's main strip or for longer stays, this large home on a residential street contains two generous, fully stocked suites. As a bonus, both have access to a shared sundeck with a BBQ and an impressive view of surrounding mountains. The Family suite includes a living room, kitchen, and dining area and has two queen-size beds, while the more lavish Honeymoon suite features a private sunroom and king-size bed with down duvet. Both options have a private bathroom, fridge, microwave, and TV and VCR, and include continental breakfast.

812 Patricia St., Jasper, AB T0E 1E0. *C* **780/852-4259.** www.austrianhaven.ca. 2 units. C$140–C$160 double. Rates include continental breakfast. Cash & traveler's checks only. Free parking. *In room:* TV/VCR, fridge, kitchen (in Family suite).

Becker's Roaring River Chalets   This family-run resort, dating back to the 1940s but modernized since, has a lot of things going for it that make it understandably popular: It's nestled in a stand of pine and offers stellar views of the adjacent (and, yes, roaring) Athabasca River and mountain scenery. The gourmet restaurant is one of the area's best. All accommodation is in log chalets ranging from rustic to refined. The cabins come in various sizes, from one room to four, with the largest deluxe cottages sleeping six to eight guests. Some have river views, and most include kitchens or kitchenettes, and a fireplace for huddling around on a chilly night. Rooms have televisions, but with so many natural distractions here, the TV will probably stay off. The downside is the sheer number of rooms crammed together. There's not much privacy or quiet here on a busy summer day.

Hwy. 95, 5km (3 miles) south of Jasper, Jasper, AB T0E 1E0 *C* **780/852-3779.** www.beckerschalets.com. 118 chalets. C$160–C$190 1-bedroom cabin; C$185–C$225 2-bedroom cabin; C$400 3-bedroom cabin. AE, MC, V. Free parking. **Amenities:** Restaurant; babysitting. *In room:* TV, fridge, hair dryer, no phone.

INEXPENSIVE

Budget travelers flock to two **Hostelling International** hostels, both reachable at P.O. Box 387, Jasper, AB T0E 1E0 (*C* **866/762-4122** or 780/852-3215; www. hihostels.ca) and open year-round. It's advisable to book well ahead in summer. The closest to town is the 80-bed **Jasper International Hostel,** on Skytram Road, 6km (4 miles) west of Jasper. It charges C$26 for members and C$29 for nonmembers. Private rooms are C$65 and C$72, respectively. Two family rooms, a barbecue area, indoor plumbing, hot showers, and bike rentals are available. In winter, ask about ski packages. A more rustic option is the **Maligne Canyon wilderness hostel,** which has no running water. It's off Maligne Lake Road, 18km (11 miles) east of Jasper, and sleeps 24; rates are C$23 for members and C$25 for nonmembers. The appeal here is immediate access to hiking, skiing, and cycling trails, since the hostel is situated above the spectacular Maligne Canyon. There's a self-catering kitchen with purified water for cooking, a refrigerator, and propane stove. More remote hostels are listed in "Backcountry Hostels," below.

IN & AROUND HINTON

If you're willing to stay a half-hour or 45-minute drive away from downtown Jasper, you can find good accommodations with markedly lower prices in the Hinton area, which is just to the east of the park gate. Here, you will find a typical array of reliable motor hotels. The **Best Western White Wolf Inn** (828 Carmichael Lane; *C* **800/220-7870** in Canada or 780/865-7777) has 42 air-conditioned rooms, most with kitchenettes. The **Black Bear Inn** (571 Gregg Ave.; *C* **888/817-2888** or

780/817-2000) features an exercise room, hot tub, and restaurant. The **Crestwood Hotel** (678 Carmichael Lane; ✆ **800/661-7288** or 780/865-4001) has a pool and restaurant. Doubles at these locations range from C$95 to C$145.

Overlander Mountain Lodge It's hard to beat the views of the Rockies from the original building of this venerable lodge at the edge of Jasper National Park, which makes a good base for exploring and relaxing. The complex is expertly decorated, adding a sheen of rustic luxury, and is aided by a friendly, professional staff. Overlander features a variety of comfortable accommodations, all with private bathrooms: there are four-plex cabins with gas fireplaces and two double beds; kitchenette rooms with queen beds; large, full-featured luxury chalets; and rooms of varied amenities within the main lodge and a newer wing, each with a view of mountains or gardens. In the old building, you'll find a bar that takes full advantage of its striking mountain setting and a lounge with large stone fireplace. The Stone Peak restaurant is noted for its showcase of regional cuisines, including venison, and lamb. For a quintessential Rocky Mountain experience, Overlander offers terrific value.

1km (½ mile) from Jasper Park's east gate, Hinton, AB T0E 1E0.✆ **877/866-2330** or 780/866-2330. www.overlandermountainlodge.com. 29 units. C$160–C$175 lodge room; C$175 cabin room; C$350 2-bedroom chalet; C$425 3-bedroom chalet. AE, MC, V. Free parking. **Amenities:** Restaurant; lounge. *In room:* Hair dryer, no phone.

CAMPING

If you're willing to rough it, camping is one of the best ways to get back to nature in Jasper National Park, which is home to 10 campgrounds—though only one (Wapiti) is open through the winter. Prices range from C$14 for rudimentary tenting sites to C$33 for full-service RV sites. Due to fire hazards, you need a special permit to camp anywhere in the parks outside the designated campgrounds. For a permit, contact the **parks information office** (✆ **780/852-6176**). Campgrounds in Jasper range from completely unserviced to those providing water, power, sewer connections, laundry facilities, gas, and groceries.

Columbia Icefield Campground The primary appeal of this small, no-frills campground is its proximity to the bulk of tourist activity at the Columbia Icefield Centre. It also opens earlier in the season and shuts down later than the nearby Wilcox Creek campground. It can get very cold here at night, so come prepared. Tents only.

106km (66 miles) south of Jasper townsite on the Icefields Pkwy. (Hwy. 93). 33 sites. C$16 site. Open mid-May to mid-Oct.

Honeymoon Lake Campground The most fortunate campers here are those who manage to secure one of the prime lakeside sites in this small, out-of-the-way campground.

52km (32 miles) south of Jasper townsite on the Icefields Pkwy. (Hwy. 93). 35 sites. C$16 site. Open mid-June to early Sept.

Jonas Creek Campground This is one of those rustic, heavily treed sites that almost make you forget you're in a campground. Beautiful but basic when it comes to amenities.

78km (48 miles) south of Jasper townsite on the Icefields Pkwy. (Hwy. 93). 25 sites. C$16 site. Open mid-May to early Sept.

9

BANFF & JASPER

Jasper National Park

Mount Kerkeslin Campground   Another primitive setup, but a top-notch view of the mountains certainly makes waking up here easier.

36km (22 miles) south of Jasper townsite on the Icefields Pkwy. (Hwy. 93). 42 sites. C$16 site. Open mid-June to early Sept.

Pocahontas Campground   This is a good place to spend the night if you're making the drive from Edmonton along the Yellowhead Highway (Hwy. 16) and are too tired to head deeper into the park. It's a large and moderately equipped campground, and the first one you'll come across as you enter Jasper National Park. Unwind at the nearby Miette Hot Springs.

44km (27 miles) east of Jasper townsite on the Yellowhead Hwy. (Hwy. 16). 140 sites. C$22 site. Open mid-May to mid-Oct.

Snaring River Campground   A cheap alternative to the pricey and crowded accommodation of the Jasper townsite, Snaring River is positively idyllic in comparison. Amenities, however, are limited to dry toilets, firewood, and kitchen shelters.

13km (8 miles) east of Jasper townsite on Yellowhead Hwy. (Hwy. 16). 66 sites. C$16 site. Open mid-May to mid-Sept.

Wabasso Campground   One of the more popular campgrounds—it's worth booking ahead at www.pccamping.ca—Wabasso is nestled picturesquely along the Athabasca River. Its 228 sites are well-equipped, including a sanitary station (with flush toilets), playground, wheelchair access, and a seasonal interpretive center.

16km (10 miles) from Jasper townsite on Athabasca Hwy. (Hwy. 93A). 228 sites. C$22 site. Open late June to early Sept.

Wapiti Campground   Wapiti is the only campground in the park with full winter access. There are 362 sites—40 with RV hook-ups and the rest reserved for tents only—and all are accessible in the winter. But be prepared to share your camping space with meandering elk—and keep your distance. In summer, it's quieter than Whistler's (see below).

4km (2½ miles) south of Jasper townsite on the Icefields Pkwy (Hwy. 93). Victoria Day weekend (late May) & mid-June to early Sept: 362 sites; C$26 site; C$30 site w/electrical hook-up. Early Oct to early May: 93 sites; C$17 site; C$20 site w/electrical hook-up.

Whistler's Campground   Whistler's may not be the most attractive or secluded place, but it's the largest campground in the park and the closest to the Jasper townsite. And its 781 campsites are often the first ones to fill up (book ahead at www.pccamping.ca). This is a camping hub, best equipped to accommodate large groups, offering interpretive programs in the high season and the most amenities for campers. There are 177 RV sites here, 77 of which offer full hook-ups. Be extra vigilant about securing your food; bears can be a problem here.

3km (1¾ miles) south of Jasper townsite on the Icefields Pkwy. (Hwy. 93). 781 sites. C$22–C$26 site; C$30 site w/electrical hook-up; C$36 site w/full hook-up. Closed early Oct to early May.

BACKCOUNTRY CAMPING

Campers looking for pleasant backcountry campsites will find more than 100 in Jasper National Park, including well-known sites on the Skyline Trail, on the Brazeau Loop, around Maligne Lake, and in the Tonquin Valley. You need to reserve a campsite before you head out on a backcountry trip. But be sure to book early: the most popular ones book up fast in early spring—reserve 3 months before your trip if you have a favored campsite in mind. Understand that when you reserve a spot to camp at a marked campsite, you select the specific site within the camping area on a first-come, first-served basis and only once you arrive on-site. Reserve by calling the **Jasper National Park** office, at ℭ **780/852-6177**, or visit the **Jasper National Park Information Centre** (500 Connaught Dr.; same telephone number). Rates are C$10 per person per night. There is a nonrefundable reservation charge of C$12.

BACKCOUNTRY HOSTELS

As in Banff, **Hostelling International** (ℭ **877/852-0781** or 780/852-3215; www.hihostels.ca/alberta) runs a number of rustic hostels in Jasper. These are all road-accessible, however, so they're not technically "backcountry." Call the main number to make reservations or for information, as the hostels themselves don't have phones. The **Beauty Creek Hostel** on the Icefields Parkway (Hwy. 93), 17km (11 miles) north of the Icefield Information Centre (87km/54 miles south of the Jasper townsite) sleeps 24 people in 2 cabins and has wood-stove heating, propane cooking, and lamplights. It is quite austere, with an outdoor toilet and no electricity or showers—authentic backcountry. It is perfect if you're interested in getting some hiking done. Rates are C$23 per person per night for Hostelling International members and C$25 per person per night for nonmembers.

The **Mount Edith Cavell Hostel** (take Hwy. 93A south from the townsite to Cavell Road; turn west and continue 13km/8 miles to the hostel, on the east side of the road) offers basic shelter in a handful of cabins in a narrow valley in the shadow of Mount Edith Cavell. There's no running water, but purified water is available for cooking (on propane stoves). And there's a refrigerator. Rates are C$23 per person per night for Hostelling International members and C$25 per person per night for nonmembers.

Where to Dine
EXPENSIVE

Andy's Bistro CONTINENTAL/CANADIAN   With a creative menu that mixes Old World and New, and an intimate (40-seat) yet casual setting, Andy's is a good compromise between high-end dining and a regular night out that's been consistently successful for years. The wine list is extensive—the whole restaurant, in fact, resembles a wine cellar. Starters on the seasonal menu may include pepper bacon–wrapped scallops and mushroom ragout with sheep cheese. Mains range from a Zurich-style veal to a "vegetarian Napoleon." One communal table for six is reserved for walk-in diners.

606 Patricia St. ℭ **780/852-4559.** Reservations recommended. Main courses C$18–C$33. MC, V. Mid-May to mid-Oct daily 5–11pm; mid-Oct to mid-May Tues–Sat 5–11pm.

Cavell's Restaurant and Terrace CANADIAN   The stunning former Edith Cavell Dining Room is the setting for a superb new dining option at the Jasper Park Lodge. The emphasis is on Canadian cuisine—regional meats, fish, and game paired with local vegetables, wild mushrooms, and berries. Bison, Arctic char, and Alberta beef are a restaurant specialty, plus a tandoori tofu and homemade mac & cheese for comfort food. Burgers, wraps, and flatbreads will please kids. The only thing better than the food is the view.

In the Fairmont Jasper Park Lodge, Old Lodge Road, 8km (5 miles) east of Jasper. ✆ **780/852-6052.** Reservations recommended. Main courses C$17–C$42. AE, DISC, MC, V. Daily 6–9pm.

Fiddle River SEAFOOD The informal dining space here belies the sophistication of Fiddle River's preparations, which go beyond just seafood to include red meat, pasta, and vegetarian dishes. But the main draw is, of course, the seafood. There's a sizable menu, but don't overlook the chalkboard list of specials, which include selections from oysters to mussels to Pacific salmon, prepared numerous ways. The sea-phobic will be sated by inventive entrees such as Alberta bison in a *chimichurri* sauce. There's also a short but well-selected wine list. The restaurant looks out on Jasper's railway station—and those inescapable mountains.

620 Connaught Dr. ✆ **780/852-3032.** Reservations highly recommended in summer. Main courses C$18–C$35. AE, MC, V. Daily 5pm–midnight.

Tekarra Restaurant ★★ STEAK/INTERNATIONAL Don't overlook this comforting space, built around a crackling fireplace in an old lodge outside town. You'll likely be very pleasantly surprised by both the sweet atmosphere and the superb food. Chef Dave Husereau's terrific menu of globetrotting cuisine has a loyal following. A playful appetizer list offers venison sliders, three tiny venison burgers, and tandoori shrimp lollipops. Mains include a macadamia nut–crusted rack of lamb and *ponzu*-marinated fish of the day. Friendly service.

Hwy. 93A, 1.6km (1 mile) east of Jasper (call for directions). ✆ **780/852-4624.** www.tekarrarestaurant. com. Reservations recommended. Main courses C$20–C$56. AE, DC, MC, V. Daily 5:30–10pm. Closed early Oct to late May.

MODERATE

Evil Dave's Grill ★ CANADIAN Don't let the name scare you: The only thing sinful about Evil Dave's cuisine is how good it is. Dave himself has moved on (or better said, he's moved back to Tekarra, above), but the upbeat chef now at the helm keeps the culinary creativity on the lighter side. Entrees include Malicious Salmon (blackened with sweet curry yoghurt), Malevolent Meatloaf, Nefarious Chicken (parmesan crusted, with salsa), and Vicious Hippy (a Portobello mushroom stuffed with artichoke, served with *panko*-crusted tofu and spun root vegetables). Best on the list for spice lovers has to be Hell's Jerk Chicken, a sweat-gland-testing take on the Jamaican traditional that's as high on flavor as it is on temperature.

622 Patricia St., Jasper, AB T0E 1E0 ✆ **780/852-3323.** Reservations recommended on weekends. Main courses C$18–C$28. AE, DC, MC, V. June–Sept daily 4–11pm; Oct–May Mon–Fri 5pm–10pm, Sat 4–11pm.

La Fiesta MEXICAN/MEDITERRANEAN Under new management, La Fiesta continues to serve up a refreshing mixture of Spanish-style tapas (calamari or tequila-and-lime mussels) and south-of-the-border classics like tacos, quesadillas, and enchiladas. Start with a jug of sangria or a white wine mimosa. The portions are large. Paella Valenciana, with pork, mussels, prawns and chicken in a tomato saffron rice, is their signature dish, although there's also a vegetarian version with grilled veggies and artichokes. Side dishes of rice and corn have a bit of a kick.

504 Patricia St. ✆ **780/852-0404.** Reservations recommended on weekends. Main courses C$13–C$29. AE, MC, V. Spring–fall daily 11:30am–11pm; winter daily 5–9pm.

Something Else INTERNATIONAL It's Greek. It's Italian. It's Creole. It's Canadian. Something Else truly aims, and largely succeeds, to be all things for all

Summer in Jasper is prime picnic season. Grab a gourmet sandwich at the extra-friendly **Patricia St. Deli** (606 Patricia St.; ✆ 780/852-4814), where they serve up "two slices of bread with heaven in between," as they say. Add chips and a cookie for C$13 and take it all out to the sandy beach at Lake Annette, to the southeast of town on the road to the Fairmont Jasper Park Lodge. You can have a swim before dining al fresco in one of the picnic areas.

people. You want *saganaki* with your jambalaya? Pizza with moussaka? Good ol' Alberta steak? You've come to the right place. This is the restaurant for families and large groups that tend to argue over what to have for lunch or dinner. Expect friendly service and reliable, well-prepared food without attitude.

621 Patricia St. ✆ **780/852-3850.** Main courses C$14–C$30. AE, DC, MC, V. Daily 11am–11pm.

INEXPENSIVE

There are a number of fine options for quick foods at the table or on the go. Besides letting you check your e-mail, **Soft Rock Café** (632 Connaught Dr.; ✆ **780/852-5850**), in the Connaught Square Mall, has omelets, sandwiches, wraps, coffee, salads, Thai food, and desserts. **Coco's Café** (608 Patricia St.; ✆ **780/852-4550**) is a popular spot for breakfast. Lunches include veggie burgers, wraps, and curries. It's a great place to mingle with the young locals.

The **Bear's Paw Bakery** (610 Connaught Dr., ✆ **780/852-2253;** 4 Cedar Ave., ✆ **780/852-3233**) is a terrific spot to fill your knapsack before a hike. The homemade breads (sourdough, baguettes, and beyond) are served at restaurants all over town. Buy fresh sandwiches, granola, delicious fruit tarts, granny smith apple pies, and a large selection of sweet baked goods alluringly laid out under glass at the counter. There are even dog treats. Another worthy gourmet cafe and pastry shop is **Café Mondo** (inside Jasper Marketplace, at 616 Patricia St; ✆ **780/852-9676**), with bagel melts, breakfast pizzas, and sweet delectables.

Jasper Pizza Place PIZZA Thin- and thick-crust pizzas from a wood-burning oven and a lively atmosphere make this a local favorite for informal dining. The main eating area is family-friendly; there's also a rooftop patio and, downstairs, a popular pool hall. Decorate your pie with your choice of four sauces and 32 toppings—some traditional, others eyebrow-raising (escargot pizza, anyone?). In addition to pizzas, there are sandwiches, wings, ribs, and pasta offerings, all with generous portions.

402 Connaught Dr. ✆ **780/852-3225.** Reservations not accepted. Pizza C$12–C$18. MC, V. Daily 11am–11pm.

Jasper after Dark

Nightlife in Jasper is largely limited to the bars and lounges found in hotels around town. By law, there is no smoking permitted at any Jasper club, even on outdoor patios.

For a post-dinner pint, head to the **Jasper Brewing Company** at 624 Connaught Dr. (✆ **780/852-4111**). Brewed on-site, there's a wide range of beers, from Union Blonde and B Hill Pilsner to Rockhopper IPA, and several others to suit your palate. There's a casually sophisticated lounge upstairs at **Earl's** (600 Patricia St, 2nd floor; ✆ **780/852-2393**), which also has the best patio in town—it's even heated!

The **Atha-B,** or just the B, is the local moniker for the Athabasca Hotel (510 Patricia St.; ✆ **780/852-3386**), home of an often crowded pool hall/sports bar (O'Shea's) and a recently renovated nightclub, which brings in DJs and live bands throughout the summer and lures a young, party-seeking crowd. With a sports-bar ambience and classic rock blaring, the **D'ed Dog Bar and Grill** (404 Connaught Dr.; ✆ **780/852-3351**) is the place you don't need to dress up to party into the night. Aptly, this is a popular spot with the summer onslaught of river and hiking guides who gather to socialize and compare notes from the trail.

Your best bet for good live music is **Pete's On Patricia,** upstairs at 614 Patricia St. (✆ **780/852-6262**), with a stream of indie rock and blues bands, as well as DJs and dancing.

Oddly enough, one of the hottest and rowdiest gathering places for the town's influx of twenty-something seasonal staffers can be found in the Fairmont Jasper Park Lodge. The noisy **Tent City Sports Lounge,** overlooking the tennis courts, is also the hangout of choice for young JPL employees.

Finally, if it's a somewhat less youthful crowd you seek, the **Downstream Bar** (620 Connaught Dr.; ✆ **780/852-9449**), a basement dive that's far from dingy, is a welcoming spot to unwind with a pint.

EDMONTON

E dmonton, Alberta's capital city, is located on the banks of the North Saskatchewan River, straddling the deep, lush river valley that has the looks of an oasis in high summer, with its sprawling green spaces. It was a settlement in pre-European times and later a key fur trading post in the 19th century. After the arrival of the railway in 1891, it developed rapidly.

Unlike its southern counterpart, Calgary, Edmonton is a decidedly low-key metropolis, with little of the flash that is Calgary's hallmark. Where Calgary is corporate, Edmonton is a government town. More liberal, it also has a marked no-nonsense, blue-collar feel to it. In general, people are more creative and unpretentious, and Edmonton has a prominent artistic side.

In many ways, Edmonton feels like a small town that happens to have a million people living in it—and most residents you encounter would count that as one of its main attractions.

Make no mistake, though: Like much of the province, Edmonton is profiting mightily from the unprecedented oil boom, and it is geographically much closer than Calgary to the source.

Chief among Edmonton's attractions is likely the almost never-ending plethora of summer festivals that the city hosts. The main star is Edmonton's Fringe Theatre Festival, second only to Edinburgh in Scotland as the largest of the worldwide Fringe festivals. Theater troupes the world over debut their best new work in Edmonton every August, and critics and aficionados flock to the city, especially the Old Strathcona theater district, to catch top-end performers strutting their stuff. The festival is part of the reason why Old Strathcona, on the southern bank of the river, across from downtown, is perhaps the most vibrant neighborhood in the city.

Old Strathcona was once its own town, and its incorporation is telling of how Edmonton grew in spurts, following a boom-and-bust pattern as exciting as it was unreliable. During World War II, the boom came in the form of the Alaska Highway, with Edmonton as the material base and temporary home of 50,000 American troops and construction workers.

The ultimate boom, however, first gushed from the ground in 1947, when a drill at Leduc, 40km (25 miles) southwest of the city, sent a fountain of crude oil soaring skyward. Some 10,000 other wells followed, and in their wake came the petro-chemical industry, and the refining and supply conglomerates. In 20 years, the population quadrupled, the skyline mushroomed with glass-and-concrete office tow-ers, a rapid-transit system was created, and a C$150-million civic center rose.

Edmonton has its head high today, with a stunning new art gallery and efforts under way to finally spruce up the downtown core, the heart of the city's continual self-improvement project.

ESSENTIALS
Getting There

BY PLANE   Edmonton International Airport (✆ 800/268-7134 or 780/890-8382; www.flyeia.com) is served by **Air Canada** (✆ 800/372-9500; www.aircanada.com); **Delta** (✆ 800/221-1212; www.delta.com); **United** (✆ 800/864-8331; www.united.com); and homegrown **WestJet** (✆ 800/937-8538; www.westjet.com), a Calgary-based carrier with several destinations across North America; among other airlines. Being a hub of international commerce, Edmonton is also served by several commuter lines.

The airport lies 29km (18 miles) south of the city on Highway 2, about 45 min-utes away. By cab, the trip costs about C$35; by the **Edmonton Sky Shuttle** (✆ 780/465-8515; www.edmontonskyshuttle.com) it's C$15 per person.

BY CAR   Edmonton straddles the Yellowhead Highway, northwestern Canada's east-west interprovincial highway. Just west of Edmonton, the Yellowhead Highway is linked to the Alaska Highway. The city is 515km (320 miles) north of the U.S. border, 283km (176 miles) north of Calgary. From Calgary, take Highway 2 north; from Banff, your best bet is through Calgary on the Trans-Canada Highway East, connecting to Highway 2 North.

BY TRAIN   The **VIA Rail station** (✆ 800/561-8630 or 780/422-6032; www.viarail.ca) is at 104th Avenue and 100th Street.

BY BUS   Greyhound buses (✆ 800/661-8747 or 780/413-8747; www.greyhound.ca) link Edmonton to points in Canada and the United States from the depot at 10324 103rd St.

Visitor Information

Contact **Edmonton Tourism** (9990 Jasper Ave. NW; ✆ 800/426-4715 or 780/496-8400; www.edmonton.com). There are also visitor centers located at City Hall and at Gateway Park, both open from 9am to 6pm, and on the Calgary Trail (Hwy. 2) at the southern edge of the city, open from 9am to 9pm.

City Layout

The winding **North Saskatchewan River** flows right through the heart of the city, dividing it into roughly equal halves. Most of this steep-banked valley has been turned into public parklands.

Like Calgary, Edmonton runs on a grid system, with streets going north-south and avenues east-west. The middle of the city is downtown at 100 Avenue and 100 Street, with corresponding numbers growing to the north and west, and declining to the south and east. Edmonton's main street is **Jasper Avenue** (actually 101st Ave.), running east-west on the north side of the river. To cross the North Saskatchewan River, you'd take the pedestrian- and car-friendly High Level Bridge south or the Low Level Bridge in either direction. Beneath the downtown core stretches a network of climate-controlled pedestrian walkways—called **Pedways**—connecting hotels, restaurants, and malls with the library, City Hall, and **Citadel Theatre.**

At the northern approach to the High Level Bridge stand the buildings of the **Alberta Legislature.** Across the bridge, to the west, stretches the vast campus of the **University of Alberta.** East of the U of A is **Old Strathcona,** a bustling neighborhood of cafes, galleries, and shops that is a haven for the hip crowd. The main arterial through Old Strathcona is **Whyte Avenue,** or 82nd Avenue. Running south from here is 104th Street, which becomes the **Calgary Trail** and leads to the airport.

West of downtown, Jasper Avenue eventually becomes Stony Plain Road, which passes near the **West Edmonton Mall,** the world's largest shopping and entertainment center, before merging with Highway 16 on its way to **Jasper National Park**.

Neighborhoods in Brief

Originally a patchwork collection of smaller cities, Edmonton can be hard to get a handle on. And while it's walkable in pockets, distances between those pockets tend to be large and hampered by steep riverbanks on either side. Still, the in-between neighborhoods offer a nice opportunity for meandering, and are different enough to suit almost any stroller's inclinations.

DOWNTOWN

Edmonton and its environs count more than a million people, but its downtown feels like it belongs to a city not even half that size. A victim of the boom/bust economic cycle of an oil town, through the '80s, Edmonton's downtown was a wasteland: With oil at an all-time low, the economy in the toilet, and the massive West Edmonton Mall drawing every potential shopper, local or otherwise, away from downtown, empty buildings nearly outnumbered those that were occupied. Property owners went so far as to knock down some of their buildings, as the property taxes for a vacant lot were significantly less than for the buildings they couldn't seem to get even a quarter full.

Much has changed since those dark days. The oil business is booming, and Edmonton's downtown, during the daytime, is a busy corporate center, with galleries, shops, and cafes to satisfy office workers. But it remains a tad impersonal,

and it often feels quite vacant in the evening hours and on weekends.

Still, some of the better chain-brand shopping in town is to be found here, anchored by the local outlet of the posh **Holt Renfrew** chain, and a concentration of the city's major art institutions, such as the **Winspear Centre,** home of the Edmonton Symphony and the Citadel Theatre, which serve as anchors to the Downtown Arts District and the stunning new **Art Gallery of Alberta.** It's also where almost all of the main hotels are. Keep an eye on downtown; Redevelopment plans are on their way.

OLD STRATHCONA/WHYTE AVENUE

This is where Edmonton comes to play. This historic district used to be a separate township but was amalgamated with Edmonton in 1912 and still contains some of the best-preserved landmarks in the city. The stretch is really only about 6 blocks wide, so it's easy to explore on foot, guided by the brochures given out at the Old Strathcona Foundation.

Undoubtedly the heaviest concentration of restaurants, bars, boutiques, and theaters to be found anywhere in the Edmonton area, the main drag through Old Strathcona is called **Whyte Avenue,** and on a summer weekend night, there's a sense of barely controlled social chaos. Street-front patios of dozens of bars and restaurants spill out onto the sidewalk, Harley riders and muscle cars with booming stereos cruise the half-dozen-block stretch over and over (and over again), and the sidewalks are packed with a game bar-hopping set looking for the next hotspot. During the day, Whyte, with its historic street fronts and collection of eclectic boutiques and cafes, is a pleasant, busy, urban stroll. Whether you want to stick around for the evening's inevitable descent is up to you, but in a new-seeming city where the car is king, Whyte Avenue is eminently walkable and filled with texture—local history with a layer of the contemporary in nice harmony.

This is also where you'll find a surfeit of independent local theaters and theater companies, as well as the **Old Strathcona Farmers Market,** at 83rd Avenue and 103rd Street.

From downtown, get to Old Strathcona on bus 46; get off around 82nd Avenue, between 103rd and 105th streets.

124TH STREET/HIGH STREET

Between Jasper Avenue (aka 101st Ave.) and 110th Avenue on 124th Street is Edmonton's High Street district (though the colorful signs that line the boulevard call it, somewhat uninventively, "The 124th Street Area"). It's a low-key and compact stretch of shops, galleries, and restaurants stretching north and west of downtown, with a cluster of older homes just off the commercial strip. While nowhere near as bustling and active as Whyte Avenue, most who choose to spend their social time here would agree that this is a good thing: There's no pounding music from wide-open bars or late-night revelers hollering at high volume after the bars close. And happy little secrets can be found here, too—like the **Blue Pear,** one of the most interesting, innovative (not to mention delicious) restaurants in Alberta, if not all of Canada.

GETTING AROUND

BY TRANSIT Edmonton Transit (☎ 780/442-5311; www.takeets.com) operates the buses and the LRT (Light Rail Transit). This electric rail service connects downtown with **Northlands Park** to the north and the University of Alberta to the south. The LRT and buses have the same fares: C$2.75 adults and children over 5; a day pass goes for C$8.25.

BY CAR In addition to the following downtown locations, **National** (10133 100A St. NW; ☎ 800/CAR-RENT or 780/890-7700), **Budget** (4612 95th St. ☎ 800/268-8900 or 780/448-2060), and **Hertz** (10815 Jasper Ave.; ☎ 780/423-3431), each have a car-rental bureau at the airport.

BY TAXI Call **Co-Op Taxi** (☎ 780/425-2525) for a ride in a driver/owner-operated cab. **24-7 Taxi** is another option (☎ 780/442-4444), as is **Edmonton Taxi** (☎ 780/462-3456).

BY BICYCLE While not as extensive as Calgary's system, Edmonton has a decent bike path network of about 150km (93 miles), including more than 100km (62 miles) worth of paths running through the river valley. This is scenic and lovely, but not terribly practical in terms of actual transportation. If you're willing to take to the city streets, be prepared for the main obstacle to Edmonton city cycling: incredibly long, painfully steep slopes into and out of the deep river valley. If you're game, you can rent a bike from **Velocity Cycle** (7208-101 Ave., ✆ **780/466-8133;** www. velocity-cycle.com) for C$50 a day.

ON FOOT Those same banks—to say nothing of the great distances between pockets of interest—make Edmonton not a terribly walkable city. But once you're in, say, Old Strathcona or the 124th Street Area (also sometimes called High Street), a stroll is a nice way around. The **Downtown Business Association of Edmonton** (✆ **780/424-4085;** www.edmontondowntown.com) offers free walking tours of the core in the summer on Mondays, Wednesdays, and Fridays between 1 and 2pm. Meet at their office at 10121 Jasper Ave. (in the Royal Bank building) 15 minutes beforehand.

[FastFACTS] EDMONTON

Airport **Edmonton International Airport** lies 29km (18 miles) south of the city on Highway 2, about 45 minutes away. For general inquiries, call ✆ **800/268-7134** (www. flyeia.com).

American Express The office at 10180 101st St. (at 102nd Ave.; ✆ **780/ 421-0608;** LRT: Corona), is open Monday to Friday from 9am to 5pm.

Area Code Edmonton and Northern Alberta are in the 780 area code. Dialing anywhere in Canada and the U.S., simply add "1" to the number you're dialing. When dialing locally in-city, you must use 10-digit dialing; add "780" before every 7-digit number.

Babysitting Hotel concierges can usually provide a list of approved sitters; higher-end or kid-friendly hotels like the **Hotel Mac-Donald** or the **Fantasyland Hotel** at West Edmonton Mall have their own internal sitters available.

Business Hours Most banks are open weekdays

10am to 4pm, and Saturdays for a few hours in the morning or afternoon. Most shopping centers are open Monday to Friday 10am to 9pm, Saturday 10am to 6pm, and Sunday noon to 5pm.

Currency Exchange Change bureaus abound, but your best bet is to use your bank card at any of the hundreds of ATMs in town. If you need to exchange cash, use one of the chartered banks: Bank of Montreal, TD Canada Trust, Scotiabank, Royal Bank, or CIBC. If you insist on using a currency exchange, you'll find Custom House Global Foreign Exchange (✆ **780/423-6000**) downtown at 10104 103rd Ave. There's also a Calforex foreign exchange bureau (✆ **780/484-3868**) in West Edmonton Mall.

Dentist Many dental clinics are open evenings and weekends. Ask your hotel to recommend one or visit the **Alberta Dental Association** website at www.abda.ab.ca to find one.

Directory Assistance Dial ✆ **411** to get local and long-distance directory help. You'll pay a fee from a private phone, but if you dial Directory at a payphone, it's free.

Doctors & Hospitals **Medicentres** offers walk-in medical services daily at 15 locations throughout the city; go to www.medicentres. com for the location nearest you. There is one downtown at 11087 Jasper Ave. (✆ **780/488-1222**). The hospital with emergency service closest to downtown Edmonton is the **Royal Alexandra Hospital** (10240 Kingsway Ave.; ✆ **780/477-4111;** bus: 9).

Emergency For fire, medical, or crime emergencies, dial ✆ **911.**

Fishing Licenses If you're planning to fish, either in the city or outside of it, you need to obtain a license. They're available at most sporting goods stores, convenience stores, and gas stations at a cost of C$26. Seniors and children 16 and under don't need a license

Libraries   The main branch of the **Edmonton Public Library** is downtown in the city's cultural district (7 Sir Winston Churchill Sq.; ℭ **780/ 496-7000;** www.epl.ca). Branches are located throughout the city, and most have Internet access.

Newspapers   The *Edmonton Journal* (www.edmontonjournal. com) and *Edmonton Sun* (www.edmontonsun.com) are the local daily papers. Arts, entertainment, and nightlife listings can be found in the weekly *See* (www.seemagazine.com).

Pharmacies   **Shoppers Drug Mart** has over a dozen locations, most open till midnight. One central location is at 8210 109th St. (ℭ **780/433-2424;** bus 6).

Police   The 24-hour number is ℭ **780/421-3333.** Dial ℭ **911** in emergencies.

Post Office   The main post office is at 103A Avenue and 99th Street (LRT: Churchill).

WHERE TO STAY

Edmonton's accommodation scene has the usual variety of predictable choices (standard chain motels like Super 8 and Travelodge, and multi-story downtown hotels like Westin, Fairmont and Sheraton), both downtown and nestled around the main highway arteries in and out of the city. Motel villages can be found clustered in the southern part of the city, where Highway 2 meets Highway 14, also known as Whitemud Drive; and also to the east and west of downtown along the Yellowhead Highway. Business-class hotels tend to cluster downtown, with a handful of interesting independents to be found in Old Strathcona. Downtown hotels are spread throughout the area, which can be quite sparsely populated in the evenings and on weekends.

For B&Bs, try **Alberta and Pacific Bed and Breakfast** (ℭ **604/944-1793**) or the **Alberta Bed and Breakfast Association** (www.bbalberta.com). Note that unless otherwise stated, Wi-Fi service is free.

Expensive

Crowne Plaza Chateau Lacombe   Centrally located downtown, the Crowne Plaza, a round 24-story tower sitting on the edge of a cliff overlooking the North Saskatchewan River, possesses some of the city's best views (best seen from La Ronde, the hotel's revolving restaurant; see p. 230). The nicely furnished standard rooms aren't huge, though the wedge-shaped design means that they are broadest toward the windows, where you'll spend time looking over the city. Riverview rooms are an extra C$18 or so; request one when booking. The Crown Plaza's Sleep Advantage program focuses on high-quality linens and pillows, plus interesting extras like relaxation CDs, "quiet floors," and aromatherapy lavender atomizers for the sheets. For just a C$30 upgrade, executive suites offer twice the square footage of standard rooms and a full living room with foldout bed—a sweet deal.

10111 Bellamy Hill NW, Edmonton, T5J 1N7. ℭ **800/661-8801** or 780/428-6611. www.chateaulacombe. com. 307 units. From C$159 double; C$219 executive suite. Additional adult $10. Weekend packages available. AE, DC, DISC, MC, V. Parking $14. **Amenities:** Revolving restaurant; lounge; cafe; coffee bar; babysitting; exercise room; room service. *In room:* A/C, TV, CD player, hair dryer, Wi-Fi.

Delta Edmonton Centre Suite Hotel   This all-suite establishment forms part of the upscale City Centre shopping mall in the heart of downtown. Without having to set foot out of doors, you can access 170 shops, plus movie theaters and an indoor putting green. Three-quarters of the windows look into the mall, so you can stand

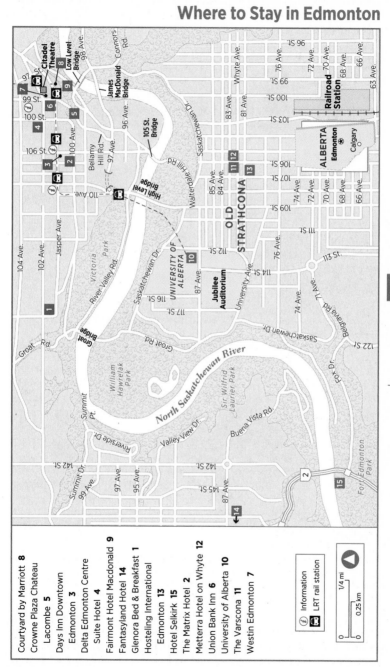

Courtyard by Marriott **8**

Crowne Plaza Chateau
Lacombe **5**

Days Inn Downtown
Edmonton **3**

Delta Edmonton Centre
Suite Hotel **4**

Fairmont Hotel Macdonald **9**

Fantasyland Hotel **14**

Glenora Bed & Breakfast **1**

Hosteling International
Edmonton **13**

Hotel Selkirk **15**

The Matrix Hotel **2**

Metterra Hotel on Whyte **12**

Union Bank Inn **6**

University of Alberta **10**

The Varscona **11**

Westin Edmonton **7**

i Information

E LRT rail station

0   1/4 mi

0   0.25 km

behind the tinted one-way glass (in your pajamas, if you like) and watch the shopping action outside. The rooms have many upgrades, but the lobby is dated. And service at the restaurant can be poor. Most units are deluxe executive suites, each with a large sitting area (with TV and wet bar) and separate bedroom (with another glass wall). If you need lots of room, or have work to do in Edmonton, these very spacious rooms are just the ticket.

Eaton Centre, 10222 102nd St., Edmonton, T5J 4C5. ☎ **800/661-6655** or 780/429-3900. www.delta hotels.com. 169 units. C$124–C$189 standard business suite; C$219 premier executive suite. Summer family discounts, weekend packages & special rates for business travelers. AE, DC, MC, V. Valet parking C$22; self-parking C$19. **Amenities:** Restaurant; bar; babysitting; concierge; exercise room; Jacuzzi; limited room service; sauna; Wi-Fi. *In room:* A/C, TV w/pay movies, hair dryer, paid Wi-Fi, minibar.

Fairmont Hotel Macdonald ★★ 👜 There's no denying that this lovely hotel is the best in town, from the unrivalled presence overlooking the North Saskatchewan River to the city's most opulent rooms and historic salons. All visiting VIPs, from royalty to rock stars, stay here. Originally opened in 1915, the restored Hotel Macdonald has retained signature elements such as its deep tubs, brass door plates, and paneled doors. Everything, including the service, is absolutely top-notch. Signature rooms have the best views and include breakfast for two. If you're unable to stay here, at least come for a summer cocktail on the patio. Needless to say, there aren't many hotels like this in Edmonton—or in Canada, for that matter.

10065 100th St., Edmonton, T5J 0N6. ☎ **800/441-1414** or 780/424-5181. www.fairmont.com. 199 units. C$299–C$329 double; C$289–C$999 suite. Weekend & off-season discounts available. AE, DC, DISC, MC, V. Parking C$22. **Amenities:** Restaurant; lounge; babysitting; concierge; concierge-level rooms; health club; indoor pool; 24-hr. room service; spa; squash court. *In room:* A/C, TV/VCR w/pay movies, hair dryer, Internet, minibar.

Fantasyland Hotel ☺ With 116 theme rooms decorated in 12 different styles, it would seem impossible to get bored at Fantasyland—which is exactly the point. An active hub for visitors eager to see what locals call "the eighth wonder of the world," West Edmonton Mall, Fantasyland is all about myth-building. Theme rooms aren't just a matter of subtle touches. Take the Truck Room: Your bed is located in the back end of a real pickup; the bench seats fold down into a child's bed; and the lights on the vanity are real stoplights. In the Igloo Room, a round bed is encased in a shell of faux ice blocks; statues of sled dogs keep you company; and the walls are painted with amazingly lifelike Arctic murals. The themes continue, through the Canadian Rail Room (train berths for beds), the African Room, and more. All luxury theme rooms come with immense four-person Jacuzzis and plenty of amenities, much of it circa 1980, when the hotel was built. The hotel offers tours of the different theme types on Saturdays at 2pm. It's not all fantasy, though: 238 large, well-furnished, non-theme rooms are divided into superior rooms, with either a king-size or two queen-size beds, and executive rooms, with a king-size bed and Jacuzzi. The rooms are large and comfortable, with new flat-screen TVs. Outdoor noise is a problem in some rooms with poor windows. The hotel's new restaurant, the **L2 Grill** (☎ **780/444-5538**) is quite good; of course, you have all-weather access to the world's second largest mall and its many eateries, as well. Kids and shoppers won't find a better option.

17700 87th Ave. (at the end of the West Edmonton Mall), Edmonton, T5T 4V4. ☎ **800/737-3783** or 780/444-3000. www.fantasylandhotel.com. 355 units. C$178–C$268 double. Additional adult C$14. Weekend & off-season packages available. AE, MC, V. Free parking. **Amenities:** Restaurant; bar; babysitting; concierge; exercise room; 24-hr. room service. *In room:* A/C, TV, fax, fridge, hair dryer, Wi-Fi.

The Matrix Hotel ★★ 👔 Forgive its sci-fi name, for there's no dystopian-future theme to be found here; rather, just a stylishly contemporary hotel with all the bells and whistles. The Matrix is the modern European sister property to the cool and stylish Metterra (see below) across the river on Whyte Avenue. Downtown, the Matrix is as urbane as Edmonton can possibly get, with its grey- and neutral-stone-toned palettes, for a modern industrial feel. Some of the spacious rooms have kitchenettes. Rooms can be tight, but they are efficient, bright, and sleek. Breakfasts are served in a cocktail lounge on the second floor, and there is a Starbucks next door. There's a daily happy hour wine and cheese tasting, which is on the house. This is by far the most interesting and modern of all the downtown hotels. Get the best rates by booking via their website.

10640 100th Ave., Edmonton, T5J 3N8. 📞 **866/465-8150** or 780/429-2861. Fax 780/426-7225. www.matrixedmonton.com. 185 units. From C$195 double; from C$295 suite. Rates include local calls, continental breakfast & evening wine & cheese. Weekend packages available. AE, DC, DISC, MC, V. Free parking. **Amenities:** Lounge; babysitting; exercise room; room service. *In room:* A/C, TV, hair dryer, Wi-Fi.

Metterra Hotel on Whyte A swanky boutique hotel in the lively Old Strathcona neighborhood, filled with students and artists, great nightlife, and dining, the Metterra is where you'll want to stay if you're in town for a festival or for soaking up the city's coolest neighborhood. The lobby sets the tone with striking art, a two-story rundle-stone wall—that would be stone from Banff's Mt. Rundle—and waterfall, while the guest rooms are large, with contemporary and Indonesian art adding some style. Some rooms offer fireplaces, others feature recliners. Rates include a continental breakfast and afternoon wine and cheese. Though not a typical business hotel, Metterra offers all the features and services sophisticated business and leisure travelers require. Be warned, though: As charming as some of the outdoor decks overlooking Whyte Avenue may be, on a Saturday night, you might like to ask for a room facing north toward downtown, instead—if you plan on sleeping, that is.

10454 82nd (Whyte) Ave., Edmonton, T6E 4Z7. 📞 **866/465-8150** or 780/465-8150. www.metterra.com. 98 units. From C$139 double; from C$249 suite. Rates include breakfast & afternoon wine & cheese. AE, MC, V. Free valet parking. **Amenities:** Fitness center; room service. *In room:* A/C, TV, fridge, hair dryer, Wi-Fi.

Union Bank Inn ★ 👔 If you're tired of unmemorable business hotels, this is a wonderful choice. The stylish Union Bank, built in 1910, now houses an elegant restaurant and intimate boutique hotel. The owner asked Edmonton's top interior designers to each design a room; the results are charming, with each unique guest room displaying its own style, colors, furniture, and fabrics. All units, however, have the same amenities, including gas fireplaces, voicemail, feather duvets, and upscale toiletries. Joining the original inn are 20 business-class rooms in a new addition—each equally idiosyncratic and uniquely designed. The older rooms aren't incredibly big, so if you're in town with work to do, ask for one of the newer and larger units. Staff are friendly; the guest experience is personalized. The restaurant/bar Madison's is a great place to meet friends (see "Where to Dine," below).

10053 Jasper Ave., Edmonton, T5J 1S5. 📞 **780/423-3600.** www.unionbankinn.com. 34 units. C$209–C$299 double. Rates include full breakfast. AE, DC, MC, V. Free parking. **Amenities:** Restaurant; bar; exercise room; limited room service. *In room:* A/C, TV, fridge, hair dryer, Internet.

The Varscona Completing the three sisters sweep of boutique hotels in Edmonton—the Metterra, Varscona, and Matrix (see above) are all affiliated—is the

Varscona, the oldest of the three and therefore the most traditionally appointed. With an old-world country style, including plush handmade pillows in every room, the Varscona strikes a contemporary balance with amenities like Bose CD players. Downstairs, **Murrieta's Bar and Grill** (✆ **780/438-4100**), with its patio open onto Whyte Avenue, is a top-notch restaurant, and an Irish pub (**O'Byrne's**, ✆ **780/414-6766**) next door is a hopping night spot.

8208 106th St. NW, Edmonton, T6E 6R9. ✆ **866/465-8150** or 780/434-6111. www.varscona.com. 89 units. From C$125 double. Rates include local calls, continental breakfast & evening wine & cheese. Weekend packages available. AE, DC, DISC, MC, V. Free parking. **Amenities:** Restaurant; lounge; babysitting; exercise room; room service. *In room:* A/C, TV, hair dryer, Wi-Fi.

Westin Edmonton   Located in the heart of the downtown office area, this modern hotel offers some of the city's largest and most comfortable rooms. A recent major facelift has brought a clean, contemporary look to the place. The beds feature custom mattresses designed for near-perfect support; showers have dual shower heads. Standard rooms come with one king-size bed or two doubles, while deluxe rooms are designed for business travelers and come with two phone lines, wireless Internet, and other telecom and amenities upgrades. Suites are gracious and large, with separate bedrooms, large dressing rooms and bathrooms, and swank sitting rooms with black leather furniture. Like at all Westins, prepare to pay for extras like parking and Internet access.

10135 100th St., Edmonton, T5J 0N7. ✆ **800/228-3000** or 780/426-3636. Fax 780/428-1454. www.thewestinedmonton.com. 413 units. From C$115 double. AE, DC, DISC, MC, V. Valet parking C$28; self-parking C$26. **Amenities:** 2 restaurants; lounge; babysitting; concierge; exercise room; Jacuzzi; indoor pool; 24-hr. room service; sauna. *In room:* A/C, TV, fridge, hair dryer, Internet, minibar.

Moderate

Courtyard by Marriott 👔   Don't let the name fool you; this is anything but a could-be-anywhere business hotel. Rooms are comfortable and well furnished, but it's the setting and facilities that really stand out. Edmontonians have voted the downtown bar and restaurant patio—cantilevered hundreds of feet above the North Saskatchewan River—as the city's top spot for outdoor drinks and dining. Located on the cliff-edge with vistas over the city center and the breadth of the valley, this Courtyard (formerly the Warwick) must have the best views in the entire chain. Just be sure to ask for a riverside view when booking your room.

1 Thornton Court (99th St. & Jasper Ave.), Edmonton, T5J 2E7. ✆ **866/441-7591** or 780/423-9999. www.marriott.com/hotels/travel/yegcy-courtyard-edmonton-downtown. 177 units. C$139–C$159 double. Parking C$22. **Amenities**: Restaurant; lounge. *In room*: A/C, TV, hair dryer, Wi-Fi.

Days Inn Downtown Edmonton 🔑   For the price, this is one of downtown Edmonton's best deals. Located just a 5-minute walk from the city center, the former motor inn has everything you need for a pleasant stay, including comfortably furnished rooms and easy access to public transport. If all you need for a night or two is a clean and basic room in a convenient location, this is a top choice. Free parking is another bonus.

10041 106th St., Edmonton, T5J 1G3. ✆ **800/267-2191** or 780/423-1925. www.daysinn-downtown edmonton.com. 76 units. C$92–C$115 double. Senior, AAA & corporate discounts available. AE, DC, DISC, MC, V. Free parking. **Amenities:** Restaurant; bar; limited room service. *In room:* A/C, TV, hair dryer, Wi-Fi.

Glenora Bed & Breakfast 🍴🛏 Located in the heart of the artsy High Street district, just west of downtown, the Glenora occupies the upper floors of a converted 1912 heritage apartment building. While lots of care has been taken to retain the period character and charm of the rooms, the rooms have been thoroughly updated—all but three have private bathrooms, and four rooms have full kitchen facilities. Most appealing is the happy mix of unique period furnishings and snappy interior design—absolutely every room is unique. There are five styles of rooms, from simple bedroom units with shared bathrooms to one-bedroom apartment suites with kitchens. Free parking, an excellent breakfast, and access to a handsome Edwardian common room and a second-story deck is included. The Glenora is an excellent value—and fun, to boot.

12327 102nd Ave. NW, Edmonton, T5N 0L8. ✆ **877/453-6672** or 780/488-6766. www.glenorabnb.com. 25 units. C$90–C$165 double. Rates include continental breakfast. AE, MC, V. Free parking. **Amenities:** Restaurant; bar; Wi-Fi. *In room:* TV/VCR, hair dryer, minibar.

Hotel Selkirk 🛏 Located inside the historic Fort Edmonton Park, this little inn manages to feel authentic and historic, yet still comfortable. While the setting is 1920, the rooms have modern furniture and plush beds. There's a two-bedroom suite on the top floor. Sit by the window and watch the trams go by. The location, right next to the river, is great for walking, biking, and running. It's quiet down here at night, and you are far from restaurants. But if you want to see the "real" history of Edmonton, you can't beat this unique inn.

1920 St., Fort Edmonton Park (on Whitemud Dr., at Fox Dr.), Edmonton, T5J 2R7. ✆ **877/496-7227** or 780/496-7227. www.hotelselkirk.com. 31 rooms. From C$141 double. Rates include breakfast & park admission. AE, DISC, MC, V. Free parking. **Amenities:** Restaurant; saloon. *In room:* A/C, Wi-Fi.

Inexpensive

Hostelling International Edmonton Well-located near the University of Alberta in the lively Old Strathcona neighborhood, this pleasant hostel has a shared and newly renovated kitchen, along with spacious common rooms. Some family rooms are available, and check-in is at 3pm. Free coffee and wireless Internet, and a good location near many festival hubs, make this a good option for budget travelers and families.

10647 81st Ave., Edmonton, T6E 1Y1. ✆ **780/988-6836.** www.hihostels.ca. 88 beds. Members C$29–C$32 bed, nonmembers C$26 members and C$36 bed non-members; C$83 members and C$85 non-members family room. MC, V. **Amenities:** Bike rental, Wi-Fi.

University of Alberta In May through August, two dorms are thrown open to visitors. Some are standard shared-bathroom rooms, single or twin, while others are single or twin with a private washroom. Also, the university has a number of hotel-style guest rooms with private bathrooms. U of A is on the LRT line, not far from Old Strathcona.

87th Ave. & 116th St. ✆ **780/492-4281.** www.uofaweb.ualberta.ca/residences/index.cfm. C$35 single w/shared bathroom, C$49 single w/private bathroom; C$45 twin w/shared bathroom, C$59 twin w/private bathroom; C$119 double. MC, V. Parking C$9. **Amenities:** Food service nearby.

WHERE TO DINE

Edmonton has a vigorous dining scene, with hip new eateries joining traditional steak and seafood restaurants. In general, fine dining is found downtown and on High Street, close to the centers of politics and business. Over in Old Strathcona, south of the river, are trendy—and less expensive—cafes and bistros. For lighter meals or coffee breaks, try the very chic new **Holt's Café** downtown (10180 101st St.; ✆ **780/425-5300**) or **Leva Cafe** (11053 86th Ave.; ✆ **780/479-5362**) near the University of Alberta, which has the best espresso in Edmonton. For pastries and café au lait in the High Street area, you can't miss **La Favorite** (12431 102nd Ave.; ✆ **780/482-7024**).

Downtown

EXPENSIVE

Hardware Grill CONTEMPORARY   This is easily one of western Canada's most exciting restaurants. The building may be historic (and within walking distance of most downtown hotels and theaters), but there's nothing antique about the dining room. Modern but not stark, the room is edged with glass partitions, exposed pipes, and ducts painted a smoky rose. There are as many appetizers as entrees, making it tempting to graze through a series of smaller dishes. A delicate, delicious bison carpaccio is served with Chevre Noir cheese, and a crispy duck-leg confit has sundried cranberries and sage. Entrees such as plank-roasted salmon with a crab crust, a demi-roasted lamb rack served cassoulet style, or herb-crusted venison loin with slow-braised short ribs practically leap off the plate with their inventive flavor combinations.

9698 Jasper Ave. ✆ **780/423-0969.** www.hardwaregrill.com. Reservations recommended. Main courses C$30–C$48. AE, DC, MC, V. Mon–Fri 11:30am–2pm; Mon–Thurs 5–9:30pm, Fri & Sat 5–10pm. Closed 1st week of July.

La Ronde ☺ CONTEMPORARY   On the 24th floor of the Crowne Plaza, the revolving La Ronde offers the best views of any restaurant in Edmonton. The Alberta-focused menu also puts on quite a show—chef Jasmin Kobajica is passionate about local organic meats and produce. The menu is rich in locally raised beef, lamb, and game prepared with a focus on indigenous flavors. Beef-lovers can choose from a AAA tenderloin with *monchego* cheese, a AAA classic prime rib, or a 227g (8-oz.) sirloin with truffle bacon sauce. Bison, lamb, curried goat, and Arctic char round out the entree options. The intensely regional menu makes a brilliant companion to the ever-changing, revolving vista of city towers and river valley. But be warned: You're paying for the view as much as the meal, and some of the dishes fail to impress. Stick with the simple stuff, and you'll be satisfied. They also have a kids menu.

10111 Bellamy Hill. ✆ 780/428-6611. www.chateaulacombe.com/laronde.php. Reservations required. Main courses C$28–C$33. AE, MC, V. Sun 10:30am–2pm; daily 5:30–10pm.

Madison's at Union Bank Inn 🏨 CONTEMPORARY   Madison's is one of the loveliest dining rooms and casual cocktail bars in Edmonton. Once an early-20th-century bank, the building's formal architectural details remain, but they now share the light-and-airy space with modern art and excellent food. The menu is contemporary, bridging continental European cuisine with regional Canadian ingredients. It features grilled and roast fish and meat, plus pasta dishes and interesting salads (one special featured smoked sablefish, watercress, avocado vinaigrette, and tomato jam). Other standouts include a pan-roasted Alberta rack of lamb and a pork tenderloin

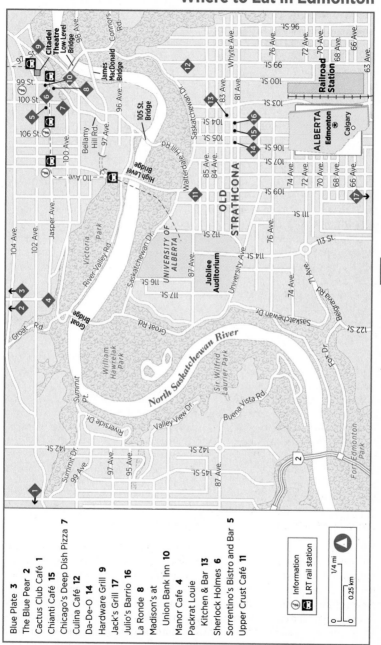

Blue Plate **3**

The Blue Pear **2**

Cactus Club Café **1**

Chianti Café **15**

Chicago's Deep Dish Pizza **7**

Culina Café **12**

Da-De-O **14**

Hardware Grill **9**

Jack's Grill **17**

Julio's Barrio **16**

La Ronde **8**

Madison's at
   Union Bank Inn **10**

Manor Cafe **4**

Packrat Louie
   Kitchen & Bar **13**

Sherlock Holmes **6**

Sorrentino's Bistro and Bar **5**

Upper Crust Café **11**

stuffed with local Saskatoon berries and gouda-stuffed pears. A six course chef's dinner runs C$85. Add wine pairings for C$50, which is a very good value. And don't miss daily breakfast and afternoon tapas menus, as well.

10053 Jasper Ave. ✆ **780/401-2222**. www.unionbankinn.com. Reservations recommended. Main courses C$34-C$39. AE, MC, V. Mon-Fri 7-10am & 11am-2pm, Sat & Sun 8-11am; Mon-Thurs 5-10pm, Fri & Sat 5-11pm, Sun 5-8pm.

Sorrentino's Bistro and Bar ITALIAN   This upscale branch of a local chain is a good addition to the downtown scene. The sophisticated dining room—flanked by the Havana Room, where Cuban cigars are available with port and single-malt Scotch—is a popular meeting place for the city's business and social elite. At lunch, order from the menu or choose sauces and noodles from a pasta buffet. The daily appetizer table features grilled vegetables, salads, and marinated anchovies. Entrees range from risotto to wood-fired pizza to the Italian classics like *osso buco* and pork saltimbocca.

10162 100th St. ✆ **780/424-7500**. www.sorrentinos.com. Reservations recommended. Main courses C$28-C$39. AE, DC, MC, V. Mon-Fri 11:30am-10:30pm; Sat 5-10:30pm.

MODERATE & INEXPENSIVE

Blue Plate ★★ ☺ DINER   Maybe Edmonton's cozy, friendly, laid-back attitude is best represented in this vegetarian-friendly diner in the Warehouse District close to downtown. The house specialties here are burgers, including the best veggie burger in town, which is stocked with good root vegetables and served with herbed mayo and a pickle. There's also a bison burger with dried blueberries and a great steak sandwich (this is Alberta, after all). They have an impressive New World–heavy wine list. It's very popular, especially on weekends, so call ahead.

10145 104th St. ✆ **780/429-0740**. www.blueplatediner.ca. Reservations highly recommended. Main courses C$14-C$26. AE, MC, V. Mon-Fri 11am-10pm; Sat 9am-10pm.

Chicago's Deep Dish Pizza ★ ☺ PIZZA   It's a long way from the Windy City to the "River City," but this joint close to the Chateau Lacombe (see "Where to Stay," above) has the best pizza in town. They are square, large, and (you guessed it!) deep. The Galaxy pizza is crammed with pepperoni, salami, mushrooms, bacon, shrimp, pineapple, and a few other surprises. Pastas and salads round out a very family-friendly meal.

10024 102nd St. ✆ **780/413-8866**. www.cddp.ca. Main courses C$14-C$18. AE, MC, V. Sun-Thurs 4pm-1:30am; Fri & Sat 4pm-3:30am.

Sherlock Holmes ENGLISH   The Sherlock Holmes is a tremendously popular English-style pub with local and regional beers on tap (as well as Guinness) and a very well-executed bar menu. The Holmes offers up a few traditional English dishes—fish and chips, steak-and-kidney pie—but there's a strong emphasis on new pub grub; the butter chicken and goat cheese quesadilla is excellent. The pub—in a charming Tudor-style building with a picket fence around the outdoor patio—is completely surrounded by high-rise towers.

Rice Howard Way (10012 101A Ave.) ✆ **780/426-7784**. www.thesherlockholmes.com. Main courses C$12-C$16. AE, MC, V. Mon-Sat 11am-3am; Sun 11:30am-11pm.

High Street

The Blue Pear ★★★ CONTEMPORARY   Tucked into an innocuous, petite strip mall just off the 124th Street stroll is this absolute gem of a restaurant that's my choice if you have but one night in Edmonton. A small room in muted gray and blue tones, the Blue Pear is the brainchild of a food-obsessed husband-and-wife team. He's the chef; she handles the hospitality. It's a perfect partnership: Over the course of a five-course meal, wonders emerge from the kitchen at perfect pace, each one leaving you breathless awaiting the next. This is simple food, with an emphasis on local ingredients, treated with respect for flavor and subtle, unique creativity: braised baby beets with Anjou pears, a goat cheese *coulis,* and candied walnuts is followed by grilled Asian marinated beef with *bulgogi* sauce and spicy cabbage puree, or a simple roasted fish of the day, with saffron-braised chickpeas, spinach, and a citrus *crostini.* It's followed by a dessert of your choice. Meals here are the fruits of a top-flight creative food mind whirring at full capacity.

10643 123rd St. ℂ **780/482/7178.** www.thebluepear.com. Reservations highly recommended. 5-course meal C$89, including dessert; 3-course meal C$59. AE, MC, V. Daily 5–11pm.

Manor Cafe INTERNATIONAL   The Manor Cafe offers one of the most fashionable outdoor dining patios in Edmonton. This longtime Edmonton favorite offers fusion and international cuisine, from Italian pastas—Manor pasta with chicken, spinach, pancetta, goat cheese, and sundried tomato cream sauce is the signature dish—to a delicious curried chicken or beef Stroganoff. Food is eclectic but always delicious.

10109 125th St. ℂ **780/482-7577.** www.manorcafe.com. Reservations recommended on weekends. Main courses C$17–C$29. AE, MC, V. Mon–Thurs 11am–10pm; Fri & Sat 11am–midnight; Sun 11am–2pm & 5–9pm.

Old Strathcona

Culina Café ★ ⓘ EUROPEAN   A few blocks from busy Whyte Avenue, this fresh neighborhood cafe has a leafy patio and healthy food. While the roots of the menu are in Ukrainian food (hearty stews, pierogies, and the like), the food is really more about simple freshness. There's a duck breast on local roasted potatoes, and Alberta beef with blue cheese and chocolate sauce. For lunch, try the Persian flatbread sandwich with roasted vegetable, hummus, and quinoa salad. Many Edmontonians say this is the best breakfast in the city. There's another location just north of downtown (at 6509 112th Ave).

9914 89th Ave. ℂ **780/437-5588.** www.culinafamily.ca. Reservations recommended on weekends and for brunch. Main courses C$13–C$27. AE, MC, V. Mon–Fri 9am–3pm, Sat & Sun 10am–2pm; Mon–Sat 5–10pm.

Chianti Café ⓘ ITALIAN   Chianti is a rarity among Italian restaurants: very good and very inexpensive. Pasta dishes include fettuccine with scallops, smoked salmon, curry, and garlic; or try one of the veal dishes (more than a dozen are offered) or seafood specials. Chianti is located in a handsomely remodeled post-office building; the restaurant isn't a secret, so it can be a busy and fairly crowded experience.

10501 82nd Ave. ℂ **780/439-9829.** Reservations required. Main courses C$14–C$22. AE, DC, DISC, MC, V. Daily 11am–11pm.

Da-De-O CAJUN/SOUTHERN   This small and hip New Orleans–style diner is authentic, right down to the low-tech jukebox at your table. The food is top-notch, with good and goopy po' boys, fresh oysters, and four kinds of jambalaya. Especially tasty is the spicy shrimp creole. Relax in a vinyl booth, listen to Billie Holiday, and graze through some crab fritters.

10548A 82nd Ave. ℂ **780/433-0930.** www.dadeo.ca. Reservations highly recommended on weekends. Main courses C$11–C$16. AE, MC, V. Mon, Tues & Thurs–Sat 11:30am–11pm; Sun noon–10pm. Closed Wed.

Julio's Barrio ★ MEXICAN   If you like Mexican food, it's worth a detour to Julio's. The food ranges from enchiladas and nachos to sizzling shrimp fajitas. This Mexican watering hole is a great place to snack on several light dishes while quaffing margaritas with friends. The atmosphere is youthful, high energy, and minimalist hip: no kitschy piñatas or scratchy recordings of marimba bands here.

10450 82nd Ave. ✆ **780/431-0774.** Main courses C$14–C$29. AE, MC, V. Sun–Wed 11:30am–11pm; Thurs 11:30am–midnight; Fri & Sat 11:30am–1am.

Packrat Louie Kitchen & Bar ★★ ITALIAN   Bright and lively, this very popular bistro has a somewhat unlikely name, given that it's one of the best casual Italian trattoria in Edmonton. Menu choices range from specialty pizzas—from a chicken *tikka* salad to smoked salmon—to fine entree salads to grilled meats, chicken, and pasta. A stocked menu of canapés by the dozen includes phyllo tenderloin bites, lemon pizza, and buffalo meatballs. Most dishes tend toward light or healthy preparations without sacrificing complexity. A rack of lamb comes with jalapeno mint jelly, and ostrich tenderloin is served with spaetzle and sour cherry *gastrique*. Right across the street from the Fringe Festival hub, you'll definitely need to reserve well in advance during the mid-August event.

10335 83rd Ave. ✆ **780/433-0123.** www.packratlouie.com. Reservations recommended on weekends. Main courses C$12–C$42. MC, V. Mon–Fri 11:30am–10pm; Sat 11:30am–11:30pm.

Upper Crust Café ✎ CAFE   Another popular neighborhood joint, the Upper Crust has the best sandwiches in town, besides well-priced entrees like vegetarian chili, lasagna, and six hearty salads. The Kaiser Filet sandwich is a classic. Or make your own deli-style on homemade molasses bread. Save room for the sticky-toffee pudding for dessert.

10909 86th Ave. ✆ **780/758-5599.** Main courses C$9–C$16. AE, MC, V. Mon–Fri 11am–9pm; Sat 9:30am–9pm.

Elsewhere

Cactus Club Café ✎ CONTEMPORARY   The best food in the West Edmonton Mall is at this Western Canadian chain that's both casual and refined. It's fun to even drop in for an afternoon cocktail. Staples like pepper-sauced steak and calamari are dependable, but there's wow-factor in more creative takes—the club sandwich has duck, chicken, and carpaccio. Service can be iffy, but under the guidance of *Iron Chef* winner Rob Feenie, the kitchen here consistently puts out fine-dining–caliber meals and average-neighborhood-diner prices. The vibe is cool and laid-back, making this a better bet than any of the other local chains like the Keg, Moxie's, or Earl's.

1946-8882 170th St. ✆ **780/489-1002.** www.cactusclubcafe.com. Reservations recommended for dinner. Main courses C$14–C$26. AE, MC, V. Daily 11am–midnight.

Jack's Grill ★ CONTEMPORARY   Ten years ago, Jack's was *the* spot in Edmonton. Lately, it's fallen down somewhat, overshadowed by the likes of Blue Plate and the Blue Pear (see above). For one, the location is not handy, tucked away in a quiet residential area in the city's south end, near the Southgate Mall. The food, though, was a trend-setter of types, relying on simple preparation, inventive flavor combinations, and tons of fresh, local ingredients before "locavore" was a word. Try the smoked lamb carpaccio crusted in rosemary with arugula and apple salad and Dijon aioli, say, or chili-rubbed grilled beef rib-eye, aged 28 days, with smoked tomato and goat cheese tortellini and creamed spinach. Think of it, perhaps, as haute comfort food—some of the best you'll find anywhere.

5842 111th St. ⓒ **780/434-1113.** www.jacksgrill.com. Reservations recommended. Main courses C$28–C$45. AE, MC, V. Mon–Sat from 5pm.

EXPLORING THE CITY

While Edmonton is eminently walkable in pockets, getting to and from those various pockets—downtown, Old Strathcona, High Street—can be a bit of a chore. Downtown and Old Strathcona are on opposite sides of the imposing river valley, with just a few bridges between them. The distance is not walkable and can take up to 30 minutes on public transit, so be sure to plan that into your day. West of downtown is High Street, a pleasant stroll where you'll find the Royal Alberta Museum, among other things, but again, don't plan to walk from downtown unless you've got time to spare. Edmonton's bus service is reliable and frequent, so rely on that instead.

Provincial Legislature   Perched with a view of the gorgeous river valley, Alberta's Legislature, the seat of the provincial government, is an impressive structure built between 1907 and 1913. Free 60-minute tours with engaging guides are offered daily for those interested in the building's Beaux Art–era architecture and decor. It's a stately monument brimming with the history of a frontier town made good and a province bursting with potential.

10800 97th Ave. ⓒ **780/427-7362.** www.assembly.ab.ca. Free admission. May to Oct 15 daily tours every hour 9am–noon & every half-hour 12:30–4pm. Oct 16 to Apr weekday tours every hour 9am–3pm & weekend tours every hour noon–4pm.

The Art Gallery of Alberta ★★   The most exciting thing to come to Edmonton since the Stanley Cup, the stunning new AGA is the C$88-million, 2,787-sq.-m (30,000-sq.-ft.) home for revolving world-class exhibits. On any given day, you could take in Degas, Picasso, and Emily Carr; there's permanent room for Alberta's top artists, as well. It is a champion of First Nations contemporary art (think artists like Jane Ash Poitras and Carl Beam) and has been an incubator for curating talent that has gone on to larger institutions all over the country and around the world.

2 Sir Winston Churchill Sq. (at the corner of 102A Ave. & 99th St). ⓒ **780/422-6223.** www.youraga.ca. C$12 adults, C$8 seniors & students, C$8 children 7–12, free for children 6 & under. Tues–Fri 11am–7pm; Sat & Sun 10am–5pm. Closed Mon.

Fort Edmonton Park ☺   Fort Edmonton Park literally reconstructs four distinct eras of Edmonton's history. Perhaps most interesting is the complete reconstruction of the old Fort Edmonton fur trading post from the turn of the 18th century. This vast wooden structure is a warren of rooms and activities: blacksmiths, bakers, and other guides ply their trades. On 1885 Street, you'll see Frontier Edmonton, complete with saloons, general store, and Jasper House Hotel, which serves hearty pioneer meals. 1905 Street celebrates the agricultural boom years of the early 19th century, when Edmonton teemed with new immigrants and was named provincial capital. On 1920 Street, sip an old-fashioned ice-cream soda at Bill's confectionery and see the changes wrought in the rural West by World War I. You can't miss the midway, with rides for kids of all ages. If the variety of activities at Fort Edmonton appeals to your family, consider spending a night at the park's Hotel Selkirk (see

Edmonton Attractions

Citadel
Theatre

Low Level
Bridge

98 Ave.

Connors Rd.

97 St.

99 St.

100 St.

106 St.

100 Ave.

110 Ave.

James
MacDonald
Bridge

96 Ave.

Bellamy
Hill Rd.

97 Ave.

105 St.
Bridge

High Level
Bridge

Saskatchewan Dr.

Walterdale
Hill Rd.

83 Ave.

81 Ave.

85 Ave.

84 Ave.

74 Ave.

72 Ave.

70 Ave.

68 Ave.

66 Ave.

96 St.

76 Ave.

72 Ave.

70 Ave.

68 Ave.

66 Ave.

63 Ave.

Whyte Ave.

100 St.

103 St.

104 St.

105 St.

106 St.

107 St.

109 St.

111 St.

113 St.

**Railroad
Station**

**OLD
STRATHCONA**

Jasper Ave.

104 Ave.

102 Ave.

Victoria
Park

River Valley Rd.

Saskatchewan Dr.

112 St.

116 St.

117 St.

87 St.

**UNIVERSITY OF
ALBERTA**

114 St.

University Ave.

**Jubilee
Auditorium**

76 Ave.

74 Ave.

71 Ave.

Belgravia Rd.

Saskatchewan Dr.

122 St.

Groat Rd.

**Groat
Bridge**

Summit
Pt.

William
Hawrelak
Park

Groat Rd.

North Saskatchewan River

Sir Wilfrid
Laurier Park

Buena Vista Rd.

Fox Dr.

Fort Edmonton
Park

Riverside Dr.

Summit
Dr.

Valley View Dr.

99 Ave.

97 Ave.

95 Ave.

142 St.

145 St.

142 St.

145 St.

87 Ave.

156 St.

The Art Gallery of Alberta **4**
The Edmonton Queen
Riverboat **5**
Fort Edmonton Park **9**
John Janzen Nature Centre **8**
Provincial Legislature **3**
Muttart Conservatory **6**
Royal Alberta Museum **2**
Telus World of Science **1**
The Valley Zoo **7**

ⓘ Information
🚉 LRT rail station

1/4 mi

0.25 km

ALBERTA
Edmonton ⊛
Calgary

10

"Where to Stay," above). A C$10-million expansion in 2010 brings a new replica of the Capital Theatre and more evening events.

On Whitemud Dr. (at Fox Dr.). ℰ **780/496-8787.** www.fortedmontonpark.ca. C$14 adults, C$11 seniors & youth 13-17, C$7.75 children 2-12; C$42 families. Mid-May to late June Mon–Fri 10am–4pm, Sat & Sun 10am–6pm; late June to early Sept daily 10am–6pm. Closed early Sept to mid-May, except for Christmas Dec 20-23.

The Edmonton Queen Riverboat ☺   It may not do much to help you get your bearings, but the Edmonton Queen is a great opportunity to ride the fast-running waters of the North Saskatchewan river through the lush and scenic valley right in the middle of downtown. Edmonton never looks as good as it does from the river's surface. Late afternoon sailings include dinner.

9734 98th Ave. ℰ **780/424-2628.** www.edmontonqueen.com. Daytime cruises C$18 adults, C$15 seniors & children 11-17, C$11 children 3-10; dinner cruises C$50 adults, C$40 seniors & children 11-17, C$22 children 3-10. Boarding times: Fri & Sat (& Thurs after June 21) 11am, 2 & 5:30pm; Sun noon, 3 & 5:30pm.

John Janzen Nature Centre ☺   Sharing a parking lot with Fort Edmonton Park, the Janzen Centre is a storehouse of knowledge on Edmonton's natural history, as well as how to co-exist with nature in an urban setting. It's ideal for kids, with baby bunnies and chicks on hand for them to fondle, and all kinds of year-round programs and classes, like "Butterfly Frolic" and "This Ark Called Earth." There are also 4km (2.5 miles) of interpretive trails signposted with all kinds of nature knowledge.

Fox Dr. & Whitemud Dr. ℰ **780/496-8787.** C$2 adults, C$1.65 seniors & youth 13-17, C$1.35 children 2-12; C$6.75 families. Summer Mon–Fri 9am–6pm; spring, fall and winter Mon, Wed & Fri 9am–4pm. Call for information on specific programs & times/dates.

Muttart Conservatory   Four glass pyramids rise up from the deep snow on the south bank of the North Saskatchewan River in the depths of an Edmonton winter. Inside, 700 species of plants, from arid to tropical, flourish despite the weather. The Muttart, a city-operated property, is an oasis for Edmontonians starving for a bit of greenery in the long, cold winter that the city's northern location always brings. Architecturally stunning and nicely curated to reflect three climatological zones— arid, temperate, and tropical—the Muttart is a welcome refuge, a place where it's moderate summer all year round.

9626 96A St. ℰ **780/442-5311.** www.muttartconservatory.ca. C$11 adults, C$8 seniors & youth 13-17, C$5.25 children 2-12; C$32 families.

Royal Alberta Museum ★   Expertly laid out, this 18,500-sq.-m (199,132-sq.-ft.) modern museum displays Alberta's natural and human history in three permanent galleries. Wild Alberta represents Alberta's diverse natural history with astonishingly lifelike dioramas and interactive displays utilizing computers, microscopes, and other hands-on tools. It's a good place to gain some knowledge about what you're going to see if you're heading to the Rockies. The Gallery of Aboriginal Culture tells the 11,000-year story of Alberta's First Nations inhabitants, incorporating artifacts, film, interactive media, and Native interpreters. The Natural History Gallery has fossils, minerals, and a live-bug room.

12845 102nd Ave. ℰ **780/453-9100.** www.royalalbertamuseum.ca. C$10 adults, C$8 seniors, C$7 students, C$5 children 7-17, free for children 6 & under; C$28 families. Sat & Sun half-price admission 9–11am. Daily 9am–5pm.

Telus World of Science ☺ This is one of the most advanced science centers in the world. Its wonders include an **IMAX theater,** the largest planetarium theater in Canada, high-tech exhibits (including a virtual-reality showcase and a display on robotics), and an observatory open on clear afternoons and evenings. Exhibits include a journey through the human body (including the Gallery of the Gross!) and Mystery Avenue, where young sleuths can try their hands.

11211 142nd St., Coronation Park. ℂ **780/451-3344.** www.edmontonscience.com. C$14 adults, C$12 seniors & children 13-17, C$9.50 children 3-12; C$55 families. Summer daily 10am-7pm; Sept 7-mid-June Sun–Thurs & holidays 10am-5pm, Fri & Sat 10am-7pm. Bus: 17 or 22.

The Valley Zoo ☺ Not as sprawling and impressive as the Calgary Zoo (see p. 102), Edmonton's Valley Zoo, nestled in Sir Wilfrid Laurier Park near the river, is nonetheless a diverting activity amid the lush green surroundings of the North Saskatchewan river valley. More than 100 exotic, endangered, and native animals are here, including rare red panda twins, born in May 2008.

13315 Buena Vista Rd. (87th Ave.). ℂ **780/442-5311.** www.valleyzoo.ca. May 10 to Oct 11 C$11 adults, C$8 seniors & children 12-17, C$5.25 children 11 & under; C$32 families. Oct 14 to May 30 C$8 adults, C$6 seniors & children 2-12; C$24 families. Sept to May 9 9:30am–4pm; May 10 to June 27 9:30am–4pm; June 28 to Aug 9:30am-6pm.

10 OUTDOOR ACTIVITIES & SPECTATOR SPORTS

Edmonton likes to call itself "the city of champions," and there's a good historical claim to it. From 1984 to 1990, the Edmonton Oilers, led by all-time greats Wayne Gretzky and Mark Messier, won the Stanley Cup, the National Hockey League championship, five times. Meanwhile, the Edmonton Eskimos, the city's Canadian Football League team, have won the Grey Cup championship 13 times, including an unmatched five consecutive wins between 1978 and 1982, and most recently in 2005—facts Edmontonians love to lord over their rivals to the south in Calgary, where sporting success has been nowhere near so frequent.

Edmonton, on a flat plain 3½ hours east of the Rocky Mountains, has nowhere near the plethora of outdoor activities as Calgary, but the network of parks that run along the river valley provide ample opportunity for in-city communing with nature. The 48km (30-mile) city stretch along the North Saskatchewan River has 22 major parks, earning it the nickname "the Ribbon of Green." It is also the largest expanse of urban parkland in North America, with about 100km (62 miles) of bike paths. Be warned: Dogs are *not* allowed at any of the city parks' picnic areas.

Parks & Outdoor Areas
NORTH RIVERBANK

Hermitage Park Until 1969, the land that is now Hermitage Park, part of the Ribbon of Green along the river valley, was cattle ranchland. At that time, the city started buying up parcels of land and converting it to parkland. Now, Hermitage Park, in the city's northeast, on the north bank of the river, is a grassy expanse of riverbank where you can launch kayaks or other watercraft, fish, or just loll in the grass and let the day drift lazily by. Hermitage also has 14 archaeological sites, where fire pits, stone tools, and butchered bison and deer bones have been found, left by nomadic hunters thousands of years ago. In 1987, Hermitage was a casualty of a vicious tornado that tore much of its foliage away; a monument commemorates the thousands of volunteer hours spent nursing the park back to health.

North of the Yellowhead Trail, just off Victoria Trail NW.

Rundle Park Rundle Park is on the north bank of the river in the northeast part of the river valley, just south and west of Hermitage Park, but separated from it by Rundle Golf Club. The park features large, open grassy areas, plentiful hiking and cycling trails, soccer and football fields, baseball diamonds, tennis courts, and a sand volleyball court. There's also a man-made lake—handy to cool off in after all that activity. You'll also find a footbridge here, to the south bank of the river and Gold Bar Park.

Park entrance at 28th St. & 118th Ave.

Dawson Park A smaller park on the Ribbon of Green, Dawson Park borders on Jasper Avenue east of downtown. It's notable for an innovative path system, designed by Edmontonian Glen Norton specifically for the visually impaired. The path is lined with raised wooden edgers that users can tap with their cane to stay on track. There are seven signs along the trail, all of them in Braille, as well as conventional signage.

Park entrance at 8940 102A Ave.

Sir Wilfrid Laurier Park At 83 hectares (205 acres), it's one of Edmonton's largest. You'll find Edmonton's Valley Zoo here, but the park is short on other amusements, like sporting fields. Rather, it's just a nice, natural expanse, with cycling and walking paths carved throughout its lush greenery.

Park entrance at Buena Vista Rd. NW, south of 87th Ave. NW.

SOUTH RIVERBANK

Gold Bar Park The park is in the city's east end on the south bank of the river. It extends from the bank of the North Saskatchewan River to 50th Street to the south. Like Hermitage, Gold Bar—so named because prospectors would pan for gold on the riverbank before the turn of the 20th century—was used for cattle ranching until the city took it over in 1969. Now, most of the cattle you'll find here is on the grill of the many BBQ pits to be found by happy weekend burgermeisters at this popular family recreation spot. Extending south along the river bank from Gold Bar is Gold Stick Park, a slender finger of grassland poking as far south as 101st Avenue NW.

The park is busy, with baseball and soccer fields, a pond, a 10km (6.2-mile) walking trail loop, and a footbridge across the river to Rundle Park. In the winter, there are excellent cross-country ski trails and outdoor skating rinks.

It's sometimes smart to book a picnic site in advance—there are only 30—which you can do at Edmonton's website, www.edmonton.ca.

Park entrance at 4620 105th Ave.

Capilano Park Moving west along the south bank, you'll find Capilano Park, a nicely treed park with plenty of hiking trails, a boat launch for canoeing and kayaking in the river, and a footbridge to the north bank that lets you off at Ada Avenue.

Park entrance at 109th Ave. & 50th St.

Queen Elizabeth Park   This larger park on the south bank features a summertime magnet—a large, and often crowded, outdoor swimming pool. Covering 31 hectares (75 acres), the park has been described as one of the city's major showpieces. Surrounded by lush greenery as the river rushes by, the downtown skyline looming across the river to the north, it's easy to see why. It's also connected to Kinsmen Park, to the west, where you'll find a pitch 'n' putt, sports fields, tennis courts, and the **John Walter museum** (1066 91A Ave.; ☏ **780/496-2925**), which features the three original Edmonton homes Walter, a prominent entrepreneur and city father, built for himself here.

Park entrance at 10380 Queen Elizabeth Park Rd.

William Hawrelak Park   Just north and west of the University of Alberta is this smaller park, on an elbow of river as it winds through the city. Named for a three-term Edmonton mayor, William Hawrelak Park has an artificial lake and the Heritage Amphitheatre, where such summer events as the Freewill Shakespeare Festival take place.

Park entrance at 9930 Groat Rd.

Whitemud Park   Whitemud is a naturalized park, and the thick growth here underscores that fact. Near the river, you'd swear you were in a pristine wilderness location—if not for the downtown tower poking up over the south bank to the east. Whitemud is adjacent to Fort Edmonton Park, the historical village, so you could easily make a day of touring the historical site, followed up by a lazy picnic in the park by the river.

Park entrance at 13204 Fox Dr.

Spectator Sports

Edmonton Oilers   The Oilers were founded in 1971 as part of the upstart World Hockey Association, which was envisioned as a rival league to the NHL. But with teams in smaller centers like Cincinnati and Indianapolis, the league failed to catch on and was dissolved in 1979. A handful of WHA teams made the jump to the NHL, the Oilers being one of them. In 1978, with the league on the verge of collapse, Edmonton acquired 17-year-old Wayne Gretzky from the Indianapolis Racers, a team that would fold just a few months later. In his first NHL season, as an 18-year-old, Gretzky scored 137 points. He would go on to the greatest career of all time, scoring 2,857 points, and would be the leader and centerpiece of an Oilers team, with Mark Messier, Paul Coffey, and Grant Fuhr, that would win multiple Stanley Cups and rank among the greatest ever. This "dynasty" won the Cup in 1984, 1985, 1987, 1988, and 1990.

Today's Oilers are less flashy, but they're a young, feisty lot who play in front of some of the loudest, most passionate—if somewhat spoiled—fans the world has to offer. If you go, be prepared to be showered in history of past glories by whomever you might sit next to; Edmontonians take their hockey very seriously, and they expect you to do the same.

Rexall Place, 7424 118th Ave. NW. ☏ **780/471-7210**, or 780/414-4625 for tickets. www.edmontonoilers.com.

Edmonton Eskimos   Edmonton's beloved Eskies, as they're known, are perhaps the most successful CFL franchise of all time. With 13 Grey Cup victories, they've

Outdoor Activities & Spectator Sports

EDMONTON

THE battle OF ALBERTA

In the pantheon of great sporting rivalries, the long-running enmity between the Calgary Flames and the Edmonton Oilers is one of the best. The Oilers joined the NHL in 1979, when the now-defunct World Hockey Association was absorbed into the NHL, and Calgary got its NHL franchise in 1980, when the Flames relocated from Atlanta. They've been at each other's throats ever since. The rivalry peaked in the '80s and early '90s, when the Oilers defeated the Flames in the playoffs in 1983, 1984, 1988, and 1991, on their way to two of their five Stanley Cups. The Flames, meanwhile, exacted sweet revenge in 1986, when Edmonton defenseman Steve Smith banked the puck into his own goal late in the deciding Game 7 of their playoff series, giving the Flames the victory. The Flames went on to lose that year in the Stanley Cup final but finally picked up their own championship victory in 1989. The last time the teams met in the playoffs was in 1991, and it came down to overtime in game 7 to decide the winner, scored by Flames nemesis and super-pest Esa Tikkanen.

Through the '80s, Alberta was often called "Death Valley" by visiting teams, which often played both clubs on the same trip, for the sheer dominance that both teams exhibited. It's said that the Flames, with their own superstar line-up including Hall of Famers like Al MacInnis and Joe Mullen, would have built their own dynasty if not for the power of their rivals to the north.

Those heady days are in the past now, as both teams have fallen far. Calgary missed the playoffs seven times through the '90s but bounced back to make it four seasons in a row from 2004 to 2007, though with little success. The Oilers are in the midst of their own slump, missing the playoffs four years in a row, starting in 2007 and finishing dead last in 2010. But when these two teams play, the intensity kicks up a couple of notches, regardless of their fortunes; it's always a hot ticket in either town.

established themselves as the second of the twin pillars of Edmonton's self-anointment as the "city of champions." The CFL game—Canada's top pro football league—has subtle differences to the one played in the National Football League, such as a larger field and only three downs, rather than four. But aficionados argue that the extra room and need to take to the air more often only serve to make the game more exciting. Some players who flourished in the NFL were CFL stars first, and the Eskimos boasted a marquee quarterback in Warren Moon, who starred here, piling up championships before becoming an NFL impact player in Houston and Minnesota. The Eskimos play at Commonwealth Stadium, a 60,000-seat outdoor stadium just a dozen or so blocks north of downtown. While popular, games rarely sell out and are always reasonably priced. It's not a bad way to spend a sunny summer evening.

11000 Stadium Rd. NW. ✆ **780/448-1525,** or 780/448-3757 for tickets. www.edmontoneskimos.com.

Edmonton Capitals   Formerly known as "the Cracker Cats," the Capitals are Edmonton's entry in the minor pro Golden Baseball League. They play at a small stadium called Telus Field, near downtown on the north bank of the river.

10233 96th Ave. ✆ **780/409-3701,** or 780/414-4625 for tickets. www.capsbaseball.ca.

Edmonton Rush   The Rush joined the National Lacrosse League in 2006 and, in fine Edmonton fashion, immediately initiated hostilities with their southern rivals, the Calgary Roughnecks, opening the Battle of Alberta on another front. It's a tough, aggressive and fast sport that may not appeal to all. But if you like American football or rugby, you'll be interested in checking out lacrosse. The Rush play at Rexall Place, where the Oilers also play.

312–11523 100th Ave. NW. ☎ **780/433-1181.** www.edmontonrush.com.

ORGANIZED TOURS

With its ridiculously long addresses (10230 101st St.) and awkward way of counting off its sprawling blocks (sts. and aves. start at 100 in central downtown, and count up as they go out), it's not a bad idea to take a tour, if only to get your bearings.

Peter's Edmonton Tours (☎ **780/904-6973**) provides small-group tours (up to seven people) of about 4 hours that can be tailored to suit your interests, though it does include stops at the beautiful Provincial Legislature building and Edmonton City Hall. Tour prices are C$45 adults, C$40 seniors, and C$20 children.

Edmonton Canoe (☎ **480/470-5353**; www.edmontoncanoe.com) offers the unique opportunity to explore the city from the surface of the North Saskatchewan River. Your guide will lead you on a paddle starting in nearby Devon, Alberta and into downtown, where, from the water's surface, the looming skyscrapers up the tall riverbanks are an imposing sight indeed. These tours are offered June to September on weekends only and cost C$50 per person for day trips from Devon to Edmonton.

New to town, **Segway Edmonton** (☎ **877/433-7347**; www.segwayedmonton. com) has 2-hour river valley tours on, you guessed it, those stand-up electric things called Segways. Tours cost C$90 per person and start at Government House Park. Riders must be 14 years of age or older and weigh at least 30kg (66 lb.).

For those less outdoorsy—or completely indoorsy—**Riester Explorer Tours** (☎ **780/475-6675**) will take you on a 6-hour tour of massive **West Edmonton Mall** (see p. 243). With more than 800 stores, it can be a little overwhelming, even for the most devout shopaholic, so a little hand-holding can't hurt. Tours are C$29 per person.

SHOPPING

Edmonton, like Calgary, is flush with oil money, though Edmontonians are a little more loath to be showy about it. As a result, the shopping scene is considerably more low-key (not counting West Edmonton Mall, of course, about which nothing is low-key at all). Still, there are options for the fashionista, from the newly expanded Holt Renfrew downtown to the trendy independent boutiques of Old Strathcona.

Downtown

Here, you'll find a handful of modest-sized, multilevel malls occupying the first and second floors of a handful of downtown office towers. Some are better than others, but you'll find most of the staples here. Edmonton's largest mall downtown is **Edmonton City Centre** (10222 102nd St; ☎ **780/426-8444**), with about 170 stores and four levels, including large retailers like the Bay, Winners, HBC Home

Outfitters, and Eddie Bauer. Other malls include **Manulife Place** (10180 101st St.; ✆ **780/420-6236**) and **Commerce Place** (Jasper Ave. at 102nd St.; ✆ **780/944-1222**). Between them, you'll find all the chain-brand staples—Roots, Club Monaco, the Gap, and a Shopper's Drug Mart.

The crown jewel of Edmonton downtown shopping, though, is the city's only **Holt Renfrew** store (10180 101st St. NW; ✆ **780/425-5300;** www.holtrenfrew. com), a posh Canadian department store chain. Think Neiman Marcus, and you've more or less got it: high-priced brands like Jil Sander, Giorgio Armani, Hugo Boss, and Paul Smith, arrayed in luxurious, if somewhat cramped, environs. Smaller than its Calgary counterpart, the Edmonton installment underwent a major renovation in 2008—the better to serve, perhaps, Edmontonians' increasingly deep pockets.

Whyte Avenue

The party's here at night, but in the day, some of the better, more unique retail options to be found in Alberta are here. Start with **Gravity Pope** (2–10442 82nd Ave.; ✆ **780/439-1637;** www.gravitypope.com), an of-the-moment shoe boutique with sister stores in Calgary and Vancouver. On Whyte (actually 82nd Ave. in Edmonton's numerical scheme), you'll find everything from books (a two-story outlet of the national big box chain **Chapters,** at 10504 82nd Ave., is here), antiques, fresh produce at the farmers' market, hippie wear, hip-hop outfitters, high-priced designer gear, and in one memorable spot, a dusty old Scottish goods shop that's doubtless been on Whyte Avenue since the city's origins as a Scots-settled northern outpost.

It's a nice nod to history, but Whyte's shopping options are almost entirely contemporary: **Colourblind** (10544 Whyte Ave.; ✆ **780/431-0981**) has trendy and eco-friendly fashions; **Method Streetwear** has all the gear for the hip-hop set (10313 82nd Ave.; ✆ **780/433-1167**), whereas **Bamboo Ballroom** (8206 104th St.; ✆ **780/439-1363;** www.bambooballroom.com) is a chic, sleek, California-inspired women's denim boutique with jewelry and clothing from chic local designers, as well.

High Street/124th Street

A little more on the mature side, 124th Street nonetheless offers some interesting retail options. You'll find a high concentration of art galleries here, like the Edmonton branch of nationally renowned **Douglas Udell Gallery** (10332 124th St.; ✆ **780/488-4445;** www.douglasudellgallery.com), which features a good complement of contemporary Canadian art, as well as historical work. 124th Street is something of Edmonton's Design District, as well, if not formally so, with highlights like the Agnes Bugera Gallery (12310 Jasper Ave; ✆ **780/482-2854;** www.gallerywalk.com), which showcases modern Canadian artists. There's also a massive **Mountain Equipment Co-Op** here (12328 102nd Ave. NW; ✆ **780/488-6614;** www.mec.ca), the wildly popular Canadian outdoor equipment chain that offers quality goods at decent prices in its massive, supermarket-sized stores—often complete with climbing walls.

West Edmonton Mall

This is the big one. It may not be the largest mall on Earth anymore (the Mall of America took that title from it in the early '90s, and others in China, the Philippines, and surely something in Dubai have since surpassed it, as well), but for a time, West Edmonton Mall (8882 170th St. ✆ **800/661-8890** or 780/444-5200. www.wem. ca), which opened in 1981, defined the enclosed, indoor shopping experience. Whether that's something to aspire to is a matter of taste and preference, of course, but what can't be denied is the sheer imposing-ness of this massive retail city in Edmonton's west end.

Locals used to call it the "eighth wonder of the world." It contains 800 stores and services—many of them the chain-brand shops you'd expect, though the mall courts Edmonton-area exclusives, such as Abercrombie & Fitch, Coach, and H&M—and 100 eateries. Truth be told, it can get a little overwhelming; you could literally spend days in here and not see everything—not to mention the sun.

As a contained universe, it's fascinating; West Edmonton is the ultimate attempt to caricaturize reality, complete with themed areas—the mall has a "Europa Boulevard" with cafes mimicking the Champs d'Elysee and "Bourbon Street," an unfortunate collection of touristy big-chain restaurants with no New Orleans connection whatsoever, like the Olde Spaghetti Factory. The old IKEA space is now filled with an imitation "Chinatown." It's Disney-like in its replication.

As a tourist attraction, though, it can start to feel like *The Truman Show*, the film in which Jim Carrey starred as a man trapped in a perfect, artificial reality that everyone but him knew wasn't real. It's also definitely looking a little rough around the edges—it's 30 years old, and there's only so much of it that can be renovated each year. It's no longer a nice mall for strolling; cleanliness in public spaces can also be an issue.

Shopping? It seems almost secondary. West Edmonton Mall looks and sounds more like a theme park than a shopping center. In a space equal to 48 city blocks, it houses the world's largest indoor amusement park, including a titanic rollercoaster, bungee-jumping platform, and enclosed wave-lake, complete with a beach and enough artificial waves to bodysurf on. It has an 18-hole minigolf course, a huge ice-skating palace, 19 movie theaters, a lagoon with performing dolphins, and a submarine adventure ride to the "ocean floor." You can take it all in from 10am–9pm every day but Sunday, when it is open from 11am–5pm.

Roll your eyes all you want, but do go for at least a rollercoaster ride or a waterslide. You have to see the West Edmonton Mall to believe it.

EDMONTON AFTER DARK

To get a read on what's going on in Edmonton's vibrant cultural scene, pick up a copy of *See* (www.seemagazine.com), the local free arts and entertainment weekly. There, you'll find listings for movies, art openings, upcoming concerts, clubs, and theater.

In the downtown cultural district, the **Winspear Centre** (4 Sir Winston Churchill Sq. NW; ✆ **780/428-1414;** www.winspearcentre.com) is home to major cultural organizations like the **Edmonton Symphony** (✆ **780/428-1414;** www. edmontonsymphony.com), the **Edmonton Opera** (✆ **780/429-4040;** www. edmontonopera.com), and many big-name traveling performers. The **Citadel Theatre** (9828 101A Ave.; ✆ **780/425-1820;** www.citadeltheatre.com) is the city's premiere live theater venue in a city known for theater, with a resident company that's generally acknowledged to be among the country's best.

Edmonton's theater scene is world-renowned, with a massive annual Fringe Festival that all but takes over the city every August. If you're not in town for the Fringe, there are a smorgasbord of local theater troupes—far too numerous to list here—to choose from year-round, performing at a variety of formal stages and informal venues, like pubs. Check your copy of *See* to see what's current.

Nightlife

Downtown, you've got to be careful not to get caught when the streets fold up at night, but Whyte Avenue, always busy during the day, kicks it up a notch after dark. **Bar Wild's** (10551 Whyte Ave; ✆ 780/504-7777) name says it all—it's the Whyte Avenue night-time scene in a nutshell. Bar Wild draws a young crowd, many of them U of A students, bent on drowning the week's mind-expanding educational experience in beer. The **Black Dog Freehouse** (10425 Whyte Ave; ✆ 780/439-1082) is a popular, pubby spot in the summertime, with its large rooftop patio, while **Devlin's Cocktail Lounge** (10507 Whyte Ave; ✆ 780/437-7489) is Whyte Avenue spiffed up for the young professional set, with its look-at-me front windows out on to the Whyte Avenue stroll.

You'll find live music on weekends at some of the many, many pubs on Whyte, like the venerable **Blues on Whyte** (10329 Whyte Ave; ✆ 780/439-3981), the **Empress Ale House** (9912 Whyte Ave; ✆ 780/758-1164), or the **Backdraught Pub** (8307 99th St.; ✆ 780/430-9200), whereas the **Pawn Shop** (10551 Whyte Ave, 2nd floor; ✆ 780/432-5058) is one of the best venues for both the local and popular traveling indie bands.

And Whyte Avenue really is one-stop bar-hopping: If you're looking for dance clubs, there's a plethora of those here, too. **Suite 69** (8232 Gateway Blvd.; ✆ 780/439-6969) is an upstairs dance club one block off Whyte Avenue, featuring popular local DJs; **Krobar** (10551 Whyte Ave; ✆ 780/916-1557) cranks up the intensity with club music that's loud, fast, and hard.

For a quiet drink, you're best off at one of the many restaurants, just sitting at the bar. **Packrat Louie** (see "Where to Dine," earlier in this chapter) is one of the best; the old building, with its exposed brick, is a cozy oasis and shelter from the socializing storm that exists just outside.

11 | NORTHERN ALBERTA

Stretching north of Edmonton and comprising a rugged landscape of forest, muskegs, and fens—the wetlands that provide the cradle for the area's remarkable biodiversity—the northern part of Alberta is a vast, sparsely populated hinterland. During the short summers, insects can be ferocious; during the long winters, Northern Alberta routinely experiences extreme, Arctic-like temperatures of–40°F (–40°C) or worse.

Yes, it's intimidating, but consider this: The Canadian North is also one of the most rugged, untouched wilderness areas in the world. Wildlife abounds; roads are few. Not long after leaving Edmonton, the high prairie gives way to the rocky, rugged, and thick boreal forest. This mixed woodland covers half of the entire province and is home to hundreds of species of birds and mammals large and small, from muskrats to moose.

For the nature lover, this can be a paradise. Far from the well-worn trails of Banff and Jasper, for example, Wood Buffalo National Park, the country's largest, is virtually untouched by humanity; this has as much to do with its extremely isolated location as the fact that, from Alberta, it's utterly inaccessible by road—access is only by water or by air, via helicopter or float plane; there's a rough road skirting its edge farther north, from the Northwest Territories. The result is much like being in a time machine: traveling back thousands of years for a glimpse at a world without us. Few such places exist on Earth.

In addition, adventurous sport fishers can find plenty of opportunities to drop in on any one of hundreds of remote northern lakes, via fishing charters on float planes; those inclined toward water sports will find the mighty Athabasca River, which empties at its northern end into Lake Athabasca, to be a spirited waterway lined, for the most part, with pristine wilderness.

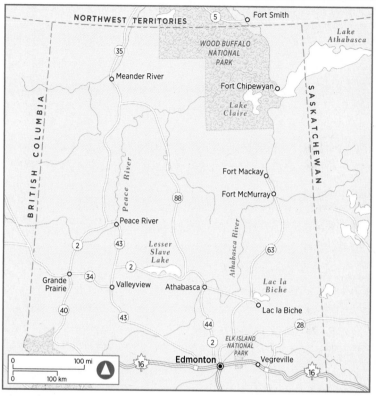

It's that "most part," though, that contains the most intrigue; equal parts fascinating and appalling, the Athabasca runs right through the middle of Alberta's massive oil sands developments, where thousands of tons of mucky sand, laden with oil, are dug up daily by hundreds of machines twice the size of the average suburban house; the oil is then separated using cataclysmic volumes of river water and chemicals. Just north of Fort McMurray, the oil sands are a sight to behold—for sheer scale, if nothing else. They're both an impressive engineering feat and disturbing testament to mankind's ability to alter the planet as it suits us.

FORT MCMURRAY

Located 435km (270 miles) northeast of Edmonton along a mostly two-lane—and heavily traveled—highway, Fort McMurray is the heart of Alberta's current oil boom, not to mention, in many ways, the engine of the modern Canadian economy. A booming outpost by anyone's measure, it's the fastest-growing city in a province of fast-growing cities; in 2006, the population of Fort McMurray was about 65,000 people; by 2012, it's expected to almost double, to 120,000.

That would be impressive all by itself, but especially so when you consider that Fort McMurray was only 25,000 people in the mid-'90s. This is a boomtown if there's ever been one, and there's one reason for it: oil. The average annual income here was C$135,000 in 2010, which is C$31,000 more per year than in wealthy Calgary and C$41,000 more per year than in the financial capital of Toronto. People here are raking in the dough these days, but there are costs. Some statistics show the cancer rate here is 30% higher than in the rest of Alberta, for example. Officials are quick to downplay these warning signs; it is certainly hard to get any real story here, as even the residents are eager to convince visitors that this is a great place to live.

The 170 billion barrels of oil hidden in these oil sands are no sudden discovery, even if the wealth they now beget is relatively new; when settlers first arrived here in the late 18th century, the native Cree people used the mucky bitumen to seal their canoes. People have been trying to turn a profit from the thick, oily glop for nearly a century; the problem has always been not that it's impossible to extract the oil from the muck, but rather that it's never really made economic sense—until recently.

With oil sitting at or below C$30 a barrel up until the late '90s, it cost more to produce oil here than it could be sold for. But all that has changed in recent years, and radically so; with oil frequently over C$75 a barrel (it peaked just above C$140 in the summer of 2008), oil-sands refining not only makes sense, but also is an extraordinary cash cow. Workers flock from all over the country to capitalize on extraordinarily high wages—as much as C$25 an hour to work in a fast-food restaurant; an easy six figures to drive a truck for an oil services company—and still, the labor shortage is the biggest story here. Oil companies simply can't get enough people to do all the work that needs to be done.

A reason for that is the pace. With oil prices high and looking to stay that way, major oil companies from all over the world have set up shop here, staking claims to various plots with the intention of digging up as much ground as possible, and as quickly as possible. What comes up, as anyone in the oil patch will tell you, must come down, and with that as the prevailing sentiment, you shouldn't be surprised to find a scar in the boreal landscape as large as England—about 140,000 sq. km (54,054 sq. miles), all told. It's not a pretty sight.

That's not the total area dug up already, but rather is the amount of oil-sands leases approved by the Alberta government. Oil-sands development is tricky and messy; it's carbon-intensive, first requiring the removal of forests and muskeg to clear the sand, and then much processing and refining before it's ready for market. This process makes it the fastest-growing source of greenhouse gas emissions in Canada. It's also dependent on prices set far away, and it's cyclical. A short economic slowdown in 2009 took some of the explosiveness out of the Fort McMurray boom.

For all its wealth, the city feels more like a dead-end town, with a semi-abandoned downtown area, sprawling faceless suburbs, and a handful of places to eat. The town's two big employers—Suncor and Syncrude—fund everything from the shiny

NORTHERN OUTDOOR adventures

One of the principal paradoxes of the northern region is the fact that, while it's one of the most rapidly industrializing zones on Earth, it also contains some of the most untouched wilderness on the planet. The Athabasca River delta—fed by the very river that some fear is being bled dry by the oil sands—is the second-largest river delta on Earth, after the Amazon, and contains a startling array of biodiversity. Deer, moose, elk, some south-ranging caribou, bears, wolves, moose, lynx, martens, wolverines, foxes, beavers, and snowshoe hares are but a few of the wild mammal species found here. Common bird species include sandhill cranes, hawks, eagles, and owls. And, in Wood Buffalo National Park to the far north, you'll find the last free-roaming wild buffalo herd in North America.

As such, it's an ideal place for those in search of sport fishing or wildlife viewing to head "into the wild." Most excursions into the North are arranged from Fort McMurray, the natural jumping-off point. Distances, however, can range from 120km (75 miles) to 650km (404 miles).

If fishing is your goal, a handful of remote lodges will fly you in via float plane for an all-inclusive adventure, fishing for northern pike, lake trout, and walleye in the pristine northern lakes of the Canadian Shield—as unspoiled as it gets. **Andrew Lake Lodge and Camps** (✆ 780/464-7537; www.andrewlake lodge.com) offers fly-in 3- and 7-day packages for hunting, fishing, or canoeing starting at C$1,095 per person from Fort McMurray. **Indian Head Camp** (✆ 780/743-2171; www.indianhead camp.com), a collection of rustic log cabins on Steward Lake, offers fishing packages starting at C$2,000 per person for 4 days. **Mikisew Sport Fishing** (✆ 888/268-7112 or 780/743-8218; www.mikisewsportfishing.com) offers trips to more than a dozen remote lakes all over the North, with 5-day packages starting at C$1,299 per person.

For a comprehensive list of all fishing tour operators, consult www.alberta sportfishing.com.

new recreation center to music festivals. They're doing what they can to bring life to town. This is not a place to visit for those interested in charming small towns, and although there are some swell trails around town, it's not going to appeal to hikers. Instead, "Fort Mac" is a rough-living masculine frontier overloaded with transient get-rich-quick seekers, many of whom often fly home to Edmonton or Newfoundland. But still, difference-makers are trying to lay the groundwork for a better future. Twenty years from now, Fort McMurray could be a northern jewel; it could also be a toxic mess, mostly abandoned in the wake of expended oil reserves and a turn to alternative energy. But, if nothing else, it's fascinating in that it represents the crux upon which our future as a society will pivot.

Essentials

GETTING THERE

BY CAR From Edmonton (435km/270 miles from Fort McMurray), take Highway 28A north past Egremont; then turn north on Highway 63, which will take you directly to Fort McMurray. The drive can be done in a comfortable 4 hours, but the road is plagued with heavy equipment haulers taking huge loads up to the oil sands. It's also extremely busy since the boom—and therefore quite dangerous. Don't drive it at night.

BY BUS Greyhound Canada (ℂ 800/661-8747 or 780-420-2424; www. greyhound.ca) runs buses from Edmonton to Fort McMurray three times daily. The trip takes about 5 hours, and the cost is C$67 per person one-way.

BY PLANE Air Canada (ℂ 800/247-2262; www.aircanada.ca) runs four direct flights daily from Edmonton to Fort McMurray; fares range from C$109 to C$169 each way. They also have three daily flights direct from Calgary to Fort McMurray for between C$129 and $159 each way and one daily direct flight from Toronto to Fort McMurray for roughly C$440 each way. **WestJet** (ℂ 800/937-8538; www.westjet.com) runs two direct flights daily from Edmonton to Fort McMurray, with fares between C$99 and C$194 each way.

VISITOR INFORMATION

The **Fort McMurray Tourism Bureau** (400 Sakitawaw Trail; ℂ 800/565-3947 or 780/791-4336; www.fortmcmurraytourism.com) is located just south of town along Highway 63. Here, you'll find information about anything you can possibly do in and around Fort McMurray. Staff are friendly, helpful, and super keen to assist any actual tourists; there's a ton of travel here, but the vast majority is related to the oil business. Staff can help find you a room or a restaurant, or hook you up with tour operators plying the northern wilderness regions. They might be able to point you in the direction of an official oil sands tour, but be advised: These take place only at the companies' behest; as of summer 2010, Suncor, one of the oldest oil sands operators and the only one giving tours of its massive facility, was

Northern Lights

To the Inuit, the aurora borealis were spirits on their way to heaven. In Siberia, they were children playing football in the sky with the skull of a walrus. Then there's the popular Western notion that God lights the path to heaven at night so that lost souls have an easier time finding it.

Believe what you will (there is no complete scientific explanation, believe it or not!), but the aurora borealis, or Northern Lights, are among the most eerie, spectacular sights you can imagine. They can be simple flickers or steady light—if you're really lucky, they'll flash and dance across the sky. They're completely unpredictable but, true to the name, the farther north you go, the more stunning they become, and Northern Alberta is one of the best places to see them.

From Fort McMurray, there are three tour operators that specialize in Northern Lights–viewing: **Alta-Can Aurora Tours Inc.** (ℂ 780/452-5187; www.altacan.ab.ca) and **Aurora Tours** (ℂ 780/334-2292; www.picturetrail.com/stuross).

Tours tend to run from early fall through the winter to early spring—the Northern Lights are rarely visible in warmer temperatures—and tend to stretch over a few days. Most are based in Fort McMurray, usually at one of the hotels, with out-tripping in the evenings for viewing. Contact operators directly for packages, tours, and rates.

A weekend IN FORT MCMURRAY

Fort McMurray's oil sands have received substantial media coverage around the world. It's only natural that folks from as close as Edmonton or as far as Australia would be interested in checking out the world's second largest oil reserve. The local tourism bureau has wisely set up a weekend trip from Edmonton that includes two nights' accommodation in Fort McMurray, a tour of the Suncor facility, and entrance into the Oil Sands Discovery Center. This makes the trip easy for curious Albertan weekenders, as well as long-distance travelers who want to add "Fort Mac" to their itinerary, along with Jasper, for example. In 2010, it was being offered on weekends from mid-May through September. Packages start at C$159 per person and don't include transportation to Fort McMurray (the closest airport is Edmonton, but there are flights from other destinations, as well; see "Getting There," above). Contact the **Fort McMurray Tourism Bureau** (400 Sakitawaw Trail; © **800/565-3947** or 780/791-4336; www.fortmcmurray tourism.com) for rates and to confirm what tours are available.

offering tours from May to August on Saturdays only, at C$35 per person. The tours are not a given, and as Suncor's public relations strategy evolves, their openness to tourists will likely also change. See also "A Weekend in Fort McMurray" (see above) for package tour information.

The landscape around Fort McMurray is chillingly primal; nestled in the Athabasca River valley, thick pine forest surrounds most of the town. There is very little road access beyond Highway 63, which runs north-south through the middle of town.

To the south is thick boreal forest—a sight in and of itself, though there's next to nothing but wilderness and a few places to pitch a tent or park an RV. You'll find **Engstrom Lake Provincial Recreation Area** (© 780/743-7437), with campsites (at C$20 a night) and fire pits near the water, 80km (50 miles) south and east along Route 881; closer, the **Hangingstone River Provincial Recreation Area** (© 780/743-7440) has C$18 campsites, 35km (22 miles) south on Highway 63.

The main attraction—if you want to call it that—is north of town. If the wind's blowing the wrong way, you can smell it well before you see it—a thick, sulfuric stench hanging in the air. As you cross the Athabasca River on the ever-widening Athabasca Bridge, you'll pass an exit for Fort McMurray's lone subdivision (which is very large, like everything around here). Then, you're on the road to the second-largest oil deposits on Earth.

Don't worry. You can't possibly miss it. Suddenly, the forest peels back, and endless piles of exposed black dirt cover the horizon in every direction. You're in Syncrude and Suncor territory, the first two companies on the oil sands way back in the '60s. On your right is Suncor, behind a strictly-monitored entrance gate. Further ahead, you'll see a massive crane—we're talking five or six stories high, with a bucket the size of a house—just outside the security fences of the Syncrude site, at their impressive **Giants of Mining** outdoor exhibit. This is both a stab at public education and some bald-faced hubris; the crane sits next to a tiny parking lot, with a cursory description of its function, for the curious. Whatever the intent, it is an astonishing piece of machinery—made all the more so by the fact that, from where it sits, you can see dozens of the working models spread out across the dull gray sprawl of sand that stretches as far as the eye can see. It's simple enough to just pull your vehicle over to the side of the highway and watch the machines at work.

Of course, to truly appreciate the scope of what you're seeing, you need to see it from the air. **McMurray Aviation** (*©* **780/791-2182;** www.mcmurrayaviation.com) can arrange a 1-hour aerial tour of the city and the plants for C$165 per person (minimum 4 people).

Across the wide lanes of Highway 63 (taking the new overpass built to streamline the busy road loaded with workers changing shifts at the various mines that run 24 hours a day) is another public gesture by Syncrude—a small herd of bison, grazing on pasture. The land is expended oil-sands mines that have been filled back in and replanted (oil companies call them "reclaimed" wetlands; however, not a single acre—and there are hundreds—has been certified as such by the provincial government).

Right next to the bison, "poppers"—noisy flares that fire at regular intervals to keep birds from landing on the toxic tailings from the refining process—flame into the air from the surface of the Syncrude tailings pond. The air is typically heavy with sulfuric smell. It's fair to say that these are likely not the happiest bison on Earth.

Traveling past Syncrude will take you through the heart of the oil-sands developments; Highway 63 slices right through the middle of them, so you're surrounded as you go by. The passage takes almost half an hour, so huge are the mines themselves; even the giant equipment is dwarfed by their mass.

Once you're through, you can turn off to Fort McKay, a nearby First Nations settlement that used to be positioned amidst pristine marshes and now sits right in the heart of all the development; with only 450 people, industry has sprung up all around them, the forests stripped. The community is trying to broker a deal with one of the companies to develop the ground beneath their feet—they're considering moving the community itself, for obvious reasons.

Attractions

Fort McMurray Heritage Park ☺ At the south end of town, near the community college, a shabby collection of decrepit buildings cluster in a small green space. If it weren't for the sign, you might guess this was a long-since abandoned settlement—and in some ways, it is. The buildings date from 1900 to 1940, some of them moved here for this purpose, and are plucked from Fort McMurray's rough-and-tumble early pioneer days. Fort McMurray Heritage Park certainly lacks the amenity surfeit of, say, its namesake in Calgary, but it's an interesting, if brief, diversion into some of the local history and characters that committed themselves to this distant northern outpost before there was any kind of economic imperative to be here. Here, you can see examples of the town's pioneering spirit. As you stand in the old Hill family house, a cramped wood-frame structure, try to imagine the chill of –50°F (–46°C) outside, and you'll have a taste of determination at its most extreme.

1 Tolen Dr. *©* **780/791-7575.** www.fortmcmurrayhistory.com. C$8 adults, C$5 students & seniors, free for children 4 & under. Year-round Mon–Sat 9am–5pm; summer Sun 9:30am–5pm.

> ### Bugs!
>
> One of the drawbacks of exploring the North in summer is the incredible, almost fog-like density of insects you'll encounter in all but the semi-urban areas of Fort McMurray and Grande Prairie, which (likely due in no small part to heavy industry) keep the population to near-tolerable levels. Not so in the backcountry, where horseflies, deerflies, black flies—every one of them a voracious flesh-eater—along with swarms of mosquitoes that move as large clouds do everything they can to drain the blood from your body. There's not enough insect repellent on Earth to save your skin from all of them; better to plan your visit in May, before they've hatched, or September, after a few early frosts have killed the bugs and their larvae, allowing you to observe the wild in peace.

The Oil Sands Discovery Centre ★ ☺ This museum/science center is a repository for all things oil sands, agglomerated in a fun, interactive setting, with subtle hints at public-relations efforts. Ongoing films tell the lighter side of the development, and an animated nutty professor guides kids through the science of what some have called the worst environmental catastrophe of the industrial age. Whatever its impacts, oil-sands history and science are indeed fascinating; there is a step-by-step how-to of extracting the oil from the mucky bitumen, and the real winner is a display model truck used to haul the tons and tons of bitumen from open-pit mine to refinery. This is an extraordinary machine: three stories high with tires 3m (10 ft.) in diameter, it appears to be transportation for some giant species not of this Earth. It's staggering to think that, out in the field, hundreds of them are shuttling back and forth at any given time; if nothing else, it allows you to clearly visualize the scale at which the oil sands are being mined.

515 MacKenzie Blvd. ℃ **780/743-7167**. www.oilsandsdiscovery.com. C$6 adults, C$5 seniors, C$4 children 7–17, free for children 6 & under. Open Tues–Sat 9am–5pm.

Where to Stay

Fort McMurray proper is perhaps over-served with accommodation, due to the revolving door of business travelers blowing in and out of town on short assignments in the oil sands. This is both a good and bad thing—good, in that there's little chance you won't get a room, and the vast majority of them are less than 10 years old; and bad, in that much of the accommodation has been built solely for that purpose and, as a result, is overpriced and generically corporate. Character and sincere hospitality are hard to come by. Rates are also significantly cheaper on weekends.

The Ace Inn One of the newer hotels in town, the Ace is clean, comfortable, and nondescript—basic accommodations you can rely on. Some rooms have kitchenettes, which is a good thing, as the Fort McMurray dining scene is yet to catch up with its wealth. Like many in town, it offers long-term rates, typically taken advantage of by business travelers.

9913 Biggs Ave., Fort McMurray, T9H 1S2. © **866/745-2219** or 780/715-2219. www.aceinnhotel.com. 48 units. C$149 double; C$169 double w/kitchenette. Rates include continental breakfast. AE, DC, DISC, MC, V. *In room:* TV, fridge, hair dryer, free Internet.

Chez Dubé Country Inn ★ The one bright light on the otherwise dull hotel scene is this cozy and friendly inn close to downtown. It's warmer than any other place by far. This is where visiting doctors, college professors, artists, and the like request to be put up. Rooms are themed, ranging from the Polar Room to the Cowboy Room. The Victorian Room has a claw-foot soaker tub. On the third floor, there's an executive suite that may be the most tasteful in town. Breakfasts are delicious homemade extravaganzas in a sunny room with a private chef.

10102 Fraser Ave., Fort McMurray, T9H 5C2. © **800/565-0757.** www.chezdube.com. 14 units. Sun-Thurs C$245 double, Fri & Sat C$225 double. Rates include full breakfast. AE, MC, V. **Amenities:** Small gym; free Wi-Fi. *In room:* TV, DVD player, fridge, hair dryer.

Merit Hotel 🐾 The Merit Hotel is part of a larger international chain looking to capitalize on Fort McMurray's growing wealth. The hallmarks of generic luxury are in full display here, from the overstuffed pleather couches to the faux fireplace in the lobby. Tackiness aside, it's a more homey option than any of the budget accommodations in town, though the walls are a little thin. It's also not on the highway, and it's several blocks from Fort McMurray's main drag—a good thing when you're talking about a town full of single roughnecks with time on their hands. All rooms have fridges; suites have kitchenettes and sitting rooms with a second TV.

8200 Franklin Ave., Fort McMurray, T9H 1S2. © **866/650-3678** or 866/794-4444. www.meritfort mcmurray.com. 83 units. Weekdays C$199 double; C$219 suite, two-night minimum. Weekends C$159 double; C$189 suite. Rates include continental breakfast. AE, DC, DISC, MC, V. **Amenities:** Restaurant; bar; fitness center; Jacuzzi; indoor pool. *In room:* TV, fridge, hair dryer, Internet.

The Sawridge Inn and Conference Centre Formerly a big, dusty motel, the Sawridge underwent a major facelift in recent years, adding a soaring, vaulted-ceiling lobby, restaurant, lounge, and conference facilities. That's the good news. Less good is that, once you pass through the grand façade of the Sawridge, you're back in that same dusty old motel, which has received very little attention from the face-lifters. Thus, you're paying premium prices for a hotel that, accommodation-wise, isn't really any better than the better budget options. It depends on your priorities, though; the Sawridge's lounge is far and away the nicest bar in town, and the restaurant is untouchably the best food to be found for kilometers. It's also located directly across from the Oil Sands Discovery Centre and the tourism office, which provides easy access to hook up with outdoor adventures. If you're a non-smoker, ask specifically for non-smoking rooms in the north wing.

530 MacKenzie Blvd., Fort McMurray, T9H 4C8. © **888/729-7343** or 780/791-7900. www.sawridge fortmcmurray.com. 188 units. C$190 double; C$210 suite. Rates include continental breakfast. AE, DC, DISC, MC, V. **Amenities:** Restaurant; bar; fitness center; Jacuzzi; pool. *In room:* TV, fridge, hair dryer, Internet.

Vantage Inns and Suites The Vantage is just off the Highway 63, which is either a) an actual advantage, if you're driving to and from the oil sands or b) a disadvantage, given that heavy haulers roll by 24 hours a day. Either way, the Vantage is another brand-spanking-new facility that offers the basics very well; a step up from the Ace (see above), both in amenities and pricing, it's nonetheless another good budget option.

200 Parent Way, Fort McMurray, T9H 1S2. © **866/713-4111.** www.advantagewest.ca. 83 units. C$139 double; C$199 suite. Rates include continental breakfast. AE, DC, DISC, MC, V. **Amenities:** Sports bar; fitness center. *In room:* TV, fridge, hair dryer, Internet.

Where to Dine

Let's be honest. Fort McMurray is no gourmand's paradise. Until very recently, it might even have been a food fancier's version of hell. The recent corporate invasion bumped things up to adequate, with the arrival of **Moxie's** (9521 Franklin Ave.; © **780/791-1996**), a chain roadhouse-style restaurant, and **Earl's** (9802 Morrison St.; © **780/791-3275**), a popular Western Canadian chain with a surprisingly cosmopolitan menu—Thai curries and vindaloos mixed in amid the burgers and fries.

Locals will point you to the unpretentious **Fish Place** (412 Thickwood Blvd.; © **780/791-4040**) in a strip mall amidst the suburban sprawl. It's worth finding for a huge variety of remarkably fresh fish and seafood. Since there are so many Atlantic Canadians in Fort McMurray (it's sometimes called "the second biggest city in Newfoundland"), you know the standards are high. The menu changes constantly. Homemade pies and cheesecakes make for irresistible desserts. The best hotel eating in town, however, is at the **Hearthstone Grill** at the Sawridge Hotel and Conference Centre (530 Mackenzie Blvd.; © **780/791-7100**). You can dine from a list of Alberta classics, like a beautiful bacon-wrapped Alberta beef tenderloin, a walleye fillet from the northern lakes, or pork chops from the nearby town of Trochu, all complemented by a huge stone fireplace and soaring, vaulted rough-timber cathedral ceilings. The menu also features crowd-pleasers like quesadillas, nachos, and wood-fired pizzas.. And, in Fort McMurray, where you'll surely be looking for comfort at some point, this is the place to find it.

FORT CHIPEWYAN

On the western shores of Lake Athabasca and reachable by road only in winter, when vehicles can pass over the vast frozen wetlands of the Athabasca delta without sinking into a muskeg, Fort Chipewyan is a true northern outpost. Located 277km (172 miles) north of Fort McMurray, it is the first settlement in the entire province, established by the North West Company (a fur-trading company based in Montreal) in 1788.

The fort was named for the Chipewyan First Nation who were living there at the time; the Chipewyan people, of the Dene nation, along with Mikisew Cree and Métis people, make up the vast majority of the town's population of about 900 people.

As you can imagine, there's not much to Fort Chipewyan, the town. But Fort Chip, as it's known, offers a look at a time and lifestyle far removed from modernity. They may have satellite TV, but the wilderness is just an arm's length away.

The "Emporium of the North"

One of the principal draws for Europeans to Canada was the fur trade; fortunes could be made trapping animals and exporting their pelts back to be sold to wealthy Europeans, and two companies in Canada, the Hudson's Bay Company and the North West Company, were in stiff competition. By the 1770s, the HBC raised the stakes, pushing farther westward and establishing a trading post at Cumberland House in what is now northeastern Saskatchewan; explorer Peter Pond pushed even farther west to establish a presence from Saskatchewan into what is now northern Alberta.

In 1778, native guides showed Pond the Methy Portage, which connected Hudson's Bay to the Arctic water systems and could carry traders to the rich, and then untapped, Athabasca region.

Pond had amazing success there, and other trappers quickly followed. In 1788, the North West Company set up a post called Fort Chipewyan; the post was moved to Fort Chip's current location in 1796. In the ensuing years, Fort Chip quickly became the fur trade's central hub in the Athabasca region and one of the most important such posts in all of Canada. Fur traders came to call Fort Chip "the emporium of the north," given its size and scale; the Hudson's Bay Company also built forts in the region, but with nowhere near the same success as Fort Chip.

Fort Chip is the gateway to **Wood Buffalo National Park,** which can be reached only by water; it also sits at the western end of Lake Athabasca, where the Athabasca River ends, and the sense is of being on the edge of the planet itself.

Attractions and amenities here are few, but for a taste of Fort Chip's fur-trading past, you can visit the **Fort Chipewyan Bicentennial Museum** (109 Mackenzie Ave, Fort Chipewyan, T0P 1B0; © **780/697-3844;** open Mon–Fri 9am–5pm, Sat and Sun 1–5pm; admission by donation). Modeled after an 18th-century Hudson's Bay Company store, it provides a time-warp experience of life more than 2 centuries ago in the outer reaches of the Canadian wild.

Another point of interest is the surprisingly ornate **Nativity of the Blessed Virgin Mary Roman Catholic Church,** by the water's edge. The most recent building, built in 1909, is in typical Northern French Canadian Oblate Mission style (Catholic missionaries to the north were typically French). Inside, the soaring vaulted ceiling is painted a deep celestial blue, speckled with gold stars and angelic medallions. To make deep red and purple "paint," the priests and nuns crushed cranberries and blueberries, then mixed the juice with fish oil. It's a testament of cross-cultural fermentation—Cree and Chipewyan syllabics frame the painting of the Crucifixion; it's observed by many that the Virgin Mary has distinct First Nations features. Tours can be arranged by contacting the church at © **780/697-3555.**

Getting There

BY CAR Think again. It's not impossible to drive to Fort Chipewyan—except in spring, summer, and fall, when the terrain is impassable—but it's really not easy. The winter road, over frozen wetlands, is 277km (172 miles), but it's slow going—as long as 10 hours, by most estimates. Factor in that you'll be traveling over completely untracked wilderness—that means no truck stops, gas stations, or bathrooms, folks—and, well, even if a visit to far-north Fort Chip when it's –40°F (–40°C) or worse strikes your fancy, you might want to opt for a different mode of transport.

BY AIR This is really the only option that makes sense. **McMurray Aviation** (© 780/791-2182; www.mcmurrayaviation.com) has flights from Fort McMurray to Fort Chipewyan Sunday through Friday for C$120 one-way and C$220 round-trip.

Exploring the Area

Simply put, this is not something you can do by yourself. The lake stretches out in front of you, but remember: This is a wild land, where all but the most experienced outdoor adventurer will need at least some guidance.

Fort Chip, of course, is where you go to access **Wood Buffalo National Park,** the largest expanse of protected wilderness in North America, among the largest in the world, and a UNESCO World Heritage site. Larger than the country of Switzerland, it was established in 1922 to protect the last free-roaming bison herds in the area. Largely a reserve of high boreal plain, Wood Buffalo is completely wild and destined to stay that way: The only road in Wood Buffalo is at park headquarters at its northern boundary at Fort Smith, in the Northwest Territories. There is no road access from Alberta at all, and the road from Fort Smith only skirts its edge. Access is largely by boat or float plane.

For experienced wilderness travelers, water access by boat or canoe is possible. Motorboat access is allowed along the major river corridors: **Athabasca River, Rivière des Rochers, Quatre Fourches River, Peace River,** and **Slave River.** Parks Canada offers a *Guide to Waterways in and around Wood Buffalo National Park* for further information about the river corridors. See www.pc.gc.ca/pn-np/nt/woodbuffalo/index.aspx for more information.

Park-use permits are required for any overnight stays in the backcountry; one night is C$9.80 or C$69 for the full season. The one major campground, at **Pine Lake**—classified "primitive" by the parks authority, meaning nothing like running water, toilets, or showers are available—is the only one accessible by road (from Fort Smith), at a cost of C$16 per night. Pine Lake features the only cabin in the park, a rustic log structure with a fireplace that sleeps up to eight people. It's available for C$39 per night. Meanwhile, the **Rainbow Lakes backcountry campsite,** a 6km (3¾-mile) hike from Pine Lake Road, offers the comfort of a tent pad and outhouse only. All campgrounds are open from late May to Labor Day only.

Needless to say, Wood Buffalo isn't for greenhorns. A handful of guides can be hired for long- or short-term excursions into the park; be careful to hire only those licensed by the park authority itself. The availability of licensed guides and outfitters changes from year to year—the **Visitor Reception Centre** in Fort Smith (© 867/872-7960) or Fort Chipewyan (© 780/697-3662) will be able to provide a current list of licensed park guides.

So, for all the hardship involved in a jaunt through Wood Buffalo, what do you get in return? Just a wilderness experience that's near-impossible to be rivaled anywhere. This is the anti-Banff: no tourist buses, throngs of shoppers, overpriced hotels and restaurants, or wildlife feasting on scattered Pringles that tourists should know better than to entice them with. Most of the animals here could easily live their entire lives without knowing humanity exists.

If you're up for a backcountry adventure, the park recommends a handful of destinations: **Sweetgrass Station,** accessibly by a challenging 12km (7½-mile) hike that takes you south of the Peace River on the broad plains of the delta, which sits in the middle of a vast wetland, on the shores of Lake Claire. It's prime nesting and feeding ground for many species of wetland birds, but it's also home to the park's namesake wild bison herd—the last of their kind in the world.

Naturally, a bison presence means predators, as well, so be on the lookout for wolves. If you're lucky ("lucky" depends on your level of squeamishness), you might catch a glimpse of the predator/prey relationship in the unfettered wild.

You can also get to Sweetgrass Station by canoe, after putting in at Peace Point and paddling downstream. The trip takes up to 12 hours, requiring an overnight stay somewhere along the river. Also, don't plan to paddle back to where you launched, as the current makes that virtually impossible. Plan instead to get picked up at either Hay Camp or Fort Fitzgerald, on the Peace River or Slave River, respectively.

Or, for a quick in-and-out, you can look into hiring a float plane to drop you off and pick you up at Sweetgrass Station; the parks information center in either Fort Smith or Fort Chipewyan can connect you with a reputable pilot. Prices fluctuate with demand and oil prices; but, because most airlines fly out of Fort McMurray or Yellowknife (in the Northwest Territories), it's not cheap. Out of Fort McMurray, McMurray Aviation would charge roughly C$3,000 for a six-seat plane round trip.

For the less adventure-inclined, the park also offers a small selection of frontcountry hiking trails just off the road from Fort Smith. **The Salt River Trail system** offers hikes from 750m (about half a mile) to 9km (5.6 miles) long; the **Lakeside Trail,** at 6.4km (4 miles), departs from the Pine Lake campground down into Pine Lake, where there's a sandy beach and good swimming; the **South Loop,** at 9km (5.6 miles), starts at the Salt River, on the east side of the road, and leads along a salty creek to Grosbeak Lake, a prime viewing area for waterfowl. There's also the curious natural phenomenon of the salt plains, littered with glacial erratics—large boulders left behind when the ice receded at the end of the last Ice Age.

A list of backcountry trails that range from a few days to 2 weeks to traverse is available from the parks office for the more intrepid wilderness explorer.

World's Biggest Beaver Dam

Canada's largest national park is also the home of the world's largest beaver dam. In a remote part of the park, the dam was spotted by scientists combing through satellite images. The dam is roughly 850m (2,789 ft.) long; average beaver dams are 10 to 100m (33–328 ft.) long. Parks Canada researchers say the dam is still growing but haven't been able to actually survey the dam themselves on foot since it's amidst thick marshland, leaving no room to land a plane or helicopter, let alone hike, ski, or paddle in. You can see images at the park's website, www.pc.gc.ca/pn-np/nt/woodbuffalo/index.aspx.

The Athabasca Sand Dunes

Located south of Lake Athabasca in Northern Alberta, a massive land of migrating sand, blown and shifted about by the wind, has produced one of the largest sand-dune complexes in Canada. For more than 8,000 years, the sand here has been on the move, blowing over marshes, burying forests, and filling in lakes. Active dunes are constantly on the move; stable dunes remain hidden under tall grass. Some dunes reach 35m (115 ft.) high, shifting over a meter each year. It's a magical area—it's hard to access, of course. The **Athabasca Sand Dune Ecological Reserve** is located in Maybelle River Wildland Park, 160km (99 miles) north of Fort McMurray and 26km (16 miles) east of Fort Chipewyan. Contact the park at ℭ 780/743-7437.

Where to Stay

Your options in Fort Chip are notably few, but there are a couple of comfortable places. Bordering on cozy, in fact, is the **Wah Pun B&B** (ℭ 780/697-3030), operated by Archie Waquan, the former chief of the Athabasca Tribal Council, and his wife Dawn. Archie lives well, in a large split-level home with satellite TV and high-speed Internet; behind his house, shouldering up to the dense bush that his property sits against, Archie has built several cabins that he rents to guests long- and short-term. (Archie says that writers, in particular, like his cabins—dead quiet and free of distraction.) The food is nothing short of great for so remote a location; if you ask nicely, Archie and his family might prepare some wild game for you, like moose or elk. If that's not to your liking, Archie operates the only pizzeria in Fort Chip in one of his buildings out back, complete with high-grade commercial pizza ovens. Doubles start at C$125; call for seasonal rates. Another good B&B option is the **Northern Lights B&B** (ℭ 780/697-3053; www.fortchip.com), a comfortable choice with excellent food in the center of town. Doubles are C$135.

GRANDE PRAIRIE

You may be going through Grande Prairie if you are driving the Alaska Highway. Or you could be coming here en route to a fishing lodge up at Swan Lake. Unless you are seriously keen to see all that Alberta has to offer, Grande Prairie won't likely otherwise be on your itinerary. This dusty natural-gas exploration hub 460km (286 miles) northwest of Edmonton, is the largest city for the broad Peace Region that follows the Peace River tributaries and covers northwestern Alberta and northeastern British Columbia.

Similar to Fort McMurray for its boomtown, oil-rich growth, Grande Prairie is smaller (about 50,000 people) and dependent on natural gas, as well as forestry, with several of the major Canadian lumber companies extracting timber from the boreal forests to the south.

Grande Prairie's name says much: To the north, east, and west lie huge expanses of flatland, the vast, high boreal plains. For early settlers, the land's relative lack of growth was a huge advantage for agriculture, and much of the region is still in heavy agronomical use. To the south lies thick boreal forest, plied for the lumber trade. It's also notable for being the largest city along Highway 43 (the Richardson Hwy.) between Edmonton and Fairbanks, Alaska.

And, while the area will likely never win any awards for scenery in this amazingly picturesque province, the high plains and foothills around Grande Prairie are popular places for cross-country skiing in the winter and hiking in the summer; about an hour and a half south, Grande Cache, set closer to the mountains, is the beginning of the alpine range; a little south and west of there, **Kakwa Wildland Park,** straddling the Alberta–British Columbia border, is a popular place among locals for alpine hiking.

In Grande Prairie, you'll find the same generic corporate hotels as in Fort McMurray, geared toward the comings and goings of the oil industry. They're all clustered together in the downtown area. **The Grande Prairie Inn** (© 800/661-6529 or 780/532-522; www.gpinn.com) is a relatively stylish, freshly renovated hotel with large, comfortable rooms and a very good restaurant; doubles start at C$149. Another recommended option is the **Days Inn** (© 780/532-2773; ww.daysinn.com), where doubles start at C$119.

If the dining room at the Grande Prairie Inn is a little too fancy, there's always the Alberta staple **Earl's** (9825 100th St.; © 780/538-3275), where you can rely on finding casual, well-prepared, pan-cosmopolitan food between C$14 and C$28.

APPENDIX: FAST FACTS, TOLL-FREE NUMBERS & WEBSITES

[Fast FACTS] ALBERTA

American Express   Calgary: 300–605 5th Ave. SW; ℂ 403/294-7100. Edmonton: 10729 104 Ave. NW; ℂ **780/429-7587.** Banff: 100 Gopher St.; ℂ 403/760-6900.

Area Codes   Southern Alberta: 403; Northern Alberta: 780. The area codes change to the Northern Alberta code just north of Red Deer.

ATM Networks/Cashpoints   You'll be able to find ATMs in even the smaller centers throughout the province. Overall, Alberta is thoroughly modern, and if there's a gas station, there'll be an ATM. Be wary of independent cashpoints, as the user fee can be C$2 or more; major Canadian chartered bank ATMs (CIBC, BMO, Royal Bank, TD Canada Trust, Scotiabank) typically charge non-customers C$1 to C$1.50. You'll find hundreds of these in the big cities, almost anywhere you go—in malls, office buildings, and even 7-Eleven stores (which have a nationwide deal with CIBC to carry their ATMs); even the smaller centers have many options. Look for branches on main streets or shopping plazas. For more information, see "Money & Costs," p. 37.

Automobile Organizations   Motor clubs will supply maps, suggested routes, guidebooks, accident and bail-bond insurance, and emergency road service. The **Alberta Motor Association** (ℂ 800/222-6400; www.ama.ab.ca) is the provincial arm of the **Canadian Automotive Association** (ℂ 800/866-9677; www.caa.ca), the major auto club in Canada, and an affiliate of the American Automobile Association (AAA); members can obtain maps of Alberta from either CAA or AAA. If you belong to a motor club in your home country, inquire about CAA reciprocity before you leave. You may be able to join CAA, even if you're not a member of a reciprocal club.

Business Hours   Standard business hours in Alberta, and Canada in general, are similar to those in the U.S., usually 10am to 6pm (office hours are more like 8am to 4:30pm).

Outside the cities and major tourist areas, it is common for stores to be closed on Sundays.

Car Rentals   See "Toll-Free Numbers & Websites," p. 268.

Drinking Laws   The legal age for purchase and consumption of alcoholic beverages in Alberta is 18, making it, along with Quebec, the youngest jurisdiction in North America; proof of age is required and often requested at bars, nightclubs, and restaurants, so it's always a good idea to bring ID when you go out.

Alberta also has a late "last call" (2am), so night life tends to be very pronounced here. And unlike most Canadian provinces, where liquor is sold only in government-owned stores, Alberta privatized its liquor sales in the 1990s. Specialty liquor and wine shops are found all over the province; in the cities, they often keep late hours—as late as 11pm.

Do not carry open containers of alcohol in your car or any public area that isn't zoned for alcohol consumption; the police can fine you on the spot. And nothing will ruin your trip faster than getting a citation for DUI ("driving under the influence"), so don't even think about driving while intoxicated. The legal blood alcohol level here is .08% (80 milligrams). A driver charged with impaired driving in Alberta may receive a 3-month driving suspension. If convicted, he or she will lose his or her right to drive for a minimum of 12 months and receive a fine of C$800 to C$1,200.

Driving Rules   See "Getting There & Around," Chapter 3, p. 34.

Electricity   Like the U.S., Canada uses 110 to 120 volts AC (60 cycles), compared to 220 to 240 volts AC (50 cycles) in most of Europe, Australia, and New Zealand. Downward converters that change 220 to 240 volts to 110 to 120 volts are difficult to find in Canada, so bring one with you.

Embassies & Consulates   A great many countries keep consulates in Alberta, based in both Calgary and Edmonton.

The **American consular office** is in Calgary, at Suite 1000, 615 Macleod Trail SE ((C) 403/266-8962).

Among other major English-speaking countries, the closest consular services for Australia, New Zealand, and the United Kingdom are in Vancouver.

For a complete list of consulates in Alberta, go to www.alberta.ca/home/255.cfm.

Emergencies   In life-threatening situations, call (C) 911.

Gasoline (Petrol)   Given that Alberta is a major source of oil, it may surprise you that gasoline (also known as gas in Canada, but never petrol), is expensive here. In the fall of 2010, gas was hovering around C$0.95 per liter. Taxes are already included in the posted price. One U.S. gallon equals 3.8 liters or .85 imperial gallons. Fill-up locations are known as gas or service stations.

Holidays   National holidays are celebrated throughout the country; all government facilities and banks are closed, but some department stores and a scattering of smaller shops stay open. If the holiday falls on a weekend, the following Monday is observed.

Canadian national holidays include New Year's Day, Good Friday, Easter Monday, Victoria Day (in mid- to late May, the weekend before U.S. Memorial Day), Canada Day (July 1), Labour Day (first Mon in Sept), Thanksgiving (in mid-Oct), Remembrance Day (Nov 11), Christmas Day, and Boxing Day (Dec 26). Alberta also celebrates Family Day, usually on the first Monday of August.

For more information on holidays, see "Calendar of Events," on p. 29.

Hospitals   All major Alberta hospitals offer 24-hour emergency services. A complete list of Alberta hospitals and their services can be found at www.informalberta.ca. In Calgary, **Rockyview General Hospital** ((C) 403/943-3449 for emergencies) is at 7007

14th St. SW. In Edmonton, the **University of Alberta Hospital** (✆ 780/407-8433) is at 8440 112th St.

Hotlines There are a number of medical hotlines in Alberta. They include AADAC, a 24-hour drug and alcohol abuse hotline (✆ 866/33-AADAC [866/332-2322] or 403/297-4664), Kids Help Phone (✆ 800/668-6868), Parent Help Line (✆ 866/603-9100), Poison Center (✆ 403/944-1414), Missing Children Society of Canada (✆ 800/661-6160), and Distress Center (✆ 403/266-1605).

Insurance **Medical Insurance:** Although it's not required of travelers, health insurance is highly recommended. Most U.S. health plans do not provide coverage outside the U.S., and the ones that do often require you to pay for services upfront and reimburse you only after you return home. Check your coverage before you leave.

International visitors to Canada should ensure their health coverage will cover them. Backup may be required. Good policies will cover the costs of an accident, repatriation, or death. Packages such as **Europ Assistance's Worldwide Healthcare Plan** are sold by European automobile clubs and travel agencies at attractive rates. **Worldwide Assistance Services, Inc.** (✆ 800/777-8710; www.worldwideassistance.com) is the agent for Europ Assistance in North America. Though lack of health insurance may prevent you from being admitted to a hospital in non-emergencies, don't worry about being left on a street corner to die: The Canadian health system is fully socialized, with access for all—if you're in dire need, you will be helped.

Travelers from the U.K. should carry their European Health Insurance Card (EHIC), which replaced the E111 form as proof of entitlement to free/reduced-cost medical treatment abroad (✆ 0845/606-2030; www.ehic.org.uk). Note, however, that the EHIC covers only "necessary medical treatment," and for repatriation costs, lost money, baggage, or cancellation, travel insurance from a reputable company should always be sought (www.travelinsuranceweb.com).

Travel Insurance: The cost of travel insurance varies widely, depending on the destination, the cost and length of your trip, your age and health, and the type of trip you're taking, but expect to pay between 5% and 8% of the vacation itself. You can get estimates from various providers through **InsureMyTrip.com**. Enter your trip cost and dates, your age, and other information, for prices from more than a dozen companies.

U.K. citizens and their families who make more than one trip abroad per year may find an annual travel insurance policy works out cheaper. Check **www.moneysupermarket.com**, which compares prices across a wide range of providers for single- and multi-trip policies.

Most big travel agents offer their own insurance and will probably try to sell you their package when you book a holiday. Think before you sign. **Britain's Consumers' Association** recommends that you insist on seeing the policy and reading the fine print before buying travel insurance. The **Association of British Insurers** (✆ 020/7600-3333; www.abi.org.uk) gives advice by phone and publishes *Holiday Insurance,* a free guide to policy provisions and prices. You might also shop around for better deals: Try **Columbus Direct** (✆ 0870/033-9988; www.columbusdirect.net).

Trip Cancellation Insurance: Trip-cancellation insurance will help retrieve your money if you have to back out of a trip or depart early, or if your travel supplier goes bankrupt. Trip cancellation traditionally covers such events as sickness, natural disasters, and national advisories. The latest news in trip-cancellation insurance is the availability of **expanded hurricane coverage** and **"any-reason"** cancellation coverage—which costs more but covers cancellations made for any reason. You won't get back 100% of your prepaid trip cost, but you'll be refunded a substantial portion.

TravelSafe (📞 888/885-7233; www.travelsafe.com) offers both types of coverage. Expedia also offers any-reason cancellation coverage for its air-and-hotel packages. For details, contact one of the following recommended insurers: **Travel Guard International** (📞 800/826-4919; www.travelguard.com), **Travel Insured International** (📞 800/243-3174; www.travelinsured.com), or **Travelex Insurance Services** (📞 888/457-4602; www.travelex-insurance.com).

Internet Access   Alberta's general connectedness is great; almost all hotels have wireless, and there are hundreds of hotspots province-wide. Refer to chapter 3 for more details.

Legal Aid   If you are pulled over for a minor infraction (such as speeding), never attempt to pay the fine directly to a police officer; this could be construed as attempted bribery, a much more serious crime. Pay fines by mail or directly into the hands of the clerk of the court. If accused of a more serious offense, say and do nothing before consulting a lawyer. Here, the burden is on the state to prove a person's guilt beyond a reasonable doubt, and everyone has the right to remain silent, whether he or she is suspected of a crime or actually arrested. Once arrested, a person can make one telephone call to a party of his or her choice. International visitors should call their embassy or consulate.

Legal Aid Alberta (www.legalaid.ab.ca) provides legal services for those who cannot afford their own legal representation. They can also refer you to a local lawyer if, in fact, you can afford those services.

Legal Aid Alberta has offices all over the province; the head office is in Edmonton (📞 780/644-4971).

Lost & Found   Be sure to tell all of your credit card companies the minute you discover your wallet has been lost or stolen, and file a report at the nearest police precinct. Your credit card company or insurer may require a police report number or record of the loss. Most credit card companies have an emergency toll-free number to call if your card is lost or stolen; they may be able to wire you a cash advance immediately or deliver an emergency credit card in a day or two. Visa's Canadian emergency number is 📞 800/847-2911 or 410/581-9994, the same as in the U.S. American Express cardholders and traveler's check holders should call 📞 800/678-5523. MasterCard holders should call 📞 800/622-7747 or 636/722-7111. For other credit cards, call the toll-free number directory assistance at 📞 800/555-1212.

If you need emergency cash over the weekend, when all banks and American Express offices are closed, you can have money wired to you via **Western Union** (📞 800/325-6000; www.westernunion.com).

Mail   At press time, domestic postage rates were C57¢ for both a letter or postcard. For international mail, a first-class letter of up to 28g (1 oz.) costs $C1 to the U.S. or C$1.70 overseas; a first-class postcard costs the same as a letter. For more information, go to **www.canadapost.ca**.

If you aren't sure what your address will be in Alberta, mail can be sent to you, in your name, c/o General Delivery at the main post office of the city or region where you expect to be. General Delivery is offered free of charge for up to 4 months to traveling customers. (Call 📞 866/697-6301 for information on the nearest post office.) The addressee must pick up mail in person and must produce proof of identity (driver's license, passport, etc.). Most post offices are open Monday to Friday from 8am to 6pm, and Saturday from 9am to 3pm.

Always include postal codes when mailing items in Canada. If you don't know the correct postal code, visit www.canadapost.ca to search by address.

Measurements   See the chart on the inside back cover of this book for details on converting metric measurements to non-metric equivalents.

Medical Conditions   If you have a medical condition that requires **syringe-administered medications,** carry a valid signed prescription from your physician; syringes in carry-on baggage will be inspected. Insulin in any form should have the proper pharmaceutical documentation. If you have a disease that requires treatment with **narcotics,** you should also carry documented proof with you—smuggling narcotics aboard a plane carries severe penalties in the U.S. and Canada.

For **HIV-positive visitors,** Canadian immigration law provides that a person may be denied a visa or entry to the country as "medically inadmissible" if:

(a) they are "likely to be a danger to public health or public safety"; or
(b) they "might reasonably be expected to cause excessive demand on health or social services."

According to the Canadian HIV/AIDS Legal network, "generally, neither of these grounds applies to a person living with HIV/AIDS seeking to enter the country as a visitor on a short-term basis (i.e., under 6 months).

"HIV is not a casually communicable infectious disease (unlike tuberculosis). It is Canadian government policy that people living with HIV/AIDS do not represent a danger to public health or safety by virtue of their HIV status." Departmental instructions to visa officers state that it would be "rare" that a visa applicant living with HIV/AIDS might need to be referred for an "immigration medical examination" and "rarer still" that the person would be assessed as medically inadmissible.

For more information, contact the Canadian HIV/AIDS Legal Network at 1240 Bay St., Suite 600, Toronto, ON M5R 2A7 (www.aidslaw.ca).

Newspapers & Magazines   Drugstores, grocery stores, and newsstands carry most of the major daily papers for their respective regions. There are two national newspapers in Canada, the *National Post* and *The Globe and Mail,* and both Calgary and Edmonton have large daily papers, the *Calgary Herald* and the *Edmonton Journal.*

You'll also find Canadian newsstands to be filled with American magazines, so if you're traveling from the U.S., you'll feel right at home. Major U.S. papers, like the *New York Times* and *USA Today,* are available throughout Alberta.

Passports   If you are a U.S. citizen, you have to carry a U.S. passport to enter Canada and to re-enter the U.S. from Canada.

Permanent U.S. residents who aren't U.S. citizens must have their Alien Registration Cards (green cards). If you plan to drive into Canada, be sure to bring your car's registration papers and proof of insurance.

Citizens of most European countries, former British colonies, and certain other countries (Israel, Korea, and Japan, for instance) do not need visas but must carry passports. Entry visas are required for citizens of more than 130 countries. Entry visas must be applied for and received from the Canadian embassy in your home country. For more information on entry requirements to Canada, see the Citizenship and Immigration website visitors' services page at www.cic.gc.ca/english/visit/index.asp.

The websites listed below provide downloadable passport applications, as well as the current fees for processing applications. For an up-to-date, country-by-country listing of passport requirements around the world, go to the "International Travel" tab of the U.S. State Department site at **http://travel.state.gov**. Allow plenty of time before your trip to apply for a U.S. passport; processing normally takes 4 to 6 weeks (3 weeks for expedited service) but can take longer during busy periods (especially spring). And keep in mind that if you need a passport in a hurry, you'll pay a higher processing fee.

For Residents of Australia: You can pick up an application from your local post office or any branch of Passports Australia, but you must schedule an interview at the passport office to present your application materials. Call the **Australian Passport Information Service** at © 131-232 or visit the government website at www.passports.gov.au.

For Residents of Ireland: You can apply for a 10-year passport at the **Passport Office** (Setanta Centre, Molesworth St., Dublin 2; © 01/671-1633; www.irlgov.ie/iveagh). Those under age 18 and over 65 must apply for a 3-year passport. You can also apply at 1A South Mall, Cork (© 21/494-4700), or at most main post offices.

For Residents of New Zealand: You can pick up a passport application at any New Zealand Passports Office or download it from their website. Contact the **Passports Office** at © 0800/225-050 in New Zealand or 04/474-8100, or log on to www. passports.govt.nz.

For Residents of the United Kingdom: To pick up an application for a standard 10-year passport (5-yr. passport for children under 16), visit your nearest passport office, major post office, or travel agency, or contact the **United Kingdom Passport Service** at © 0870/521-0410 or search its website at www.ukpa.gov.uk.

Police   Dial © 911 in emergencies province-wide. In Calgary, you can also dial © 403/266-1234; in Edmonton dial © 780/423-4567. The Banff RCMP can also be reached at © 403/762-2228.

Smoking   Alberta banned smoking in public places in January 2008. There is no smoking indoors in any business or establishment open to the public, including bars and restaurants. Some hotels still have smoking rooms; smoking is typically allowed on outdoor patios.

Taxes   Alberta has no provincial sales tax—the only province to do so—which makes shopping there a relative bargain. You'll still pay the 5% federal GST, and an additional 5% accommodation tax on hotel rooms.

Telephones   Many convenience stores, grocery stores, and packaging services sell **prepaid calling cards** in denominations up to C$50; for international visitors, these can be the least expensive way to call home. Many public pay phones at airports now accept American Express, MasterCard, and Visa credit cards. **Local calls** made from pay phones in most locales cost C50¢. Most long-distance and international calls can be dialed directly from any phone. **For calls within Canada to the U.S.,** dial 1, followed by the area code and the seven-digit number. **For other international calls,** dial 011, followed by the country code, city code, and the number you are calling.

Calls to area codes 800, 888, 877, and 866 are toll-free.

For **reversed-charge or collect calls,** and for person-to-person calls, dial the number 0, then the area code and number; an operator will come on the line, and you should specify whether you are calling collect, person-to-person, or both. If your operator-assisted call is international, ask for the overseas operator.

For **local directory assistance** ("information"), dial © 411; for long-distance information, dial 1, then the appropriate area code and **555-1212.**

Telegraph, Telex & Fax   **Telegraph and telex services** are provided primarily by **Western Union** (© 800/325-6000; www.westernunion.com). You can telegraph (wire) money or have it telegraphed to you very quickly over the Western Union system, but this service can cost as much as 15% to 20% of the amount sent.

Most hotels have **fax machines** available for guest use (be sure to ask about the charge to use it). Many hotel rooms are wired for guests' fax machines. A less expensive way to send and receive faxes may be at stores such as the **UPS Store** or **FedEx Kinko's.**

Time   Alberta is in the Mountain Time Zone, 1 hour later than Pacific Standard Time and 2 hours earlier than Eastern Standard Time.

North America is divided into **four time zones:** Eastern Standard Time (EST), Central Standard Time (CST), Mountain Standard Time (MST), and Pacific Standard Time (PST). Alaska and Hawaii have their own zones. For example, when it's 9am in Los Angeles (PST), it's 7am in Honolulu (HST), 10am in Denver (MST), 11am in Chicago (CST), noon in New York City (EST), 5pm in London (GMT), and 2am the next day in Sydney.

Daylight Saving Time is in effect from 1am on the second Sunday in March to 1am on the first Sunday in November. Daylight Saving Time moves the clock 1 hour ahead of standard time.

Tipping   Tips are a very important part of certain workers' income, and gratuities are the standard way of showing appreciation for services provided. (Tipping is certainly not compulsory if the service is poor!) In hotels, tip **bellhops** at least C$1 per bag (C$2–C$3 if you have a lot of luggage) and tip the **chamber staff** C$1 to C$2 per day (more if you've left a disaster area for him or her to clean up). Tip the **doorman** or **concierge** only if he or she has provided you with some specific service (for example, calling a cab for you or obtaining difficult-to-get theater tickets). Tip the **valet-parking attendant** C$1 every time you get your car.

In restaurants, bars, and nightclubs, tip **service staff** 15% to 20% of the check, tip **bartenders** 15%, tip **checkroom attendants** C$1 per garment, and tip **valet-parking attendants** C$1 per vehicle.

As for other service personnel, tip **cab drivers** 15% of the fare; tip **skycaps** at airports at least C$1 per bag (C$2–C$3 if you have a lot of luggage); and tip **hairdressers** and **barbers** 15% to 20%.

Toilets   You won't find public toilets or "restrooms" on the streets in most Alberta cities, but they can be found in hotel lobbies, bars, restaurants, museums, department stores, railway and bus stations, and service stations. Large hotels and fast-food restaurants are often the best bet for clean facilities. Restaurants and bars in resorts or heavily visited areas may reserve their restrooms for patrons.

Useful Phone Numbers   Travel Alberta (© 800/252-3782); Crisis Services Provincial Help Line (© 800-779-5057); Provincial Fire Bans/Forest Closures (© 866/394-3473); U.S. Department of State Travel Advisory (© 202/647-5225, manned 24 hrs.); U.S. Passport Agency (© 202/647-0518).

Visas   Citizens of the United States, Australia, Ireland, New Zealand, and the U.K. do not need visas to enter Canada.

A complete list of those countries whose citizens do require a visa can be found at www.cic.gc.ca/english/visit/visas.asp.

Water   Water quality is very good in Alberta, although the state of the water in the areas surrounding the Fort McMurray oil sands has been of growing concern to locals and environmentalists lately. This, however, does not apply to tap water, which is fine to drink.

Water

AIRLINE WEBSITES

MAJOR U.S. AND CANADIAN AIRLINES

Air Canada
www.aircanada.ca

Alaska Airlines
www.alaskaair.com

American Airlines
www.aa.com

Continental Airlines
www.continental.com

Delta Air Lines
www.delta.com

United Airlines
www.united.com

U.S. Airways
www.usairways.com

WestJet
www.westjet.com

MAJOR INTERNATIONAL AIRLINES

Air France
www.airfrance.com

Air India
www.airindia.com

Air New Zealand
www.airnewzealand.com

Alitalia
www.alitalia.com

American Airlines
www.aa.com

British Airways
www.british-airways.com

China Airlines
www.china-airlines.com

Continental Airlines
www.continental.com

Delta Air Lines
www.delta.com

El Al Airlines
www.el.co.il

Hawaiian Airlines
www.hawaiianair.com

Japan Airlines
www.jal.co.jp

Lufthansa
www.lufthansa.com

Philippine Airlines
www.philippineairlines.com

United Airlines*
www.united.com

U.S. Airways*
www.usairways.com

Virgin Atlantic Airways
www.virgin-atlantic.com

Index

See also Accommodations and Restaurant indexes, below.

General Index

A

AARP, 44
Academic trips, 47
Accommodations. *See also* Camping and RV parks; Accommodations Index
  Banff, 177
  best, 6–7
  Calgary, 82–89
  Canmore, 142–144
  Columbia Icefields, 199–200
  Drumheller, 124–125
  Edmonton, 224–229
  Fort Chipewyan, 259
  Fort McMurray, 253–255
  Jasper, 209–215
  Kananaskis, 140–141
  Lake Louise, 191–195
  Lethbridge, 129
  tips on, 50
  Waterton Lakes National Park, 135–137
Active vacations. *See* Outdoor activities and adventures
Adventure and wellness trips, 47
Agriculture, 22
Air Canada, 34, 36
Airplane and helicopter tours
  Canmore and Kananaskis Country, 148
  Columbia Icefields, 198
  Fort McMurray, 252
  Horseshoe Canyon, 123
Air travel, 34–36
Alberta and Pacific Bed and Breakfast, 224
Alberta Bed and Breakfast Association, 224
Alberta Children's Hospital (Calgary), 82
Alberta Country Vacations Association, 60
Alberta Dental Association, 82
Alberta Legislature (Edmonton), 221
Alberta Motor Association, 261
Alberta Outfitters Association, 59
Alberta Theatre Projects (Calgary), 115
Alpine Club of Canada (ACC), 44, 185–186
Alpine Helicopters (Canmore), 148
Alpine Stables (Waterton Lakes), 59, 134
Alta-Can Aurora Tours Inc (Fort McMurray), 250

American Automobile Association (AAA), 261
American Express, 261
  Calgary, 81
  Edmonton, 223
  traveler's checks, 39
Amtrak, 35
Andrew Lake Lodge and Camps (Fort McMurray), 249
Animal-rights issues, 46–47
APT Touring, 48
Area codes, 261
Arnold Churgin (Calgary), 113
Art Central (Calgary), 114
Artcity Festival (Calgary), 31
Art galleries
  Canmore, 147
  Edmonton, 243
  Lethbridge, 127–128
The Art Gallery of Alberta (Edmonton), 235
Art Gallery of Calgary, 97, 99
Athabasca, Mount, 198–199
Athabasca River, 257
Athabasca Sand Dunes, 259
Atha-B (Jasper), 218
Atlas Coal Mine (East Coulee), 121
ATMs (automated teller machines), 38–39, 261
Aurora (Banff), 190
Aurora Tours (Fort McMurray), 250
Automobile organizations, 261
A World of Options, 43

B

Babysitting
  Calgary, 81
  Edmonton, 223
Backcountry camping and huts
  Banff National Park, 185–186
  Jasper National Park, 214–215
Backcountry hostels
  Jasper National Park, 215
  Lake Louise area, 195
Backcountry lodges, Banff National Park, 182
Backdraught Pub (Edmonton), 245
Bactrax (Banff), 61
The badlands, 20, 22
Balance Quest, 47
Bald Hills, 203–204
Bamboo Ballroom (Edmonton), 243
Banff Accommodation Reservations, 161
Banff Airporter, 34, 172
Banff Camera Shop, 170
The Banff Centre, 172, 175
Banff Centre Festival of Mountain Films and Books, 172
Banff Fishing Unlimited, 58, 166
Banff Information Centre, 162, 166, 173
Banff International String Quartet Competition, 172

Banff Mountain Film and Book Festivals, 31
Banff Mount Norquay, 54
Banff National Park, 52–53, 157–190
  accommodations, 161–162
  arts festivals, 172
  ATMs, 169
  bird-watching, 58
  car trouble and towing services, 169
  currency exchange, 169
  emergencies, 169
  gas stations, 169
  grocery stores, 169
  laundry, 169
  medical services, 169
  naming, 168
  orientation, 159
  outdoor activities, 165–171
  permits, 169–170
  photo supplies, 170
  post offices, 170
  seasons, 161
  taxis, 170
  tours and excursions, 159, 161
  visitor information, 159
  weather updates, 170
Banff Park Museum, 175
Banff Summer Arts Festival, 30, 172
Banff townsite, 172–190
  accommodations, 177
  attractions, 173–177
  camping near, 183–186
  getting around, 173
  nightlife, 190
  orientation, 173
  restaurants, 186–189
  shopping, 177
  traveling to, 172–173
  visitor information, 173
Banker's Hall (Calgary), 113
Bankhead, 146
Barley Mill Neighbourhood Pub (Calgary), 116
Barrier Lake Visitor Information Centre, 140
Bar U Ranch (near Longview), 153
Bar Wild's (Edmonton), 245
Baseball
  Calgary, 111
  Edmonton, 241
The Bay (Calgary), 113
Bears
  Banff and Jasper national parks, 162–163
  Kananaskis Country, 149
  safety concerns, 40, 163
Beauvert Promenade (Jasper), 209
Bed and Breakfast Association of Calgary, 83
Belly River Campground (near Waterton), 136–137
Big Valley Jamboree (near Camrose), 7
Bike Calgary, 81

Restaurants